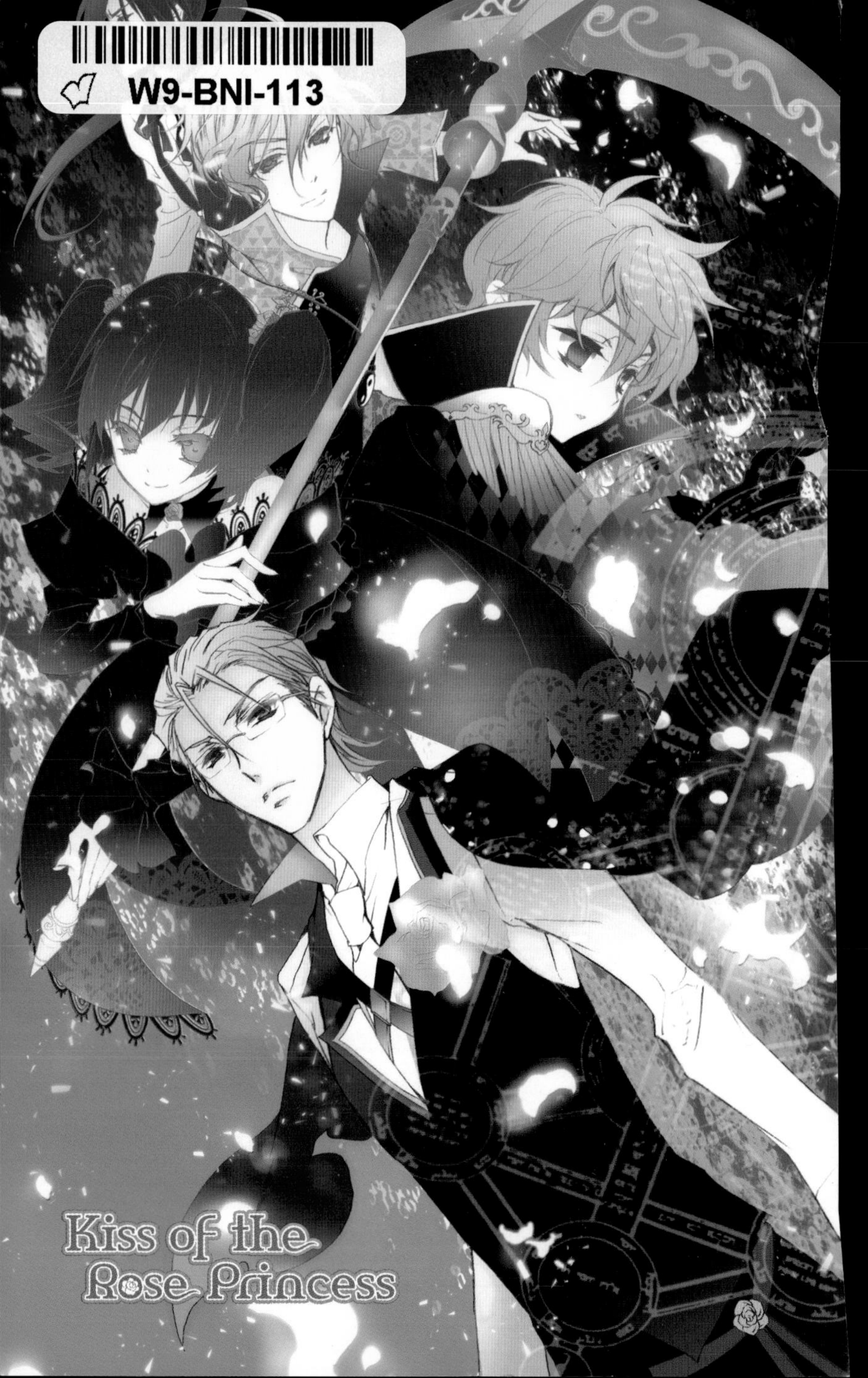
Kiss of the Rose Princess

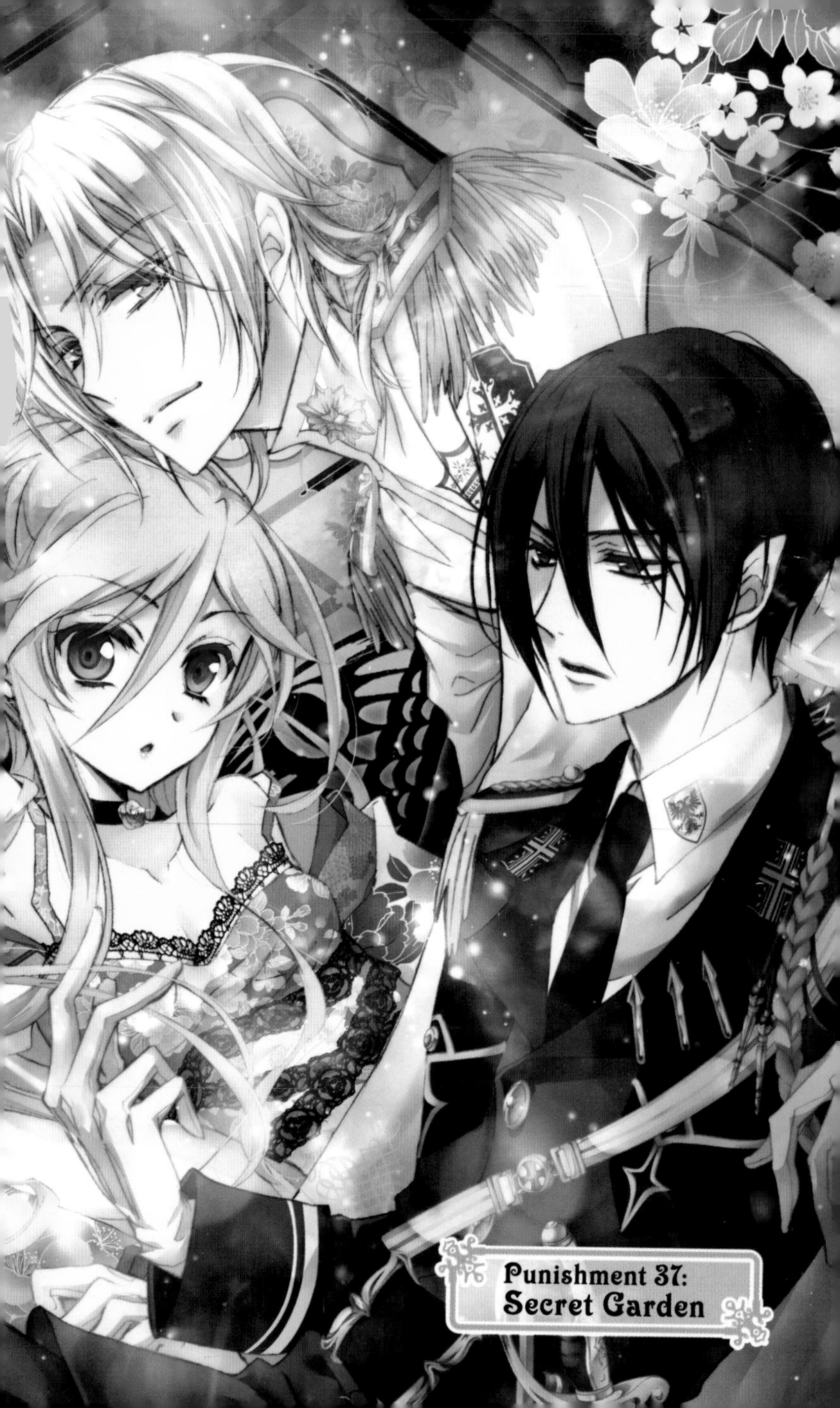
Punishment 37:
Secret Garden

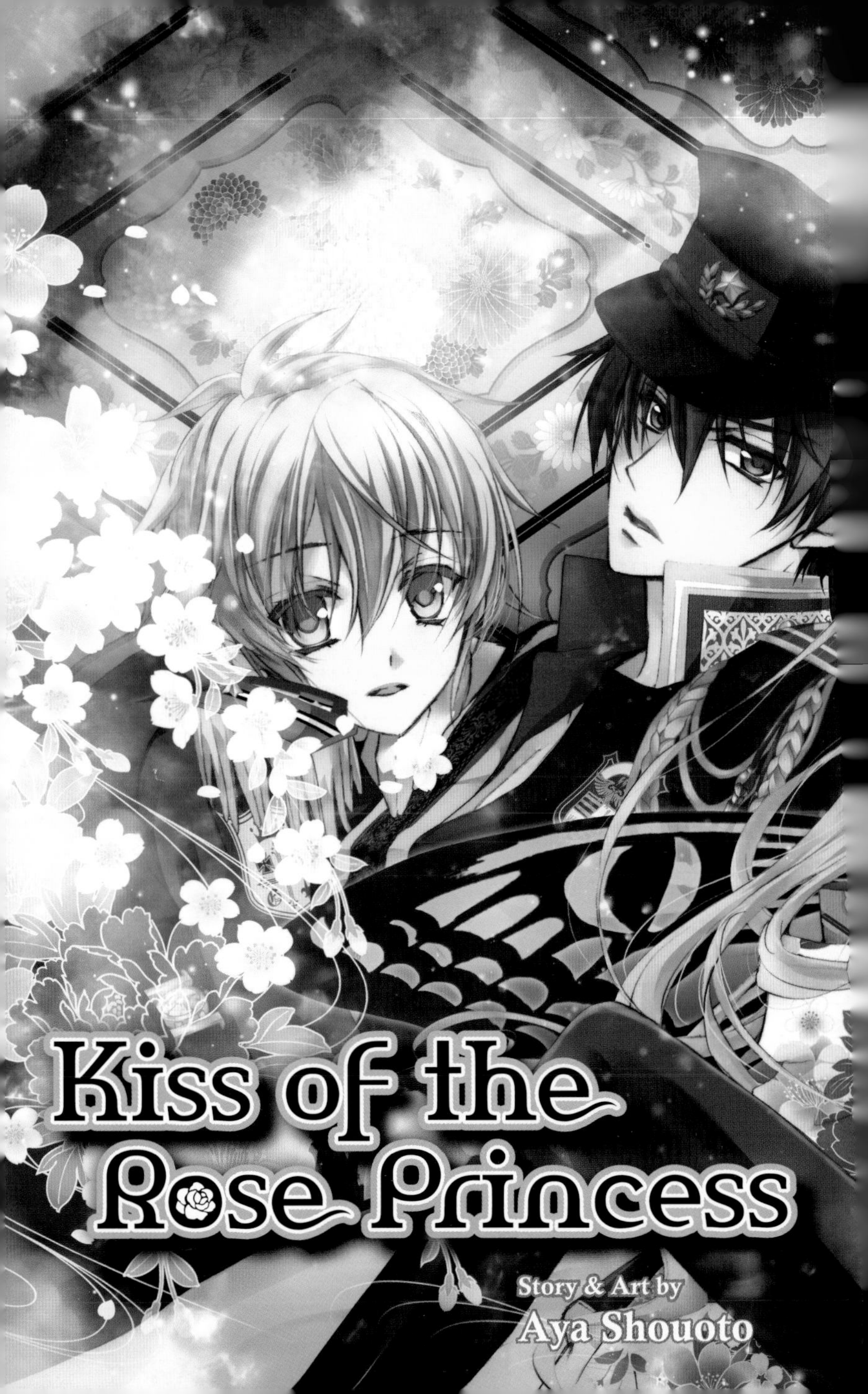
Kiss of the Rose Princess
Story & Art by
Aya Shouoto

Kiss of the Rose Princess

Contents

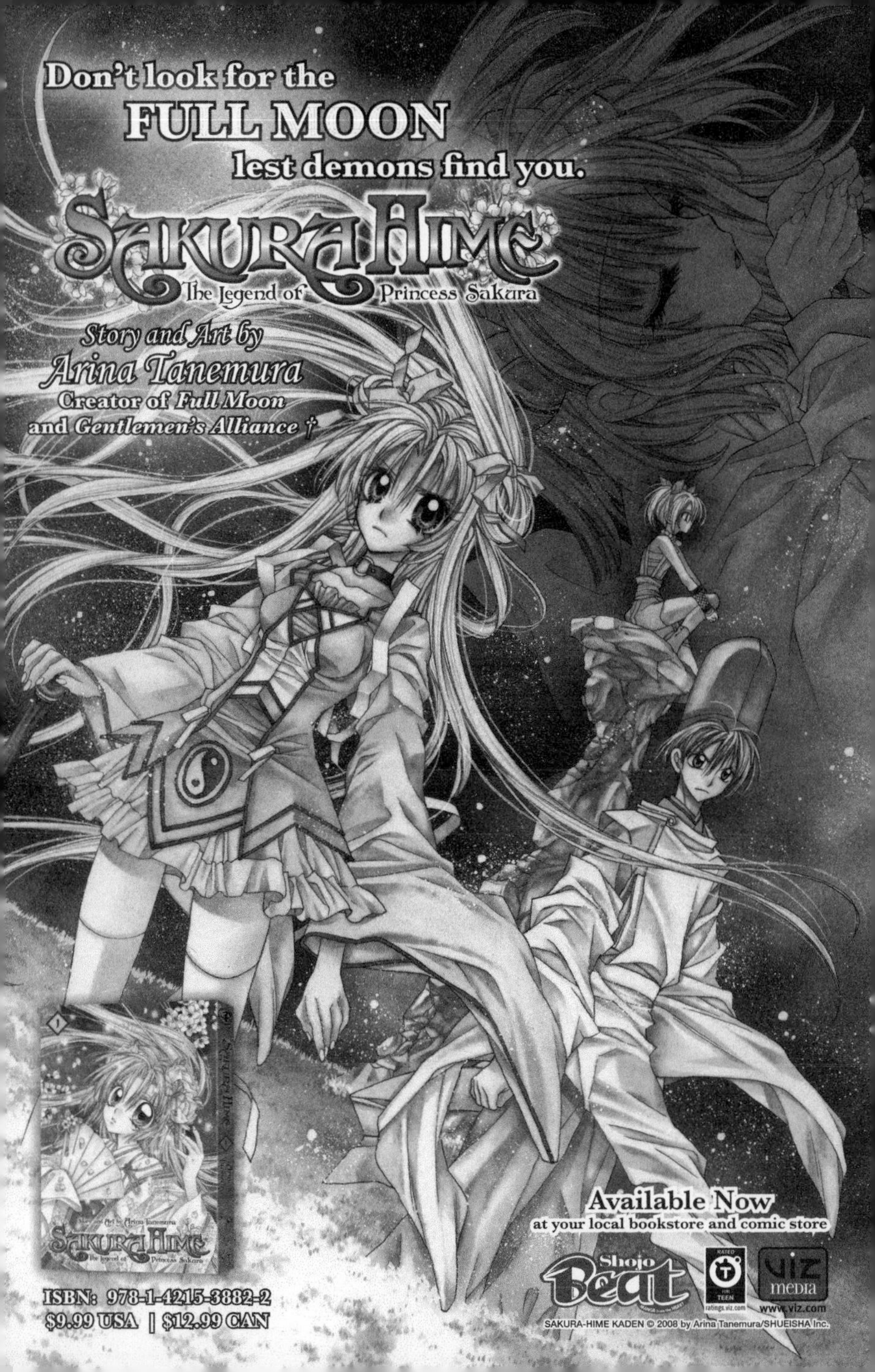
Don't look for the
FULL MOON
lest demons find you.
SAKURA HIME
The Legend of Princess Sakura
Story and Art by
Arina Tanemura
Creator of Full Moon
and Gentlemen's Alliance †
Available Now
at your local bookstore and comic store
ISBN: 978-1-4215-3882-2
$9.99 USA | $12.99 CAN
Shojo Beat
RATED T TEEN
ratings.viz.com
VIZ media
www.viz.com
SAKURA-HIME KADEN © 2008 by Arina Tanemura/SHUEISHA Inc.

Kiss of the Rose Princess

Volume 9
Shojo Beat Edition

STORY AND ART BY
AYA SHOUOTO

Translation/Tetsuichiro Miyaki
Touch-up Art & Lettering/Inori Fukuda Trant
Design/Yukiko Whitley
Editor/Nancy Thistlethwaite

KISS OF ROSE PRINCESS Volume 9
© Aya SHOUOTO 2012
Edited by KADOKAWA SHOTEN
First published in Japan in 2012 by KADOKAWA CORPORATION, Tokyo.
English translation rights arranged with KADOKAWA CORPORATION, Tokyo.

Printed in the U.S.A.

Published by VIZ Media, LLC
P.O. Box 77010
San Francisco, CA 94107

10 9 8 7 6 5 4 3 2 1
First printing, March 2016

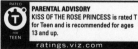

www.viz.com

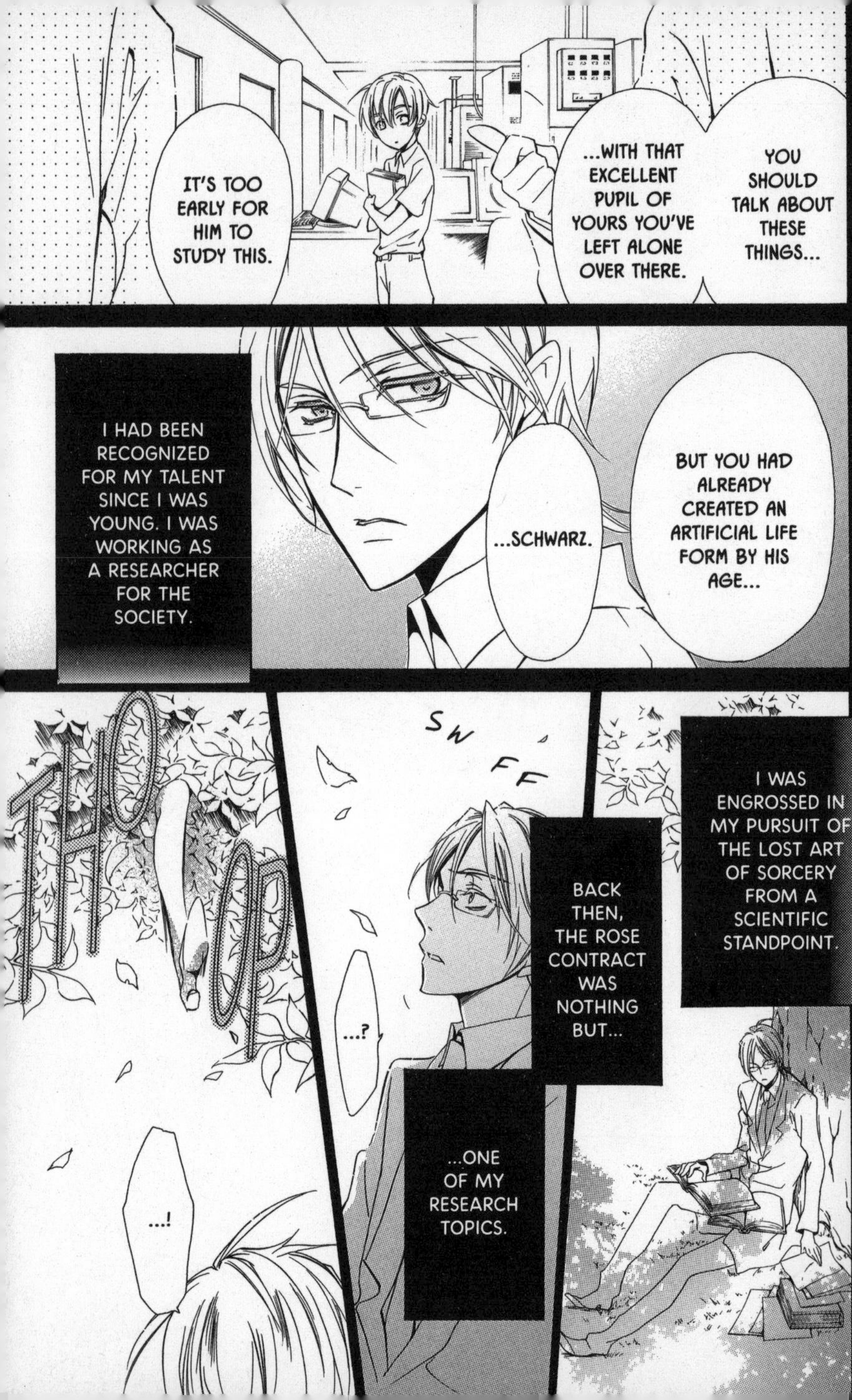
YOU SHOULD TALK ABOUT THESE THINGS...
...WITH THAT EXCELLENT PUPIL OF YOURS YOU'VE LEFT ALONE OVER THERE.
IT'S TOO EARLY FOR HIM TO STUDY THIS.
BUT YOU HAD ALREADY CREATED AN ARTIFICIAL LIFE FORM BY HIS AGE...
...SCHWARZ.
I HAD BEEN RECOGNIZED FOR MY TALENT SINCE I WAS YOUNG. I WAS WORKING AS A RESEARCHER FOR THE SOCIETY.
I WAS ENGROSSED IN MY PURSUIT OF THE LOST ART OF SORCERY FROM A SCIENTIFIC STANDPOINT.
SWFF
BACK THEN, THE ROSE CONTRACT WAS NOTHING BUT...
...?
...ONE OF MY RESEARCH TOPICS.
THOP
...!

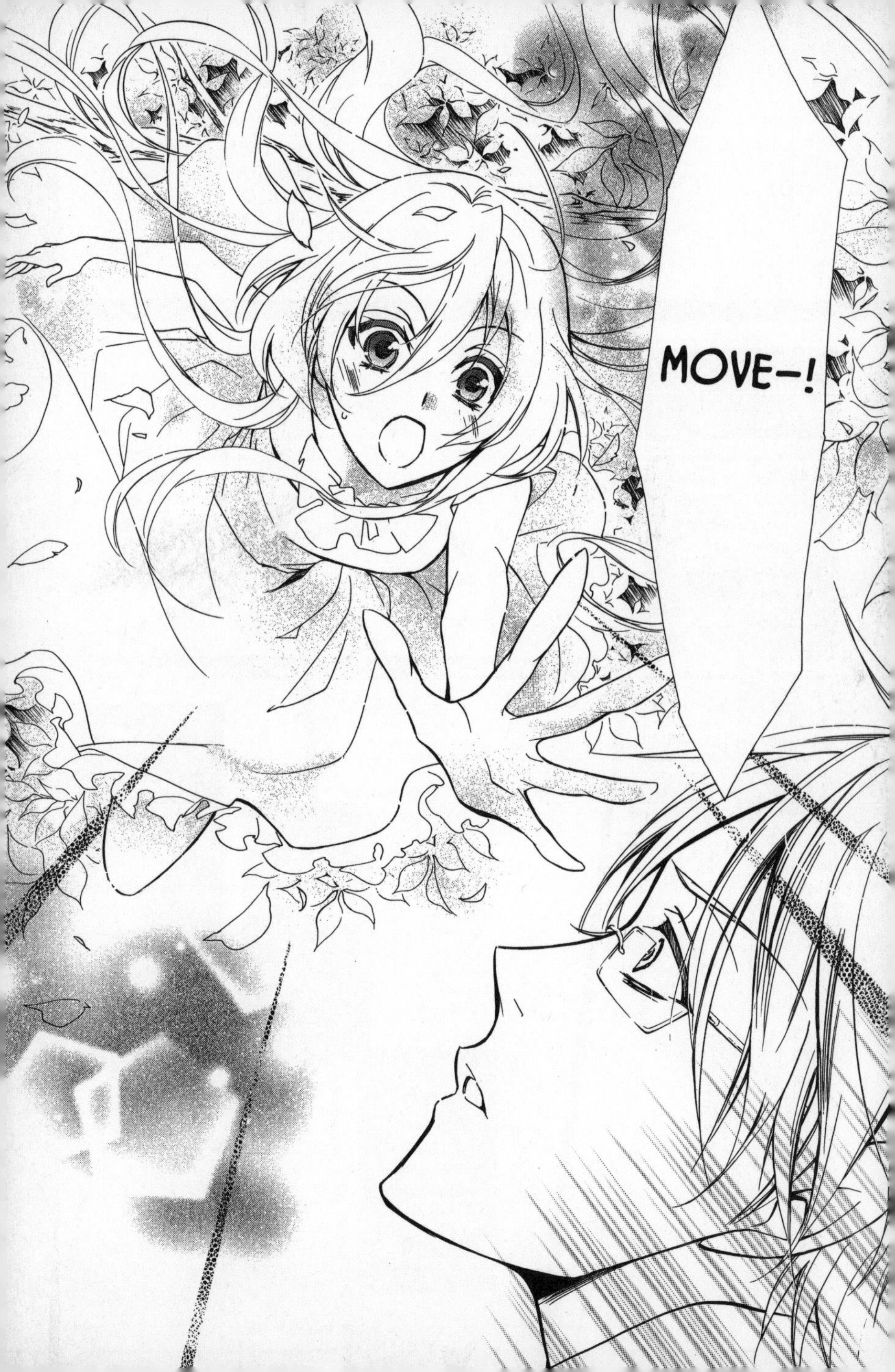
MOVE-!

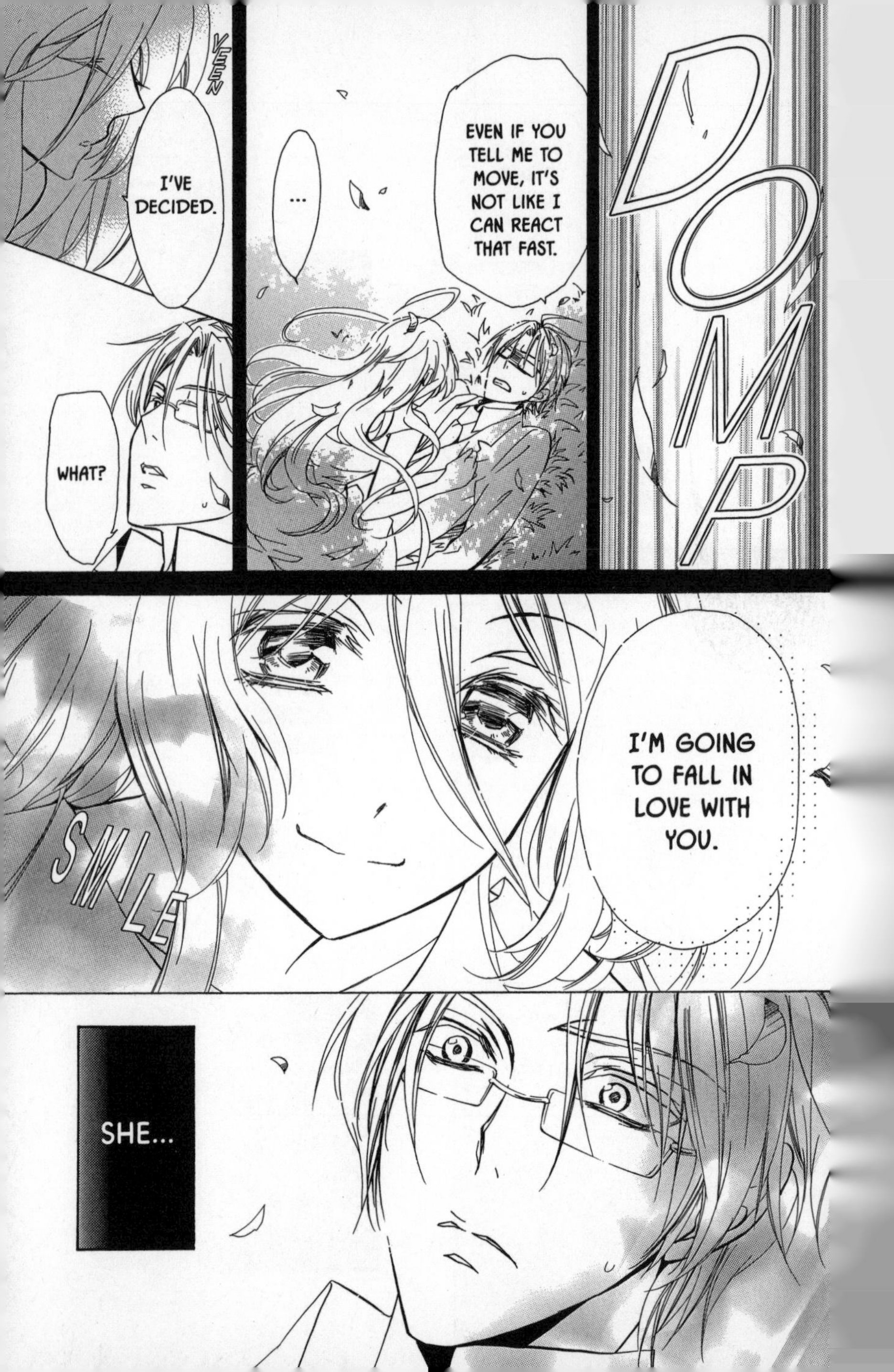
DOMP
EVEN IF YOU TELL ME TO MOVE, IT'S NOT LIKE I CAN REACT THAT FAST.
...
VEEN
I'VE DECIDED.
WHAT?
I'M GOING TO FALL IN LOVE WITH YOU.
SMILE
SHE...

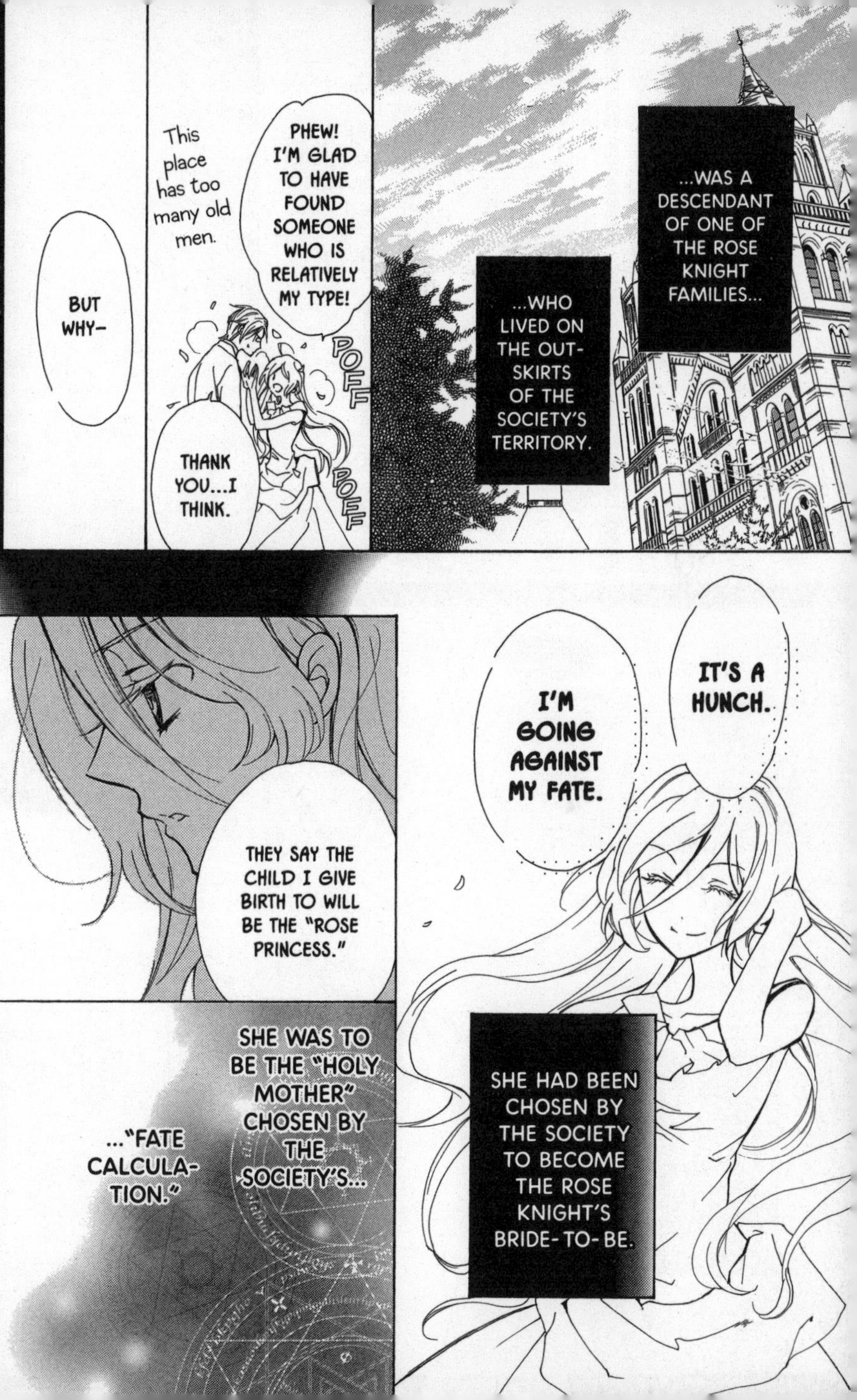
...WAS A DESCENDANT OF ONE OF THE ROSE KNIGHT FAMILIES...
...WHO LIVED ON THE OUT-SKIRTS OF THE SOCIETY'S TERRITORY.
PHEW! I'M GLAD TO HAVE FOUND SOMEONE WHO IS RELATIVELY MY TYPE!
This place has too many old men.
POFF
POFF
THANK YOU...I THINK.
BUT WHY-
IT'S A HUNCH.
I'M GOING AGAINST MY FATE.
SHE HAD BEEN CHOSEN BY THE SOCIETY TO BECOME THE ROSE KNIGHT'S BRIDE-TO-BE.
THEY SAY THE CHILD I GIVE BIRTH TO WILL BE THE "ROSE PRINCESS."
SHE WAS TO BE THE "HOLY MOTHER" CHOSEN BY THE SOCIETY'S...
..."FATE CALCULA-TION."

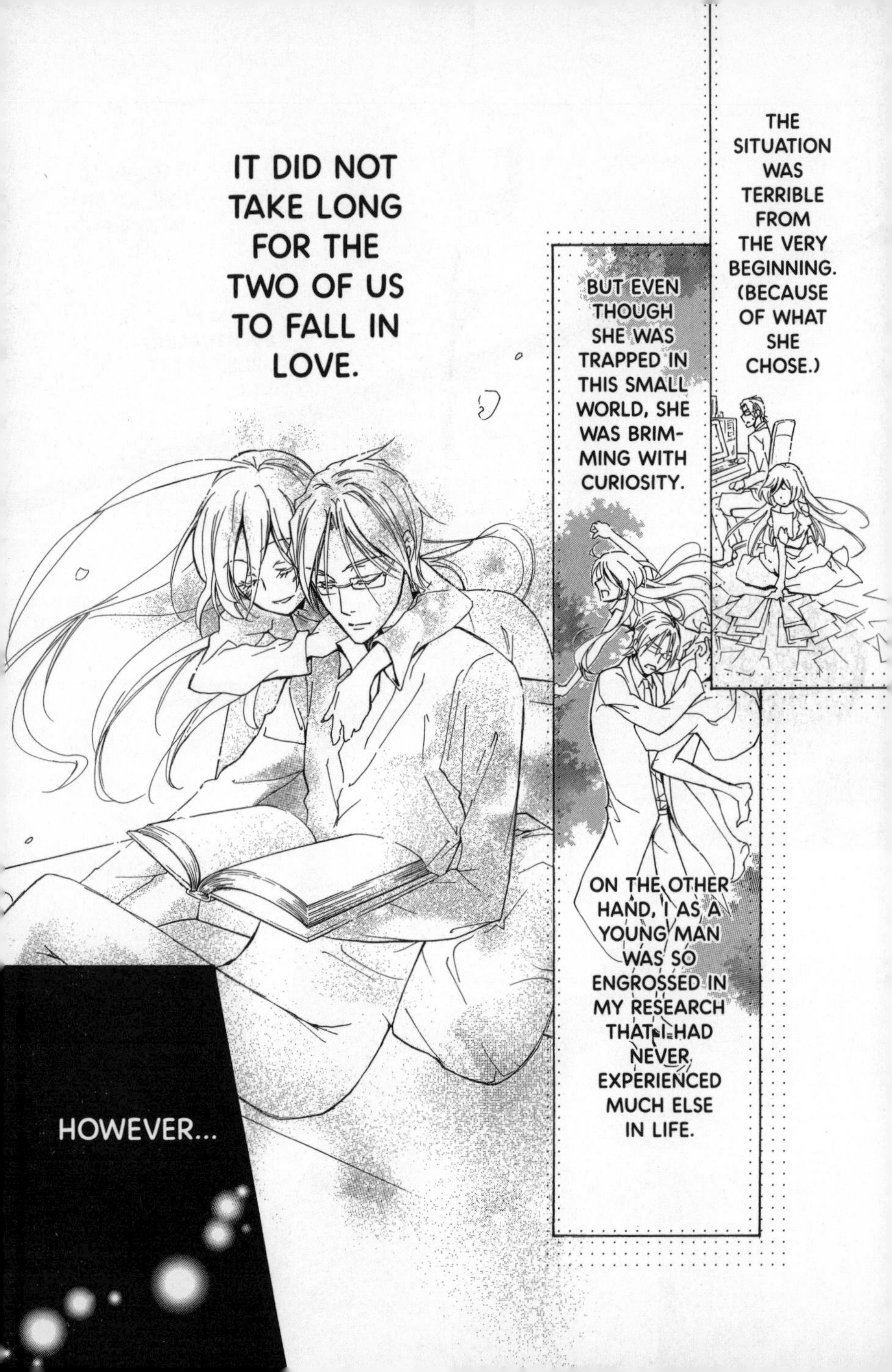
THE SITUATION WAS TERRIBLE FROM THE VERY BEGINNING. (BECAUSE OF WHAT SHE CHOSE.)
BUT EVEN THOUGH SHE WAS TRAPPED IN THIS SMALL WORLD, SHE WAS BRIMMING WITH CURIOSITY.
ON THE OTHER HAND, I AS A YOUNG MAN WAS SO ENGROSSED IN MY RESEARCH THAT I HAD NEVER EXPERIENCED MUCH ELSE IN LIFE.
IT DID NOT TAKE LONG FOR THE TWO OF US TO FALL IN LOVE.
HOWEVER...

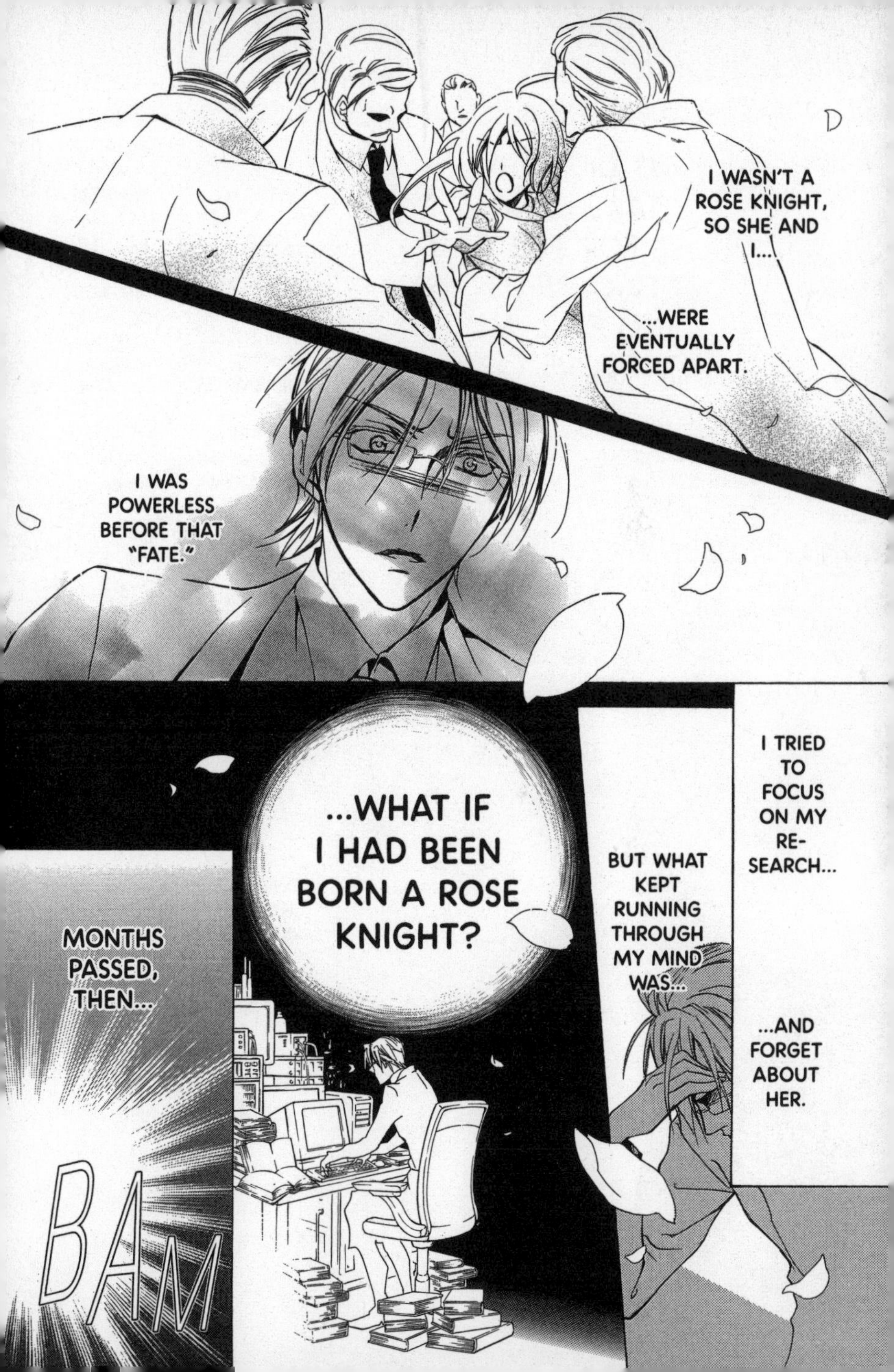
I WASN'T A ROSE KNIGHT, SO SHE AND I...
...WERE EVENTUALLY FORCED APART.
I WAS POWERLESS BEFORE THAT "FATE."
I TRIED TO FOCUS ON MY RE-SEARCH...
...AND FORGET ABOUT HER.
BUT WHAT KEPT RUNNING THROUGH MY MIND WAS...
...WHAT IF I HAD BEEN BORN A ROSE KNIGHT?
MONTHS PASSED, THEN...
BAM

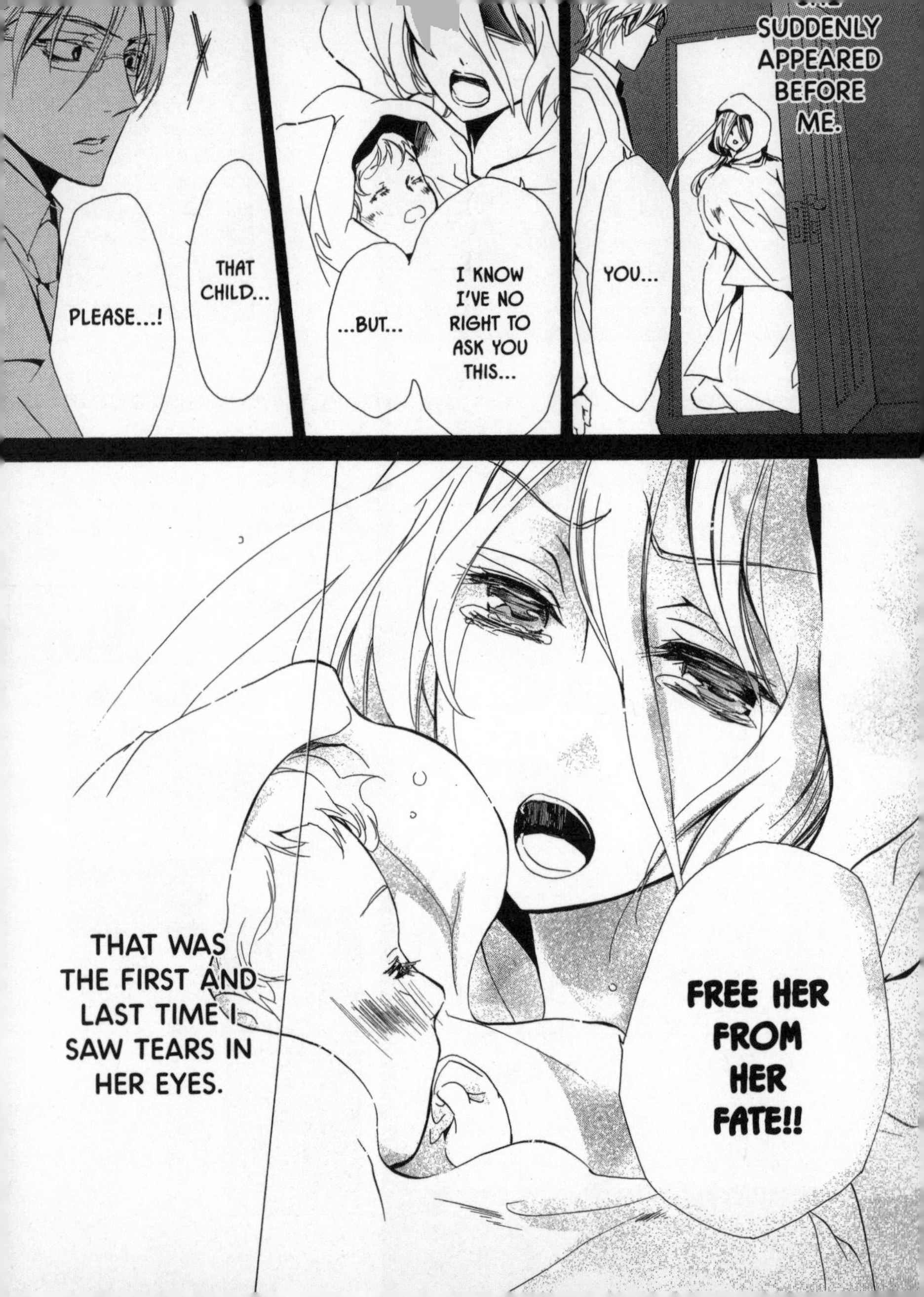
SUDDENLY APPEARED BEFORE ME.
YOU...
I KNOW I'VE NO RIGHT TO ASK YOU THIS...
...BUT...
THAT CHILD...
PLEASE...!
FREE HER FROM HER FATE!!
THAT WAS THE FIRST AND LAST TIME I SAW TEARS IN HER EYES.

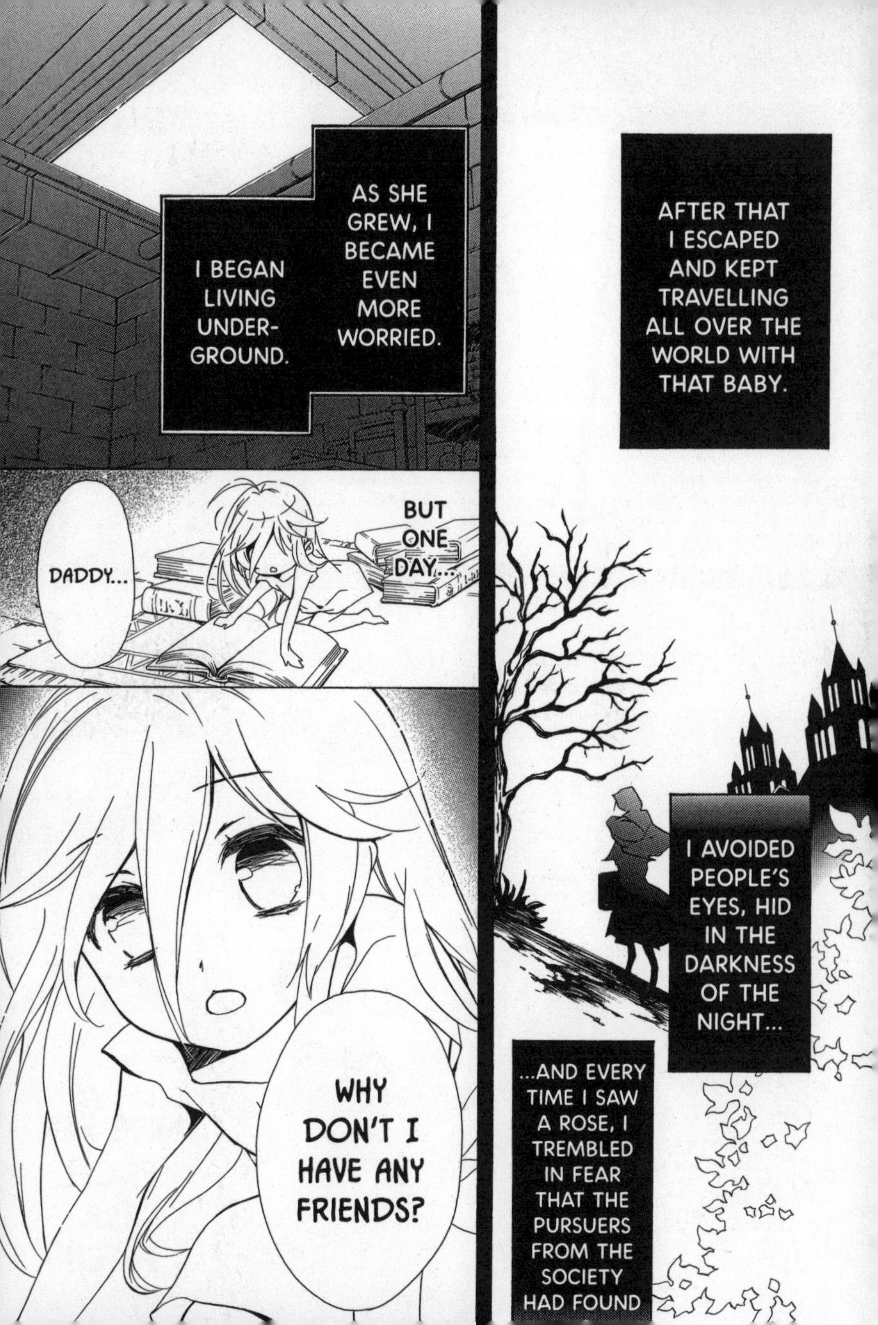
AFTER THAT I ESCAPED AND KEPT TRAVELLING ALL OVER THE WORLD WITH THAT BABY.
I AVOIDED PEOPLE'S EYES, HID IN THE DARKNESS OF THE NIGHT...
...AND EVERY TIME I SAW A ROSE, I TREMBLED IN FEAR THAT THE PURSUERS FROM THE SOCIETY HAD FOUND
AS SHE GREW, I BECAME EVEN MORE WORRIED.
I BEGAN LIVING UNDER-GROUND.
BUT ONE DAY...
DADDY...
WHY DON'T I HAVE ANY FRIENDS?

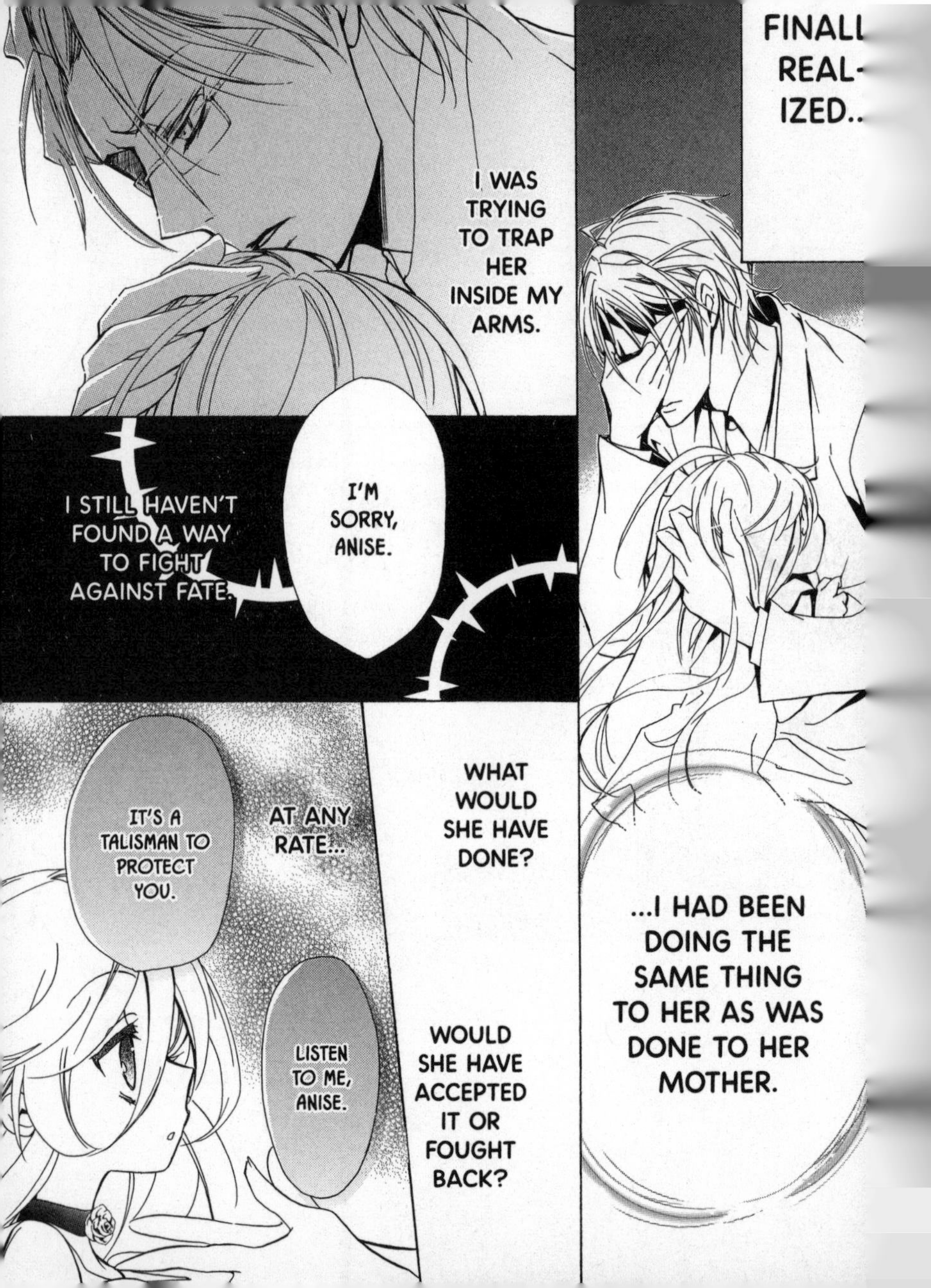
FINALL
REAL-
IZED..
...I HAD BEEN DOING THE SAME THING TO HER AS WAS DONE TO HER MOTHER.
I WAS TRYING TO TRAP HER INSIDE MY ARMS.
I'M SORRY, ANISE.
I STILL HAVEN'T FOUND A WAY TO FIGHT AGAINST FATE.
WHAT WOULD SHE HAVE DONE?
WOULD SHE HAVE ACCEPTED IT OR FOUGHT BACK?
AT ANY RATE...
IT'S A TALISMAN TO PROTECT YOU.
LISTEN TO ME, ANISE.

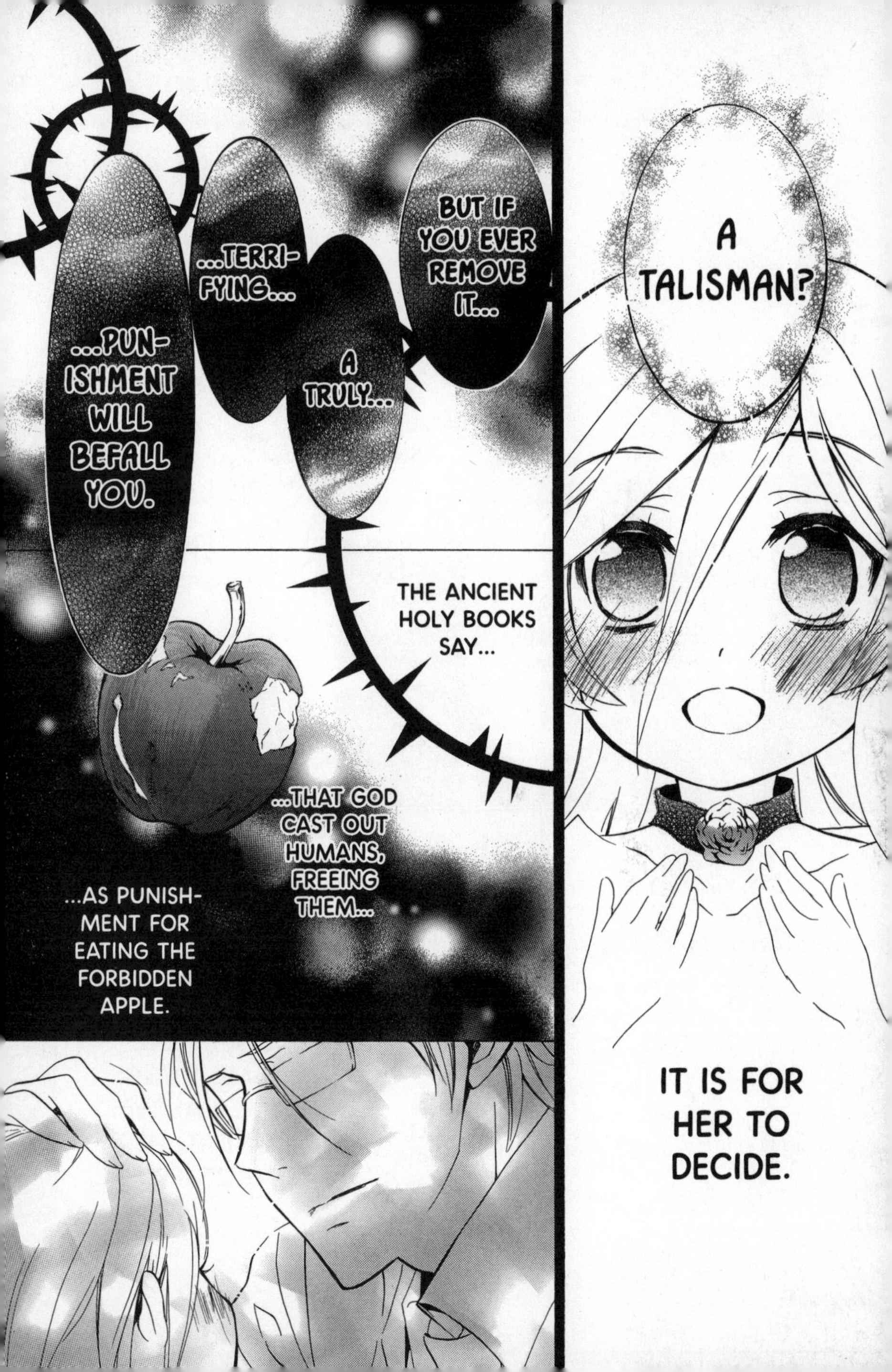
A TALISMAN?
IT IS FOR HER TO DECIDE.
BUT IF YOU EVER REMOVE IT...
A TRULY...
...TERRIFYING...
...PUNISHMENT WILL BEFALL YOU.
THE ANCIENT HOLY BOOKS SAY...
...THAT GOD CAST OUT HUMANS, FREEING THEM...
...AS PUNISHMENT FOR EATING THE FORBIDDEN APPLE.

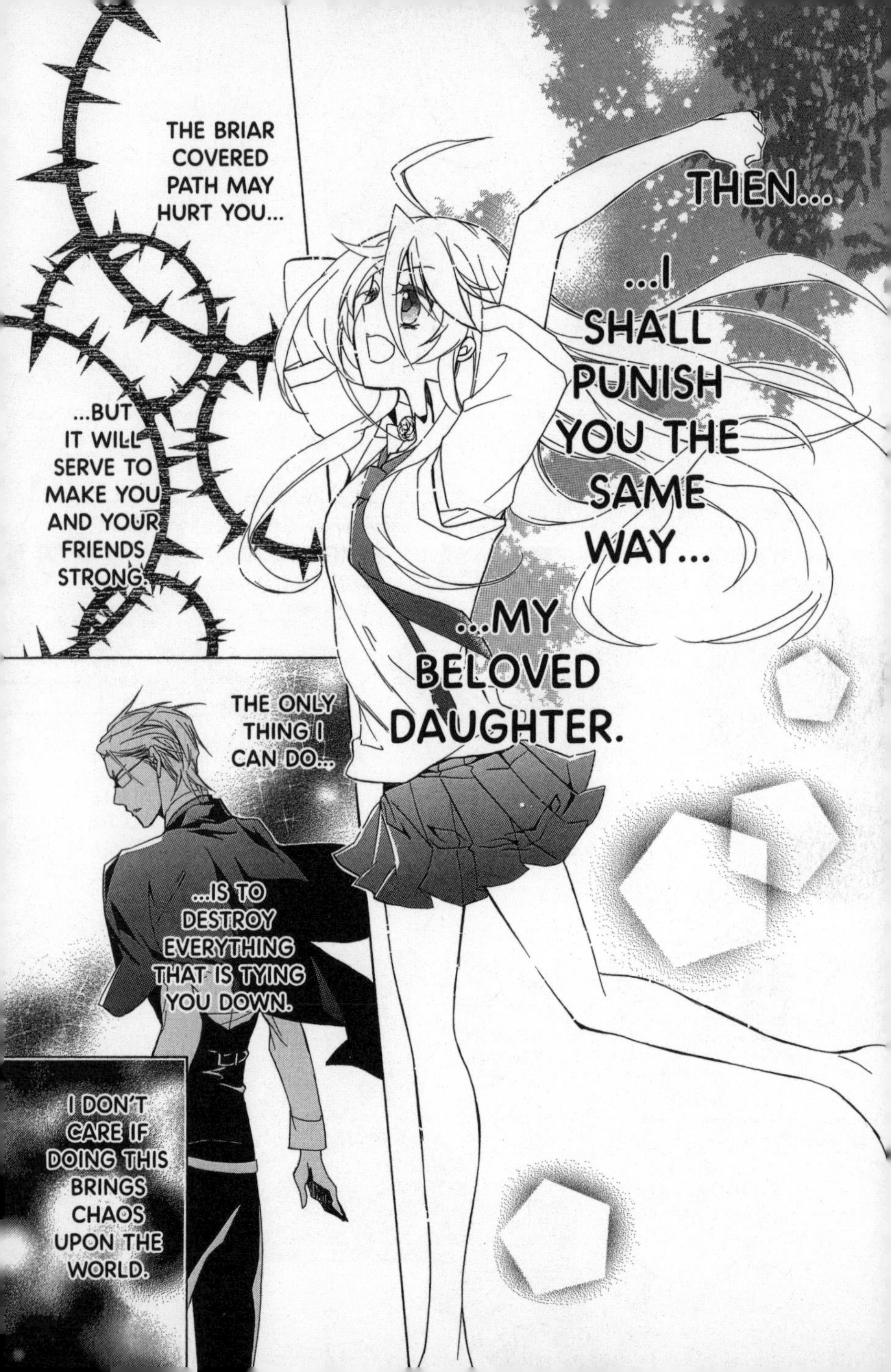
THEN...
...I SHALL PUNISH YOU THE SAME WAY...
...MY BELOVED DAUGHTER.
THE BRIAR COVERED PATH MAY HURT YOU...
...BUT IT WILL SERVE TO MAKE YOU AND YOUR FRIENDS STRONG.
THE ONLY THING I CAN DO...
...IS TO DESTROY EVERYTHING THAT IS TYING YOU DOWN.
I DON'T CARE IF DOING THIS BRINGS CHAOS UPON THE WORLD.

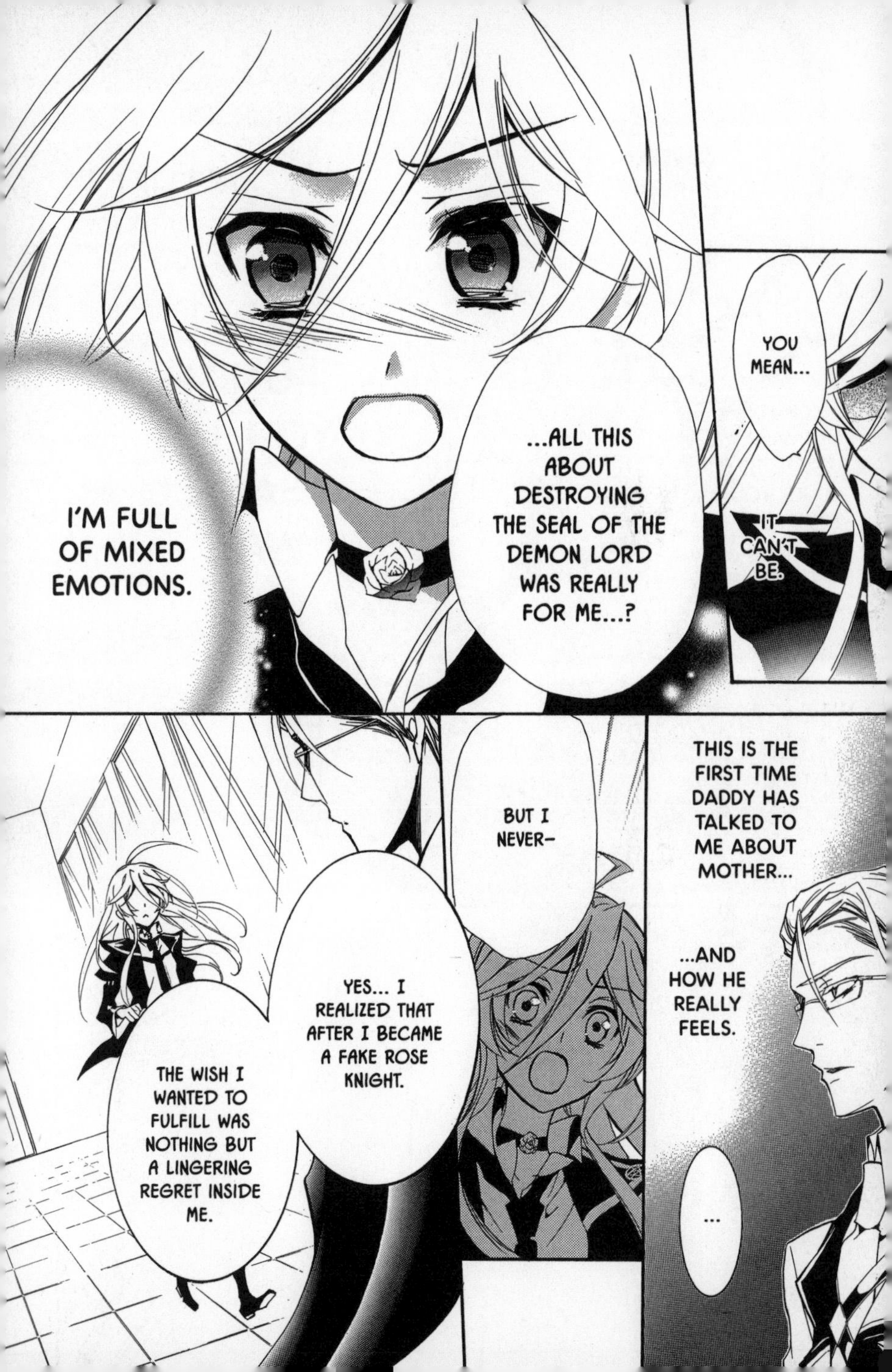
YOU MEAN...
IT CAN'T BE.
...ALL THIS ABOUT DESTROYING THE SEAL OF THE DEMON LORD WAS REALLY FOR ME...?
I'M FULL OF MIXED EMOTIONS.
THIS IS THE FIRST TIME DADDY HAS TALKED TO ME ABOUT MOTHER...
...AND HOW HE REALLY FEELS.
...
BUT I NEVER–
YES... I REALIZED THAT AFTER I BECAME A FAKE ROSE KNIGHT.
THE WISH I WANTED TO FULFILL WAS NOTHING BUT A LINGERING REGRET INSIDE ME.

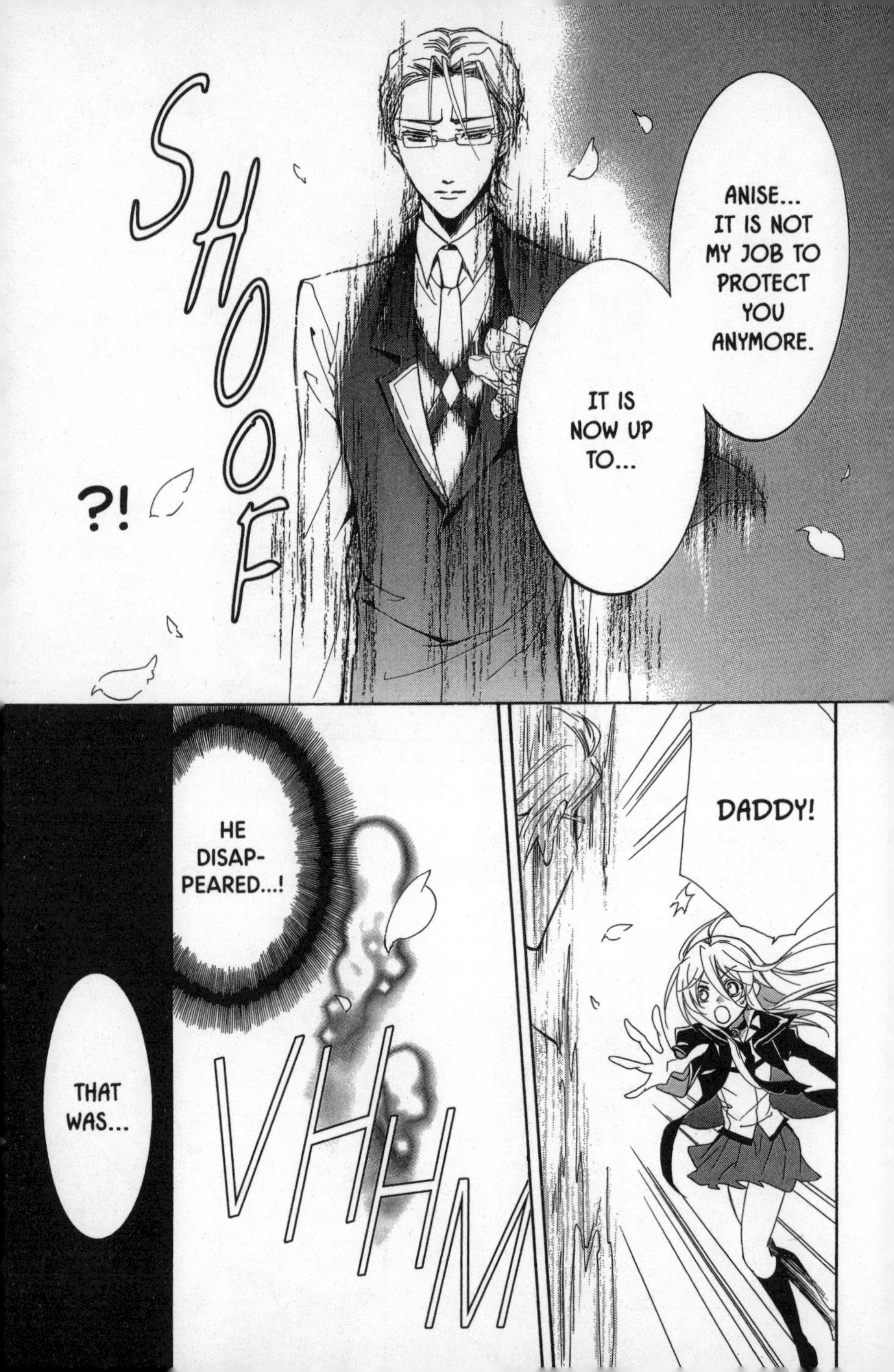
ANISE... IT IS NOT MY JOB TO PROTECT YOU ANYMORE.
IT IS NOW UP TO...
SHOOOF
?!
DADDY!
HE DISAPPEARED...!
VHHM
THAT WAS...

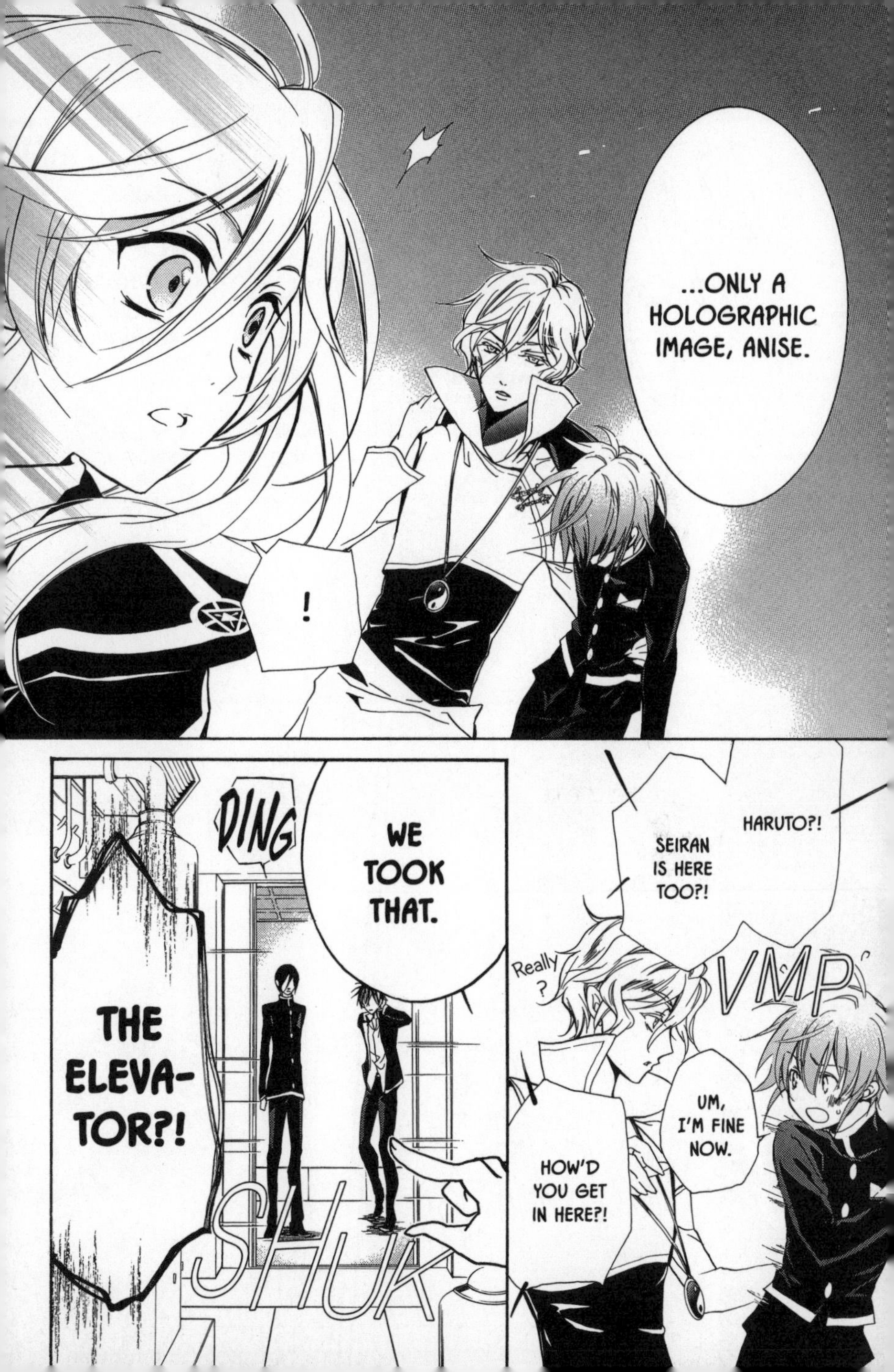
...ONLY A HOLOGRAPHIC IMAGE, ANISE.
!
HARUTO?!
SEIRAN IS HERE TOO?!
VMP
Really?
UM, I'M FINE NOW.
HOW'D YOU GET IN HERE?!
WE TOOK THAT.
DING
THE ELEVA-TOR?!
SHUK

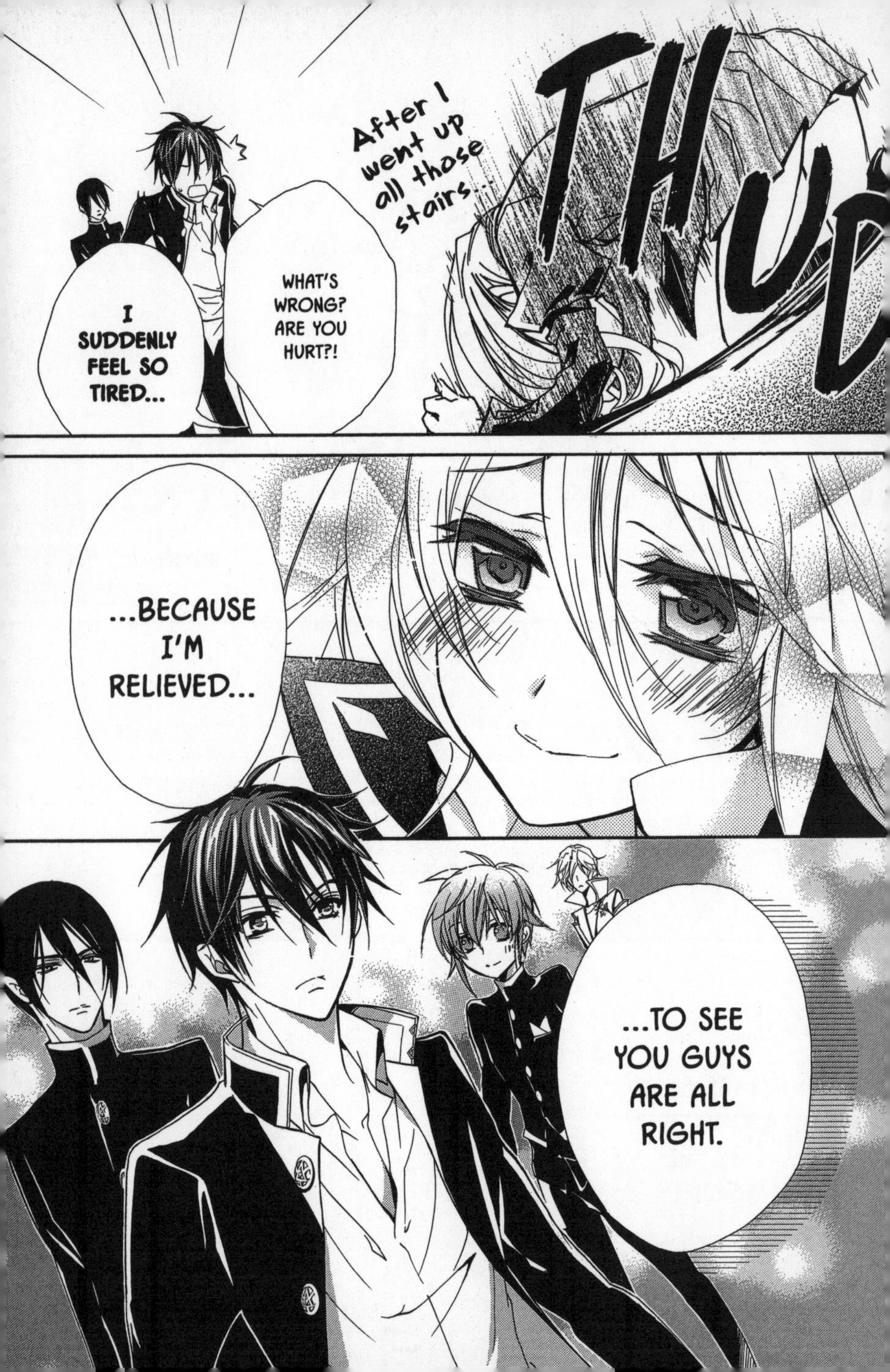
THUD
After I went up all those stairs...
WHAT'S WRONG? ARE YOU HURT?!
I SUDDENLY FEEL SO TIRED...
...BECAUSE I'M RELIEVED...
...TO SEE YOU GUYS ARE ALL RIGHT.

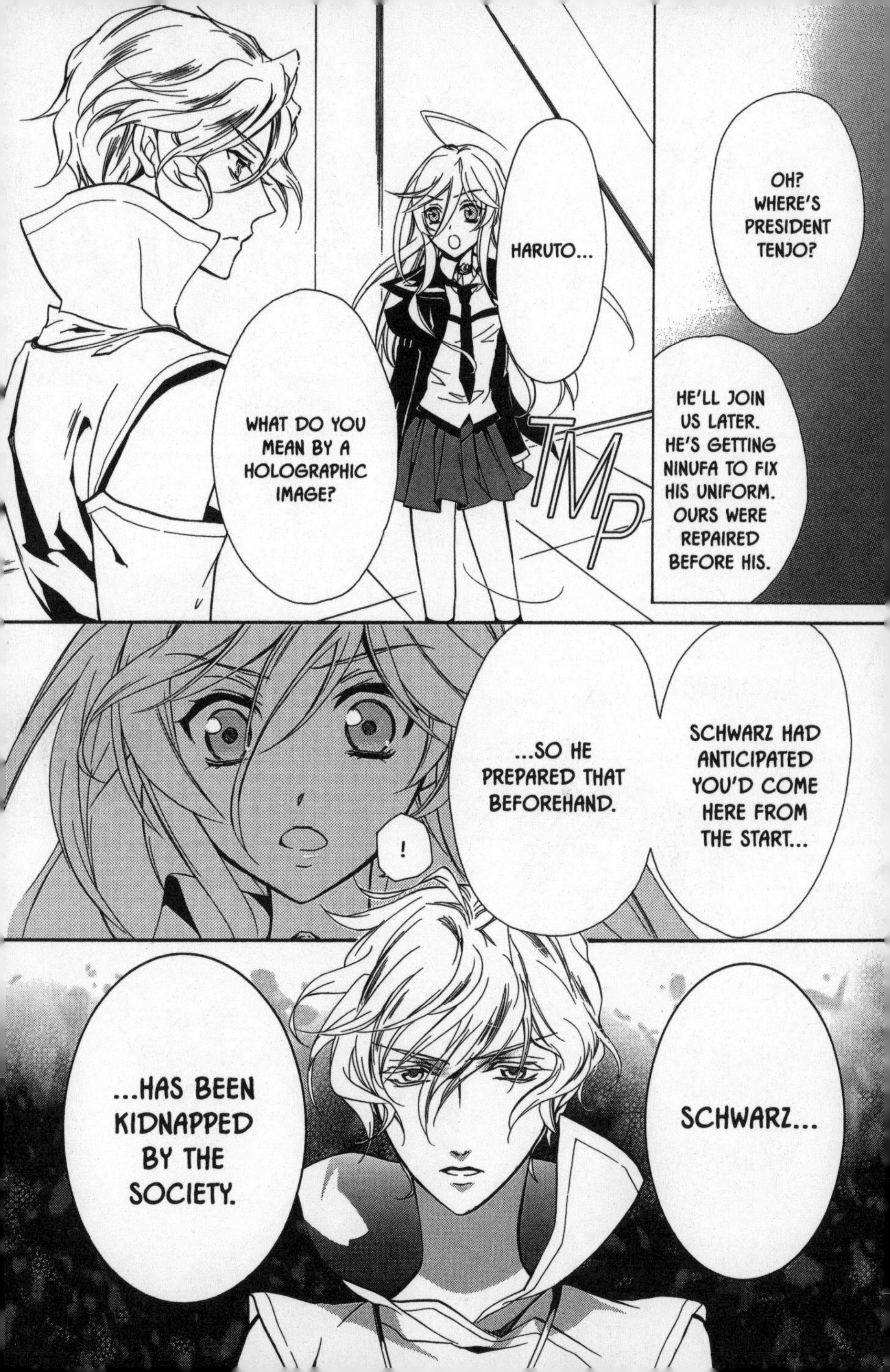
OH? WHERE'S PRESIDENT TENJO?
HE'LL JOIN US LATER. HE'S GETTING NINUFA TO FIX HIS UNIFORM. OURS WERE REPAIRED BEFORE HIS.
HARUTO...
TMP
WHAT DO YOU MEAN BY A HOLOGRAPHIC IMAGE?
SCHWARZ HAD ANTICIPATED YOU'D COME HERE FROM THE START...
...SO HE PREPARED THAT BEFOREHAND.
!
SCHWARZ...
...HAS BEEN KIDNAPPED BY THE SOCIETY.

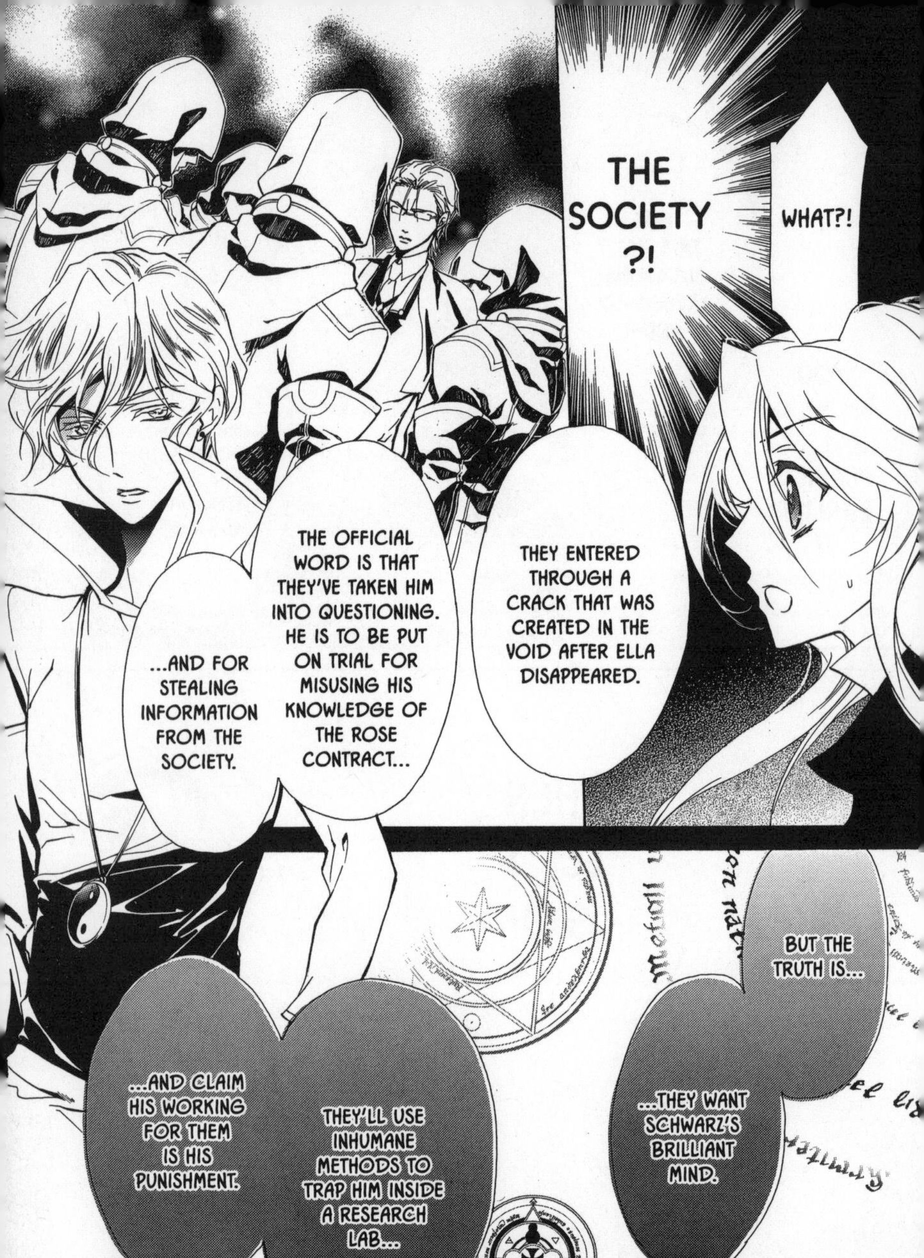
WHAT?!
THE SOCIETY ?!
THEY ENTERED THROUGH A CRACK THAT WAS CREATED IN THE VOID AFTER ELLA DISAPPEARED.
THE OFFICIAL WORD IS THAT THEY'VE TAKEN HIM INTO QUESTIONING. HE IS TO BE PUT ON TRIAL FOR MISUSING HIS KNOWLEDGE OF THE ROSE CONTRACT...
...AND FOR STEALING INFORMATION FROM THE SOCIETY.
BUT THE TRUTH IS...
...THEY WANT SCHWARZ'S BRILLIANT MIND.
THEY'LL USE INHUMANE METHODS TO TRAP HIM INSIDE A RESEARCH LAB...
...AND CLAIM HIS WORKING FOR THEM IS HIS PUNISHMENT.

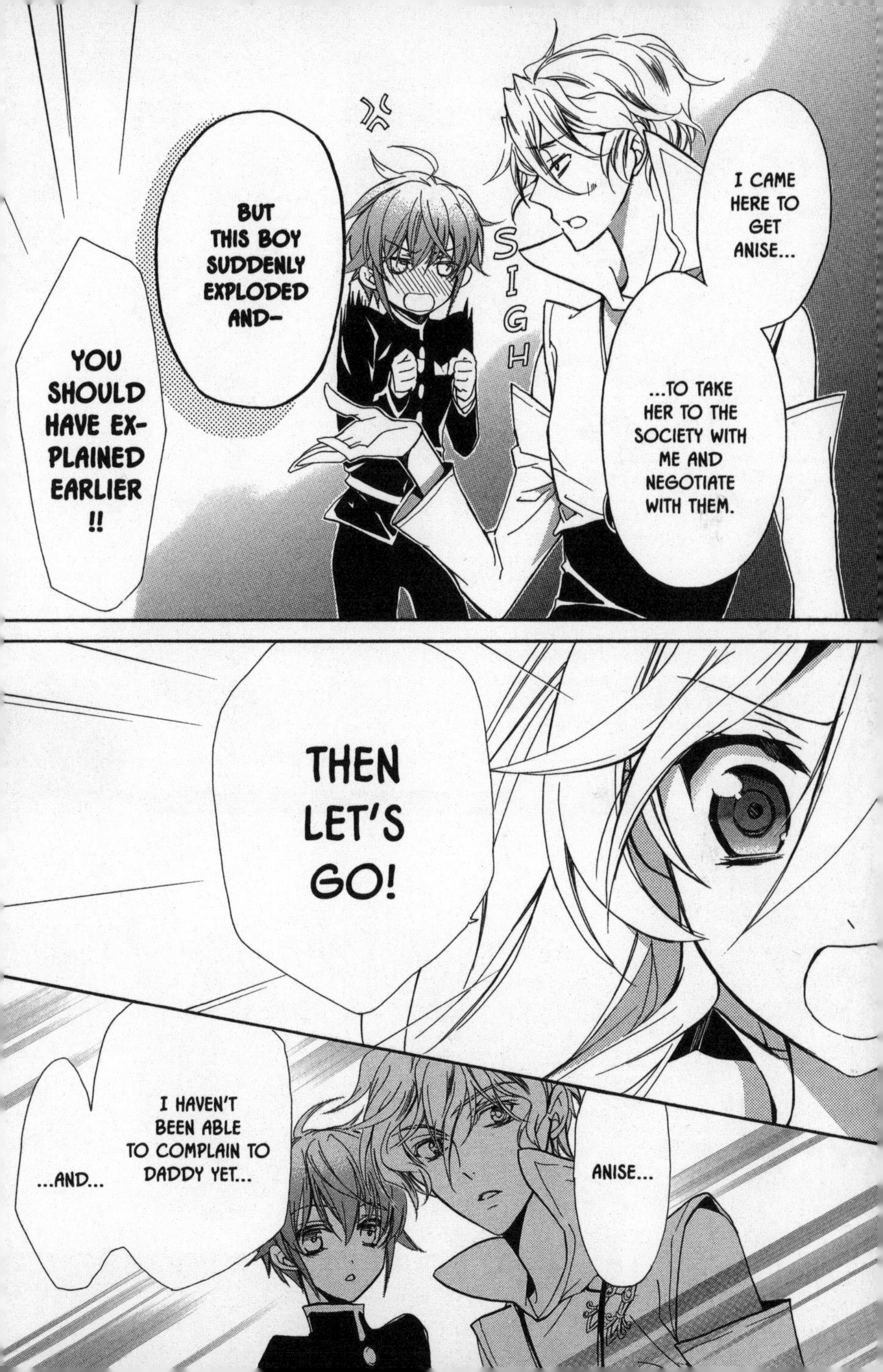
I CAME HERE TO GET ANISE...
...TO TAKE HER TO THE SOCIETY WITH ME AND NEGOTIATE WITH THEM.
SIGH
BUT THIS BOY SUDDENLY EXPLODED AND-
YOU SHOULD HAVE EX-PLAINED EARLIER !!
THEN LET'S GO!
ANISE...
I HAVEN'T BEEN ABLE TO COMPLAIN TO DADDY YET...
...AND...

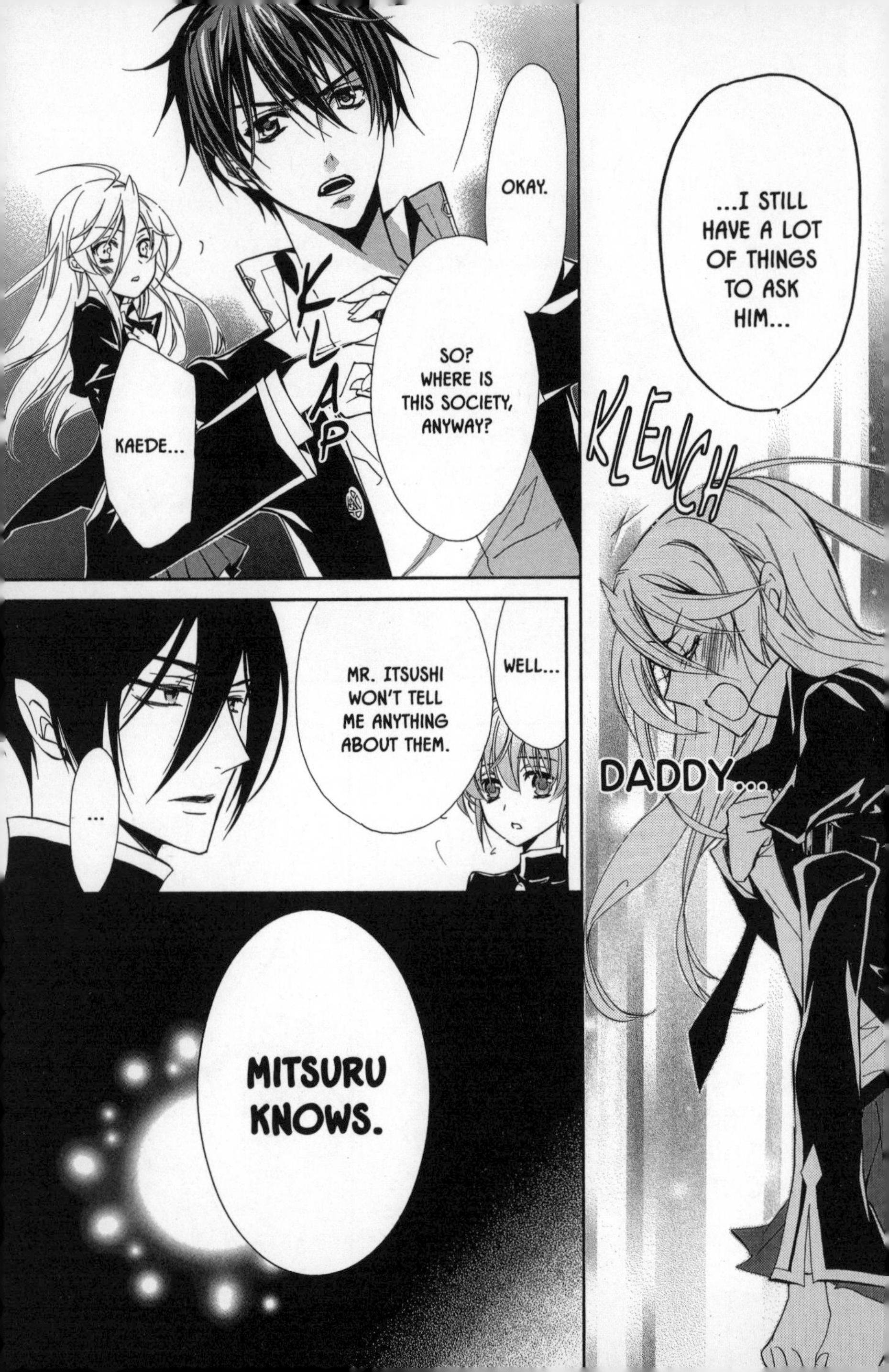
...I STILL HAVE A LOT OF THINGS TO ASK HIM...
KLENCH
DADDY...
OKAY.
SO? WHERE IS THIS SOCIETY, ANYWAY?
KLAP
KAEDE...
WELL...
MR. ITSUSHI WON'T TELL ME ANYTHING ABOUT THEM.
...
MITSURU KNOWS.

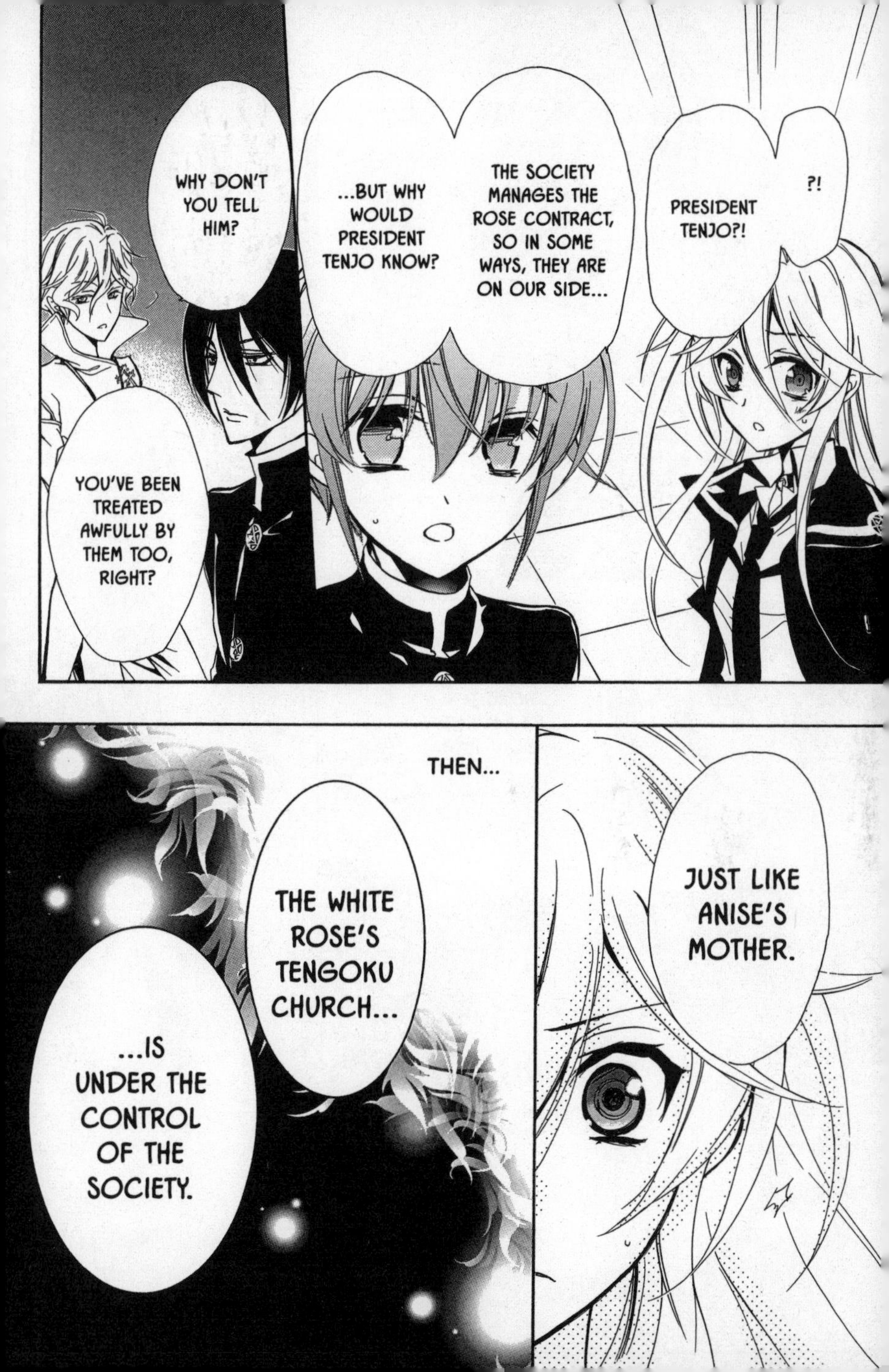
?!
PRESIDENT TENJO?!
THE SOCIETY MANAGES THE ROSE CONTRACT, SO IN SOME WAYS, THEY ARE ON OUR SIDE...
...BUT WHY WOULD PRESIDENT TENJO KNOW?
WHY DON'T YOU TELL HIM?
YOU'VE BEEN TREATED AWFULLY BY THEM TOO, RIGHT?
JUST LIKE ANISE'S MOTHER.
THEN...
THE WHITE ROSE'S TENGOKU CHURCH...
...IS UNDER THE CONTROL OF THE SOCIETY.

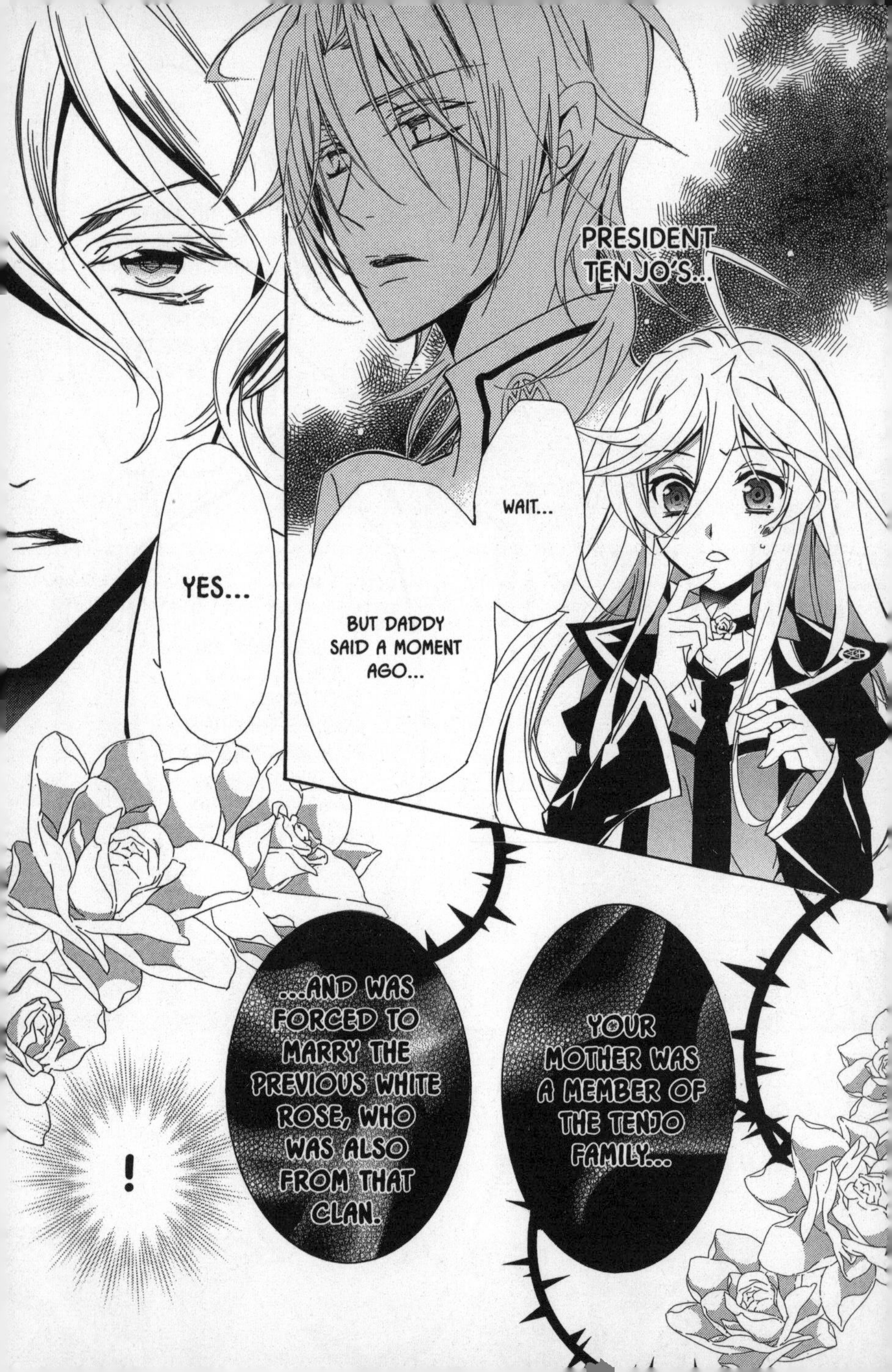
PRESIDENT TENJO'S...
WAIT...
BUT DADDY SAID A MOMENT AGO...
YES...
YOUR MOTHER WAS A MEMBER OF THE TENJO FAMILY...
...AND WAS FORCED TO MARRY THE PREVIOUS WHITE ROSE, WHO WAS ALSO FROM THAT CLAN.
!

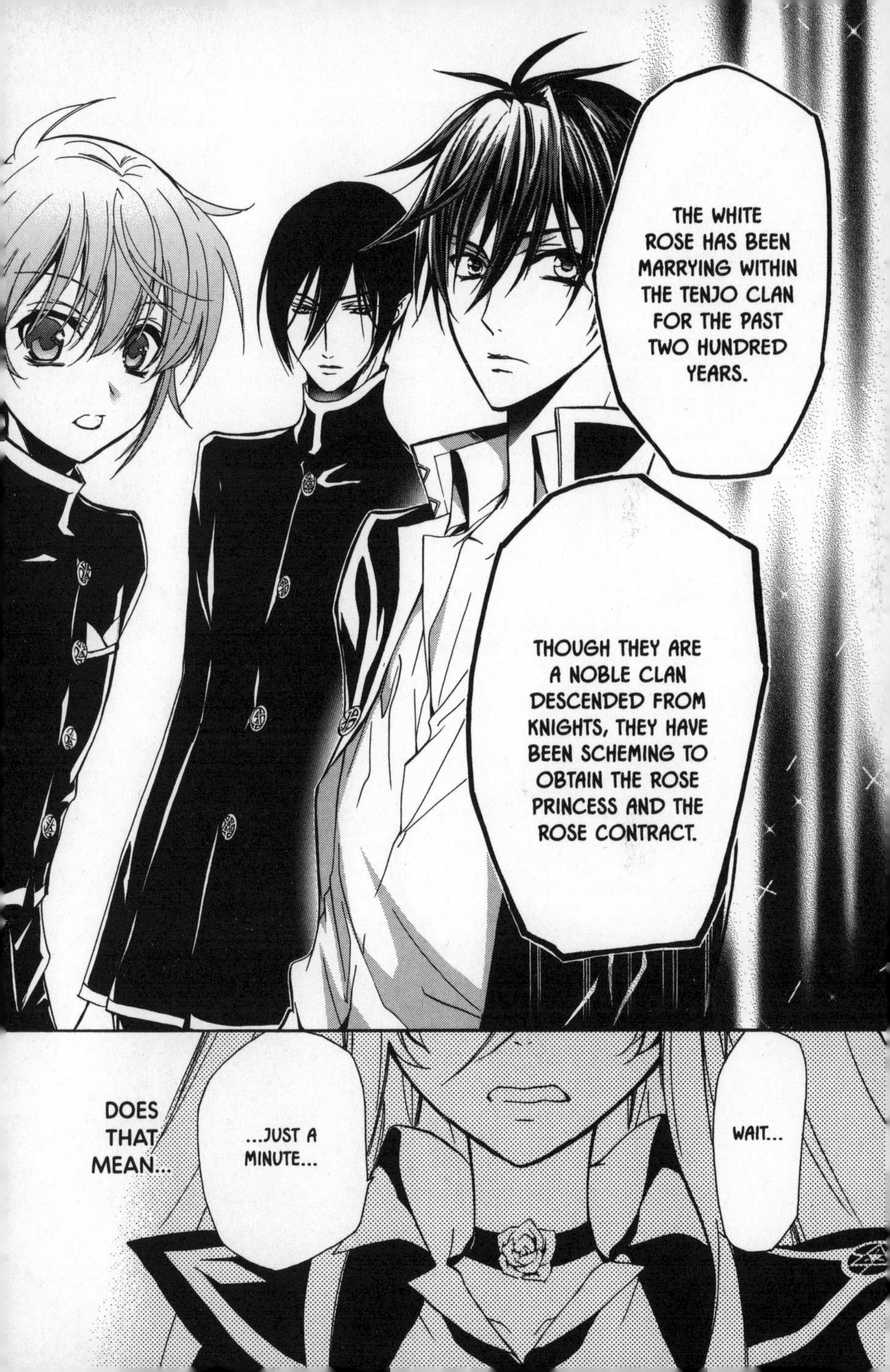
THE WHITE ROSE HAS BEEN MARRYING WITHIN THE TENJO CLAN FOR THE PAST TWO HUNDRED YEARS.
THOUGH THEY ARE A NOBLE CLAN DESCENDED FROM KNIGHTS, THEY HAVE BEEN SCHEMING TO OBTAIN THE ROSE PRINCESS AND THE ROSE CONTRACT.
WAIT...
...JUST A MINUTE...
DOES THAT MEAN...

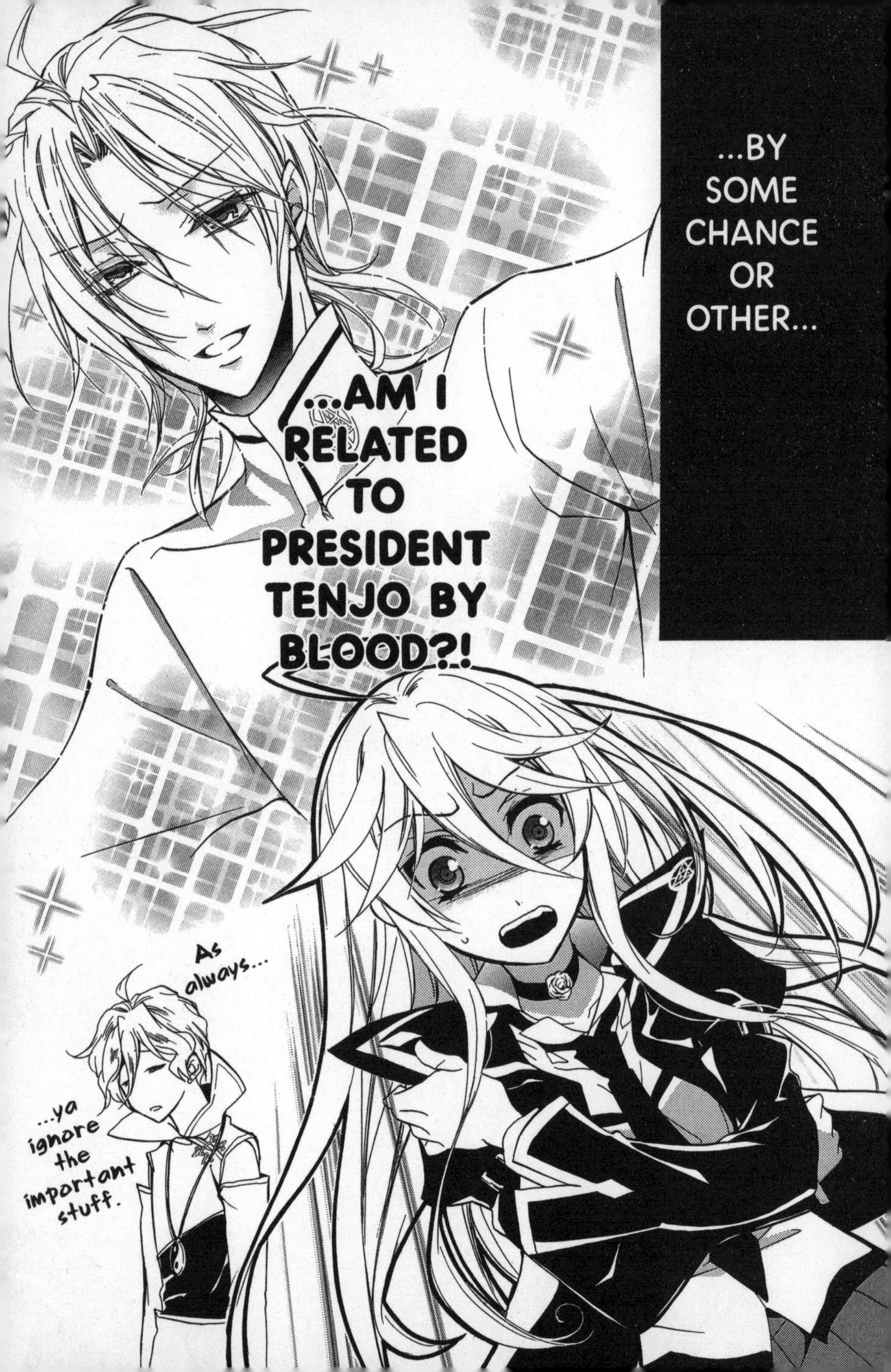
...BY SOME CHANCE OR OTHER...
...AM I RELATED TO PRESIDENT TENJO BY BLOOD?!
As always...
...ya ignore the important stuff.

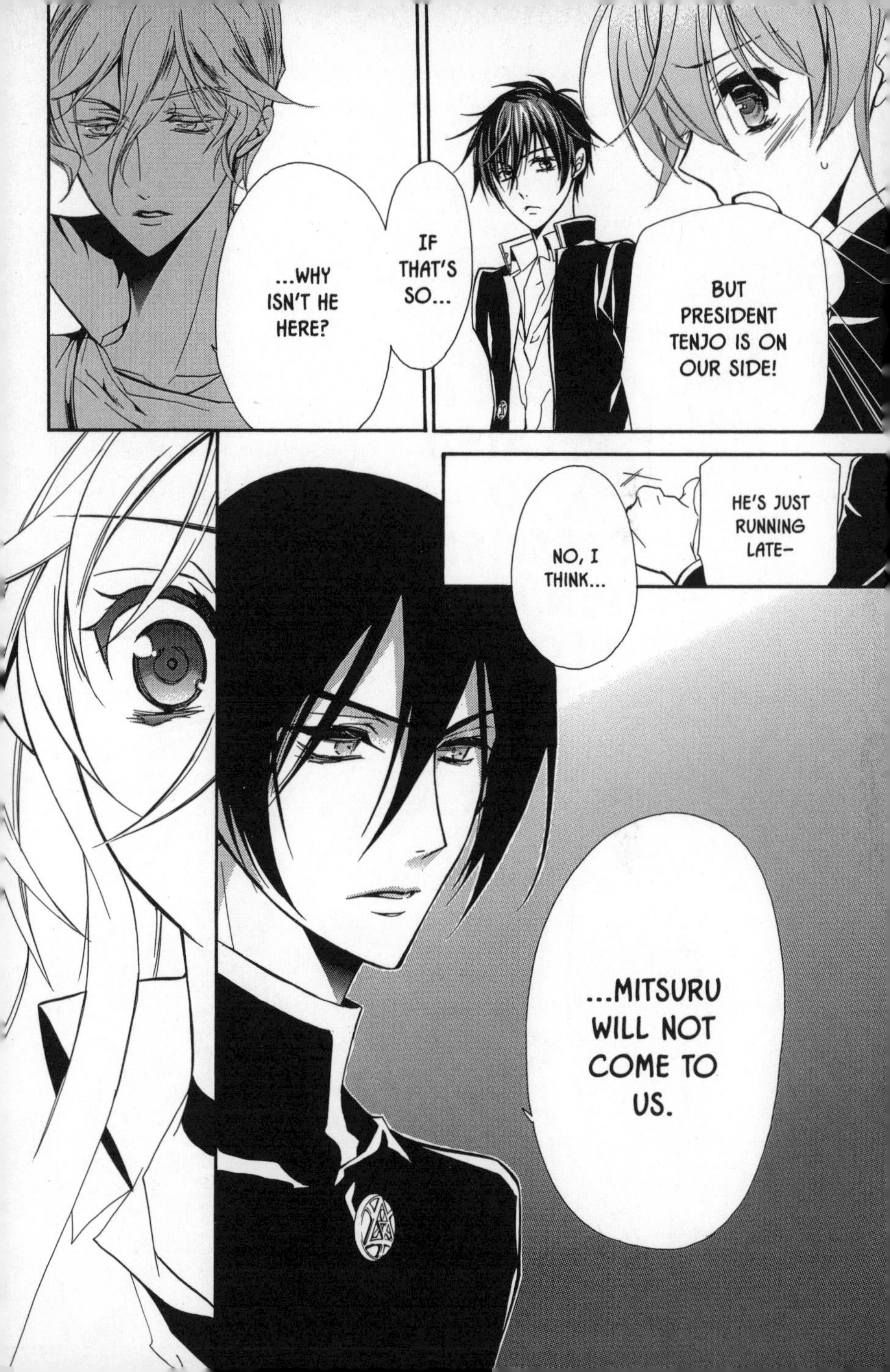
BUT PRESIDENT TENJO IS ON OUR SIDE!
IF THAT'S SO...
...WHY ISN'T HE HERE?
HE'S JUST RUNNING LATE–
NO, I THINK...
...MITSURU WILL NOT COME TO US.

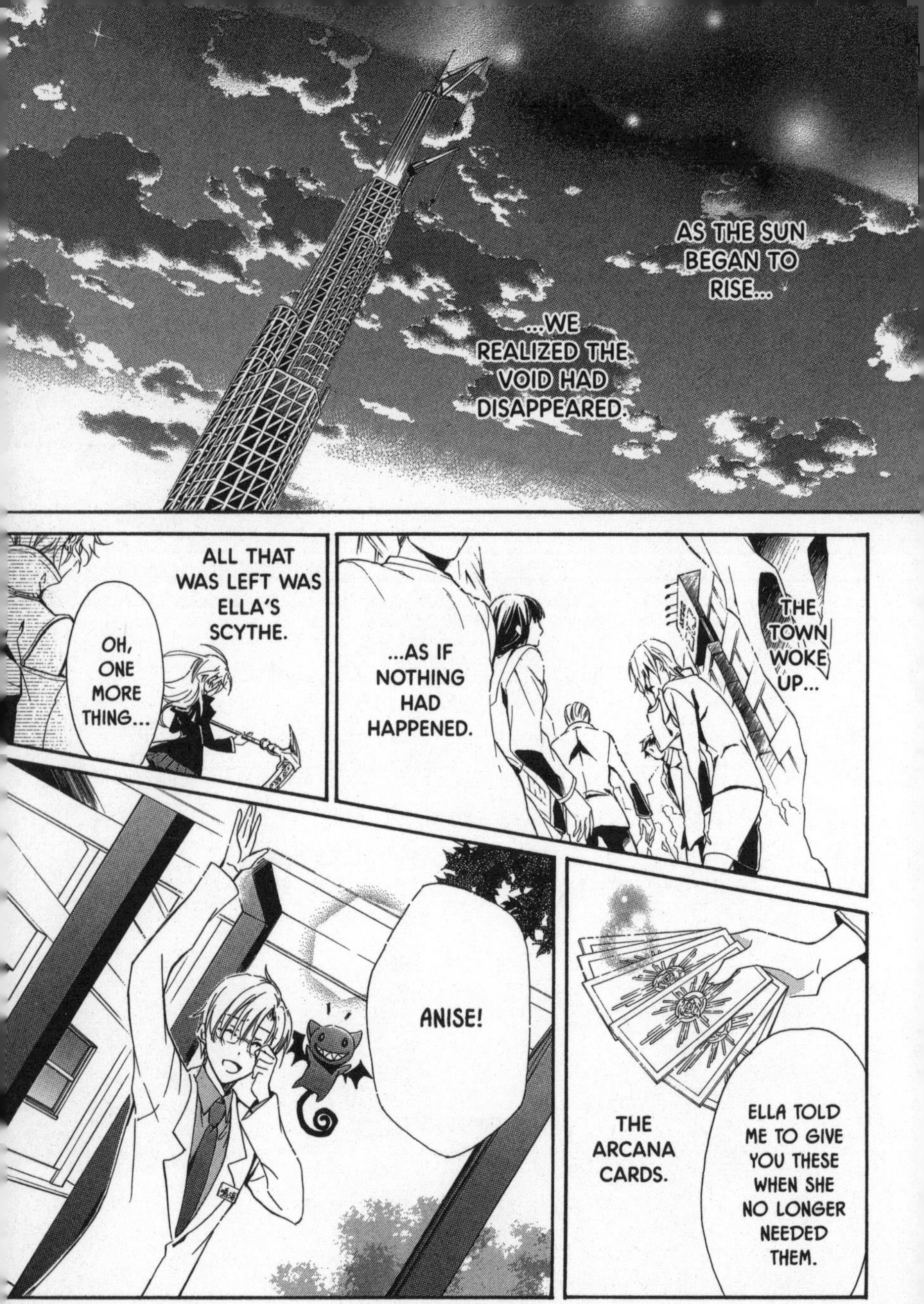
AS THE SUN BEGAN TO RISE...
...WE REALIZED THE VOID HAD DISAPPEARED.
THE TOWN WOKE UP...
...AS IF NOTHING HAD HAPPENED.
ALL THAT WAS LEFT WAS ELLA'S SCYTHE.
OH, ONE MORE THING...
ELLA TOLD ME TO GIVE YOU THESE WHEN SHE NO LONGER NEEDED THEM.
THE ARCANA CARDS.
ANISE!

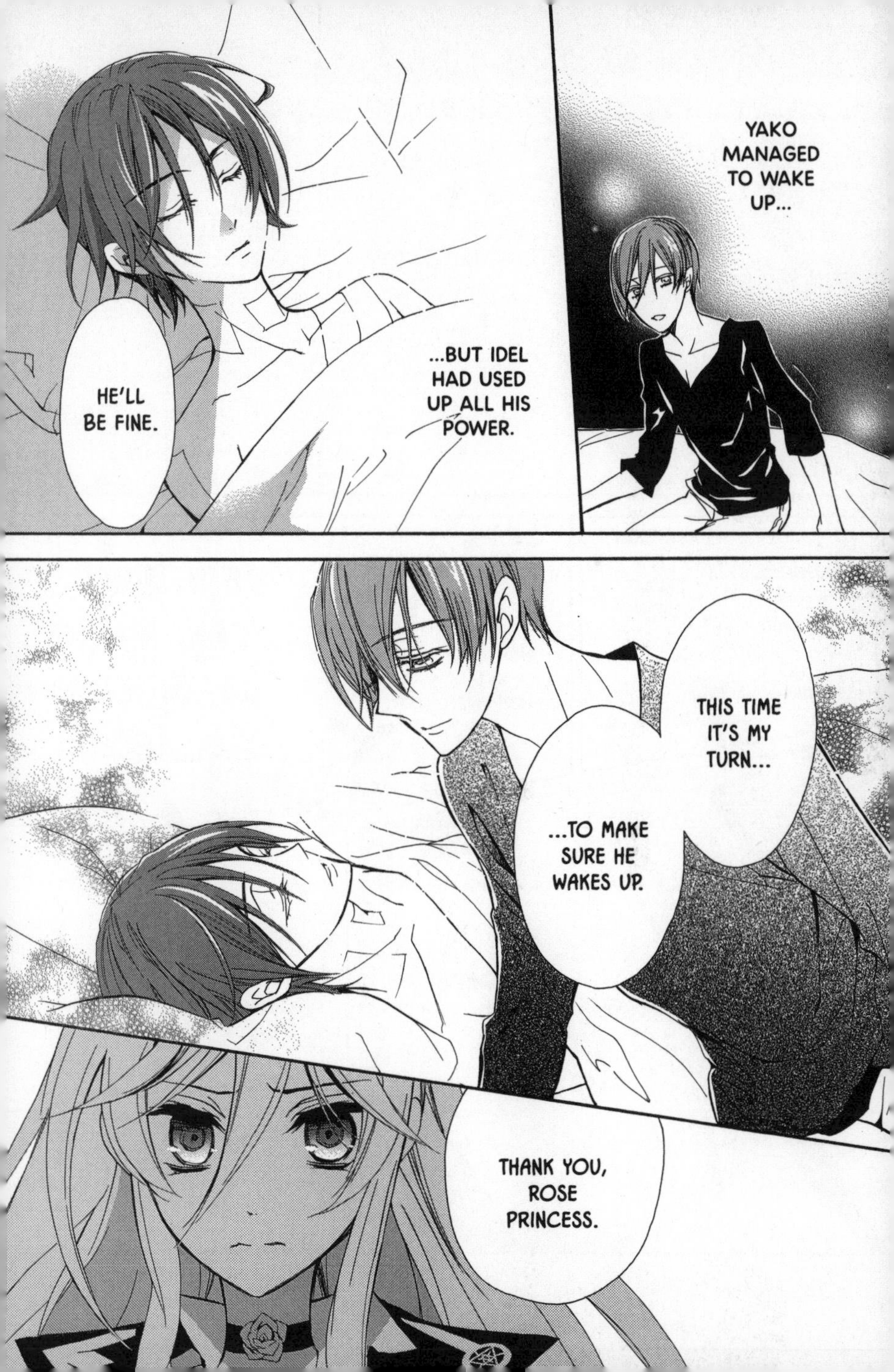
YAKO MANAGED TO WAKE UP...
...BUT IDEL HAD USED UP ALL HIS POWER.
HE'LL BE FINE.
THIS TIME IT'S MY TURN...
...TO MAKE SURE HE WAKES UP.
THANK YOU, ROSE PRINCESS.

PRESIDENT TENJO NEVER CAME.

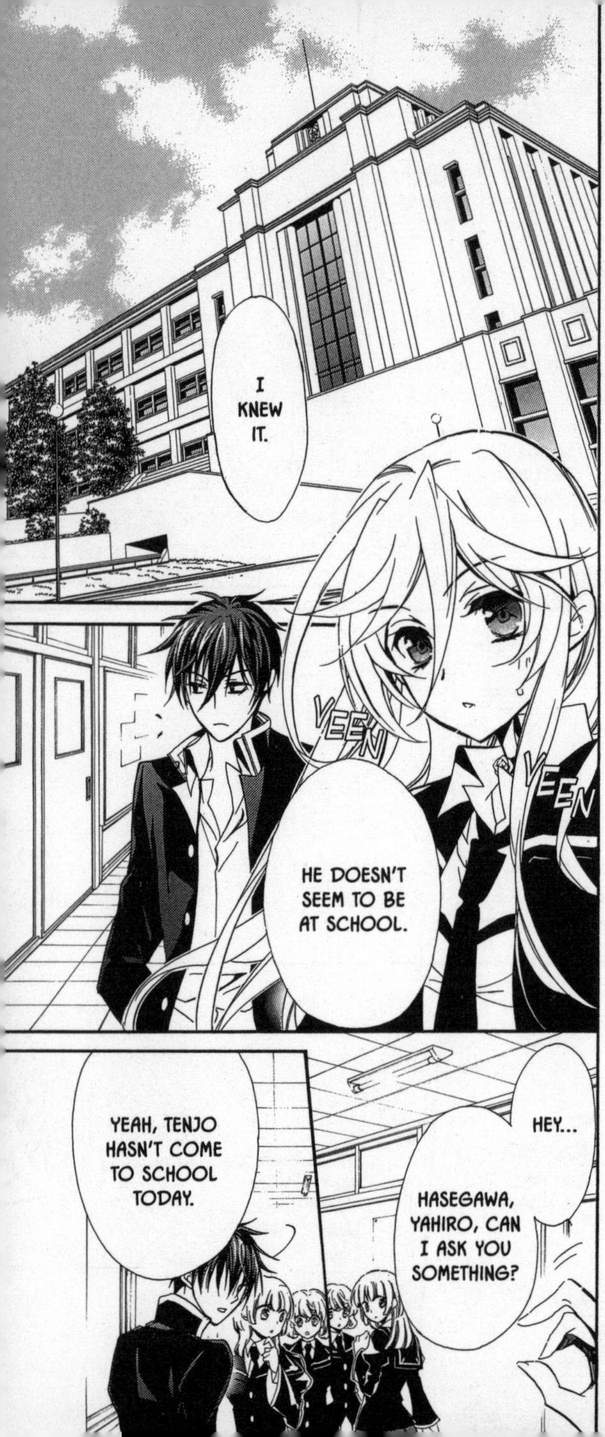
I KNEW IT.
VEEN
VEEN
HE DOESN'T SEEM TO BE AT SCHOOL.
HEY...
HASEGAWA, YAHIRO, CAN I ASK YOU SOMETHING?
YEAH, TENJO HASN'T COME TO SCHOOL TODAY.

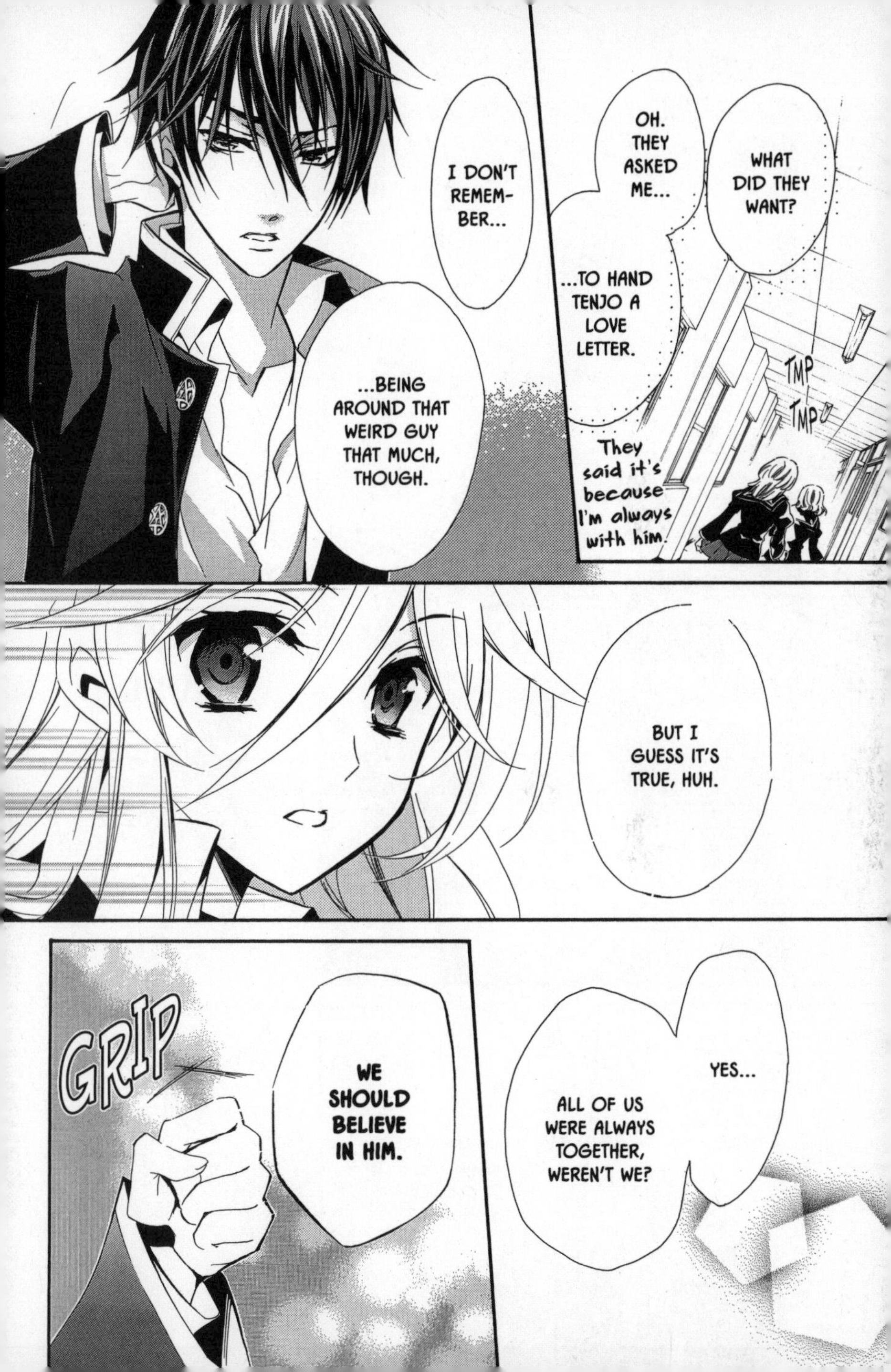
WHAT DID THEY WANT?
OH. THEY ASKED ME...
...TO HAND TENJO A LOVE LETTER.
TMP
TMP
They said it's because I'm always with him.
I DON'T REMEM-BER...
...BEING AROUND THAT WEIRD GUY THAT MUCH, THOUGH.
BUT I GUESS IT'S TRUE, HUH.
YES...
ALL OF US WERE ALWAYS TOGETHER, WEREN'T WE?
WE SHOULD BELIEVE IN HIM.
GRIP

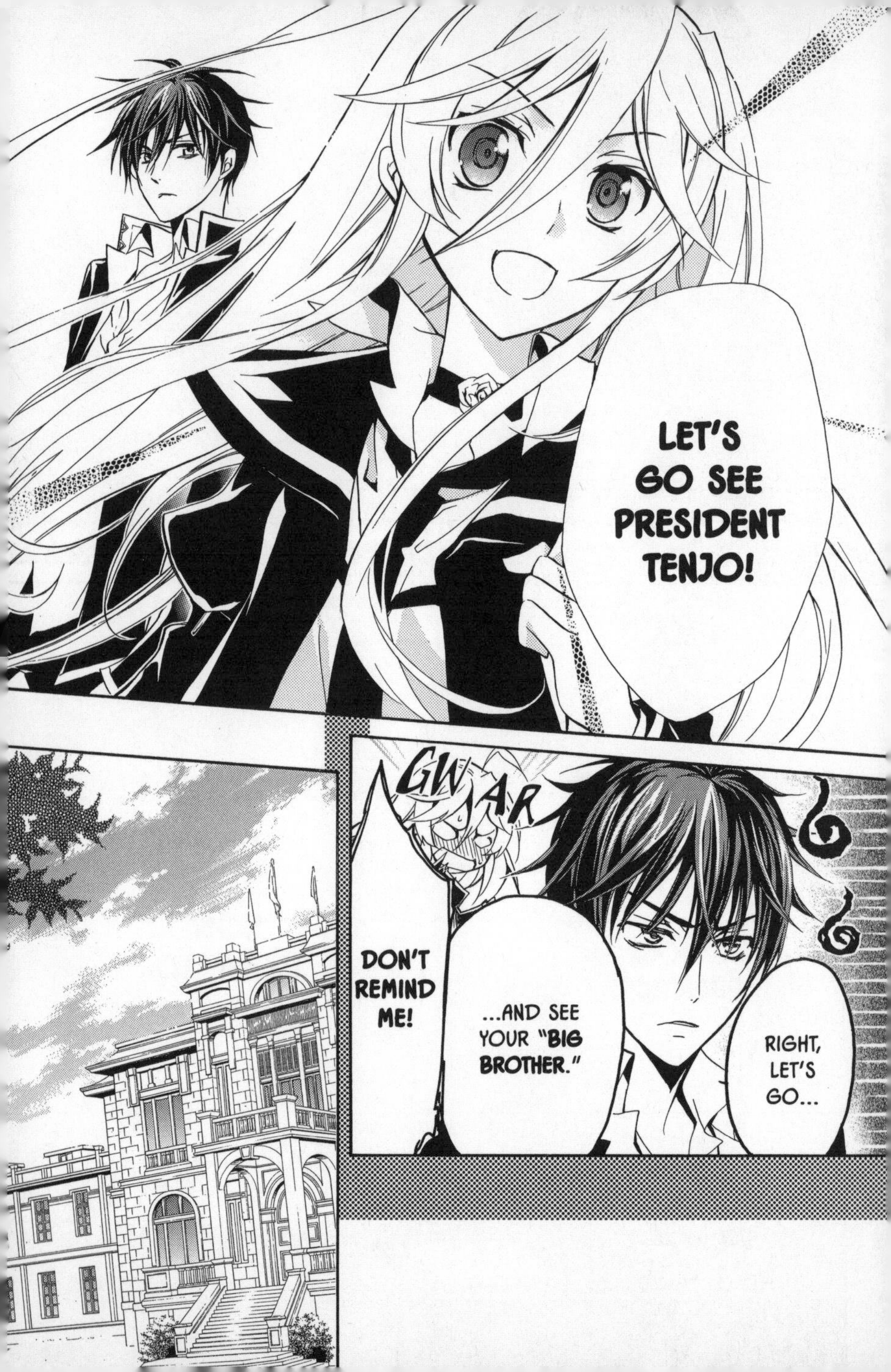
LET'S GO SEE PRESIDENT TENJO!
RIGHT, LET'S GO...
...AND SEE YOUR "BIG BROTHER."
GWAR
DON'T REMIND ME!

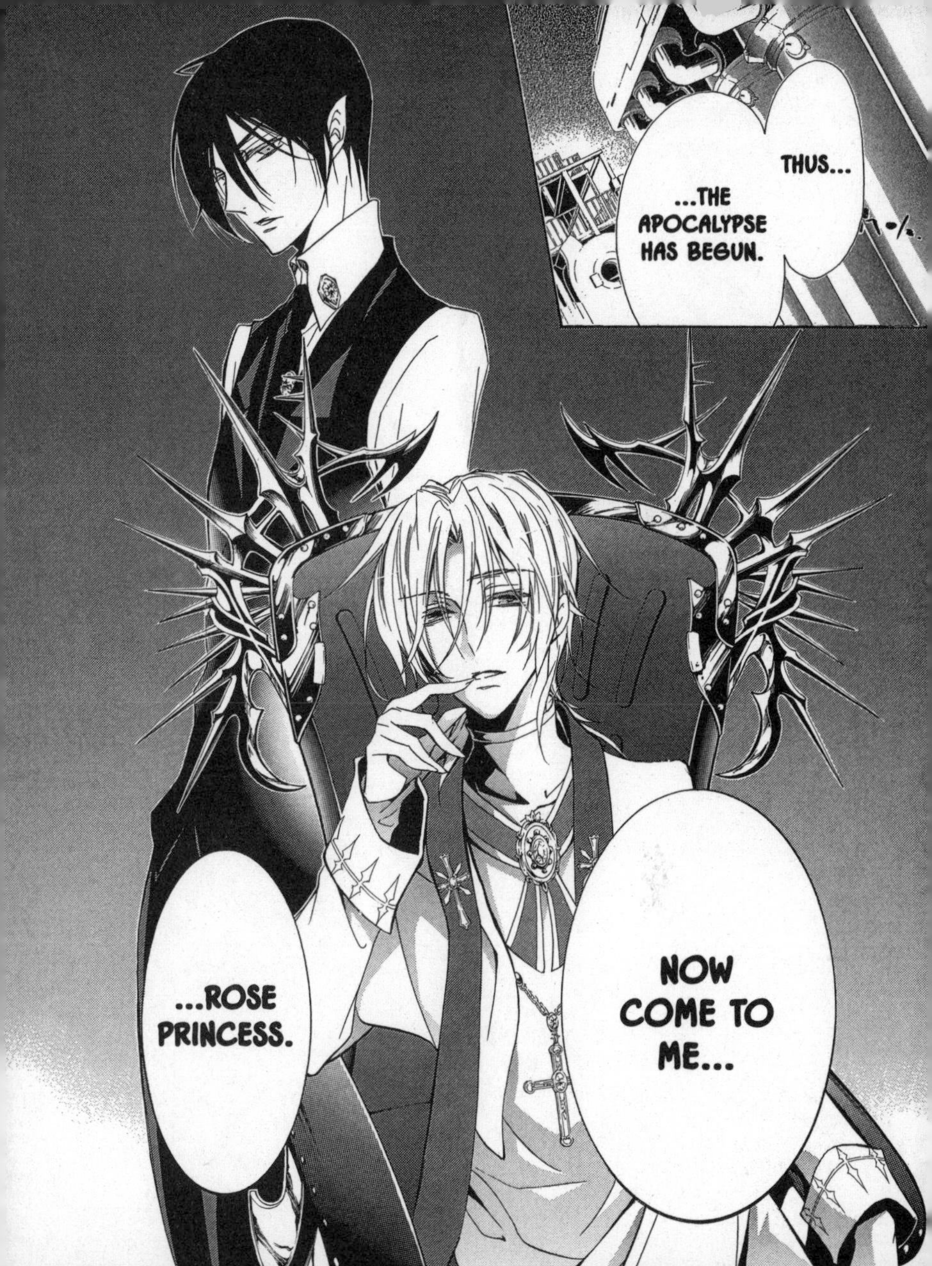
THUS...
...THE APOCALYPSE HAS BEGUN.
NOW COME TO ME...
...ROSE PRINCESS.

Kiss of the Rose Princess

Kiss of the Rose
Princess

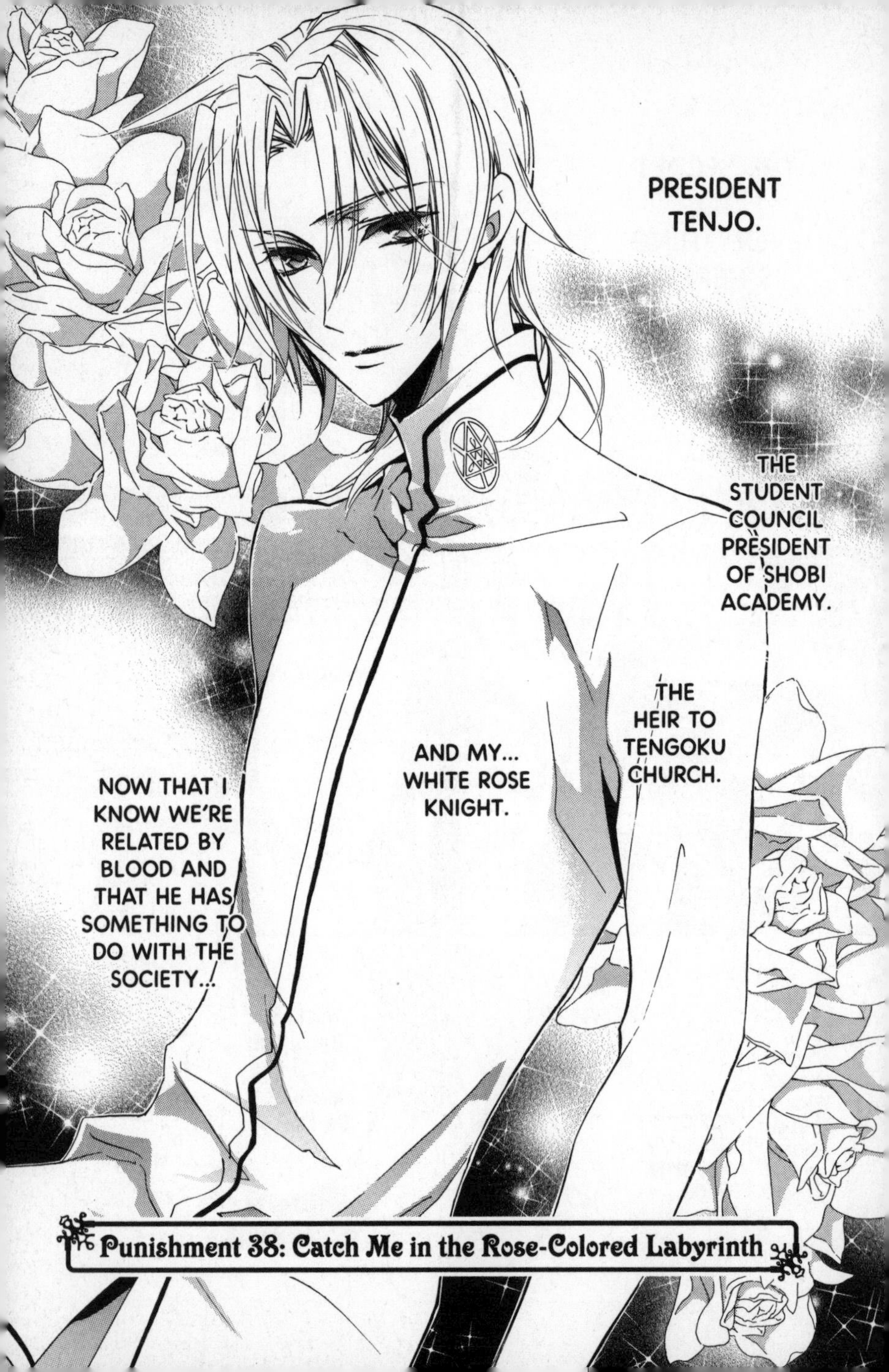
PRESIDENT TENJO.
THE STUDENT COUNCIL PRESIDENT OF SHOBI ACADEMY.
THE HEIR TO TENGOKU CHURCH.
AND MY... WHITE ROSE KNIGHT.
NOW THAT I KNOW WE'RE RELATED BY BLOOD AND THAT HE HAS SOMETHING TO DO WITH THE SOCIETY...
Punishment 38: Catch Me in the Rose-Colored Labyrinth

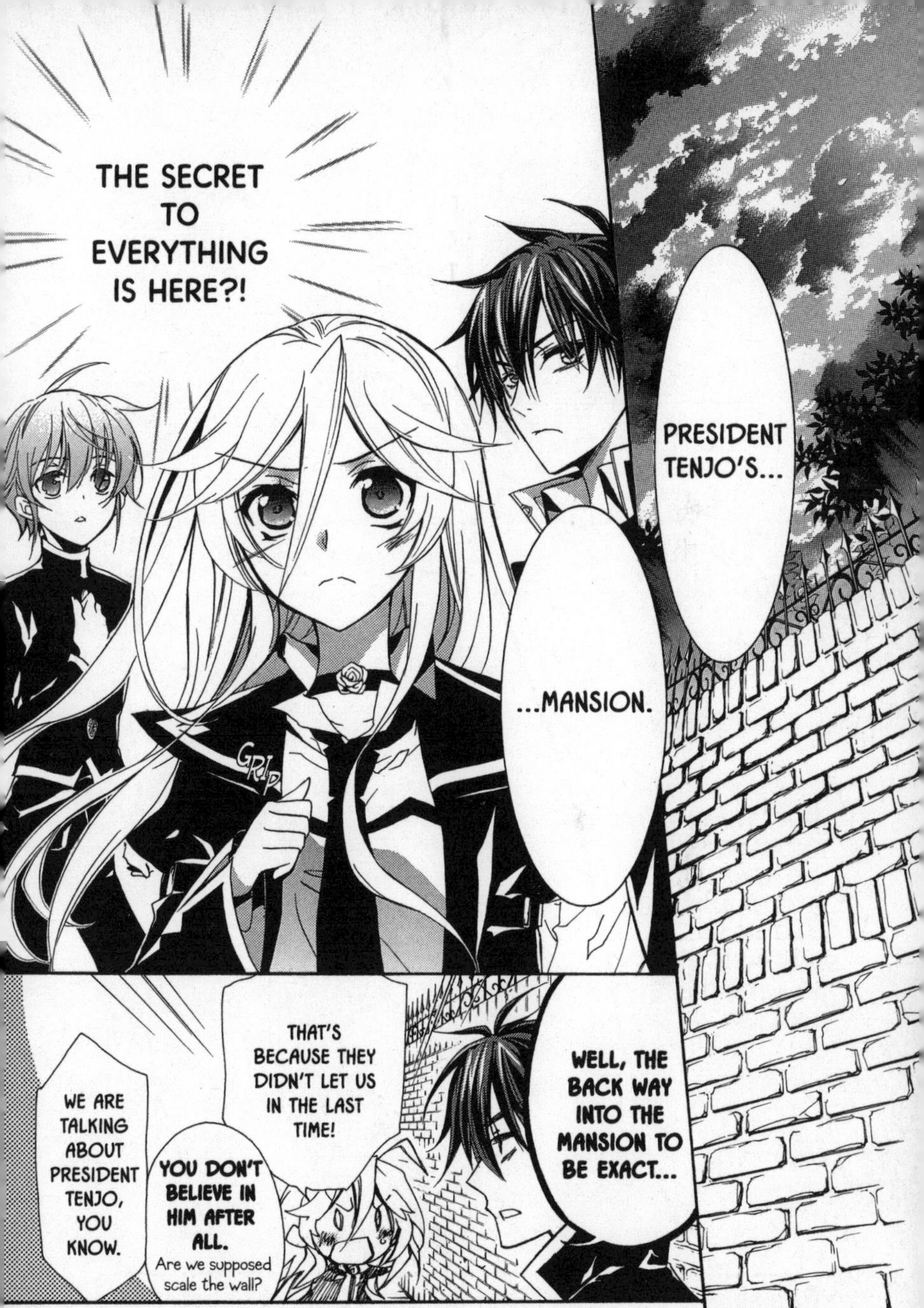
PRESIDENT TENJO'S...
...MANSION.
THE SECRET TO EVERYTHING IS HERE?!
GRIP
WELL, THE BACK WAY INTO THE MANSION TO BE EXACT...
THAT'S BECAUSE THEY DIDN'T LET US IN THE LAST TIME!
YOU DON'T BELIEVE IN HIM AFTER ALL.
Are we supposed scale the wall?
WE ARE TALKING ABOUT PRESIDENT TENJO, YOU KNOW.

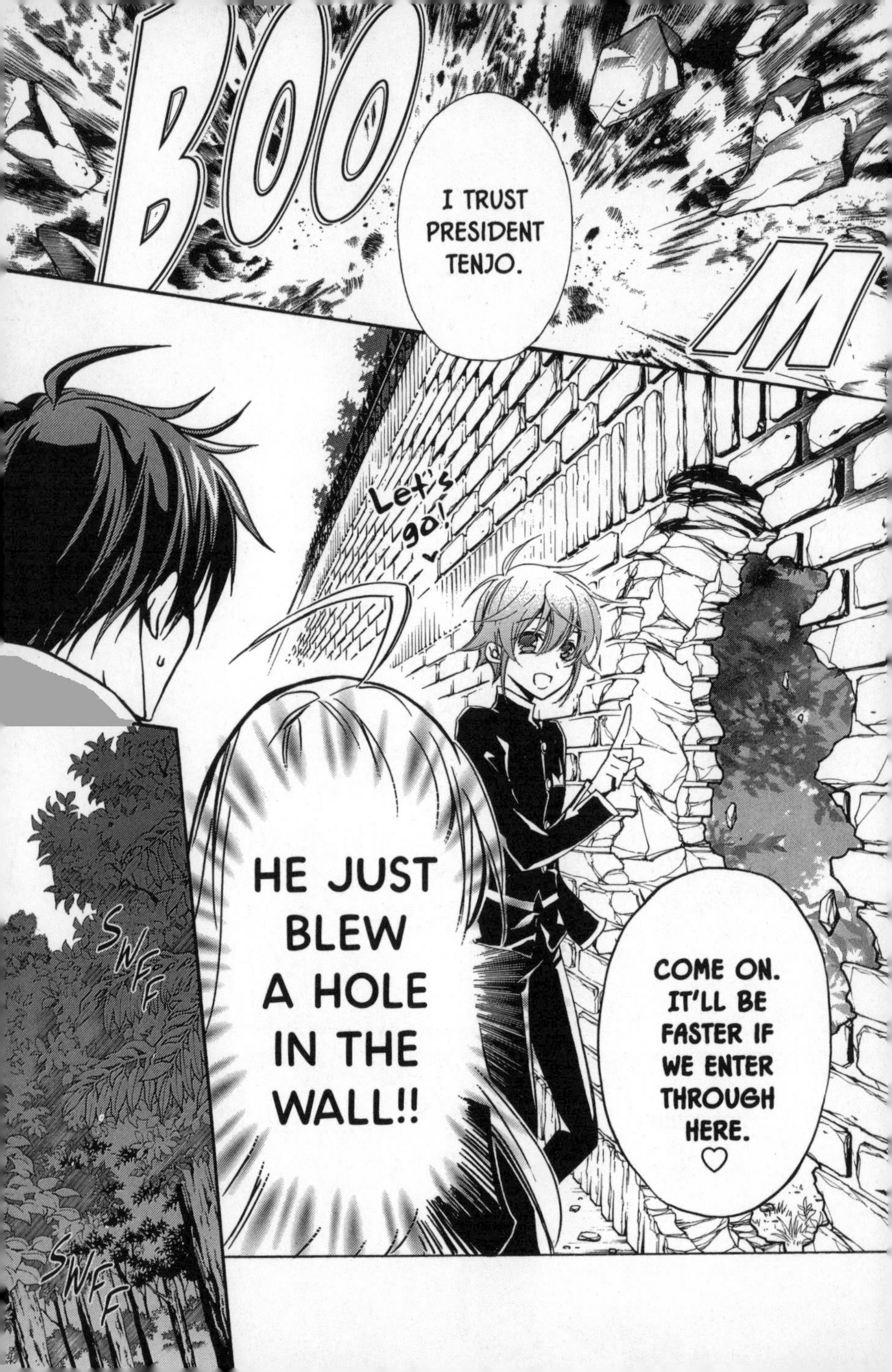
BOOOM
I TRUST PRESIDENT TENJO.
COME ON. IT'LL BE FASTER IF WE ENTER THROUGH HERE. ♡
Let's go! ♥
HE JUST BLEW A HOLE IN THE WALL!!
SWFF
SWFF

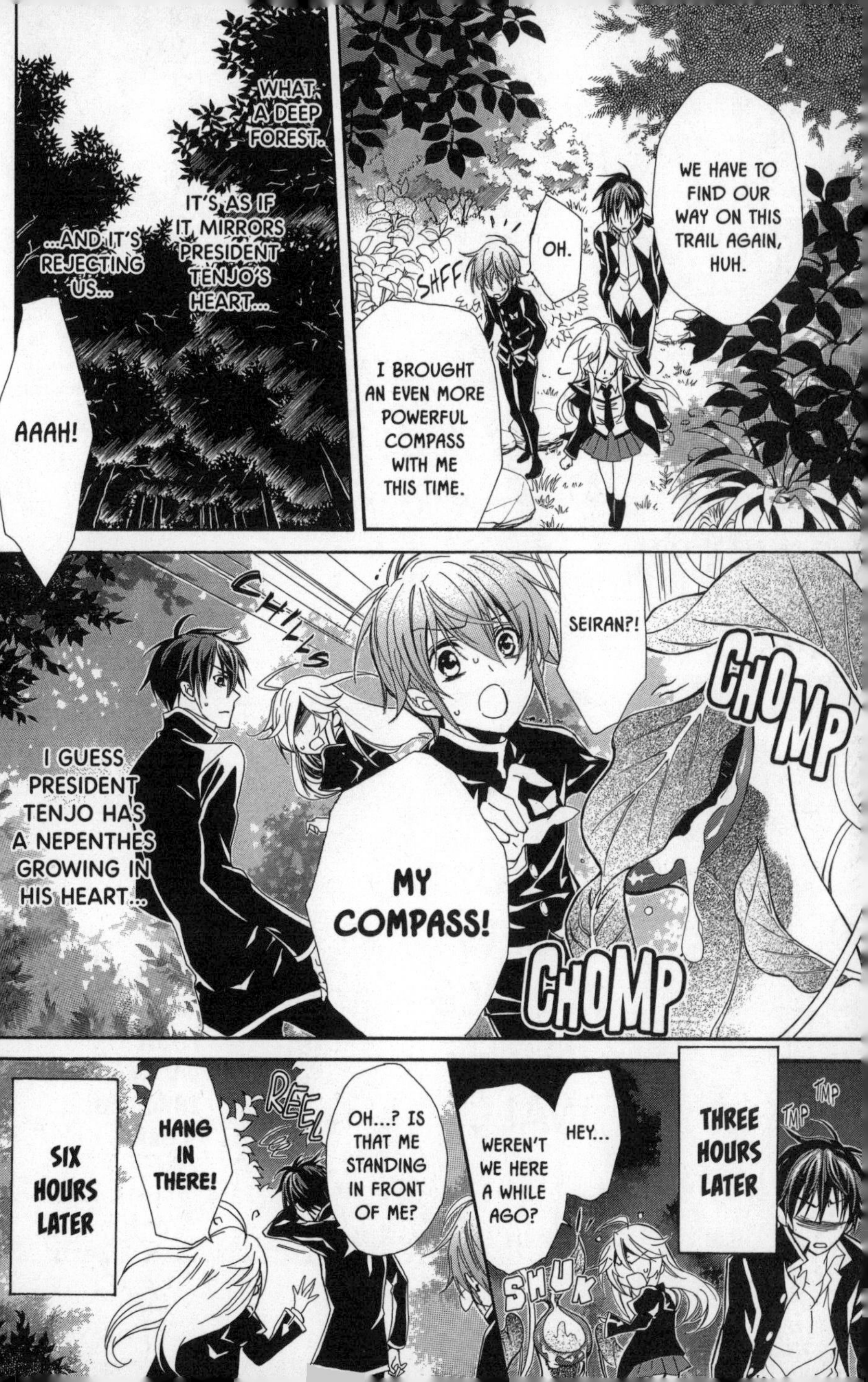
WE HAVE TO FIND OUR WAY ON THIS TRAIL AGAIN, HUH.
OH.
SHFF
I BROUGHT AN EVEN MORE POWERFUL COMPASS WITH ME THIS TIME.
WHAT A DEEP FOREST.
IT'S AS IF IT MIRRORS PRESIDENT TENJO'S HEART...
...AND IT'S REJECTING US...
AAAH!
SEIRAN?!
CHOMP
CHILLS
MY COMPASS!
CHOMP
I GUESS PRESIDENT TENJO HAS A NEPENTHES GROWING IN HIS HEART...
TMP
TMP
THREE HOURS LATER
HEY...
WEREN'T WE HERE A WHILE AGO?
SHUK
OH...? IS THAT ME STANDING IN FRONT OF ME?
REEL
HANG IN THERE!
SIX HOURS LATER

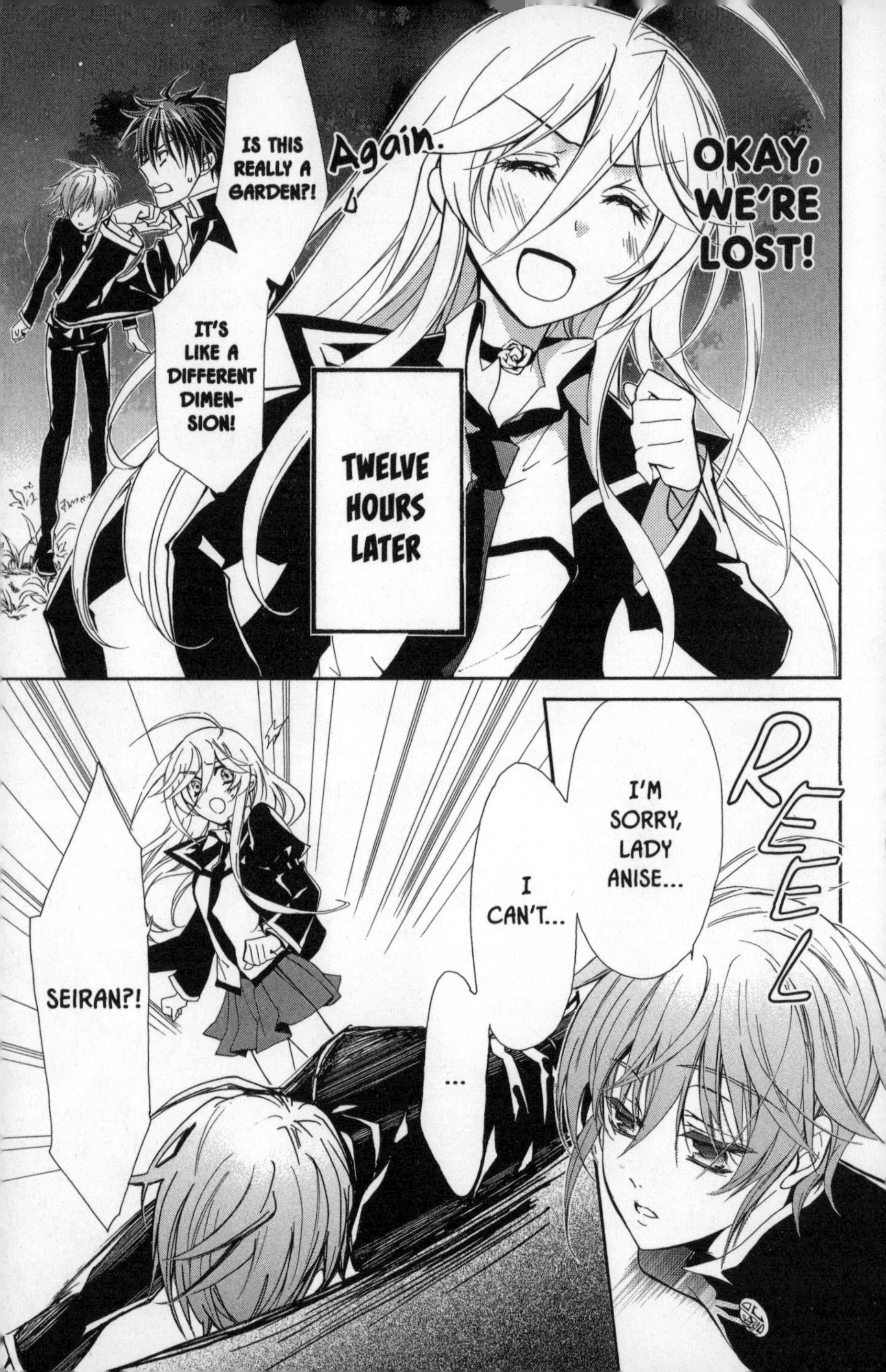
OKAY, WE'RE LOST!
Again.
IS THIS REALLY A GARDEN?!
IT'S LIKE A DIFFERENT DIMENSION!
TWELVE HOURS LATER
REEL
I'M SORRY, LADY ANISE...
I CAN'T...
...
SEIRAN?!

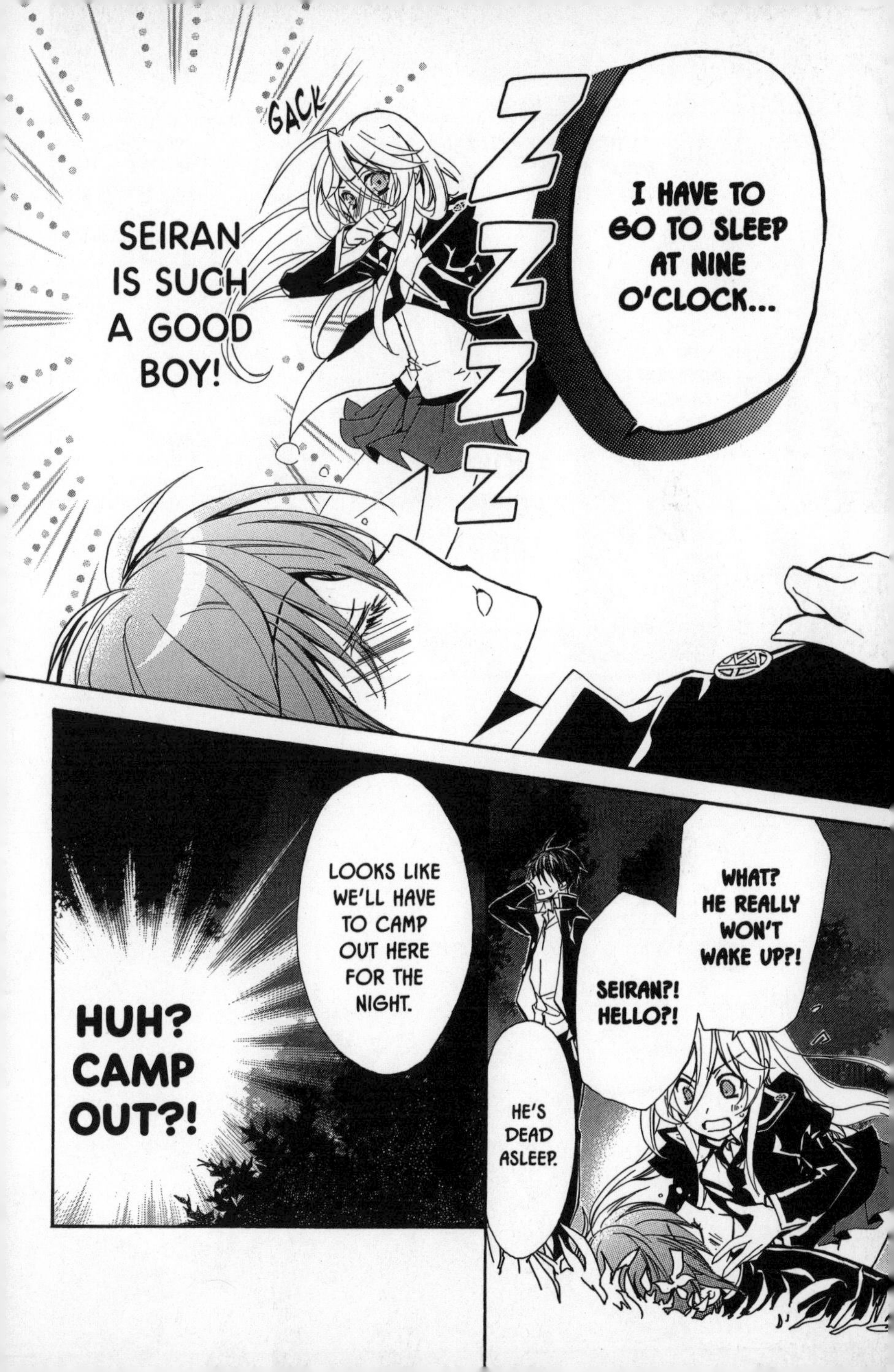
I HAVE TO GO TO SLEEP AT NINE O'CLOCK...
ZZZZZ
GACK
SEIRAN IS SUCH A GOOD BOY!
WHAT? HE REALLY WON'T WAKE UP?!
SEIRAN?! HELLO?!
HE'S DEAD ASLEEP.
LOOKS LIKE WE'LL HAVE TO CAMP OUT HERE FOR THE NIGHT.
HUH? CAMP OUT?!

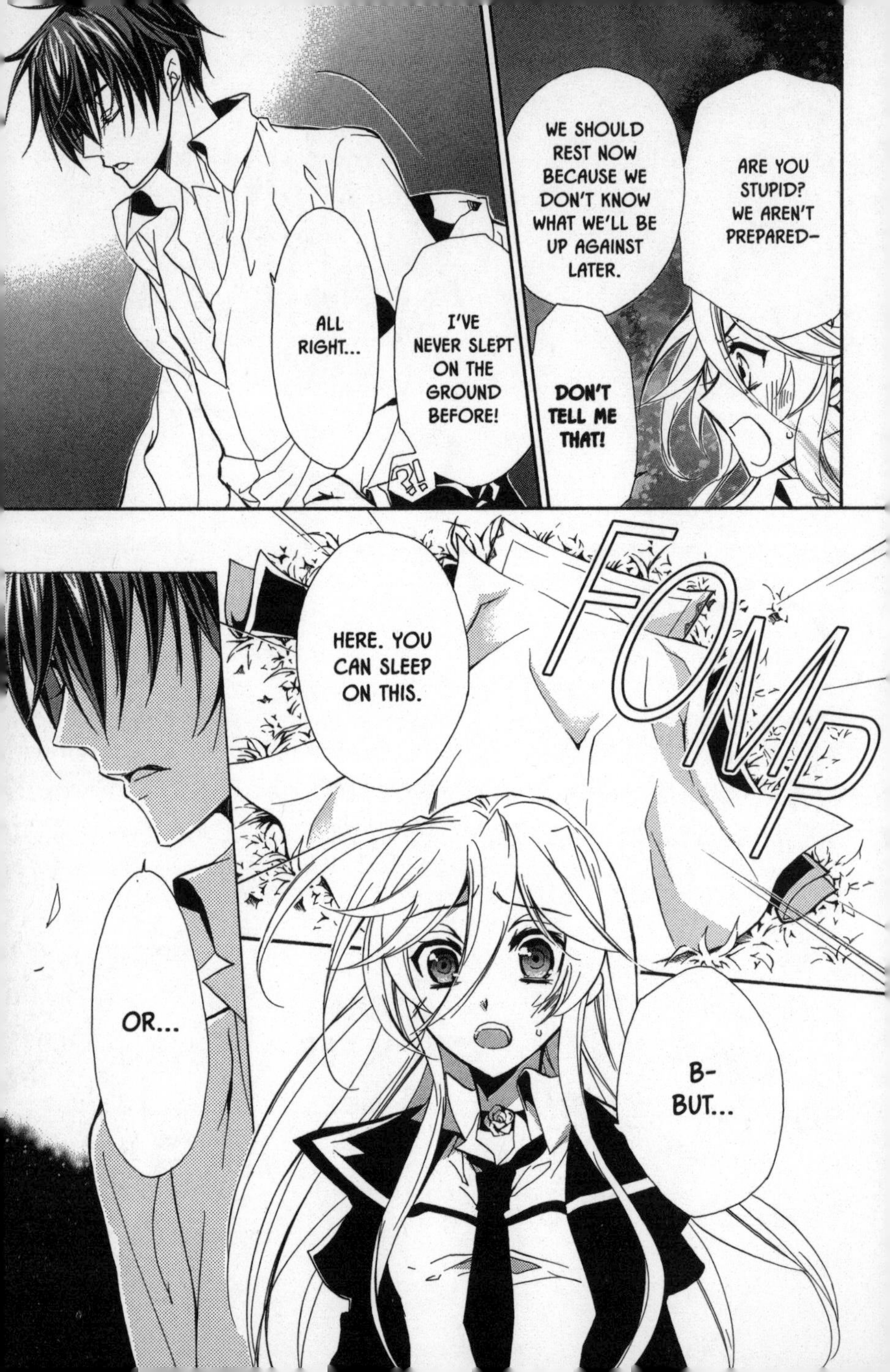

ARE YOU STUPID? WE AREN'T PREPARED—
WE SHOULD REST NOW BECAUSE WE DON'T KNOW WHAT WE'LL BE UP AGAINST LATER.
DON'T TELL ME THAT!
I'VE NEVER SLEPT ON THE GROUND BEFORE!
?!
ALL RIGHT...
FOMP
HERE. YOU CAN SLEEP ON THIS.
B-BUT...
OR...

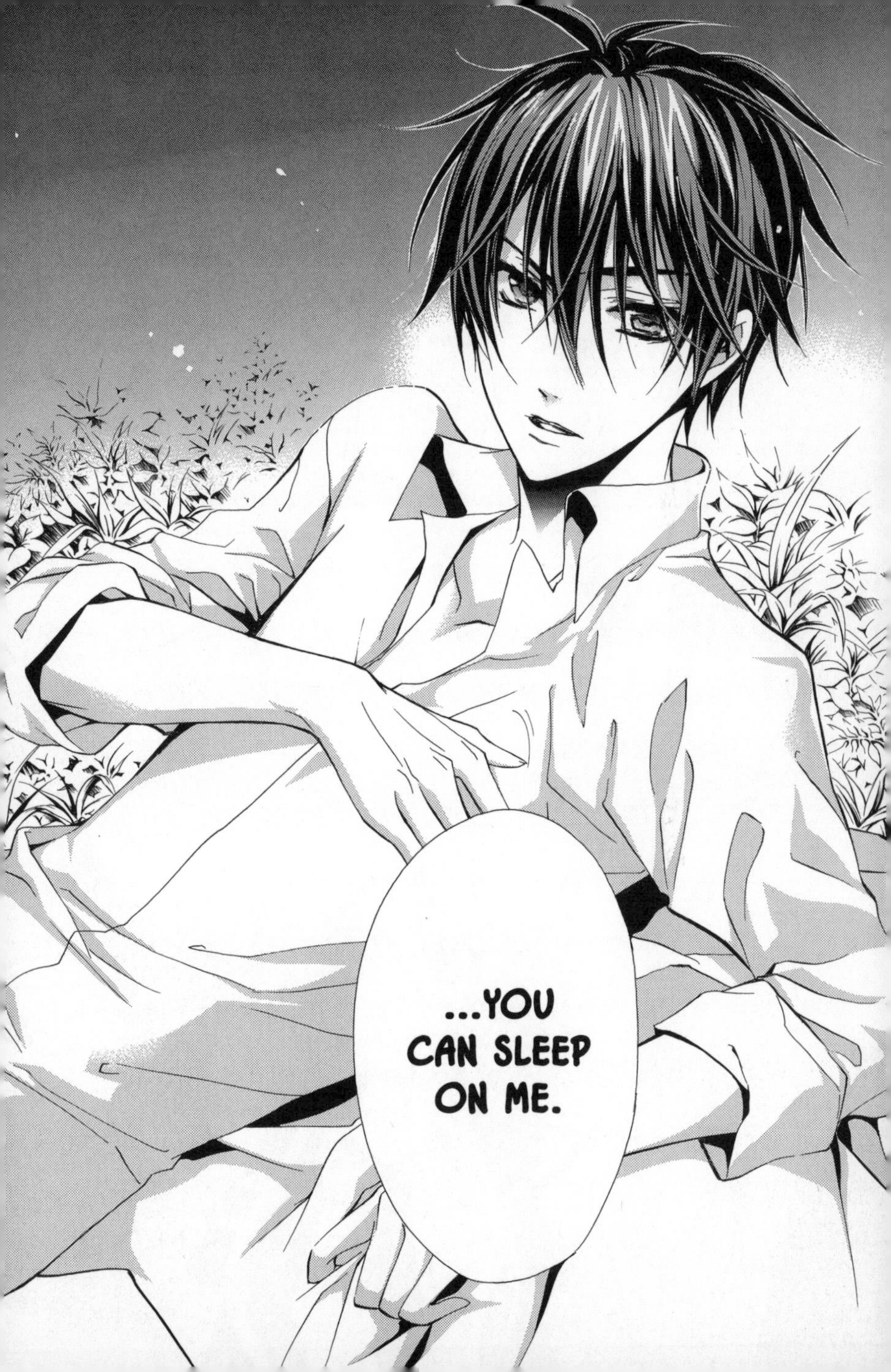
...YOU CAN SLEEP ON ME.

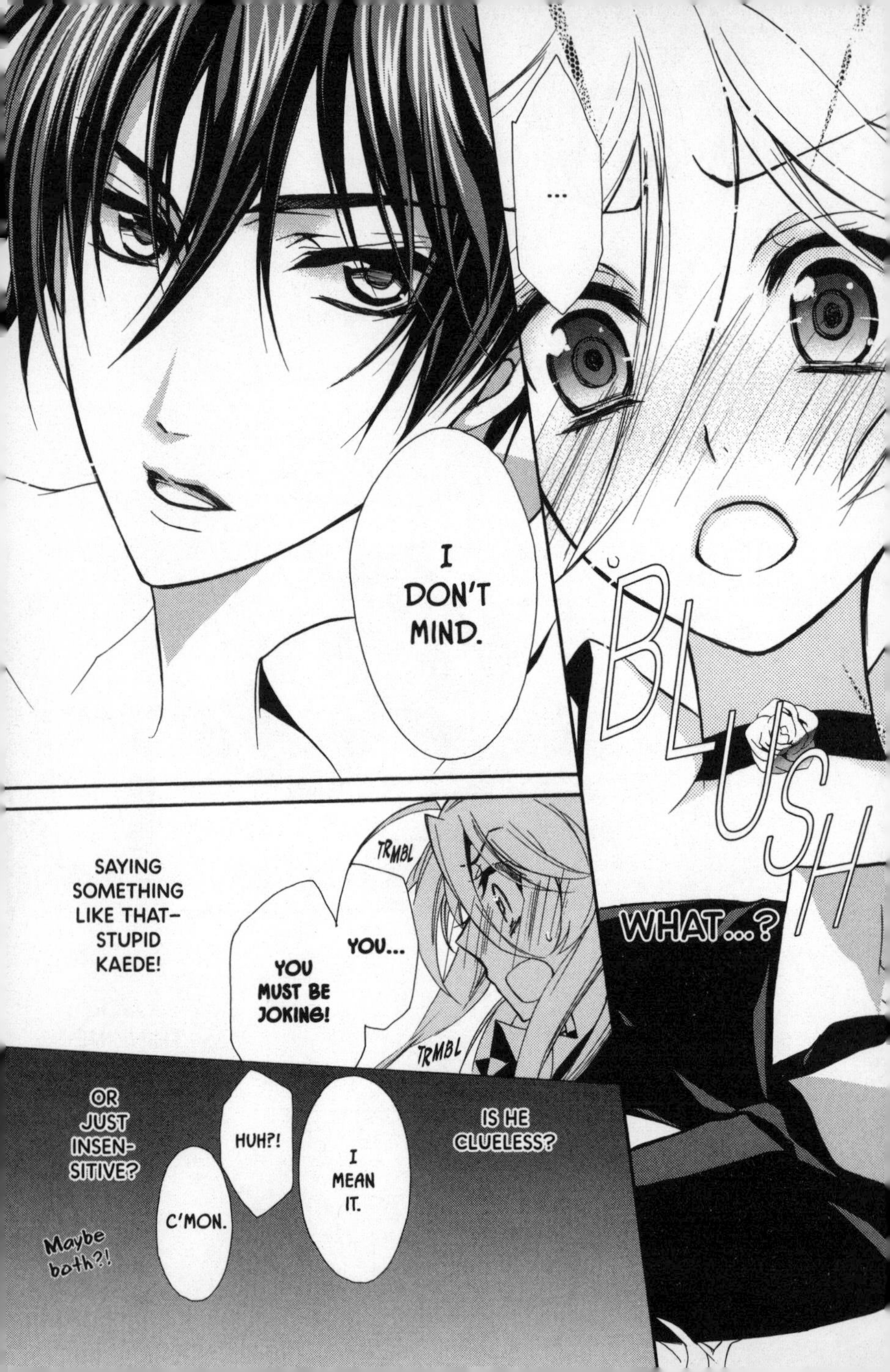
...
BLUSH
WHAT...?
I DON'T MIND.
TRMBL
YOU...
YOU MUST BE JOKING!
TRMBL
SAYING SOMETHING LIKE THAT— STUPID KAEDE!
IS HE CLUELESS?
I MEAN IT.
HUH?!
C'MON.
OR JUST INSEN-SITIVE?
Maybe both?!

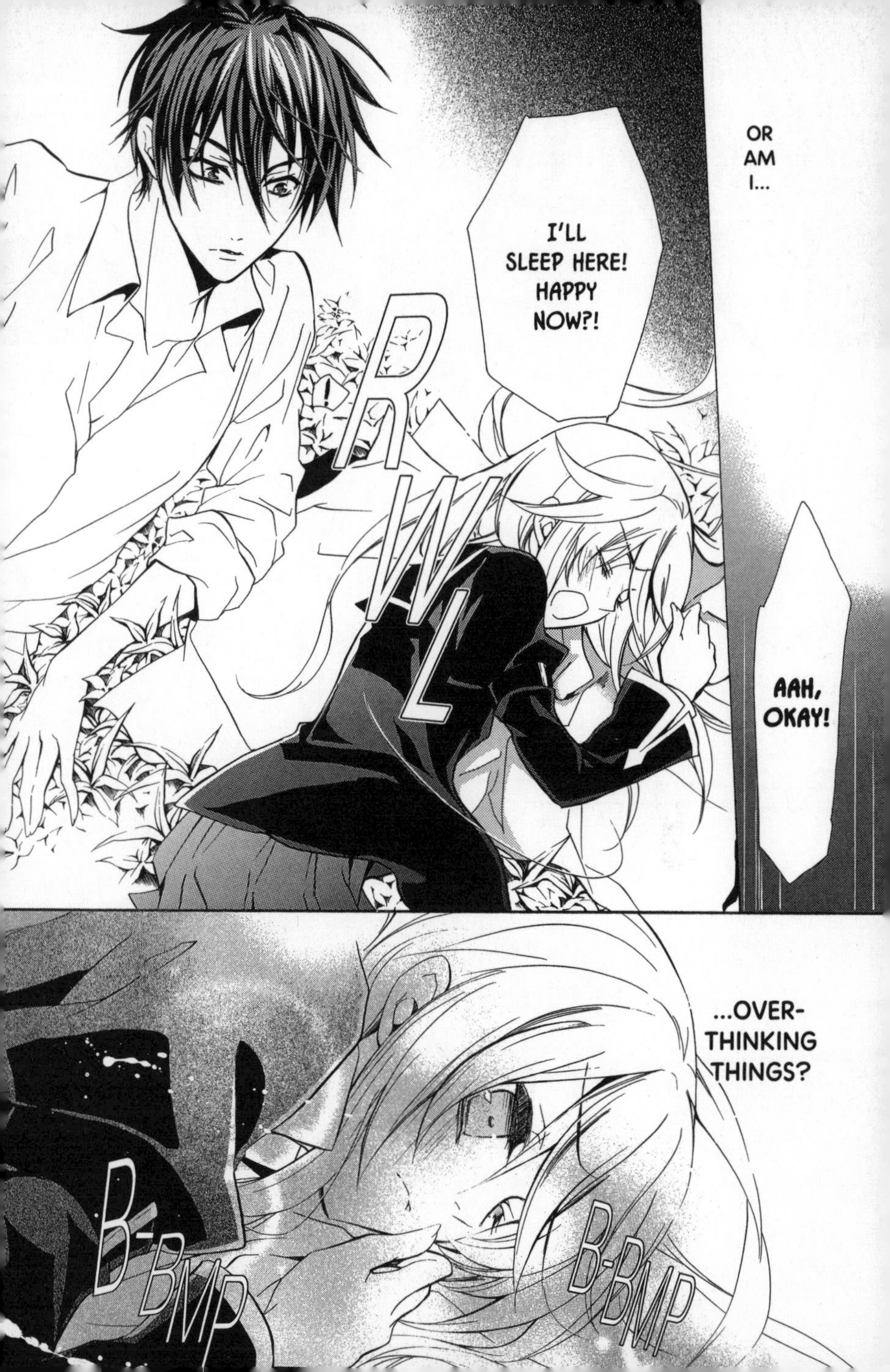
OR AM I...
I'LL SLEEP HERE! HAPPY NOW?!
RWL
AAH, OKAY!
...OVER-THINKING THINGS?
B-BMP
B-BMP

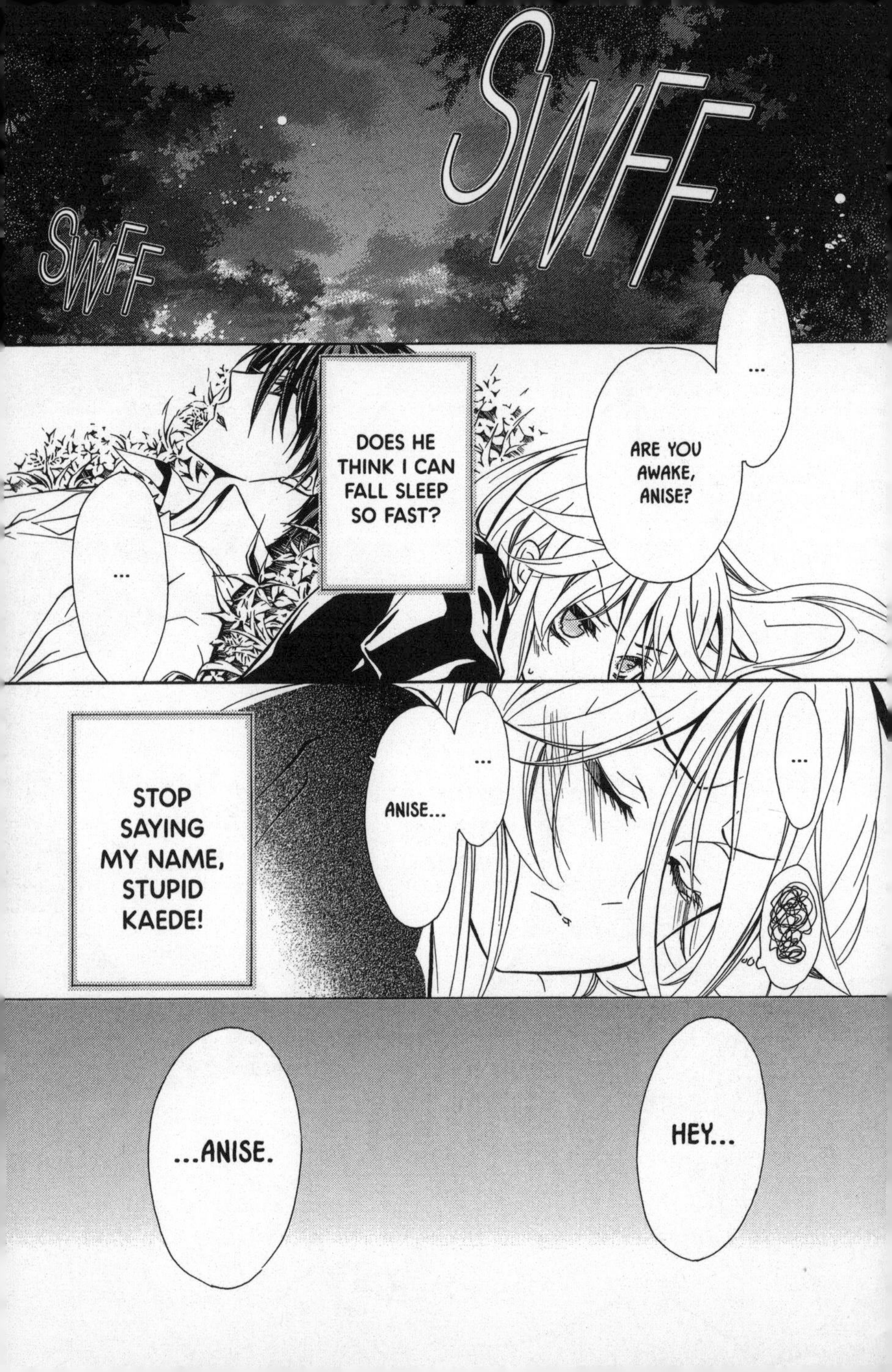
SWFF
SWFF
...
ARE YOU AWAKE, ANISE?
DOES HE THINK I CAN FALL SLEEP SO FAST?
...
...
...
ANISE...
STOP SAYING MY NAME, STUPID KAEDE!
HEY...
...ANISE.

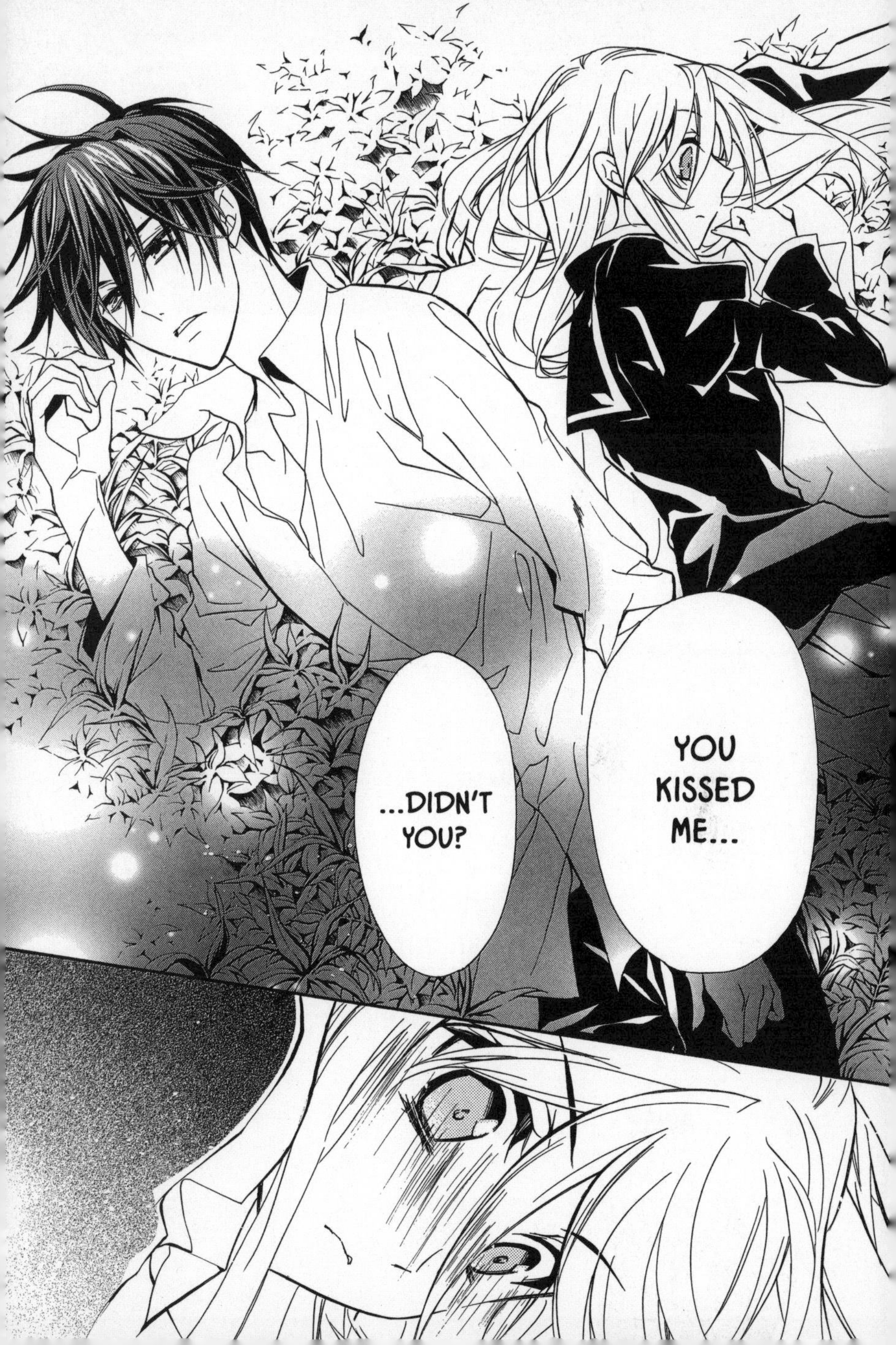
YOU KISSED ME...
...DIDN'T YOU?

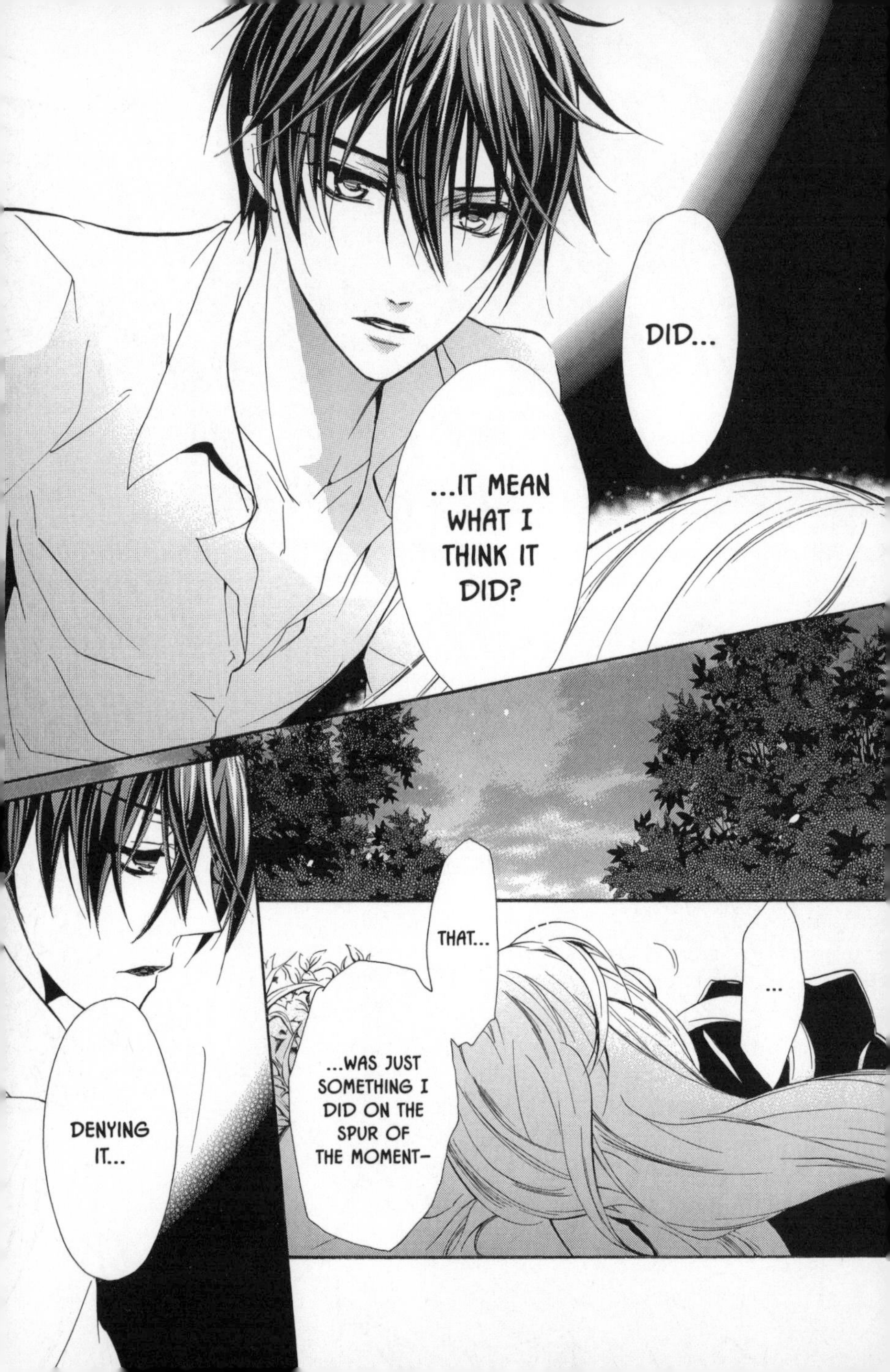
DID...
...IT MEAN WHAT I THINK IT DID?
...
THAT...
...WAS JUST SOMETHING I DID ON THE SPUR OF THE MOMENT–
DENYING IT...

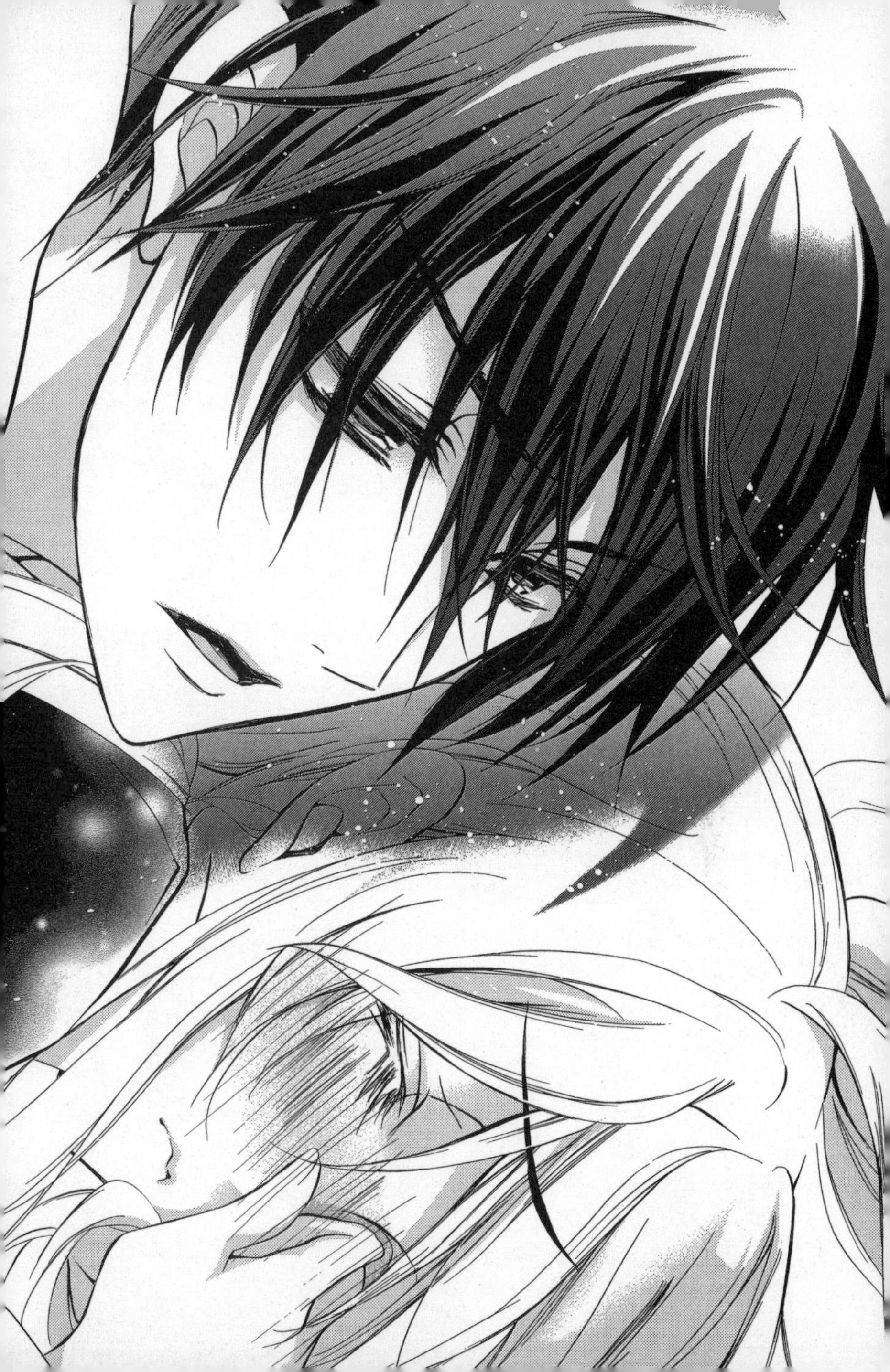

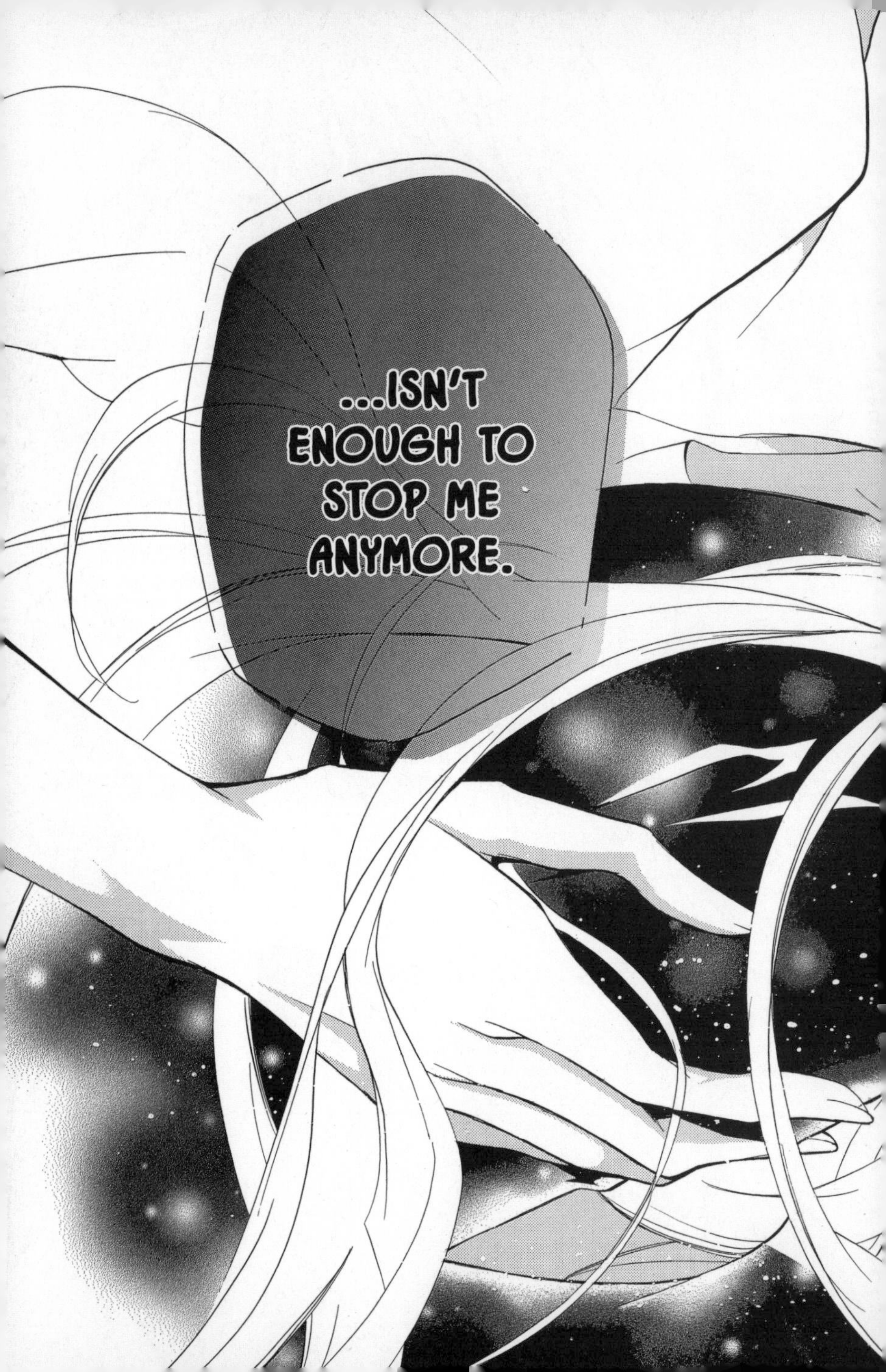
...ISN'T ENOUGH TO STOP ME ANYMORE.

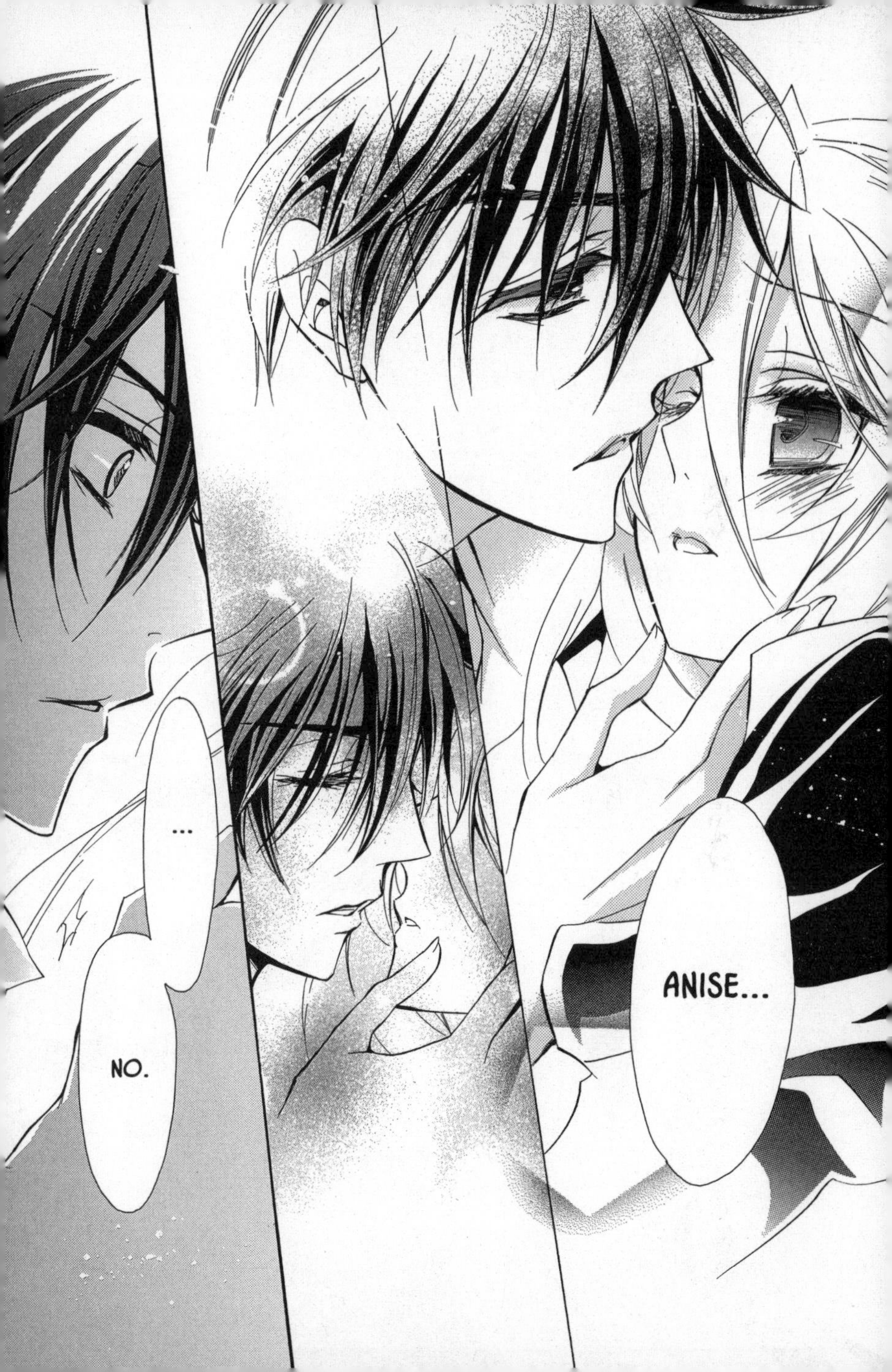
ANISE...
...
NO.

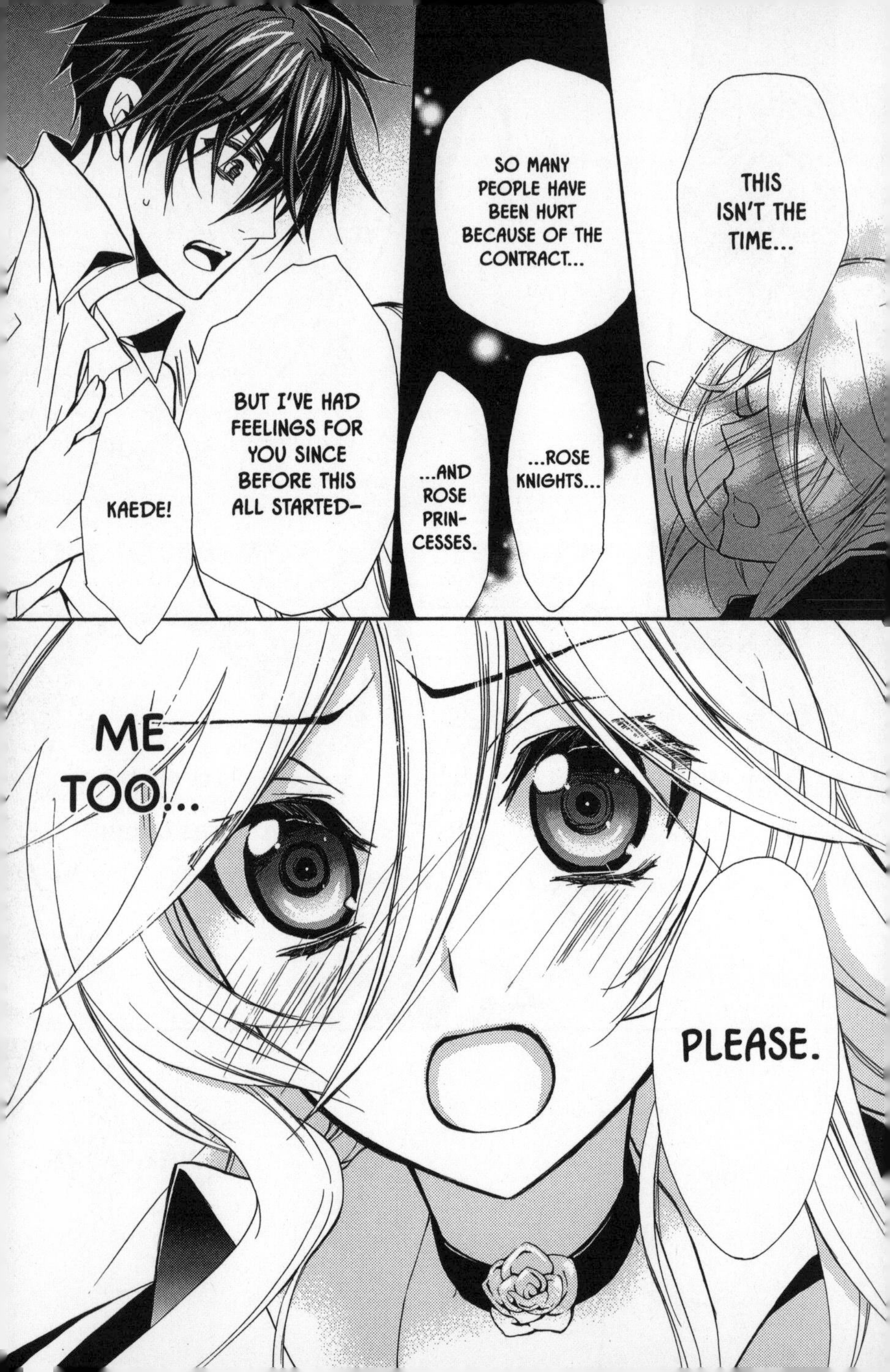
THIS ISN'T THE TIME...
SO MANY PEOPLE HAVE BEEN HURT BECAUSE OF THE CONTRACT...
...ROSE KNIGHTS...
...AND ROSE PRINCESSES.
BUT I'VE HAD FEELINGS FOR YOU SINCE BEFORE THIS ALL STARTED–
KAEDE!
ME TOO...
PLEASE.

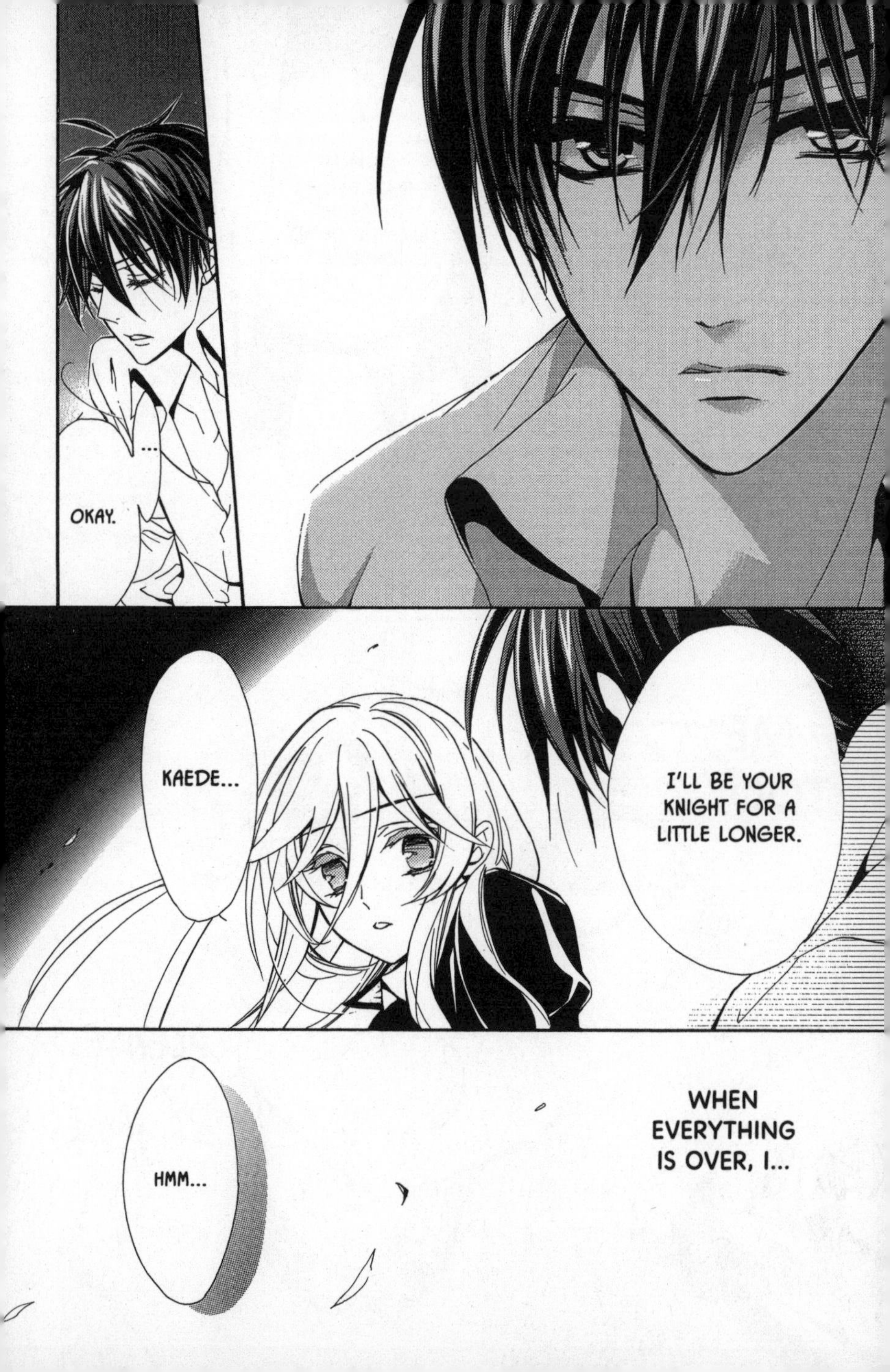
...
OKAY.
I'LL BE YOUR KNIGHT FOR A LITTLE LONGER.
KAEDE...
WHEN EVERYTHING IS OVER, I...
HMM...

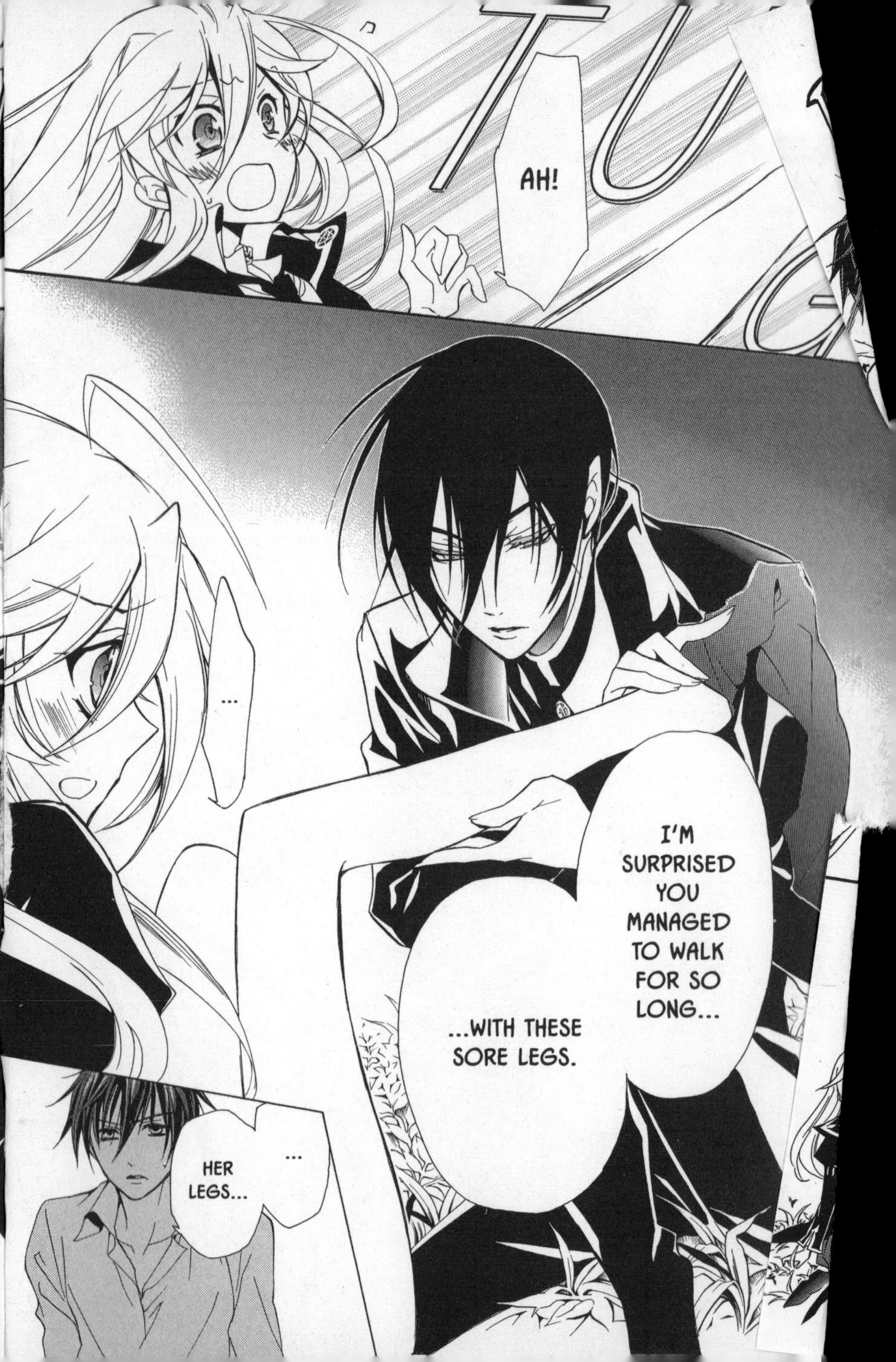
AH!
I'M SURPRISED YOU MANAGED TO WALK FOR SO LONG...
...WITH THESE SORE LEGS.
...
HER LEGS...

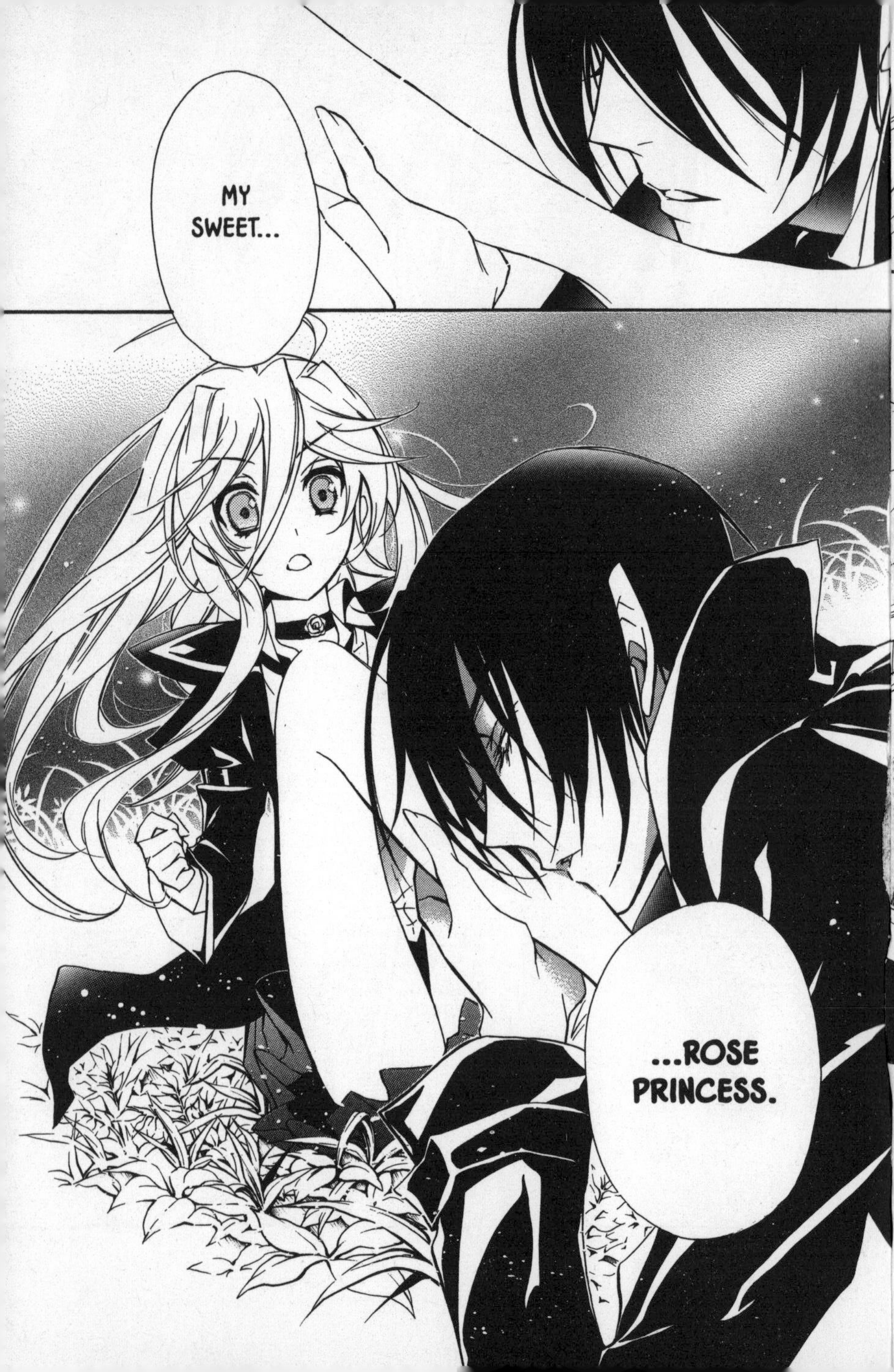
MY SWEET...
...
...ROSE PRINCESS.

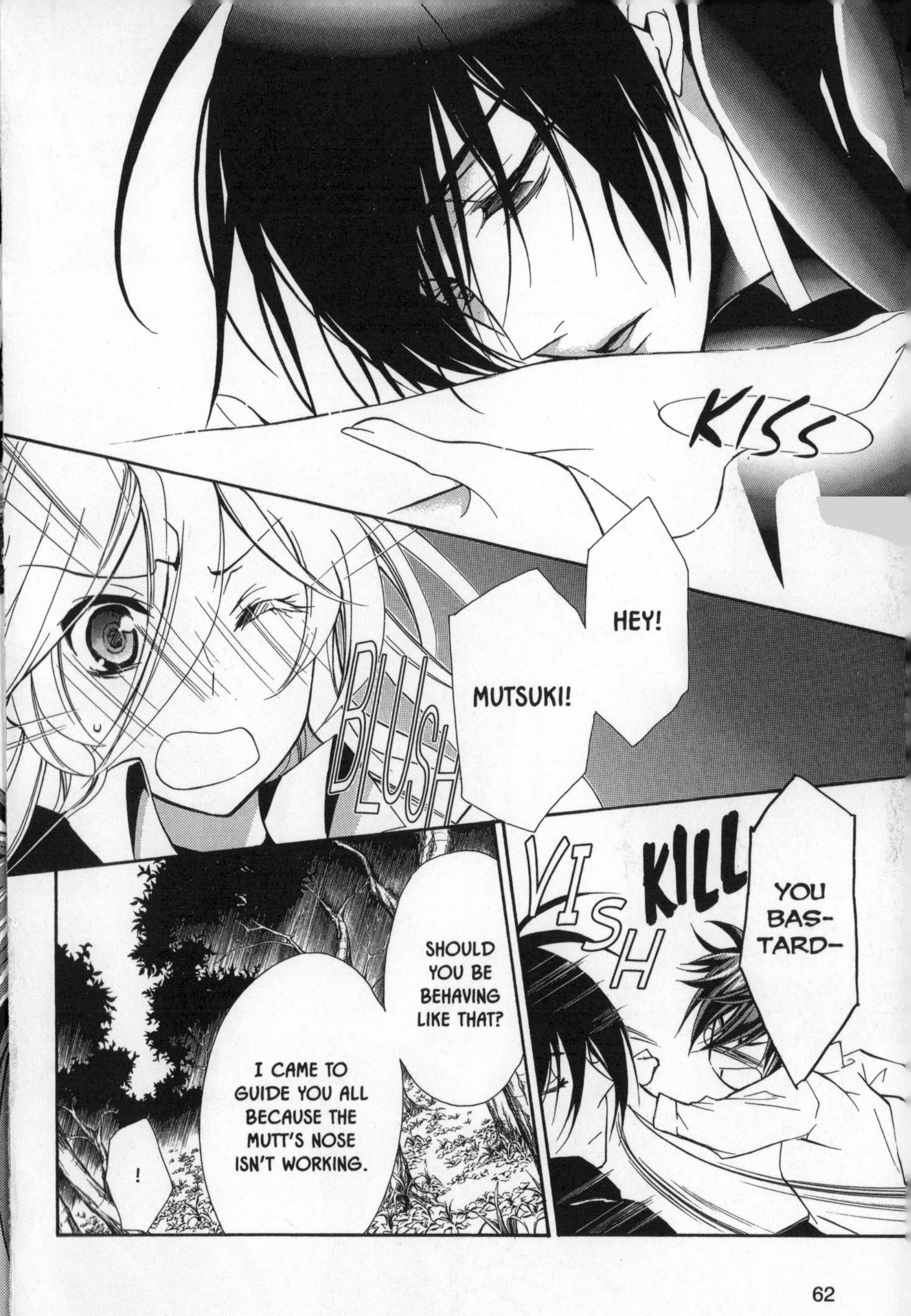
KISS
HEY!
MUTSUKI!
BLUSH
KILL
VISH
YOU BAS-TARD—
SHOULD YOU BE BEHAVING LIKE THAT?
I CAME TO GUIDE YOU ALL BECAUSE THE MUTT'S NOSE ISN'T WORKING.
!

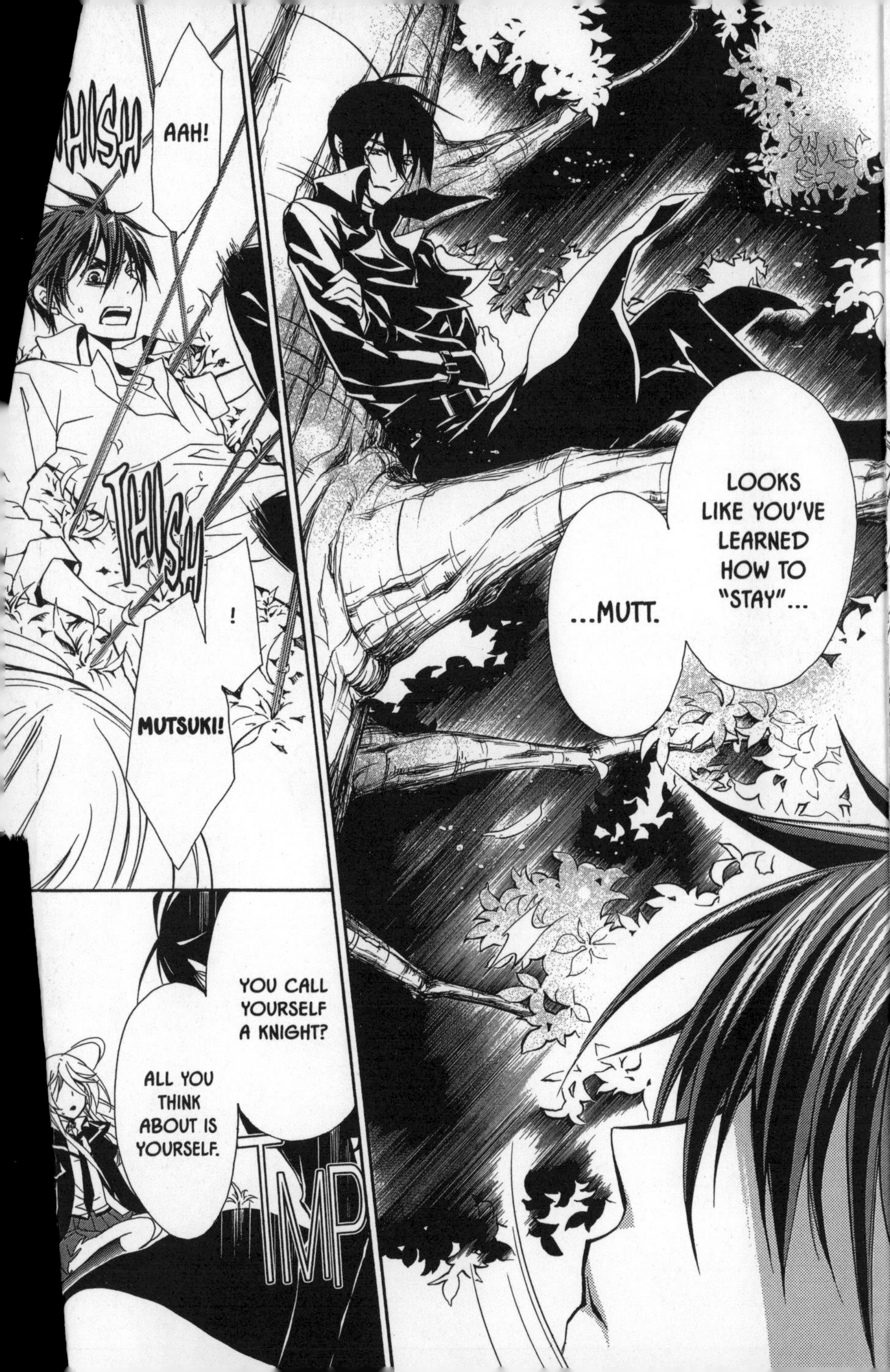
LOOKS LIKE YOU'VE LEARNED HOW TO "STAY"...
...MUTT.
HISH
AAH!
THISH
!
MUTSUKI!
YOU CALL YOURSELF A KNIGHT?
ALL YOU THINK ABOUT IS YOURSELF.
TMP

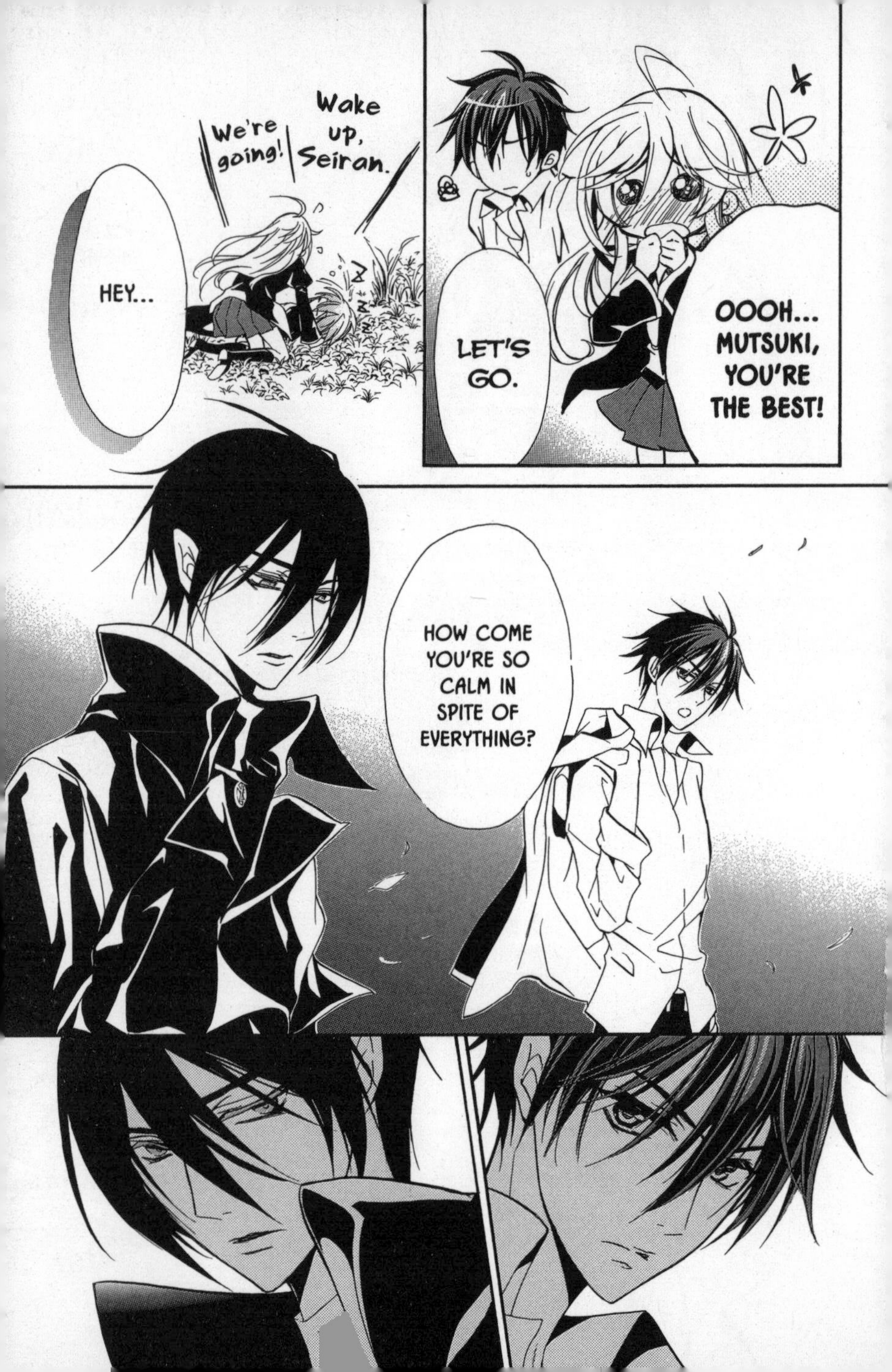
OOOH... MUTSUKI, YOU'RE THE BEST!
LET'S GO.
Wake up, Seiran.
We're going!
HEY...
HOW COME YOU'RE SO CALM IN SPITE OF EVERYTHING?

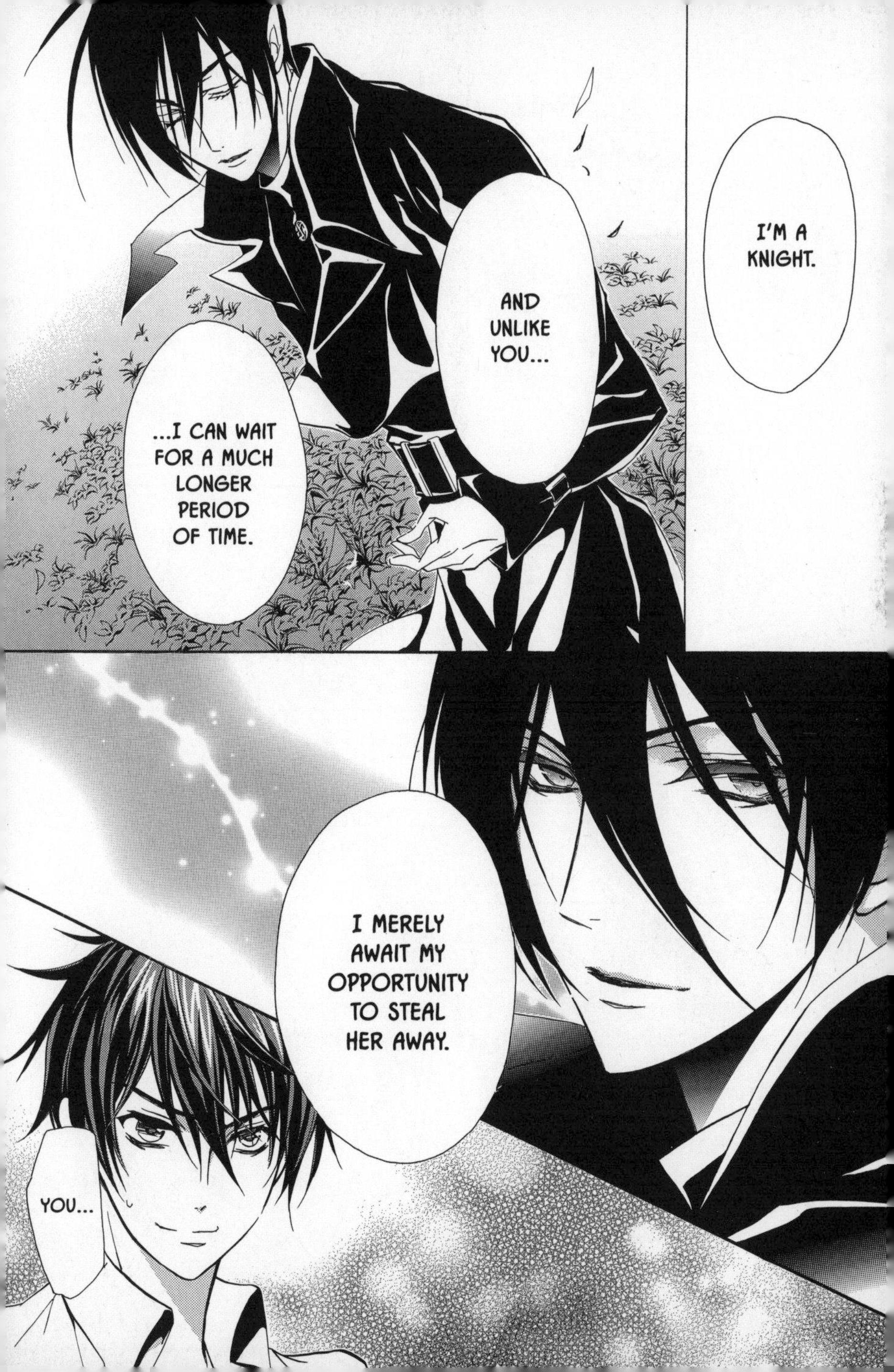
I'M A KNIGHT.
AND UNLIKE YOU...
...I CAN WAIT FOR A MUCH LONGER PERIOD OF TIME.
I MERELY AWAIT MY OPPORTUNITY TO STEAL HER AWAY.
YOU...

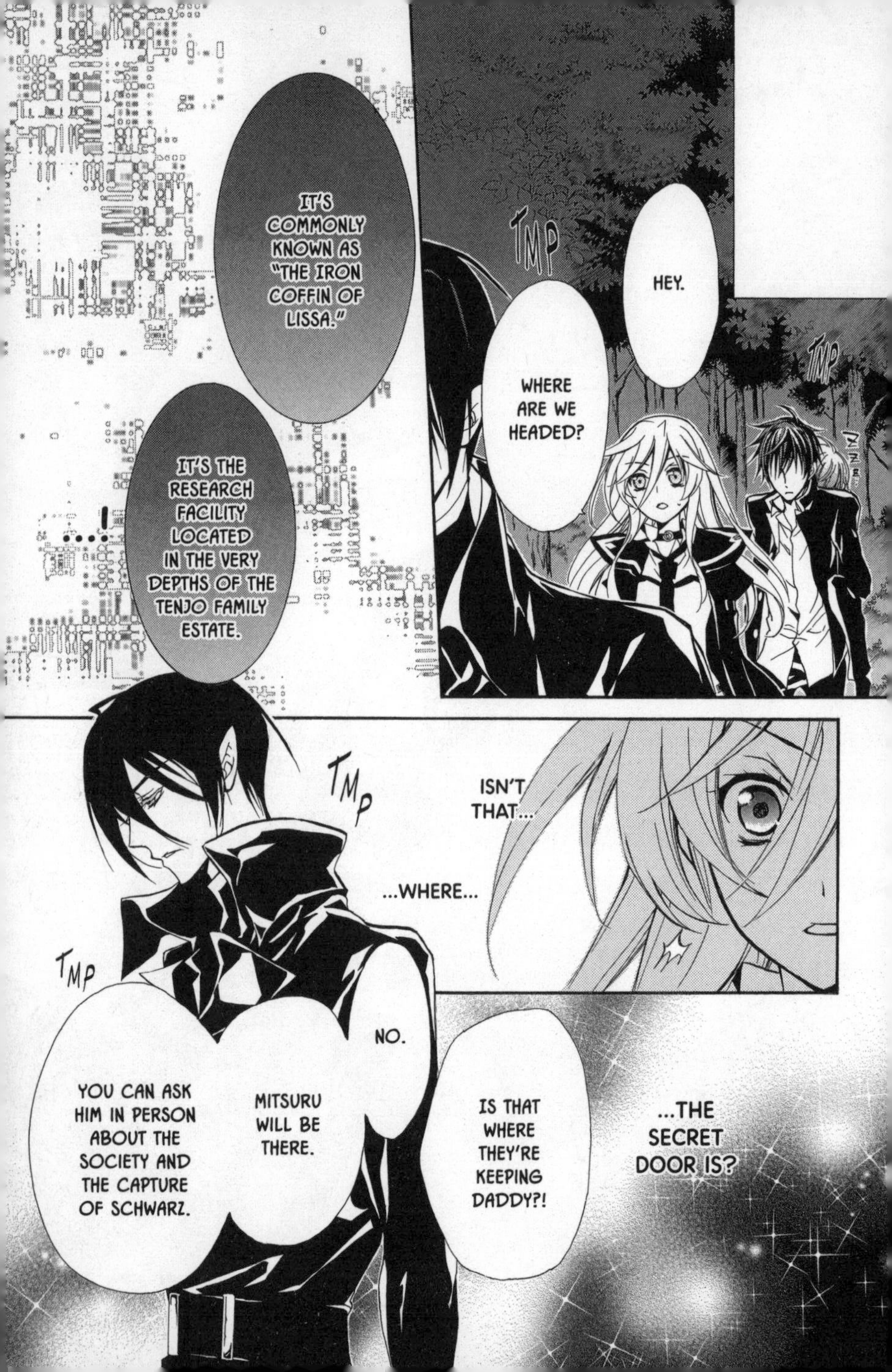
TMP
HEY.
TMP
WHERE ARE WE HEADED?
Z Z Z
IT'S COMMONLY KNOWN AS "THE IRON COFFIN OF LISSA."
IT'S THE RESEARCH FACILITY LOCATED IN THE VERY DEPTHS OF THE TENJO FAMILY ESTATE.
ISN'T THAT...
...WHERE...
...THE SECRET DOOR IS?
TMP
IS THAT WHERE THEY'RE KEEPING DADDY?!
NO.
MITSURU WILL BE THERE.
TMP
YOU CAN ASK HIM IN PERSON ABOUT THE SOCIETY AND THE CAPTURE OF SCHWARZ.

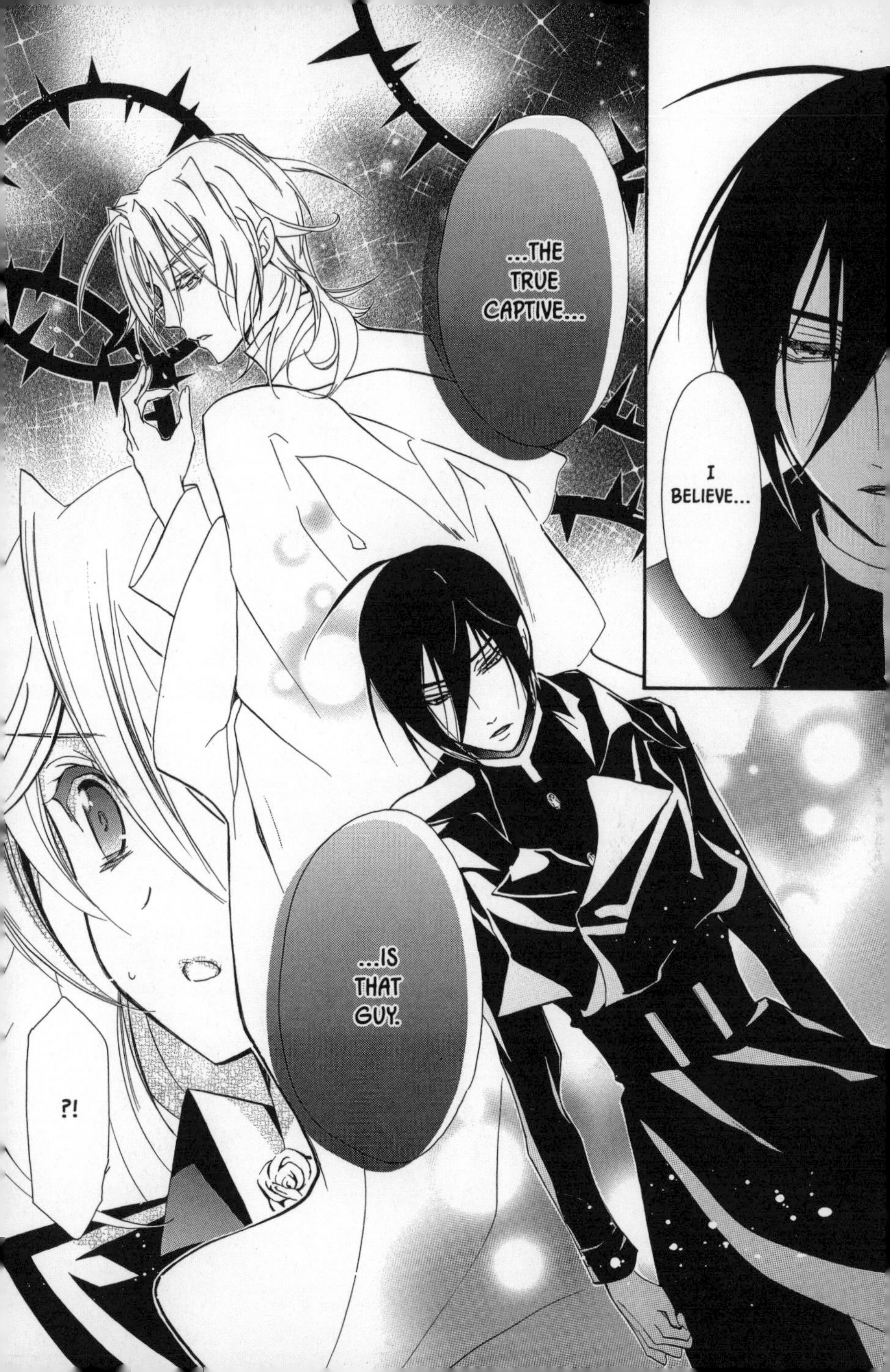
I BELIEVE...
...THE TRUE CAPTIVE...
...IS THAT GUY.
?!

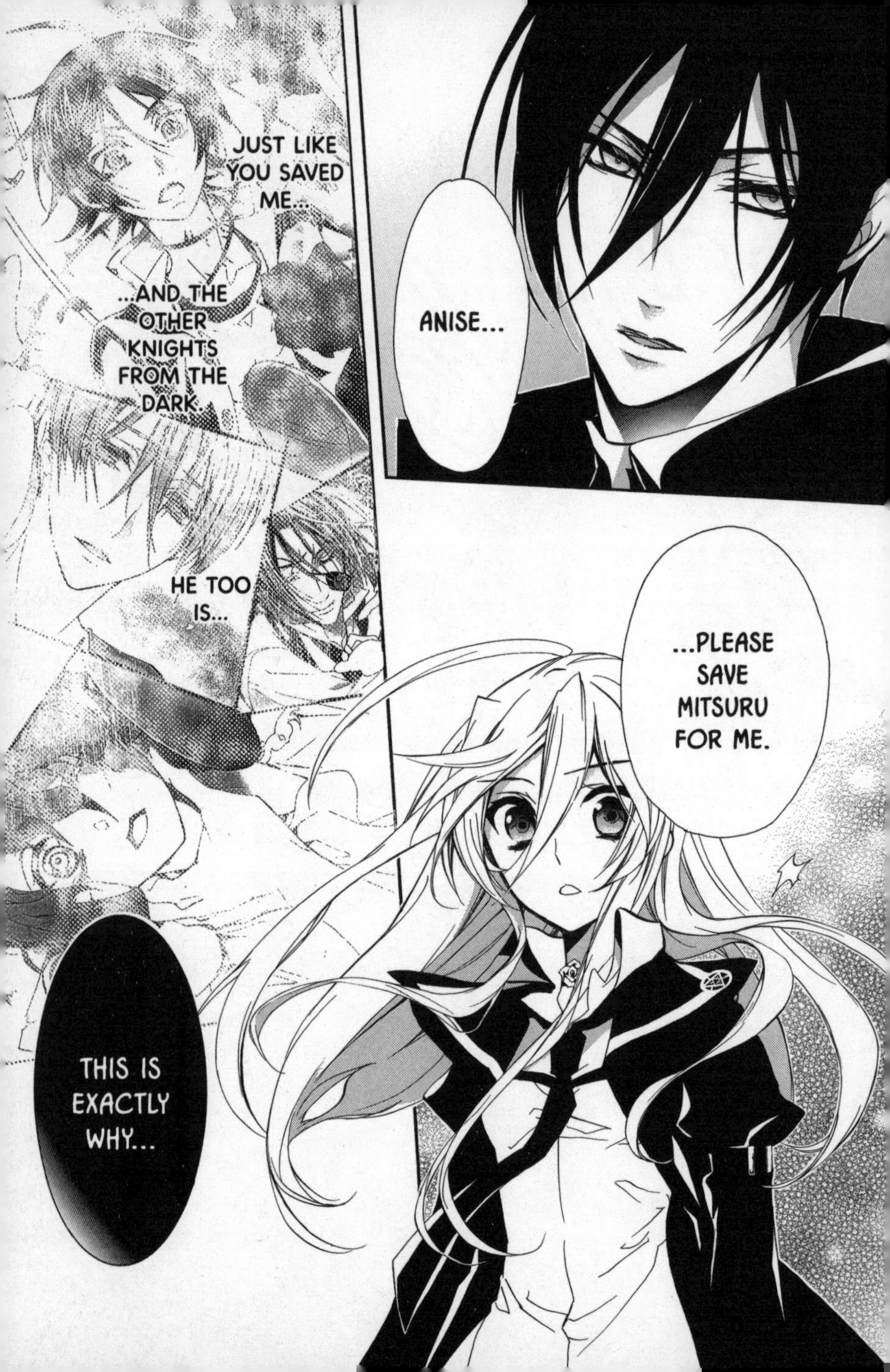
ANISE...
...PLEASE SAVE MITSURU FOR ME.
JUST LIKE YOU SAVED ME...
...AND THE OTHER KNIGHTS FROM THE DARK.
HE TOO IS...
THIS IS EXACTLY WHY...

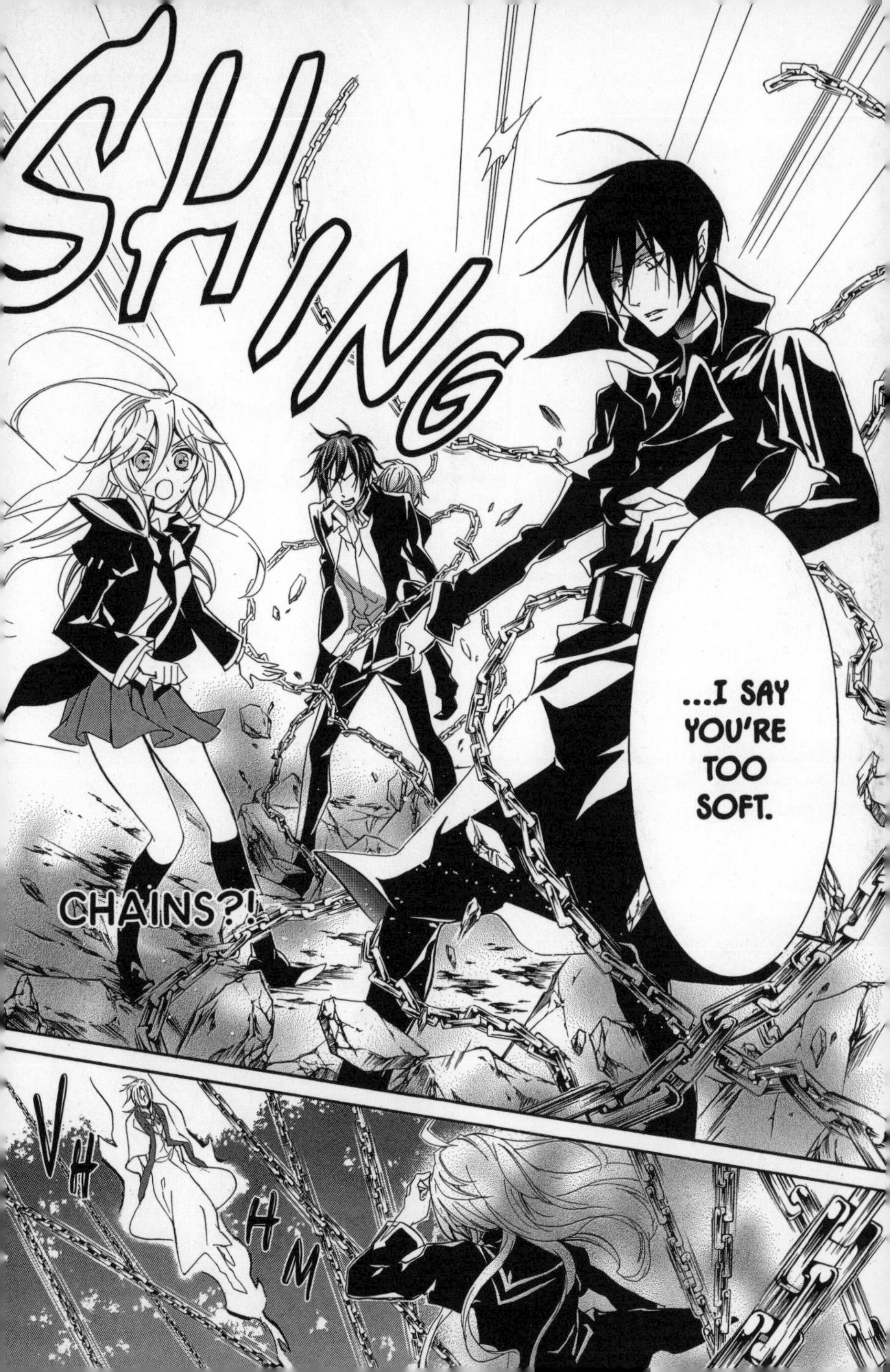
SHING
...I SAY YOU'RE TOO SOFT.
CHAINS?!
VHHM

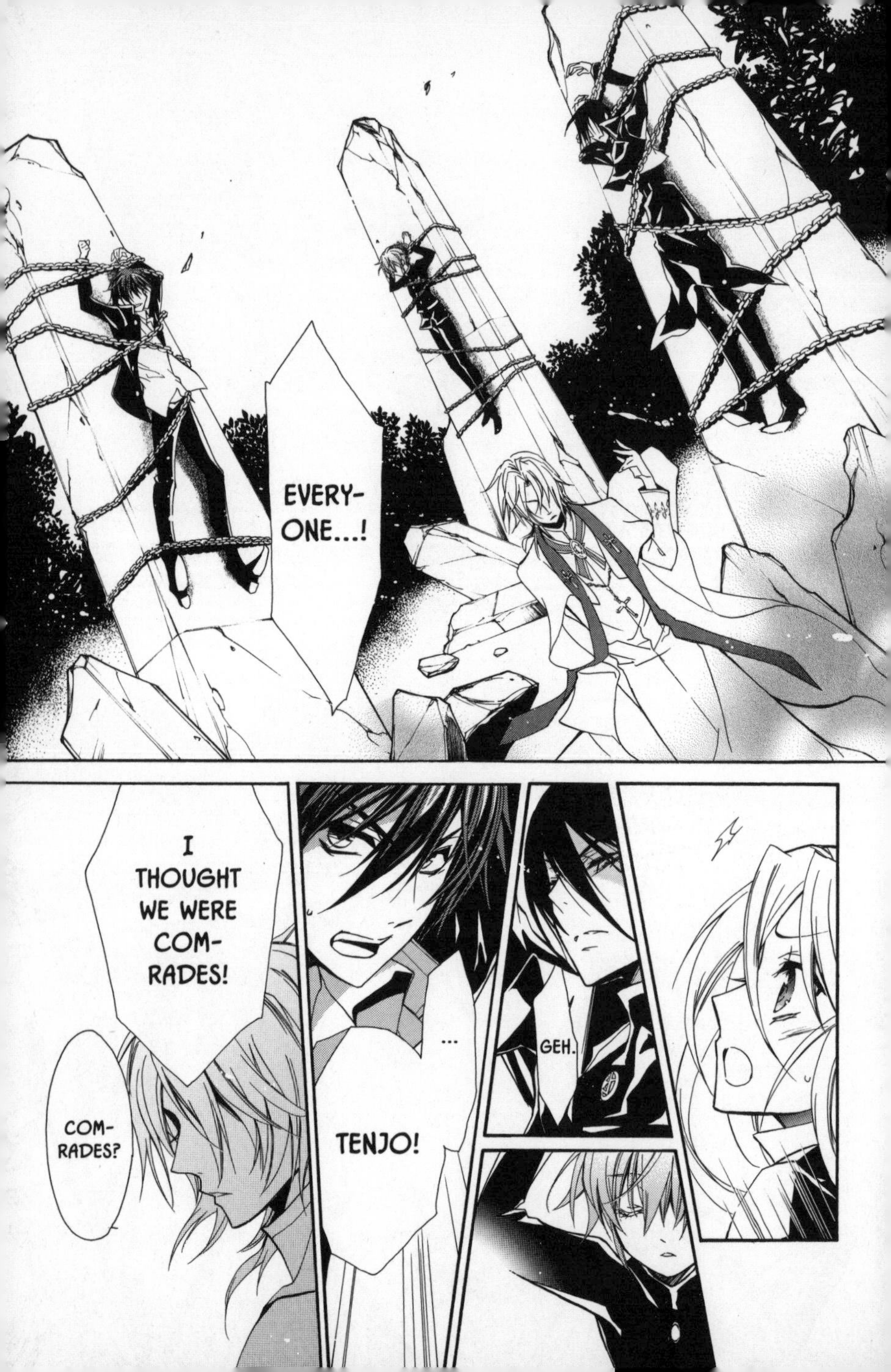
EVERY-ONE...!
GEH.
...
TENJO!
I THOUGHT WE WERE COM-RADES!
COM-RADES?

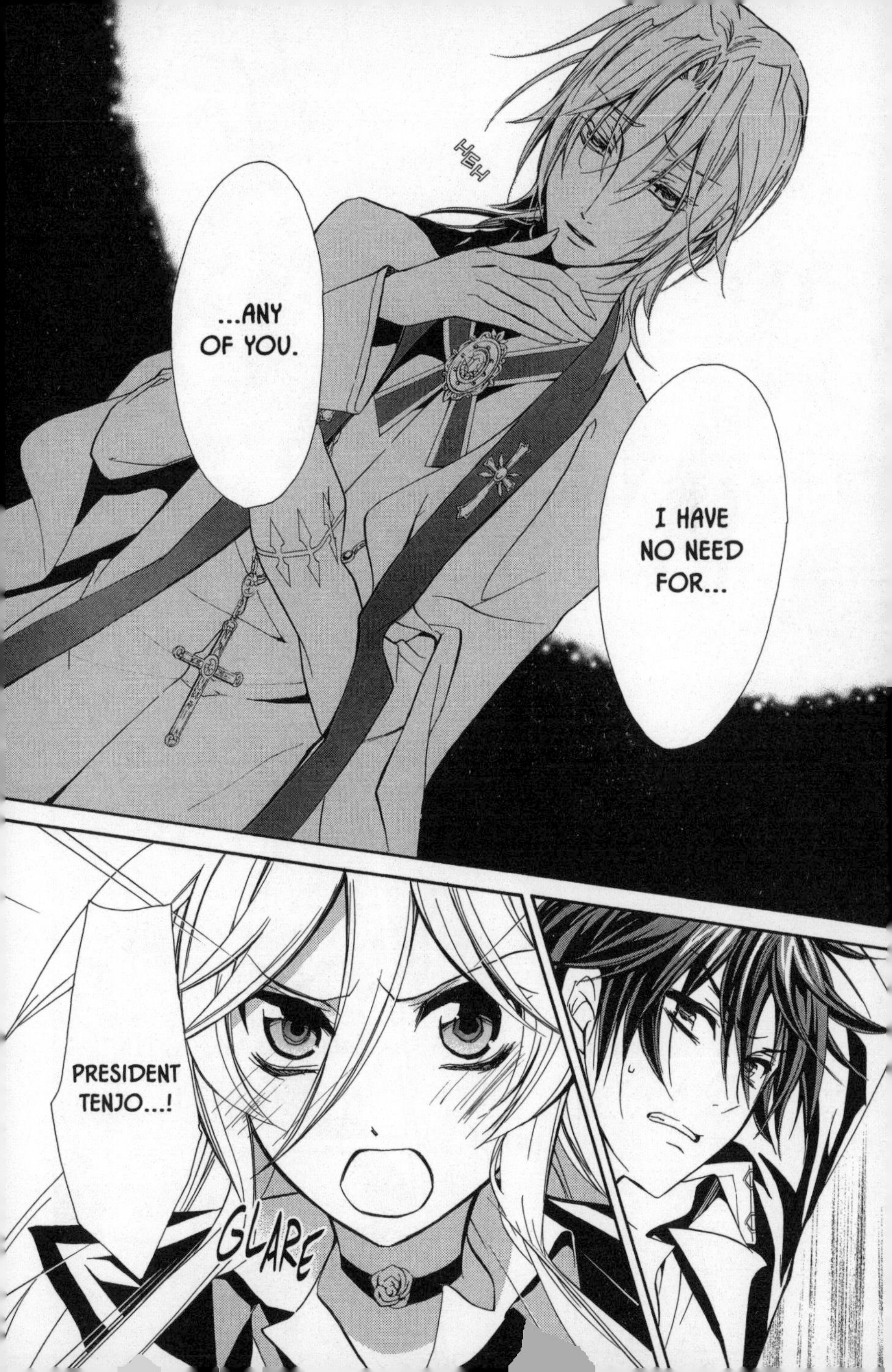
HEH
I HAVE NO NEED FOR...
...ANY OF YOU.
PRESIDENT TENJO...!
GLARE

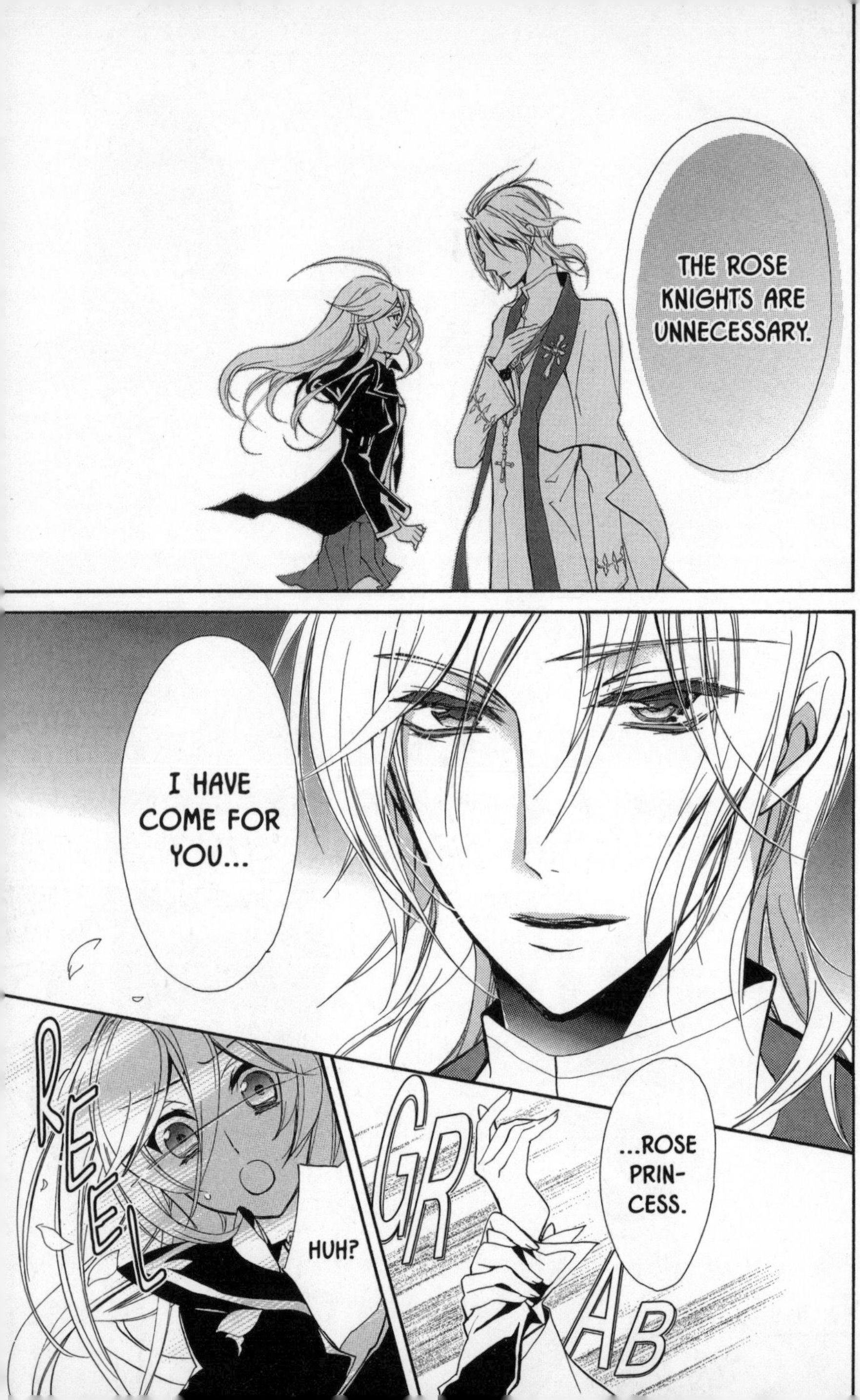
THE ROSE KNIGHTS ARE UNNECESSARY.
I HAVE COME FOR YOU...
...ROSE PRIN-CESS.
GRAB
HUH?
REEL

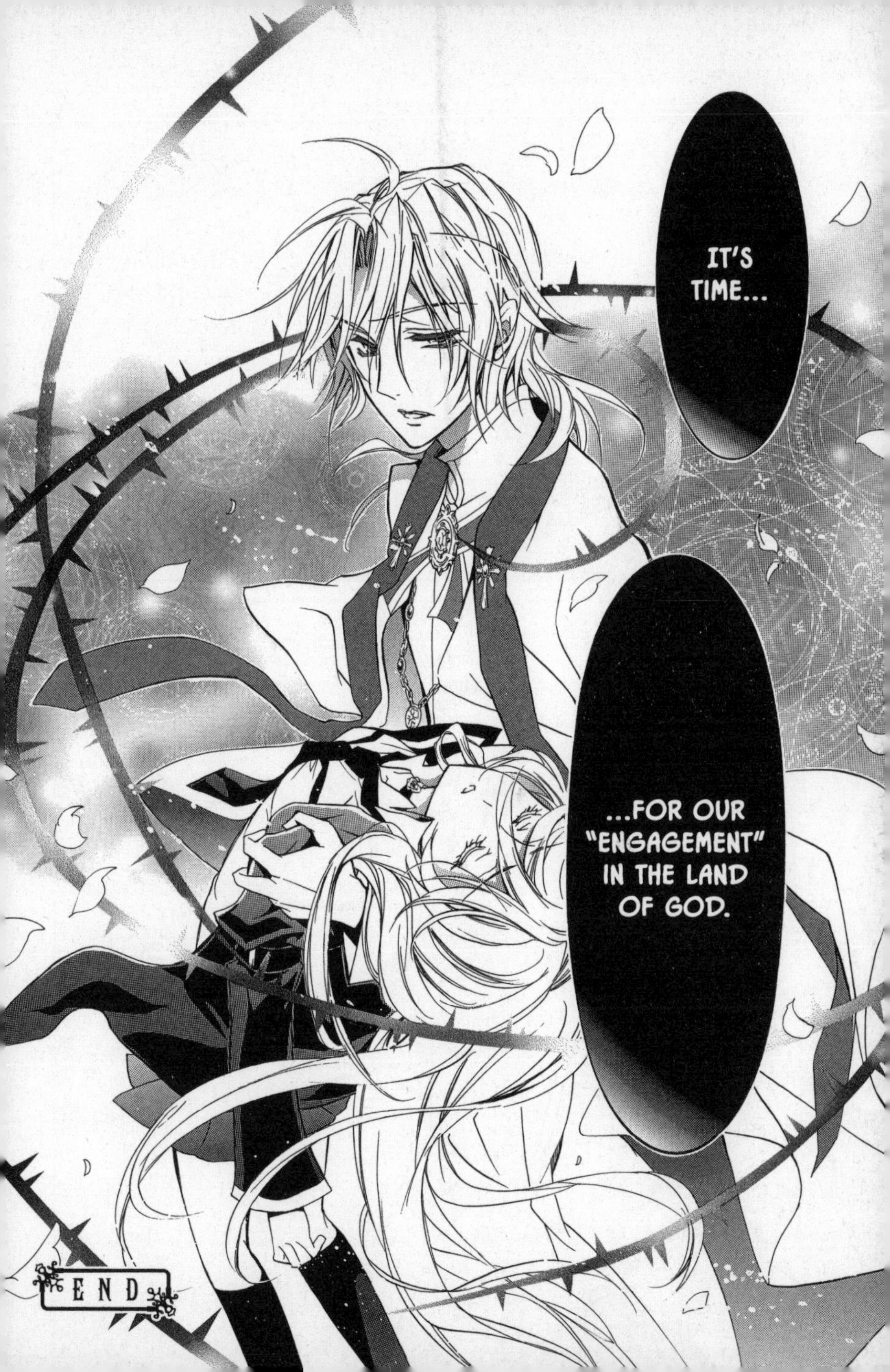
IT'S TIME...
...FOR OUR "ENGAGEMENT" IN THE LAND OF GOD.
END

Kiss of the Rose Princess

Kiss of the Rose
Princess

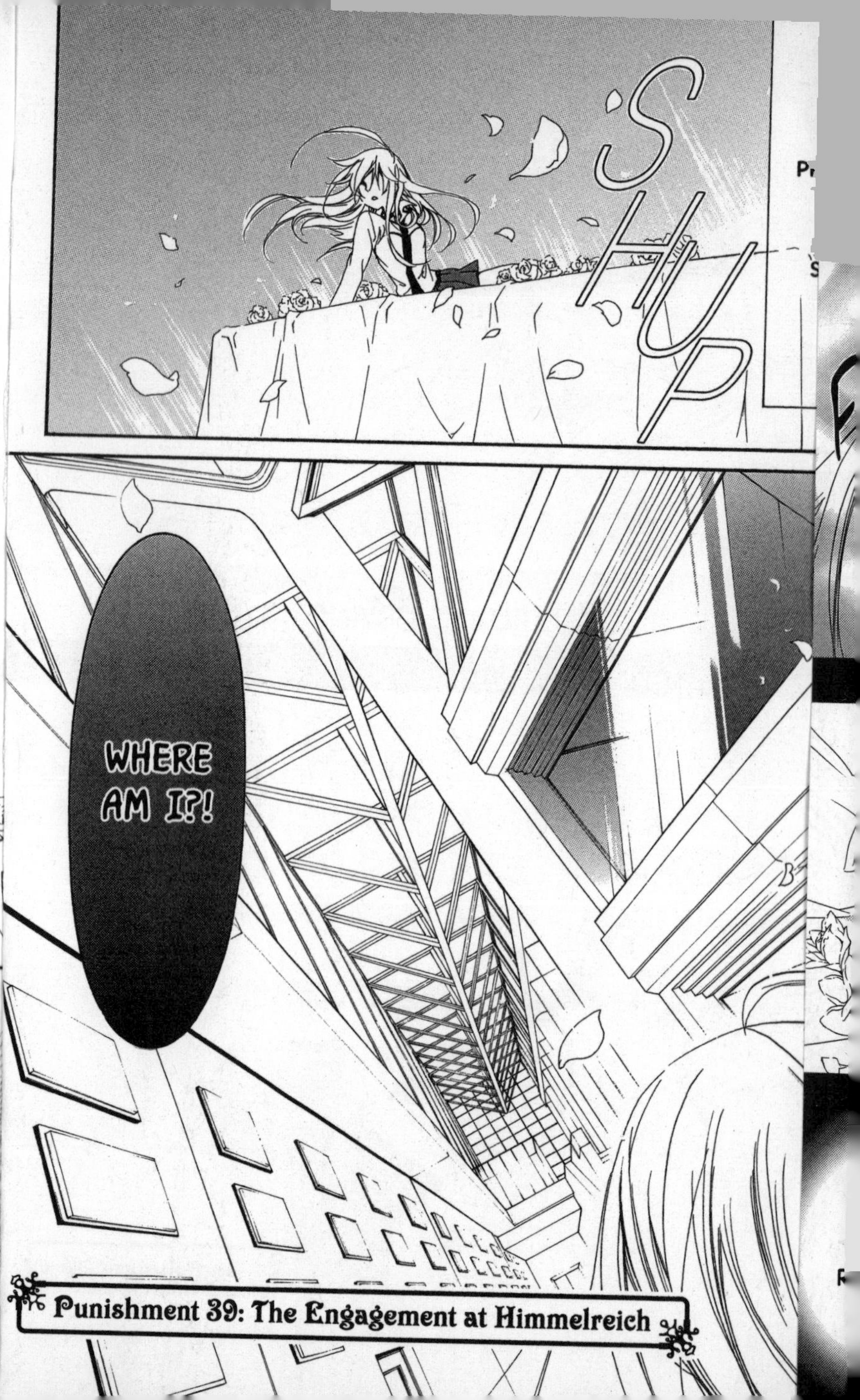
SHUP
WHERE AM I?!

Punishment 39: The Engagement at Himmelreich

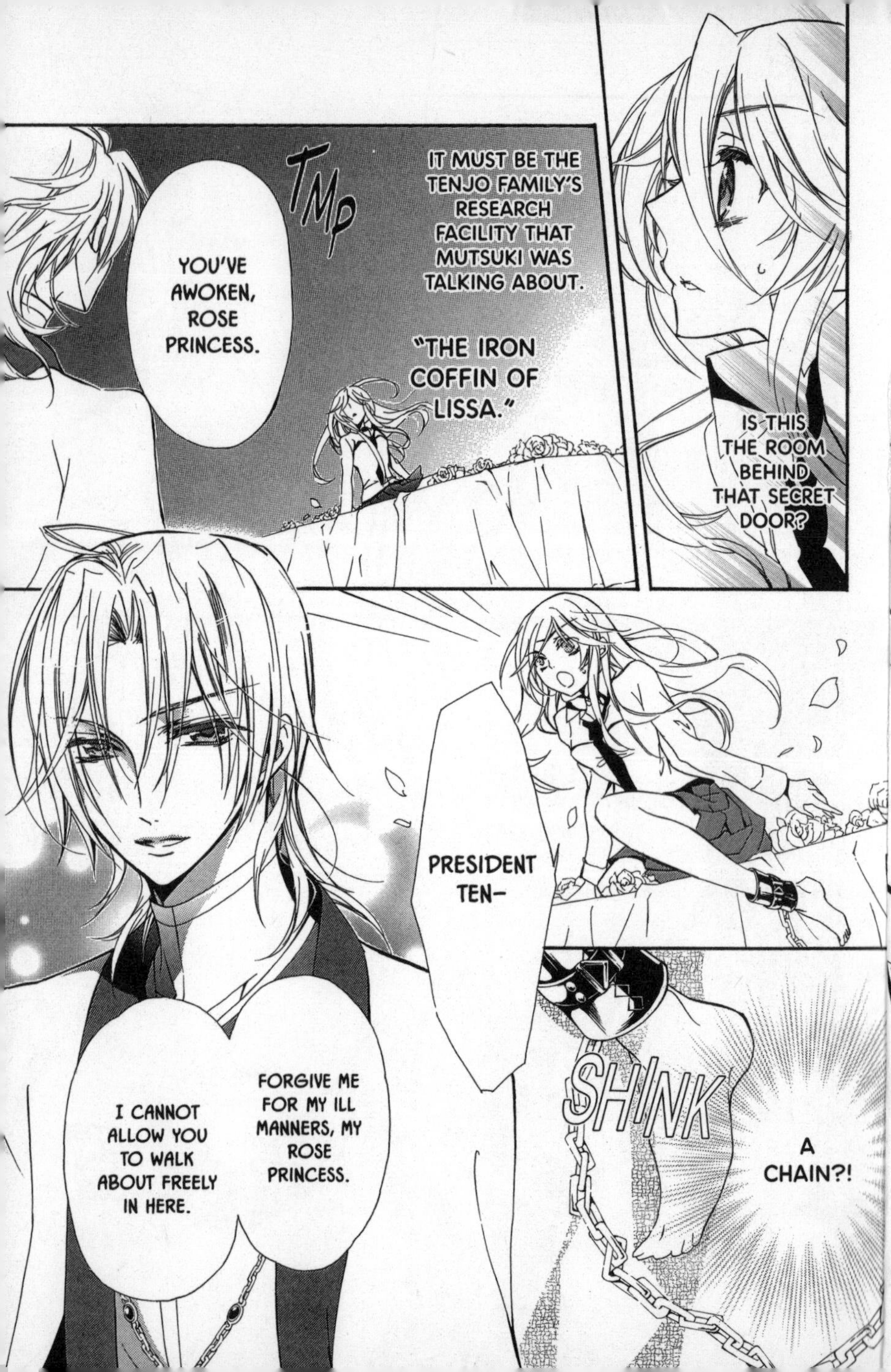
IS THIS THE ROOM BEHIND THAT SECRET DOOR?
TMP
IT MUST BE THE TENJO FAMILY'S RESEARCH FACILITY THAT MUTSUKI WAS TALKING ABOUT.
"THE IRON COFFIN OF LISSA."
YOU'VE AWOKEN, ROSE PRINCESS.
PRESIDENT TEN–
SHINK
A CHAIN?!
FORGIVE ME FOR MY ILL MANNERS, MY ROSE PRINCESS.
I CANNOT ALLOW YOU TO WALK ABOUT FREELY IN HERE.

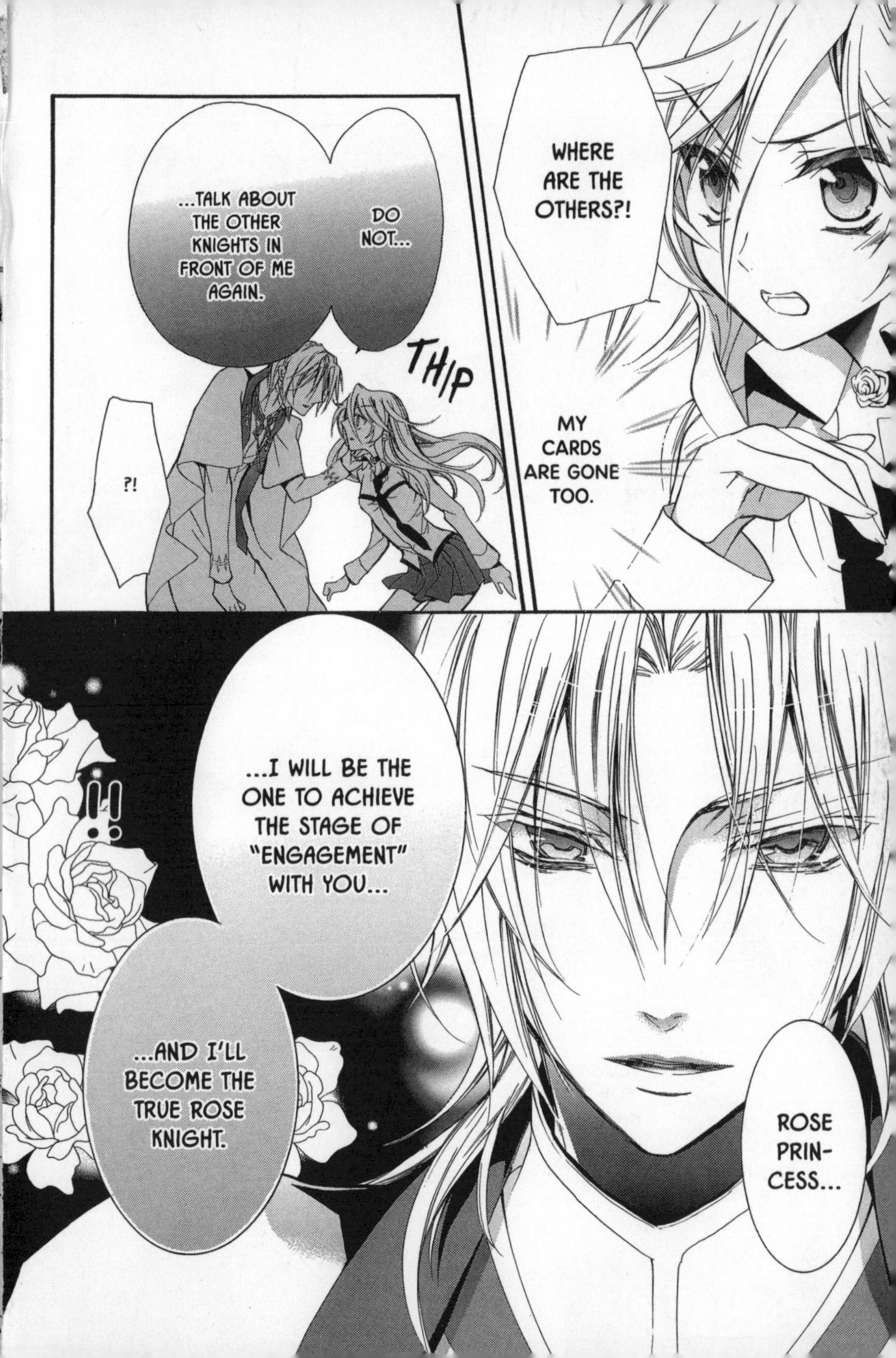

WHERE ARE THE OTHERS?!
MY CARDS ARE GONE TOO.
DO NOT...
...TALK ABOUT THE OTHER KNIGHTS IN FRONT OF ME AGAIN.
THIP
?!
ROSE PRINCESS...
...I WILL BE THE ONE TO ACHIEVE THE STAGE OF "ENGAGEMENT" WITH YOU...
...AND I'LL BECOME THE TRUE ROSE KNIGHT.
!!

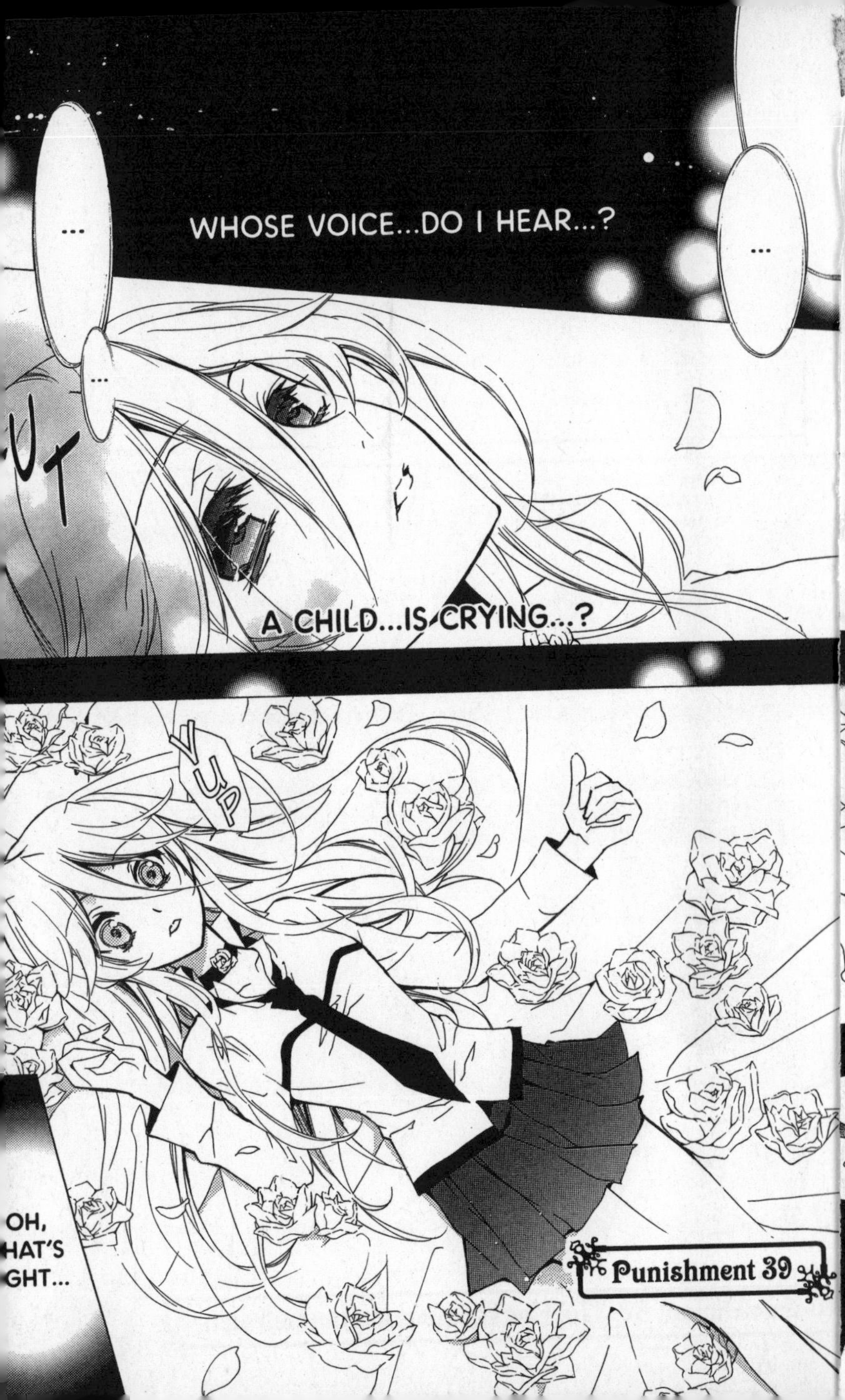

...
...
...
WHOSE VOICE...DO I HEAR...?
A CHILD...IS CRYING...?
OH,
HAT'S
GHT...
Punishment 39

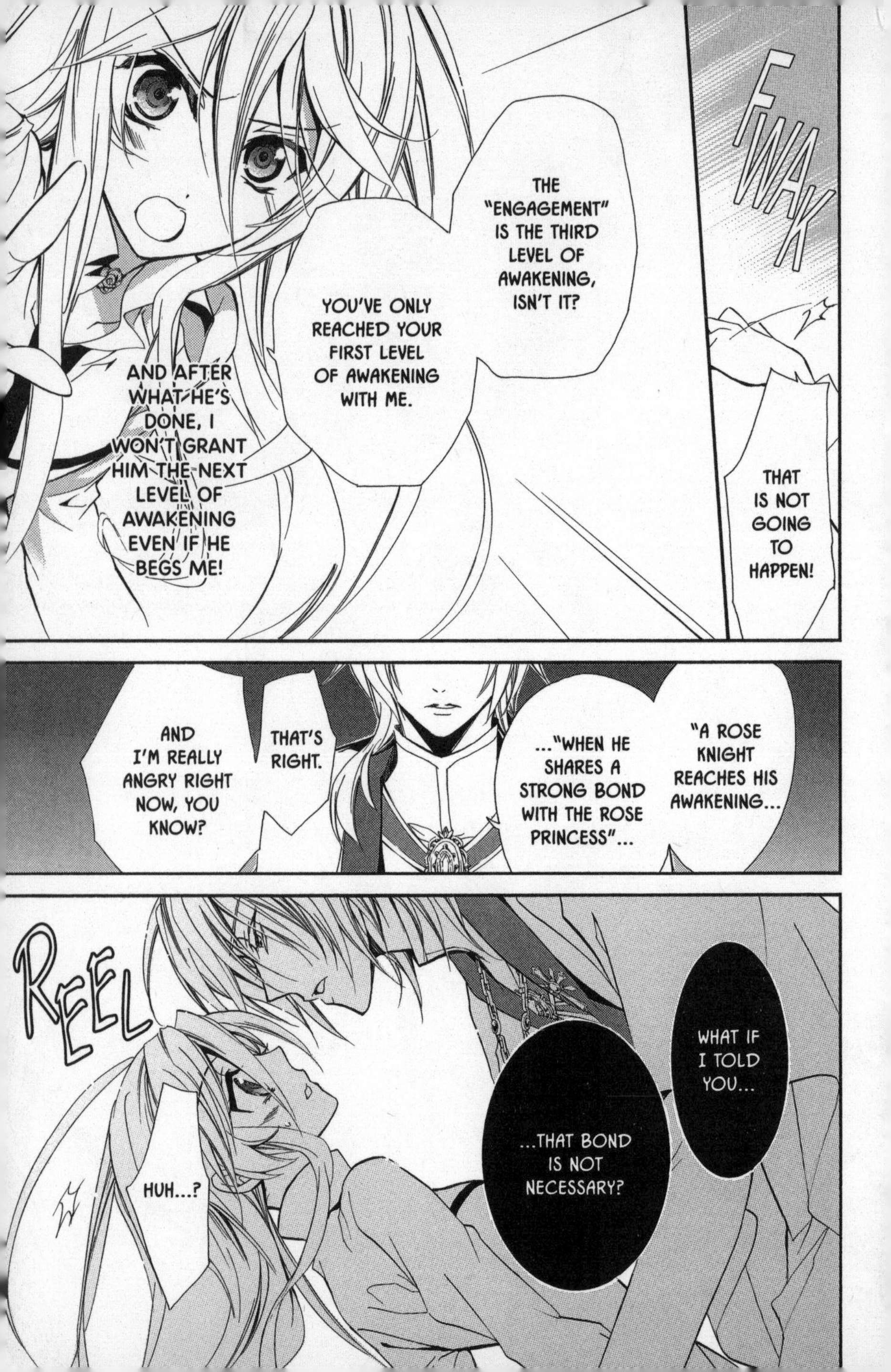
FWAK
THAT IS NOT GOING TO HAPPEN!
THE "ENGAGEMENT" IS THE THIRD LEVEL OF AWAKENING, ISN'T IT?
YOU'VE ONLY REACHED YOUR FIRST LEVEL OF AWAKENING WITH ME.
AND AFTER WHAT HE'S DONE, I WON'T GRANT HIM THE NEXT LEVEL OF AWAKENING EVEN IF HE BEGS ME!
"A ROSE KNIGHT REACHES HIS AWAKENING...
..."WHEN HE SHARES A STRONG BOND WITH THE ROSE PRINCESS"...
THAT'S RIGHT.
AND I'M REALLY ANGRY RIGHT NOW, YOU KNOW?
WHAT IF I TOLD YOU...
REEL
...THAT BOND IS NOT NECESSARY?
HUH...?

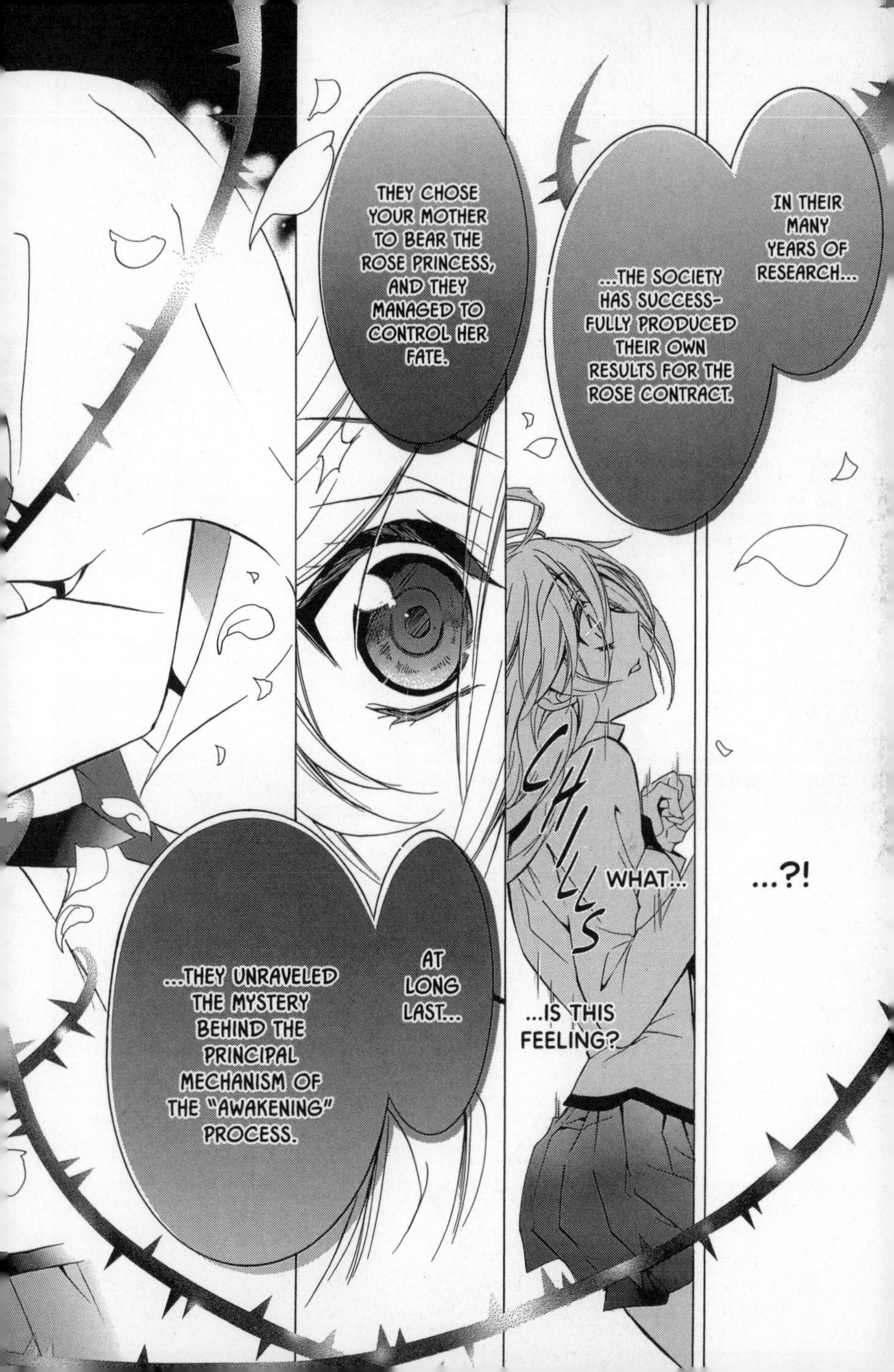
IN THEIR MANY YEARS OF RESEARCH...
...THE SOCIETY HAS SUCCESS-FULLY PRODUCED THEIR OWN RESULTS FOR THE ROSE CONTRACT.
...?!
CHILLS
WHAT...
...IS THIS FEELING?
THEY CHOSE YOUR MOTHER TO BEAR THE ROSE PRINCESS, AND THEY MANAGED TO CONTROL HER FATE.
AT LONG LAST...
...THEY UNRAVELED THE MYSTERY BEHIND THE PRINCIPAL MECHANISM OF THE "AWAKENING" PROCESS.

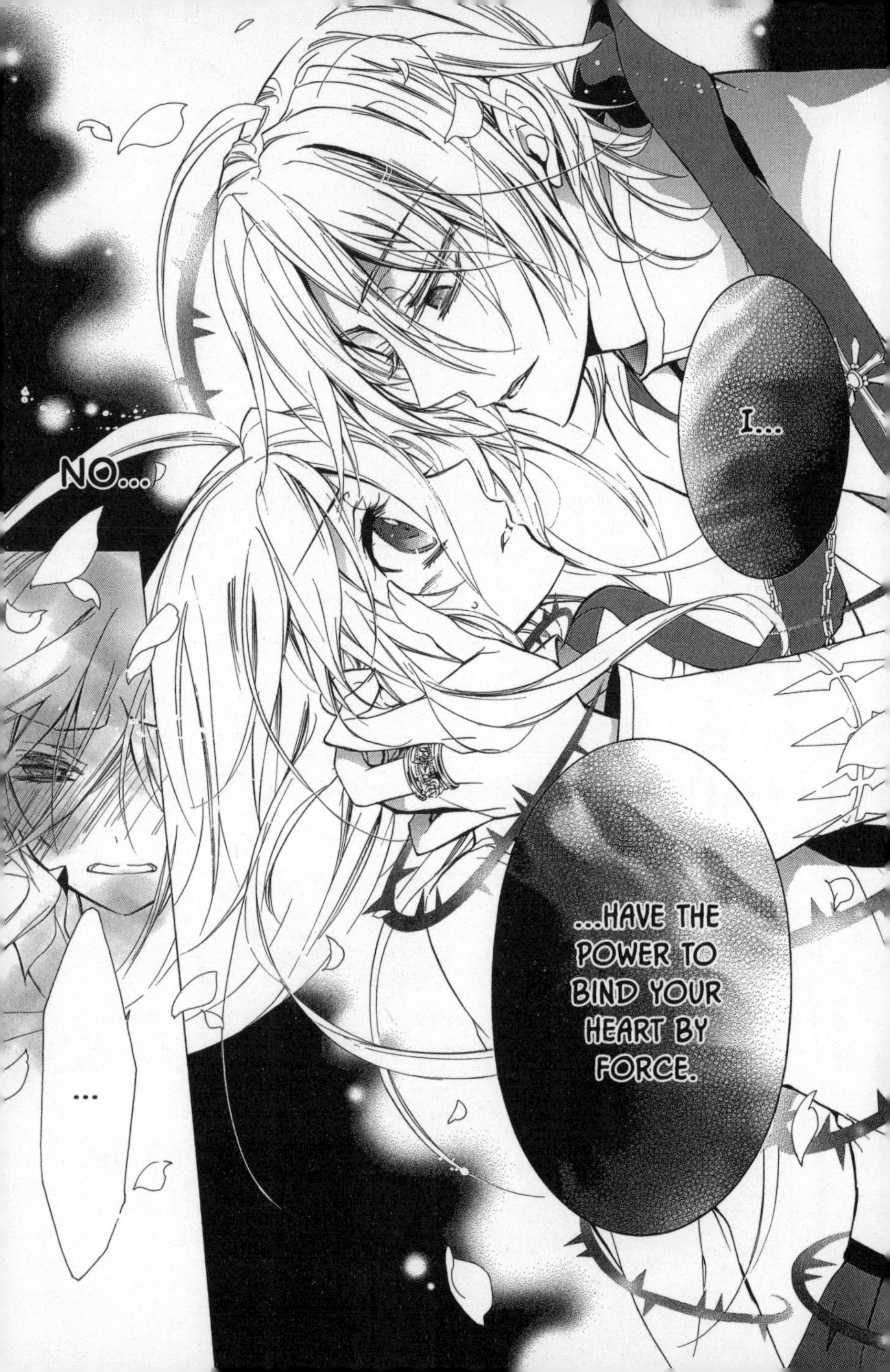
I...
...HAVE THE POWER TO BIND YOUR HEART BY FORCE.
NO...
...

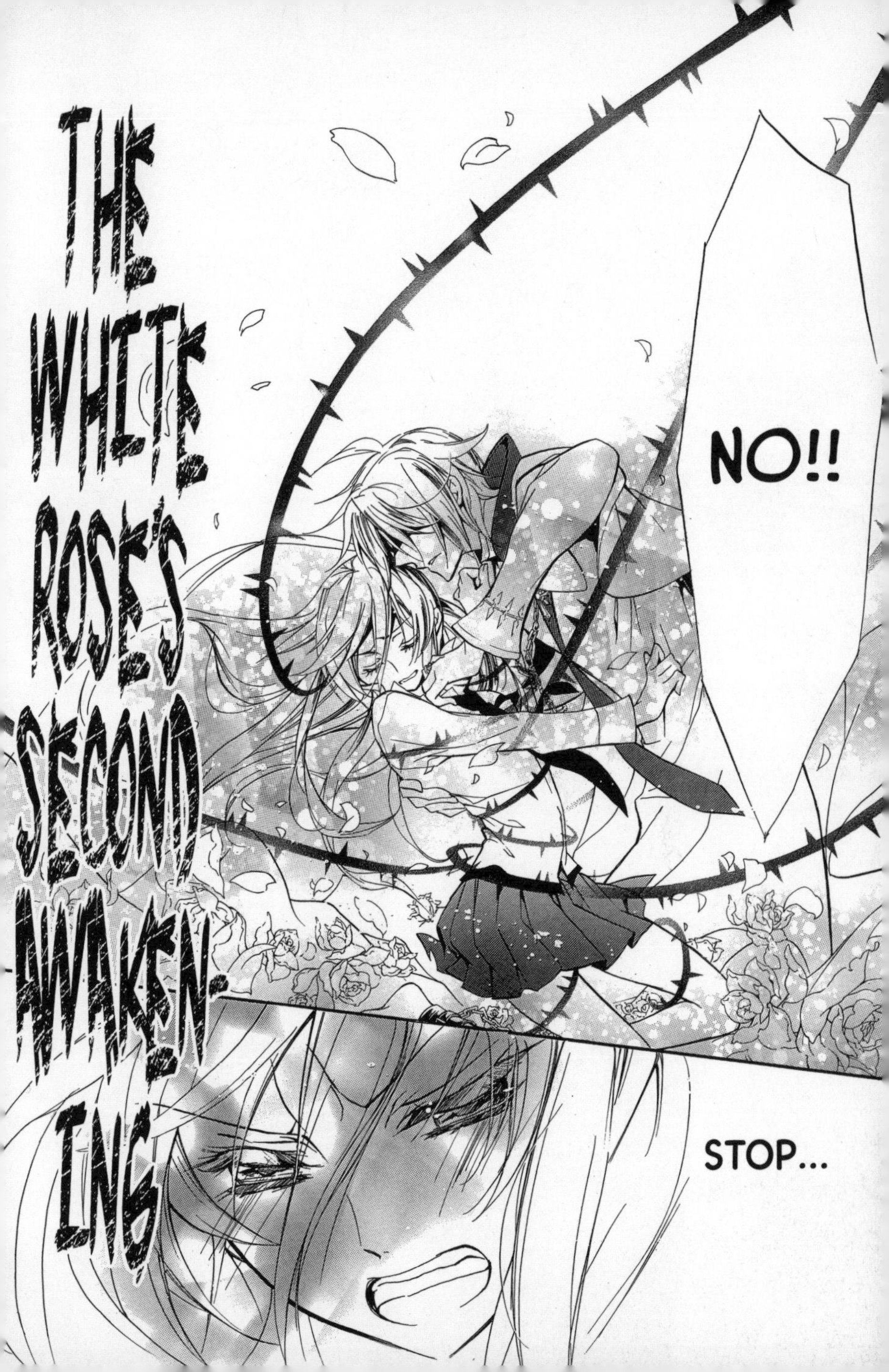
THE WHITE ROSE'S SECOND AWAKENING
NO!!
STOP...

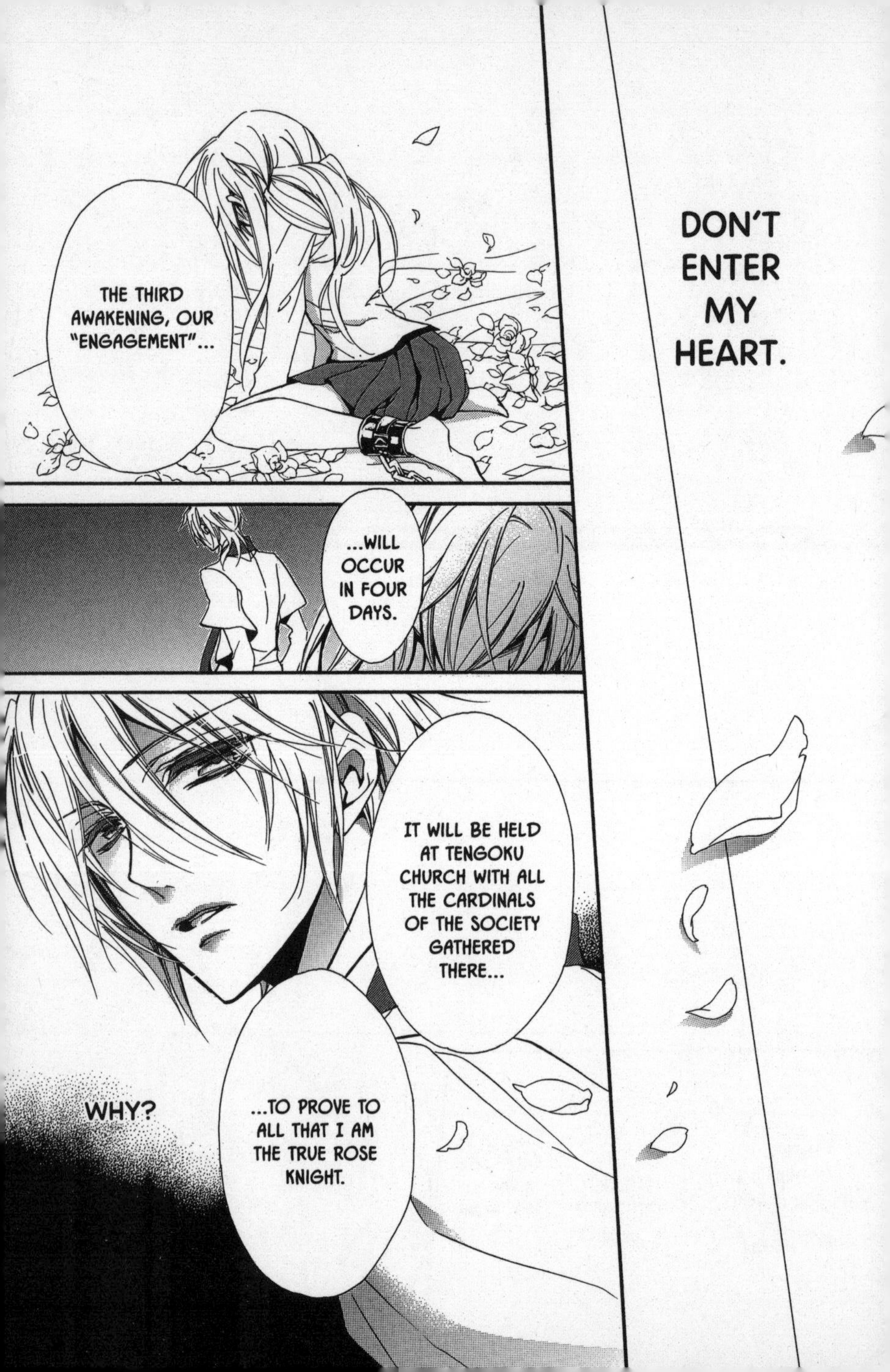
DON'T ENTER MY HEART.
THE THIRD AWAKENING, OUR "ENGAGEMENT"...
...WILL OCCUR IN FOUR DAYS.
IT WILL BE HELD AT TENGOKU CHURCH WITH ALL THE CARDINALS OF THE SOCIETY GATHERED THERE...
...TO PROVE TO ALL THAT I AM THE TRUE ROSE KNIGHT.
WHY?

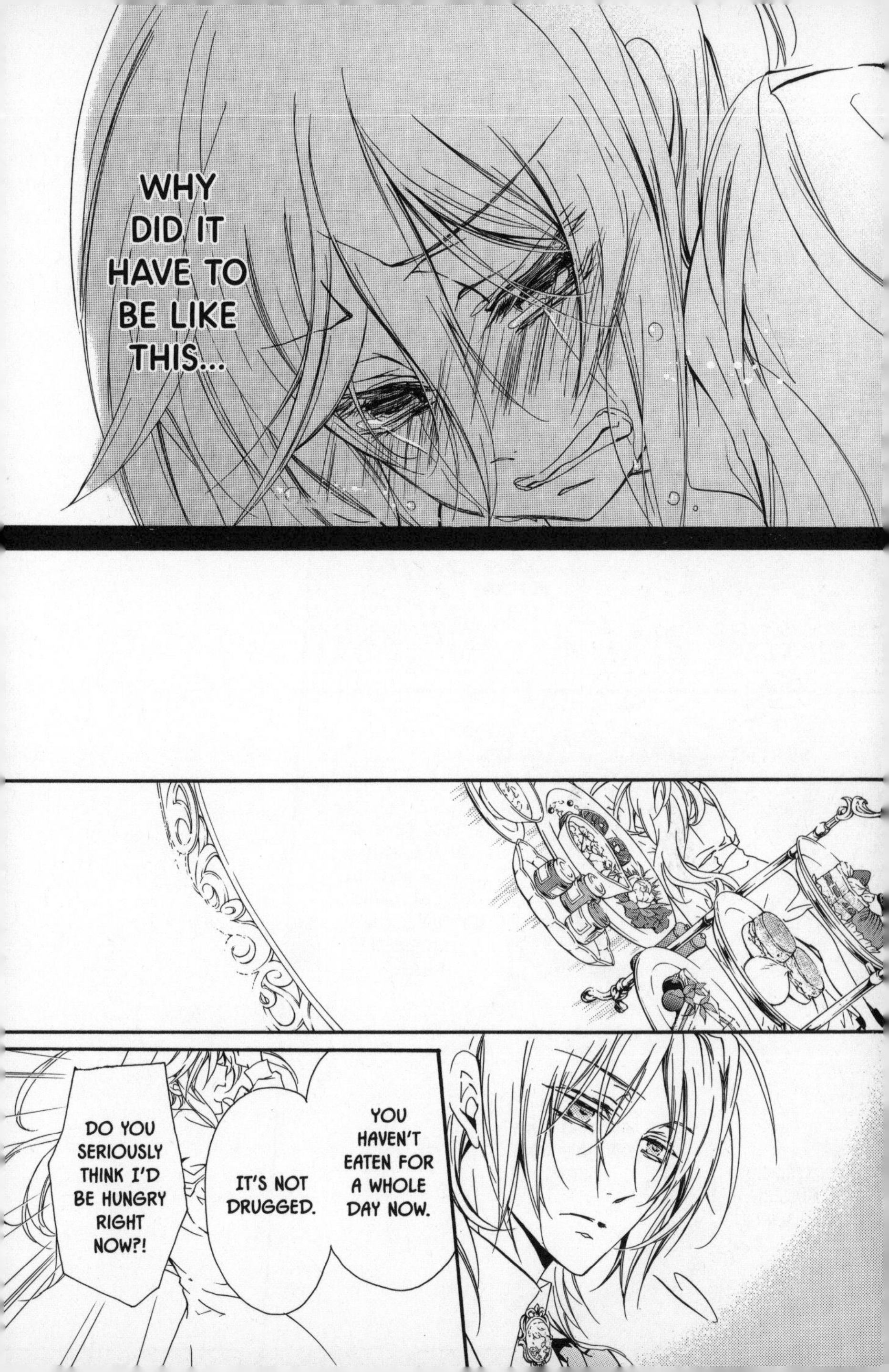
WHY DID IT HAVE TO BE LIKE THIS...
YOU HAVEN'T EATEN FOR A WHOLE DAY NOW.
IT'S NOT DRUGGED.
DO YOU SERIOUSLY THINK I'D BE HUNGRY RIGHT NOW?!

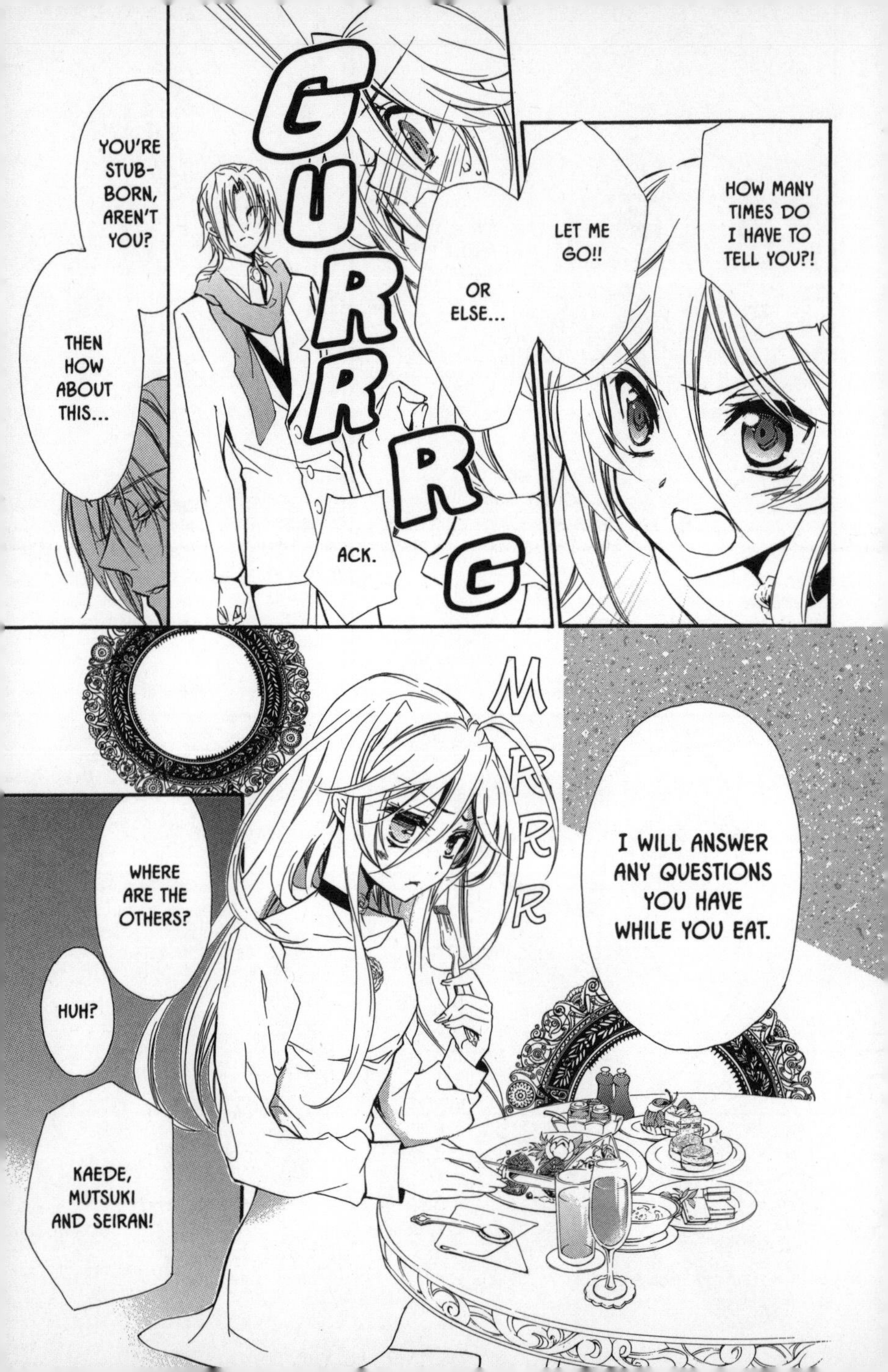
HOW MANY TIMES DO I HAVE TO TELL YOU?!
LET ME GO!!
OR ELSE...
GURRRG
ACK.
YOU'RE STUB-BORN, AREN'T YOU?
THEN HOW ABOUT THIS...
MRRRR
I WILL ANSWER ANY QUESTIONS YOU HAVE WHILE YOU EAT.
WHERE ARE THE OTHERS?
HUH?
KAEDE, MUTSUKI AND SEIRAN!

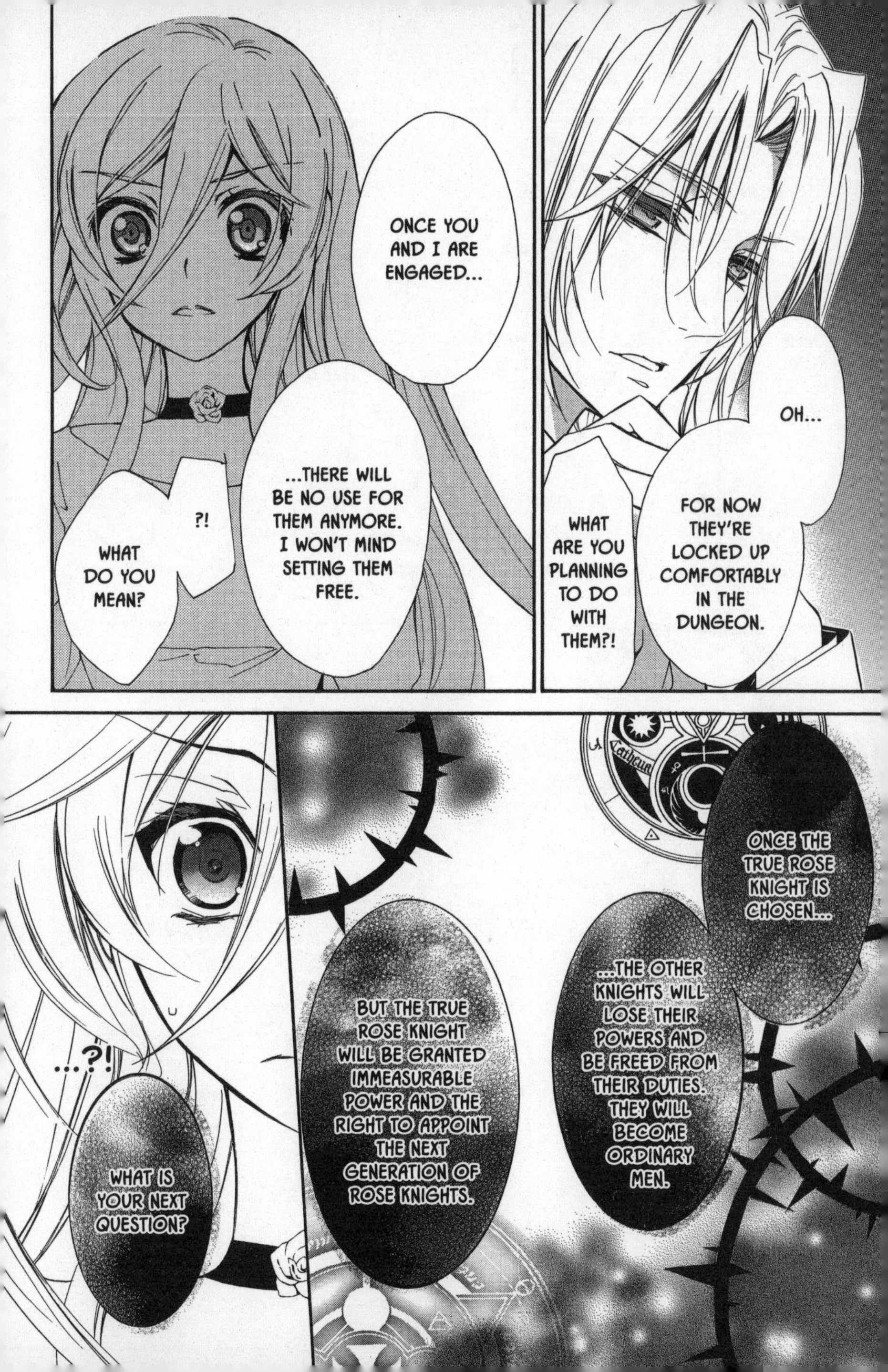
OH...
FOR NOW THEY'RE LOCKED UP COMFORTABLY IN THE DUNGEON.
WHAT ARE YOU PLANNING TO DO WITH THEM?!
ONCE YOU AND I ARE ENGAGED...
...THERE WILL BE NO USE FOR THEM ANYMORE. I WON'T MIND SETTING THEM FREE.
?! WHAT DO YOU MEAN?
ONCE THE TRUE ROSE KNIGHT IS CHOSEN...
...THE OTHER KNIGHTS WILL LOSE THEIR POWERS AND BE FREED FROM THEIR DUTIES. THEY WILL BECOME ORDINARY MEN.
BUT THE TRUE ROSE KNIGHT WILL BE GRANTED IMMEASURABLE POWER AND THE RIGHT TO APPOINT THE NEXT GENERATION OF ROSE KNIGHTS.
...?!
WHAT IS YOUR NEXT QUESTION?

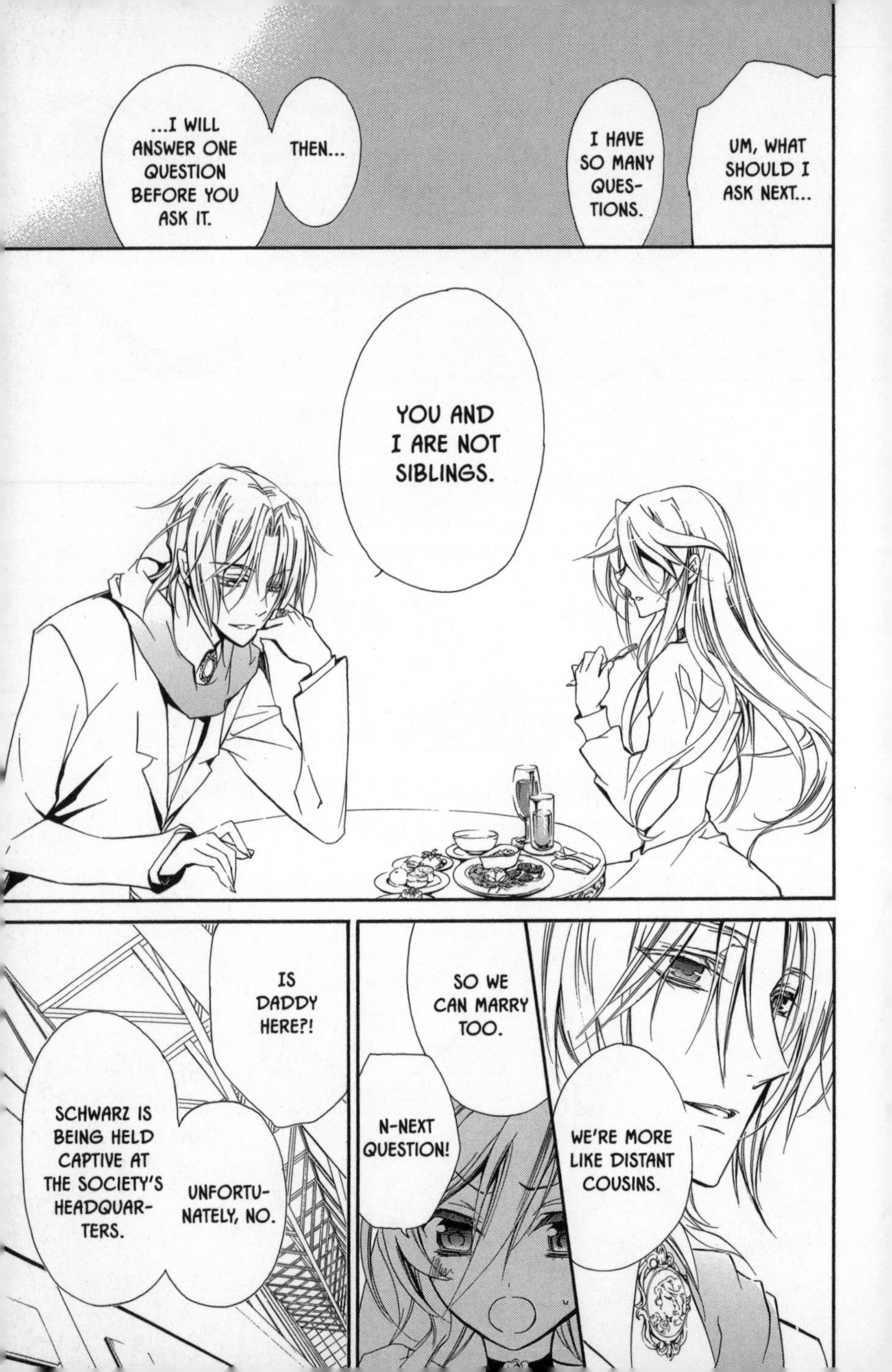
UM, WHAT SHOULD I ASK NEXT...
I HAVE SO MANY QUES-TIONS.
THEN...
...I WILL ANSWER ONE QUESTION BEFORE YOU ASK IT.
YOU AND I ARE NOT SIBLINGS.
WE'RE MORE LIKE DISTANT COUSINS.
SO WE CAN MARRY TOO.
N-NEXT QUESTION!
IS DADDY HERE?!
UNFORTU-NATELY, NO.
SCHWARZ IS BEING HELD CAPTIVE AT THE SOCIETY'S HEADQUAR-TERS.

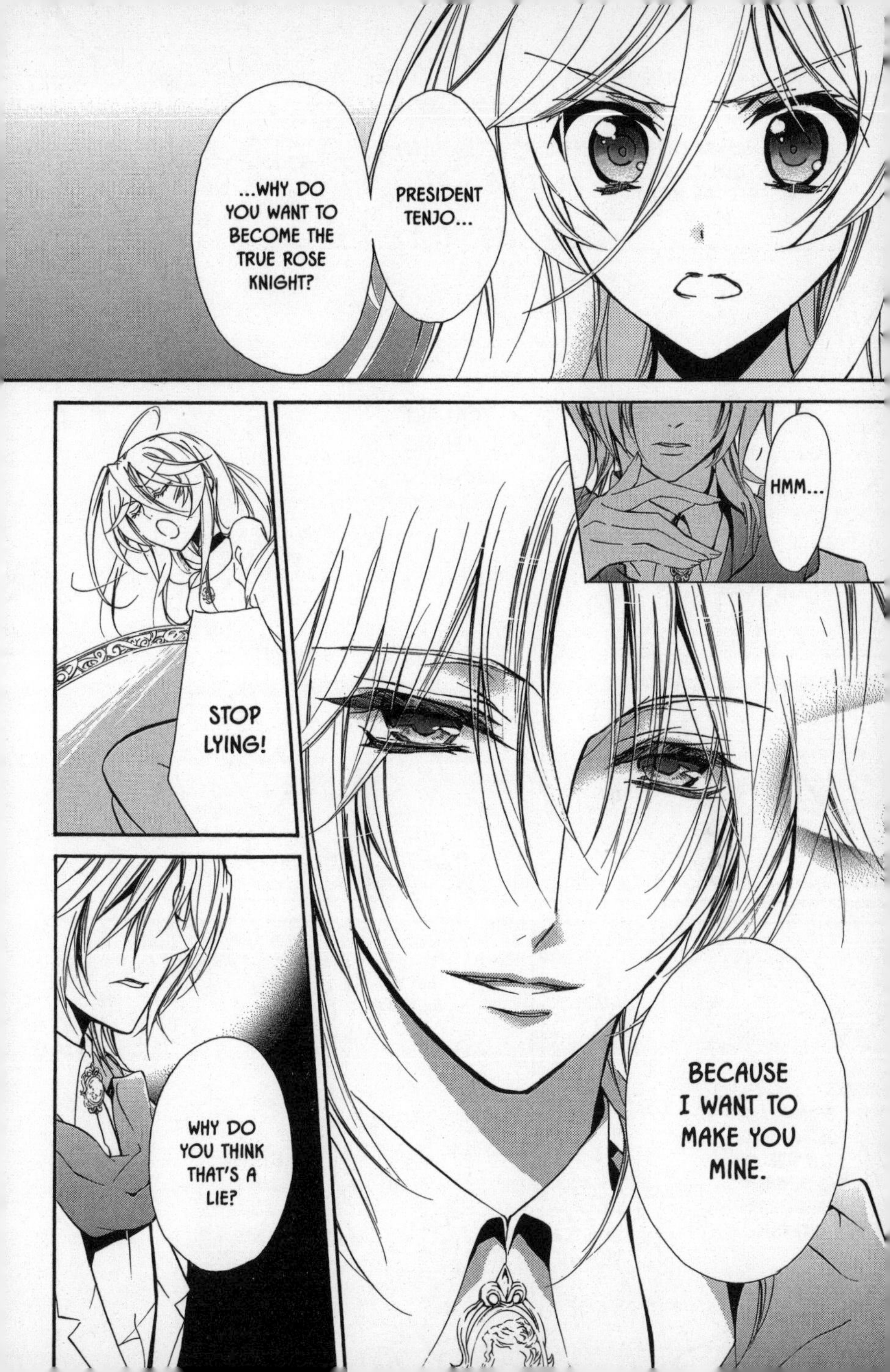
PRESIDENT TENJO...
...WHY DO YOU WANT TO BECOME THE TRUE ROSE KNIGHT?
HMM...
BECAUSE I WANT TO MAKE YOU MINE.
STOP LYING!
WHY DO YOU THINK THAT'S A LIE?

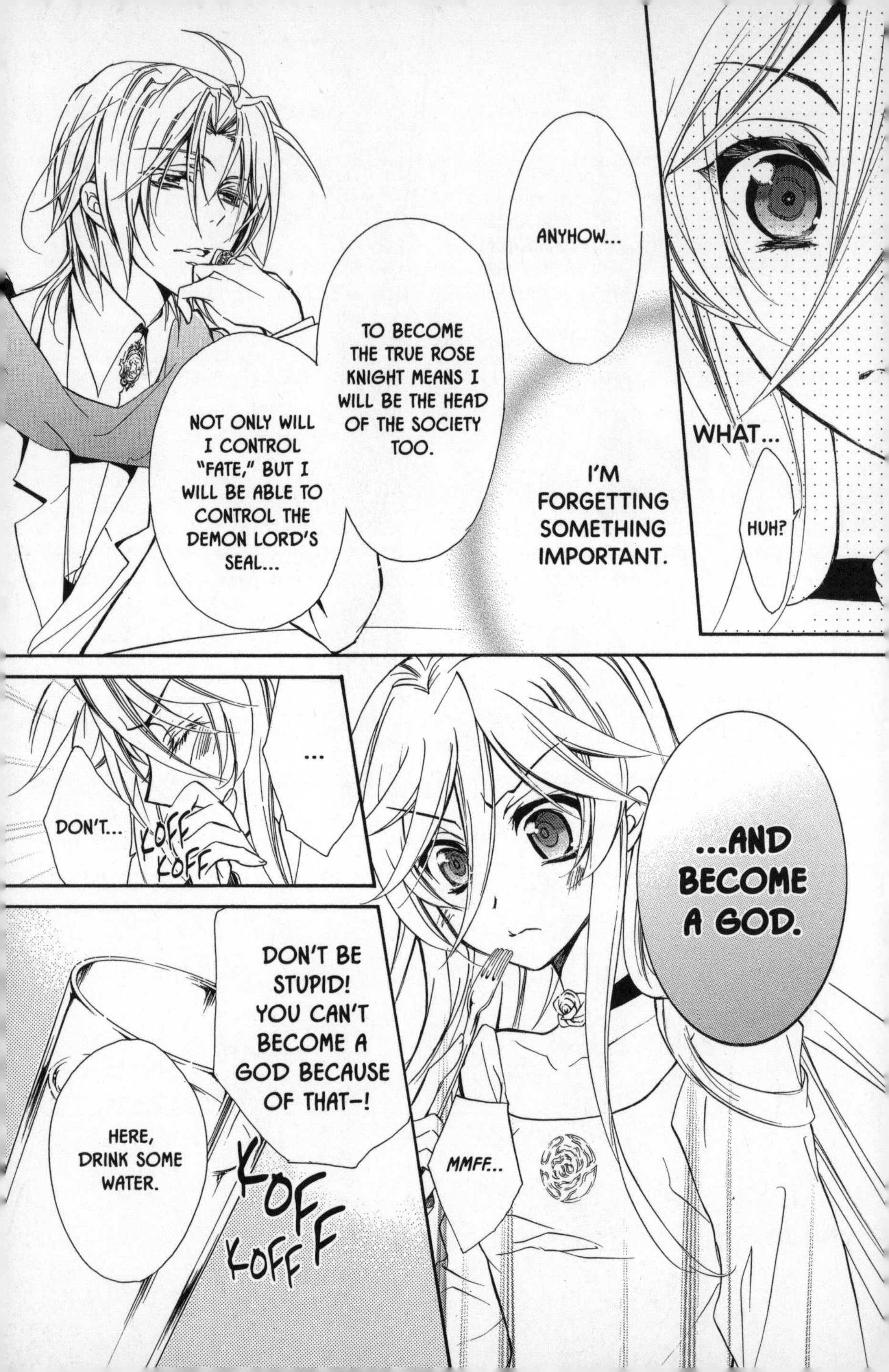
WHAT...
HUH?
I'M FORGETTING SOMETHING IMPORTANT.
ANYHOW...
TO BECOME THE TRUE ROSE KNIGHT MEANS I WILL BE THE HEAD OF THE SOCIETY TOO.
NOT ONLY WILL I CONTROL "FATE," BUT I WILL BE ABLE TO CONTROL THE DEMON LORD'S SEAL...
...AND BECOME A GOD.
...
DON'T...
KOFF KOFF
DON'T BE STUPID! YOU CAN'T BECOME A GOD BECAUSE OF THAT-!
MMFF...
HERE, DRINK SOME WATER.
KOFF KOFF

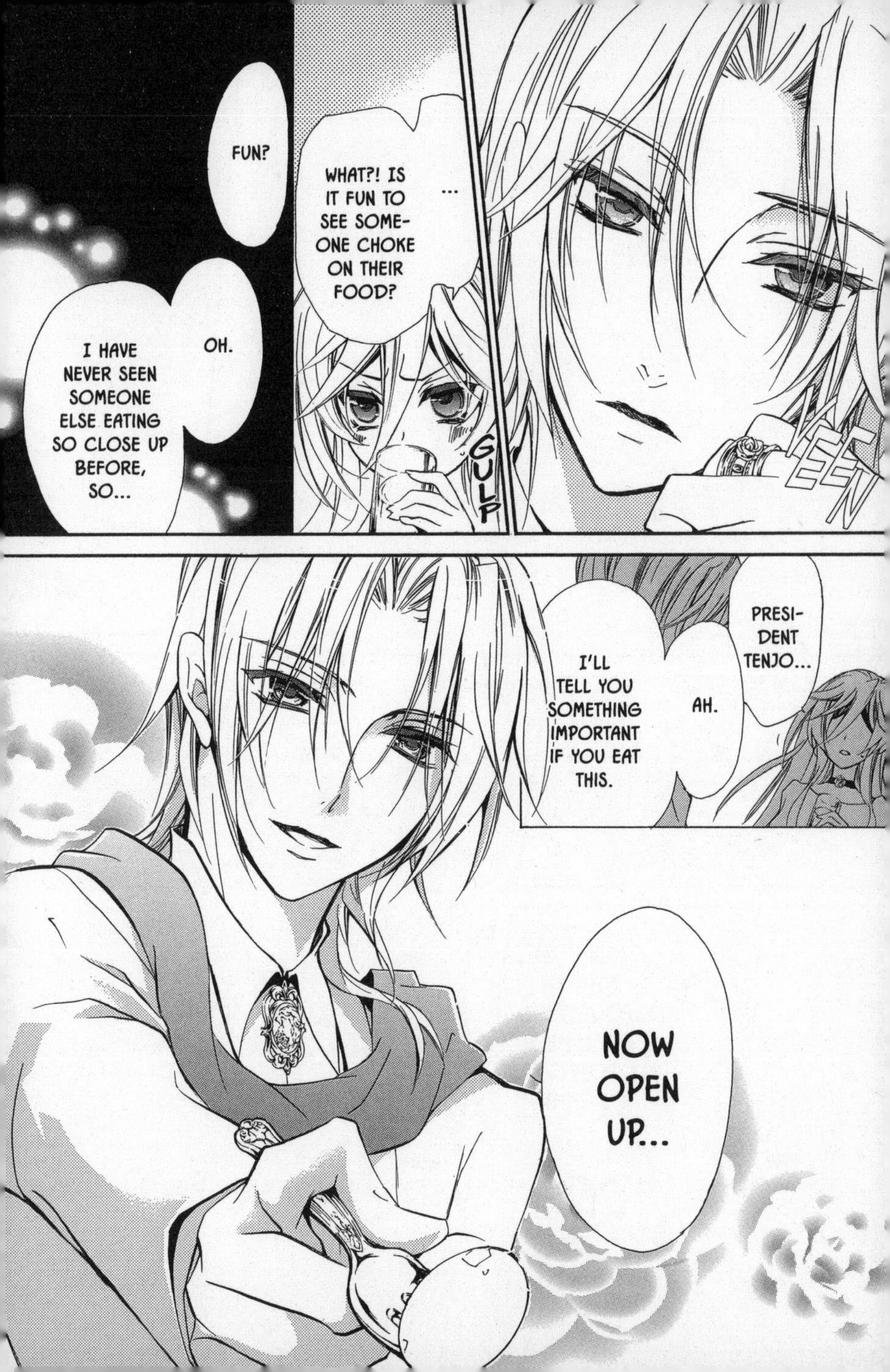
VEEEN
...
WHAT?! IS IT FUN TO SEE SOME-ONE CHOKE ON THEIR FOOD?
GULP
FUN?
OH.
I HAVE NEVER SEEN SOMEONE ELSE EATING SO CLOSE UP BEFORE, SO...
PRESI-DENT TENJO...
AH.
I'LL TELL YOU SOMETHING IMPORTANT IF YOU EAT THIS.
NOW OPEN UP...

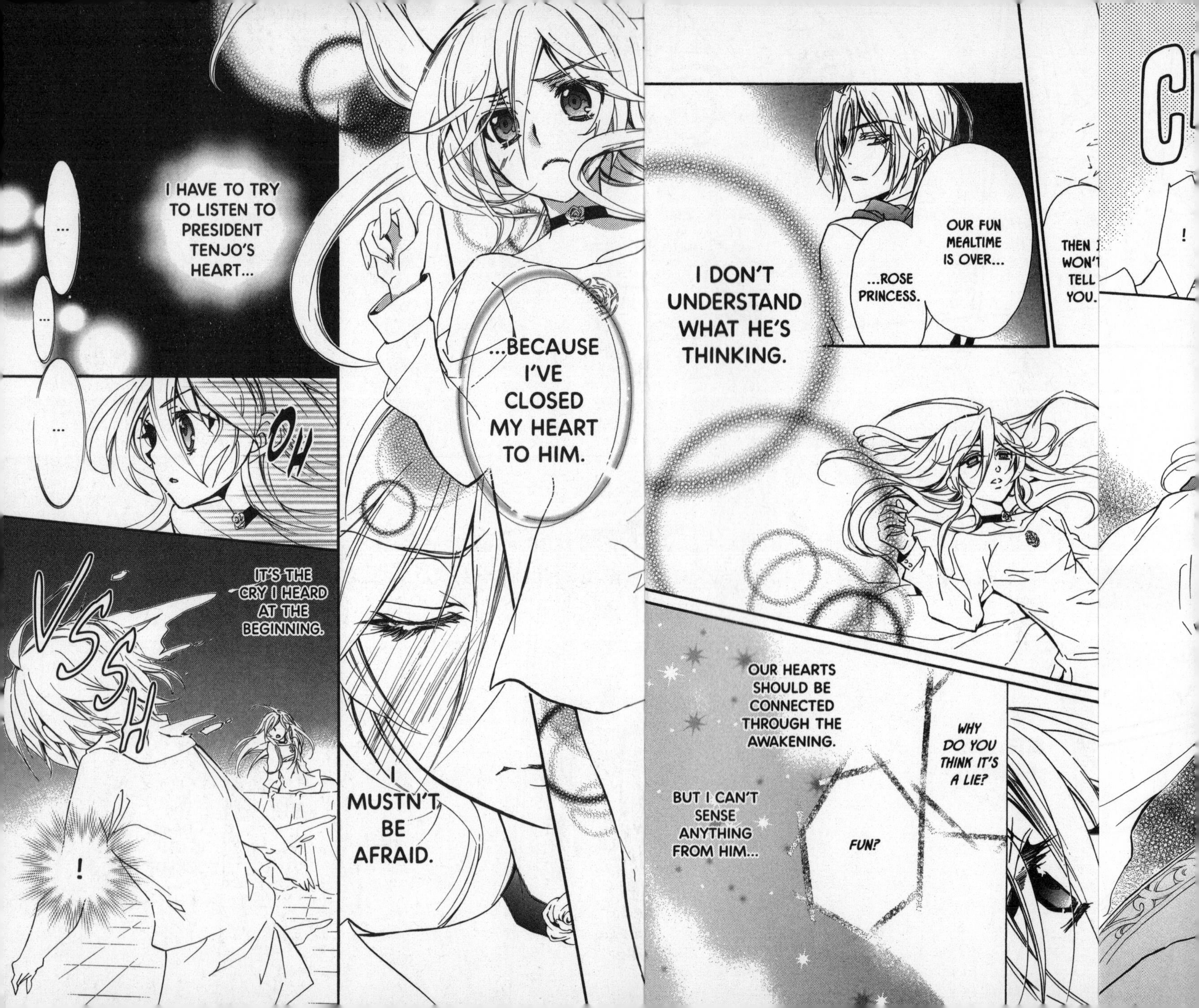
!
THEN I WON'T TELL YOU.
OUR FUN MEALTIME IS OVER...
...ROSE PRINCESS.
I DON'T UNDERSTAND WHAT HE'S THINKING.
WHY DO YOU THINK IT'S A LIE?
FUN?
OUR HEARTS SHOULD BE CONNECTED THROUGH THE AWAKENING.
BUT I CAN'T SENSE ANYTHING FROM HIM...
...BECAUSE I'VE CLOSED MY HEART TO HIM.
I MUSTN'T BE AFRAID.
I HAVE TO TRY TO LISTEN TO PRESIDENT TENJO'S HEART...
...
...
OH
...
IT'S THE CRY I HEARD AT THE BEGINNING.
VSSH
!

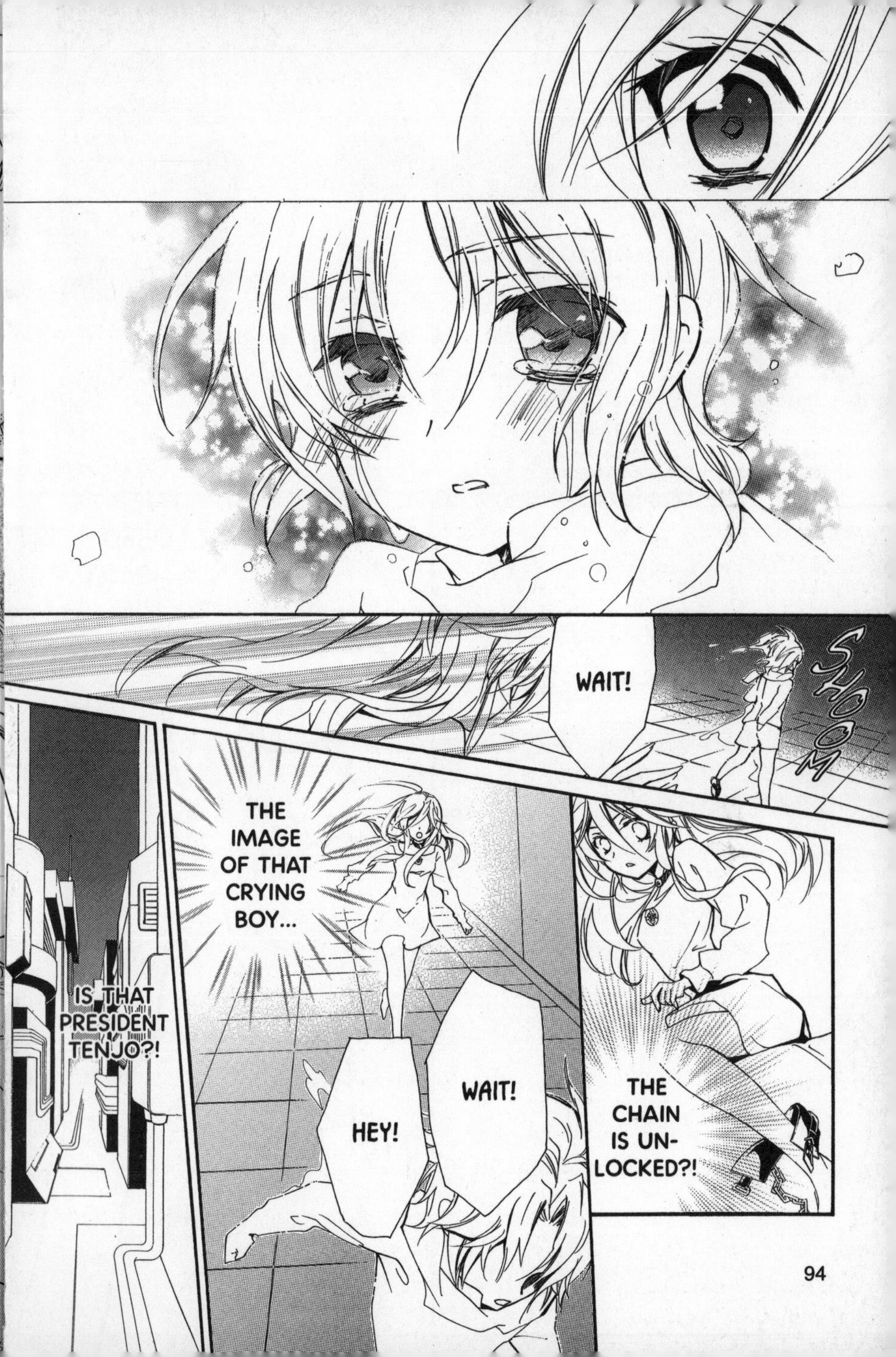
WAIT!
SHOOM
THE CHAIN IS UN-LOCKED?!
THE IMAGE OF THAT CRYING BOY...
WAIT!
HEY!
IS THAT PRESIDENT TENJO?!

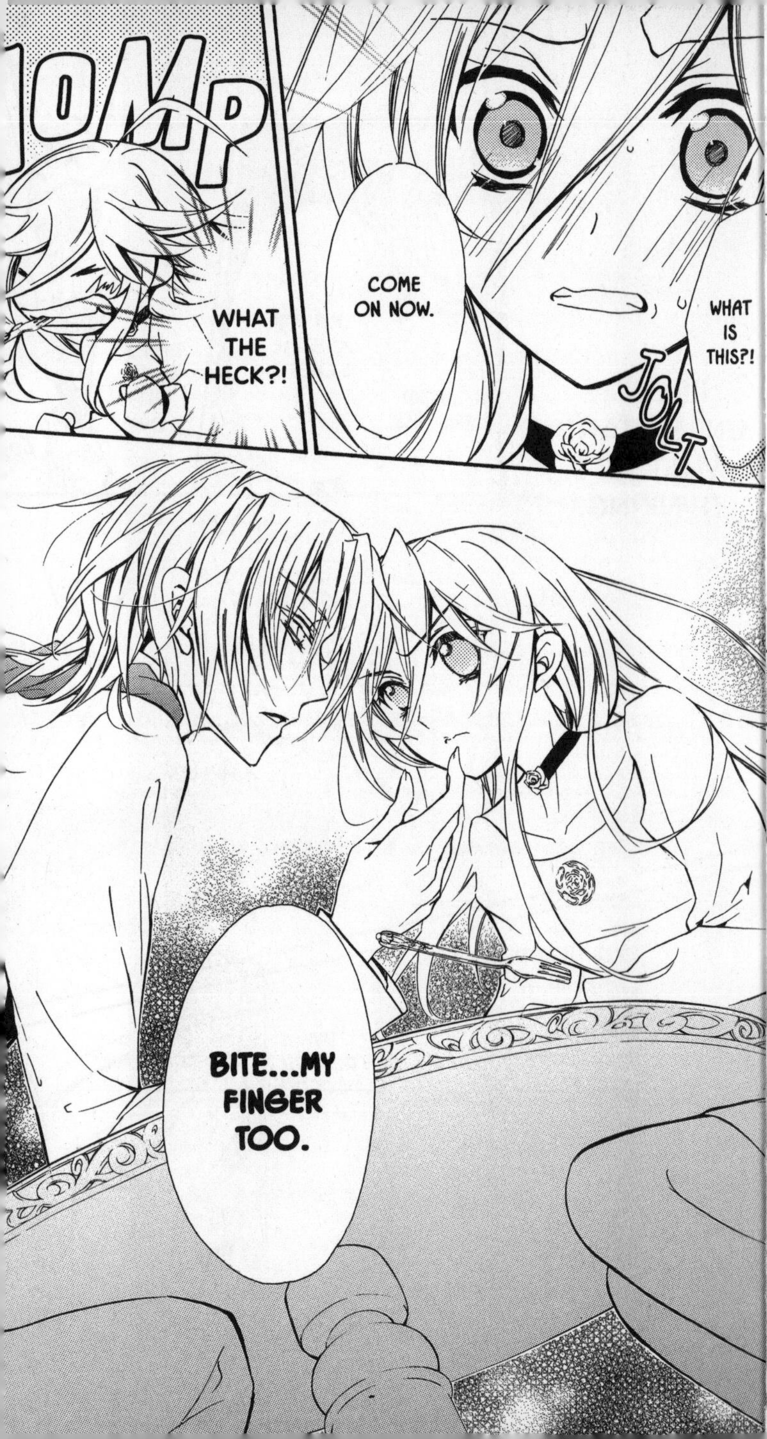
WHAT IS THIS?!
COME ON NOW.
JOLT
OMP
WHAT THE HECK?!
BITE...MY FINGER TOO.

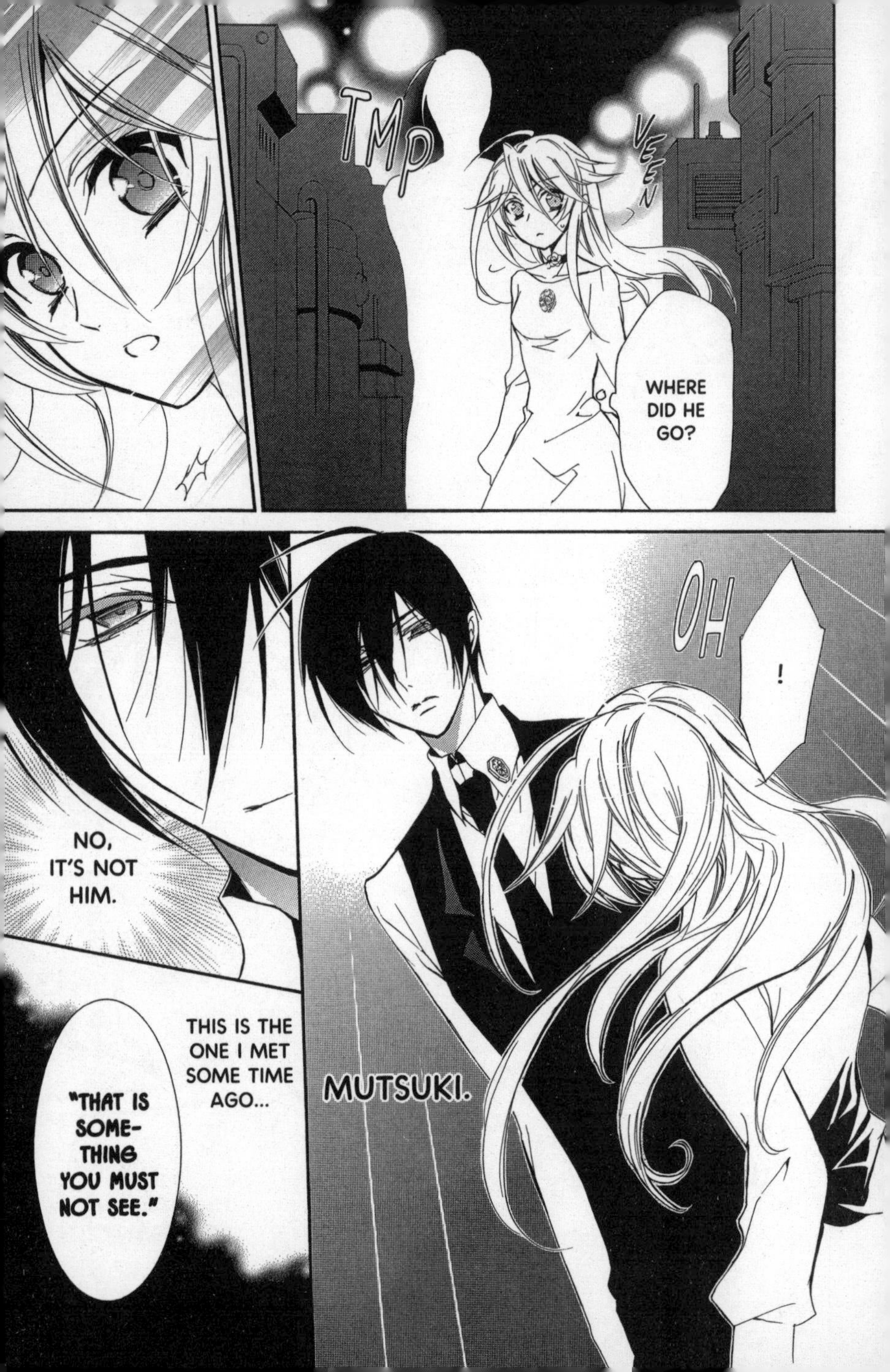
TMP
VEEN
WHERE DID HE GO?
OH
!
MUTSUKI.
NO, IT'S NOT HIM.
THIS IS THE ONE I MET SOME TIME AGO...
"THAT IS SOME-THING YOU MUST NOT SEE."

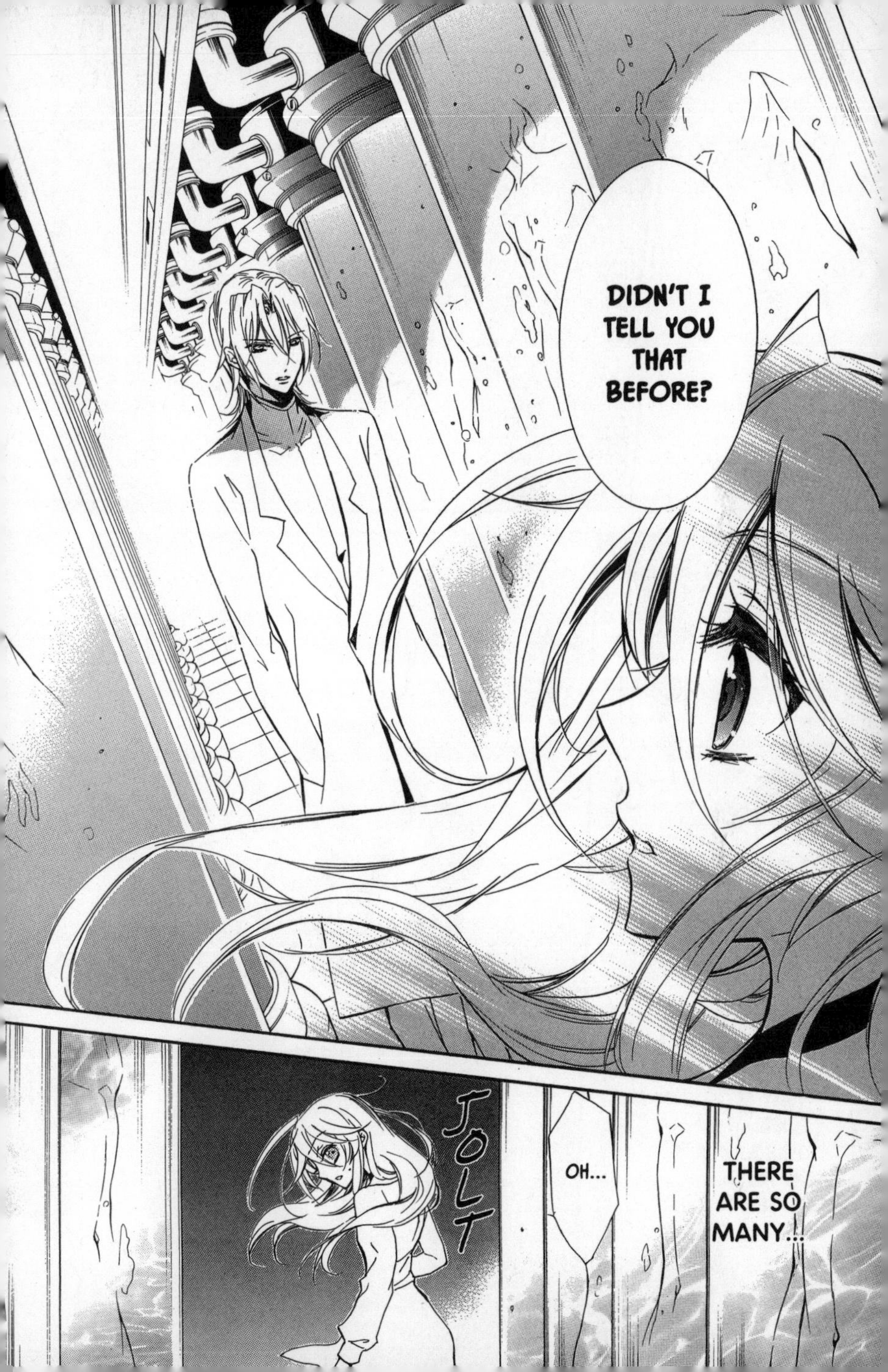
DIDN'T I TELL YOU THAT BEFORE?
THERE ARE SO MANY...
OH...
JOLT

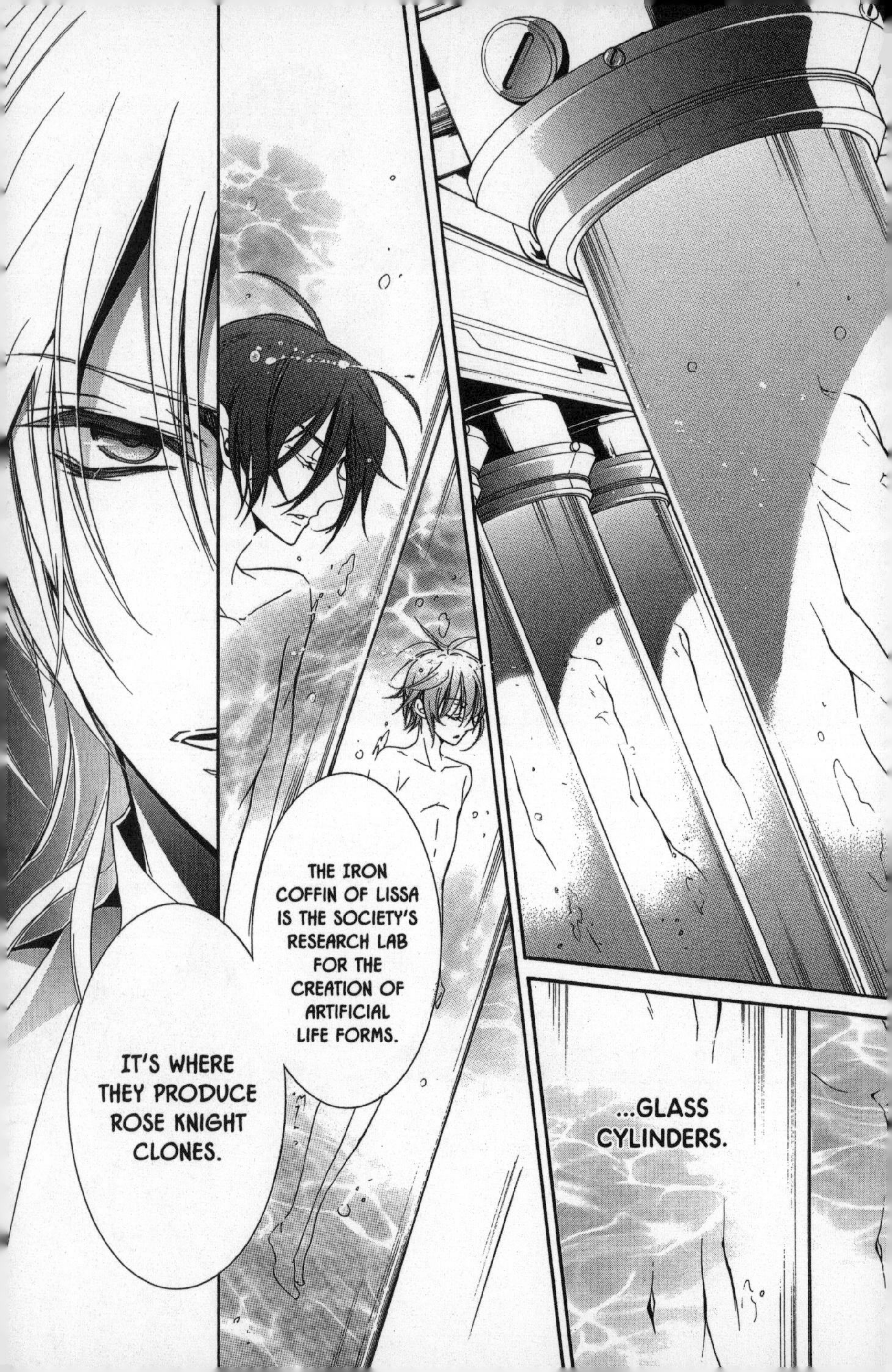
...GLASS CYLINDERS.
THE IRON COFFIN OF LISSA IS THE SOCIETY'S RESEARCH LAB FOR THE CREATION OF ARTIFICIAL LIFE FORMS.
IT'S WHERE THEY PRODUCE ROSE KNIGHT CLONES.

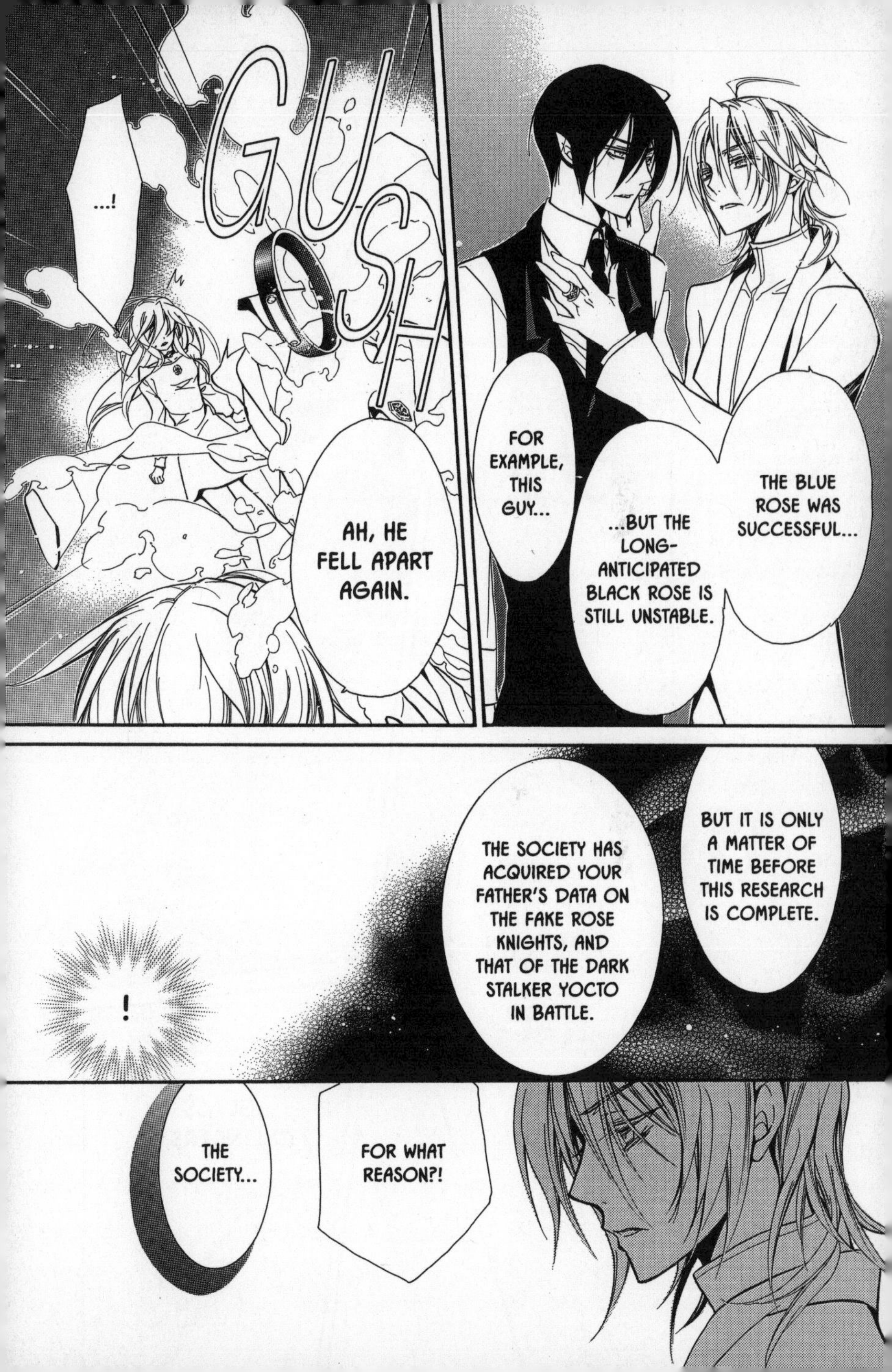
THE BLUE ROSE WAS SUCCESSFUL...
...BUT THE LONG-ANTICIPATED BLACK ROSE IS STILL UNSTABLE.
FOR EXAMPLE, THIS GUY...
GUSH
AH, HE FELL APART AGAIN.
...!
BUT IT IS ONLY A MATTER OF TIME BEFORE THIS RESEARCH IS COMPLETE.
THE SOCIETY HAS ACQUIRED YOUR FATHER'S DATA ON THE FAKE ROSE KNIGHTS, AND THAT OF THE DARK STALKER YOCTO IN BATTLE.
!
FOR WHAT REASON?!
THE SOCIETY...

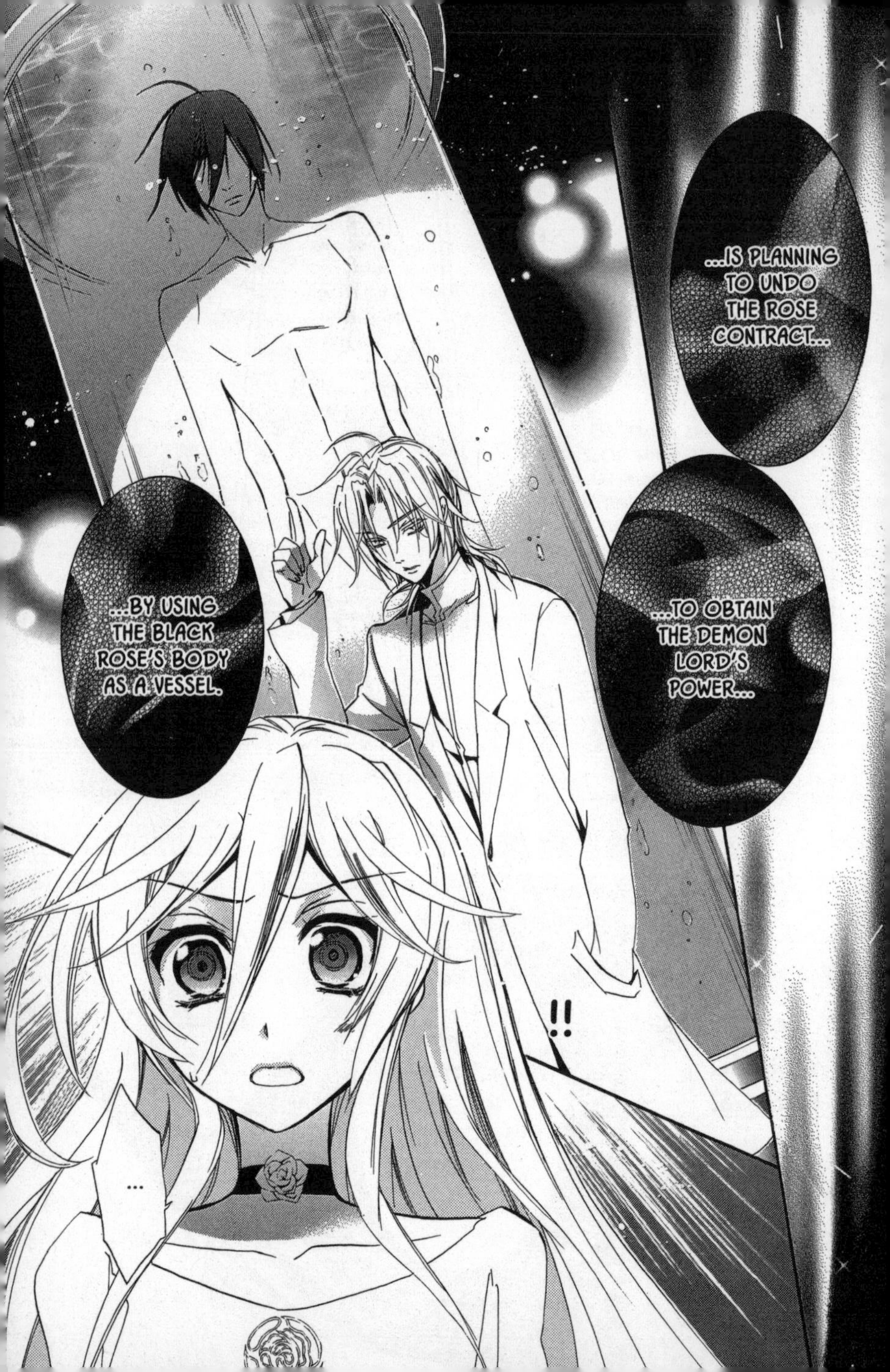
...IS PLANNING TO UNDO THE ROSE CONTRACT...
...TO OBTAIN THE DEMON LORD'S POWER...
...BY USING THE BLACK ROSE'S BODY AS A VESSEL.
!!
...

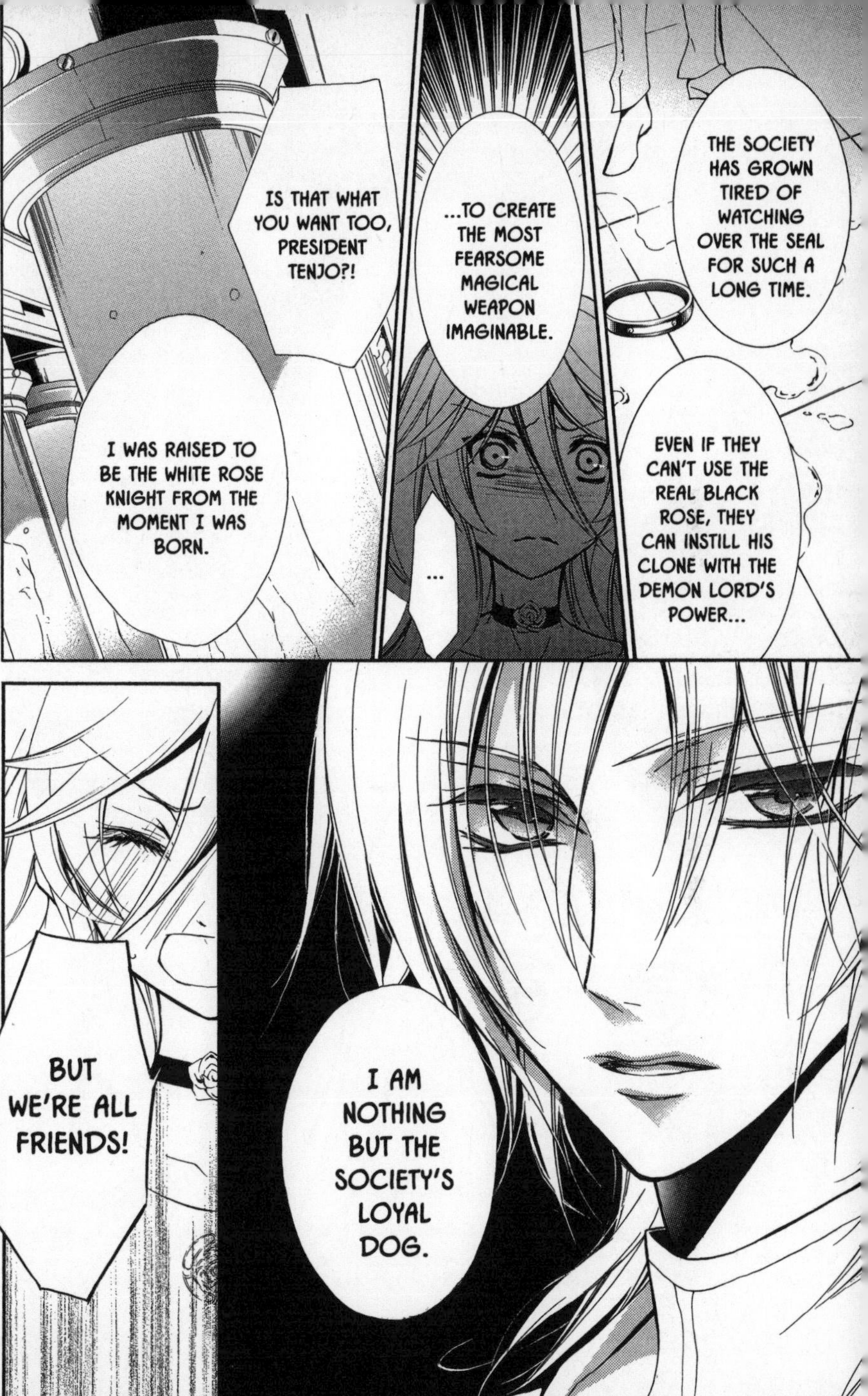
THE SOCIETY HAS GROWN TIRED OF WATCHING OVER THE SEAL FOR SUCH A LONG TIME.
EVEN IF THEY CAN'T USE THE REAL BLACK ROSE, THEY CAN INSTILL HIS CLONE WITH THE DEMON LORD'S POWER...
...TO CREATE THE MOST FEARSOME MAGICAL WEAPON IMAGINABLE.
...
IS THAT WHAT YOU WANT TOO, PRESIDENT TENJO?!
I WAS RAISED TO BE THE WHITE ROSE KNIGHT FROM THE MOMENT I WAS BORN.
I AM NOTHING BUT THE SOCIETY'S LOYAL DOG.
BUT WE'RE ALL FRIENDS!

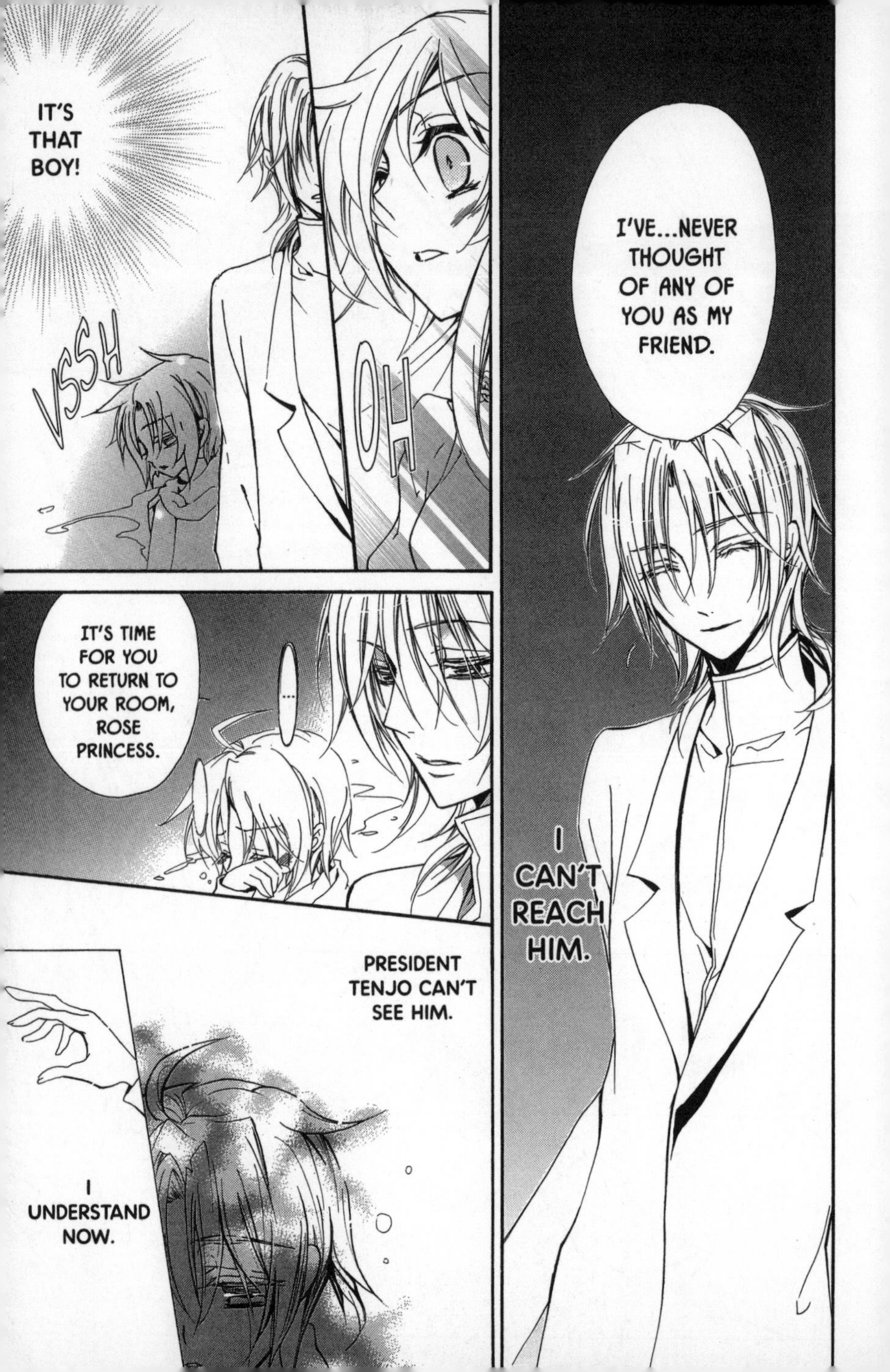
I'VE...NEVER THOUGHT OF ANY OF YOU AS MY FRIEND.
I CAN'T REACH HIM.
IT'S THAT BOY!
OH
VSSH
IT'S TIME FOR YOU TO RETURN TO YOUR ROOM, ROSE PRINCESS.
...
PRESIDENT TENJO CAN'T SEE HIM.
I UNDERSTAND NOW.

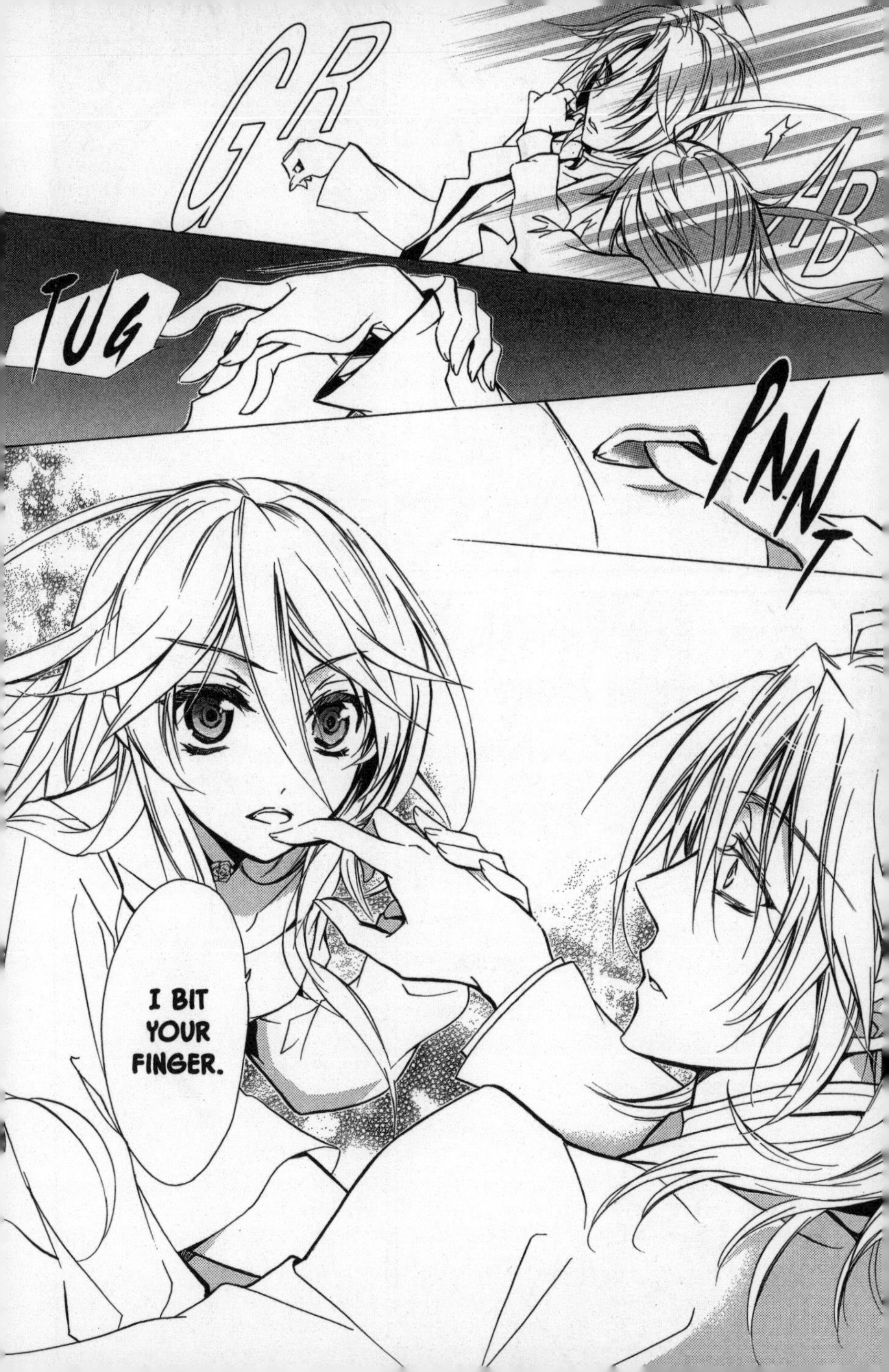
GRAB
TUG
PNNT
I BIT YOUR FINGER.

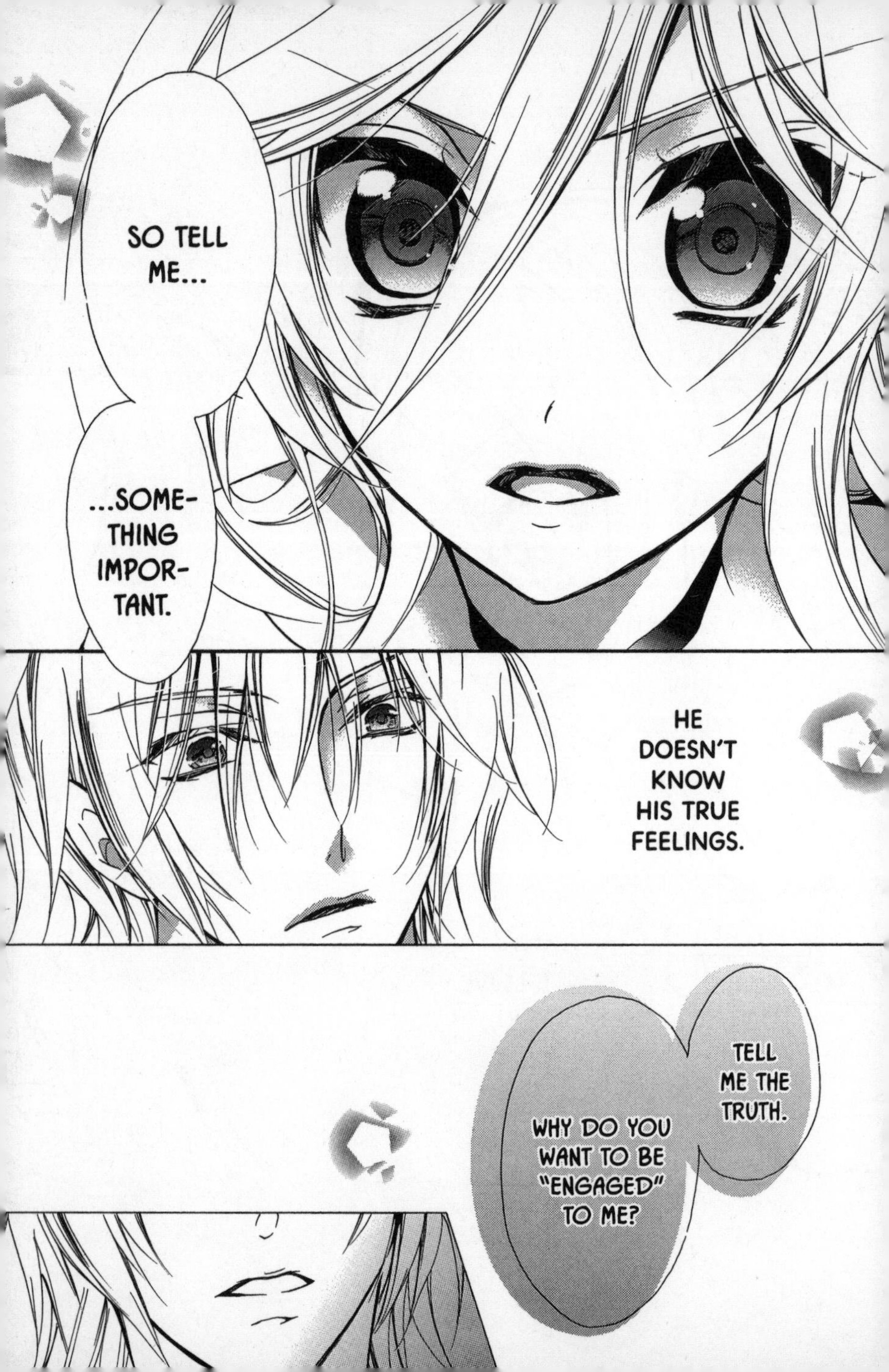
SO TELL ME...
...SOMETHING IMPORTANT.
HE DOESN'T KNOW HIS TRUE FEELINGS.
TELL ME THE TRUTH.
WHY DO YOU WANT TO BE "ENGAGED" TO ME?

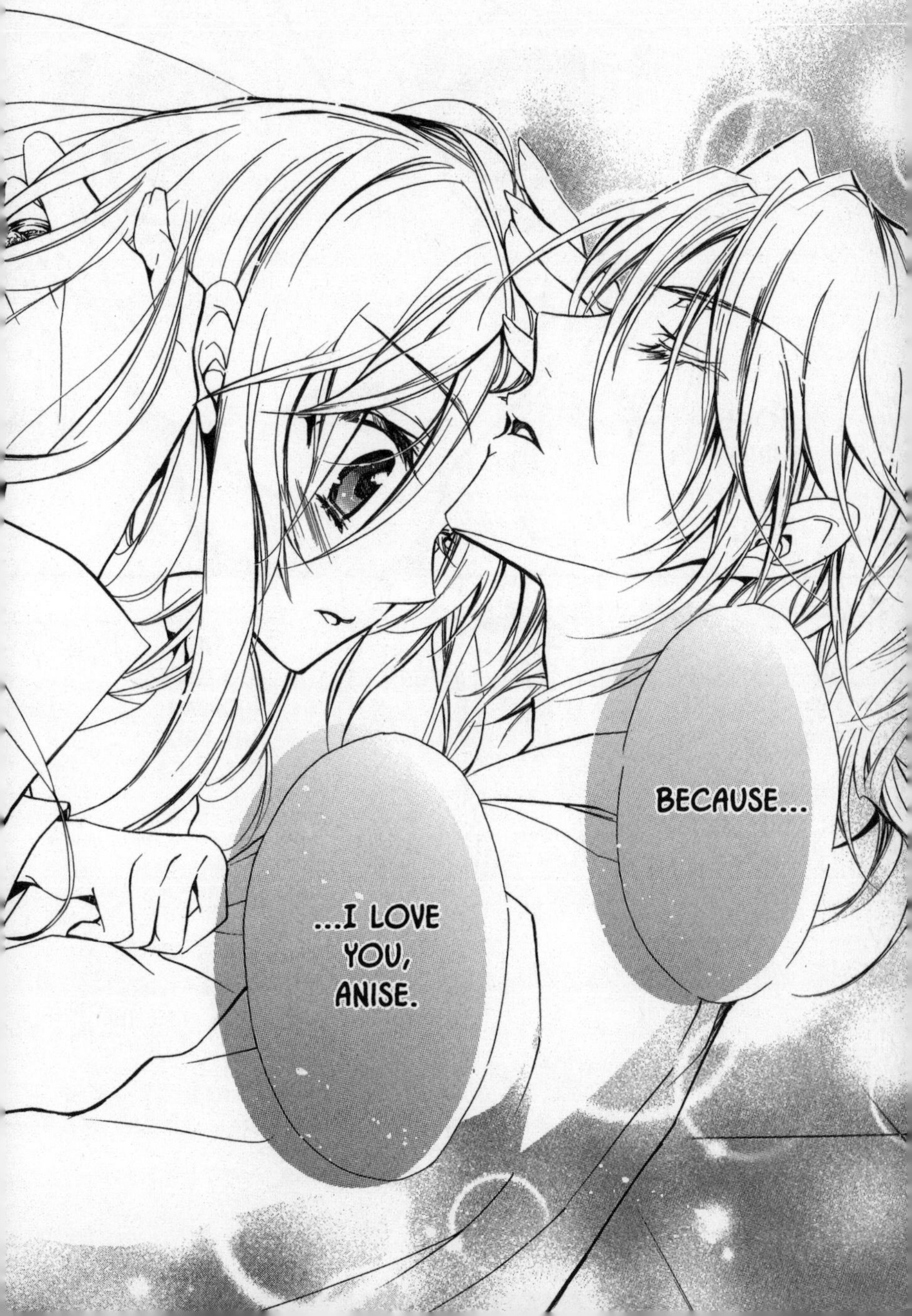
BECAUSE...
...I LOVE YOU, ANISE.

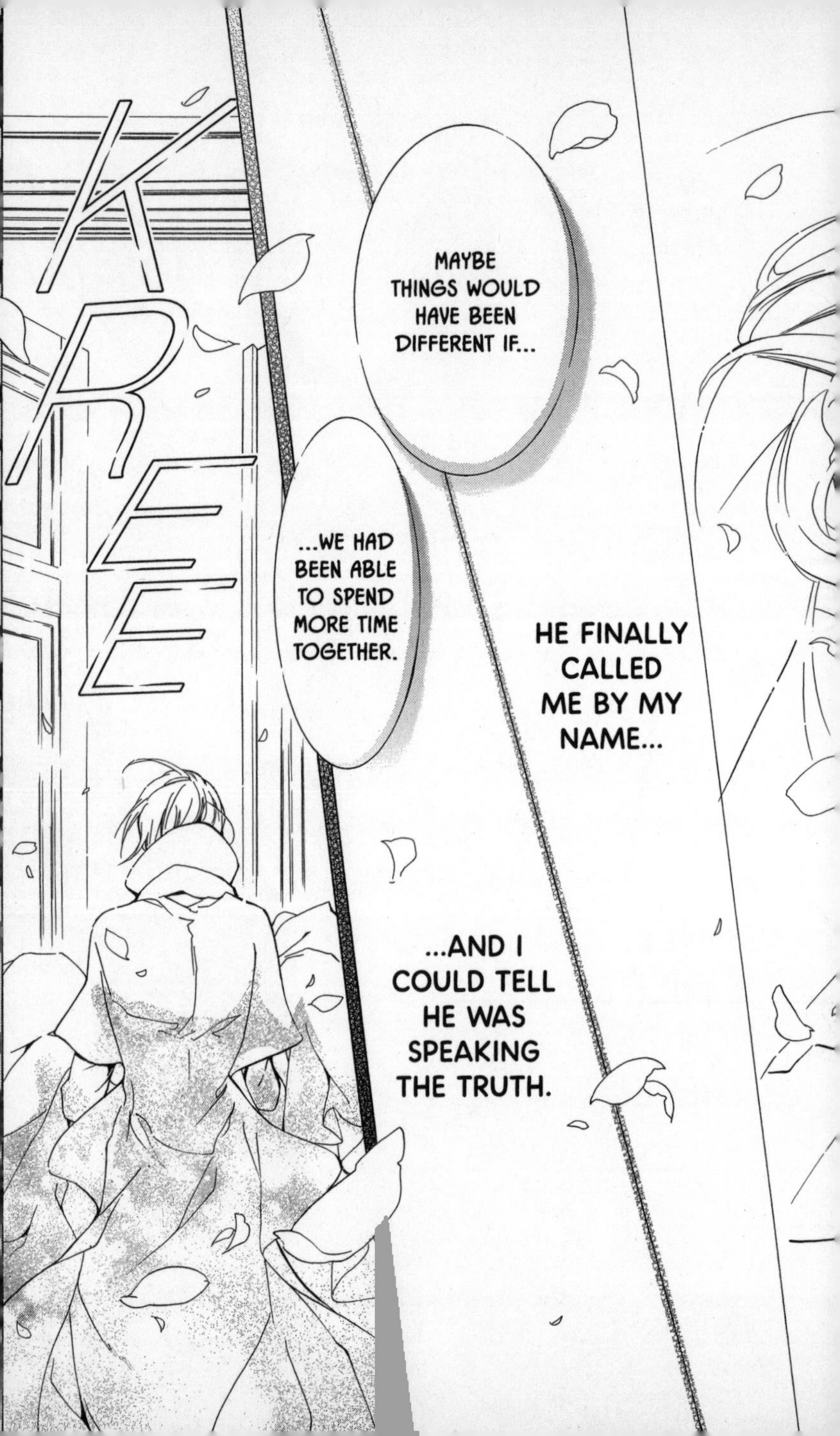
HE FINALLY CALLED ME BY MY NAME...
...AND I COULD TELL HE WAS SPEAKING THE TRUTH.
MAYBE THINGS WOULD HAVE BEEN DIFFERENT IF...
...WE HAD BEEN ABLE TO SPEND MORE TIME TOGETHER.
KREEE

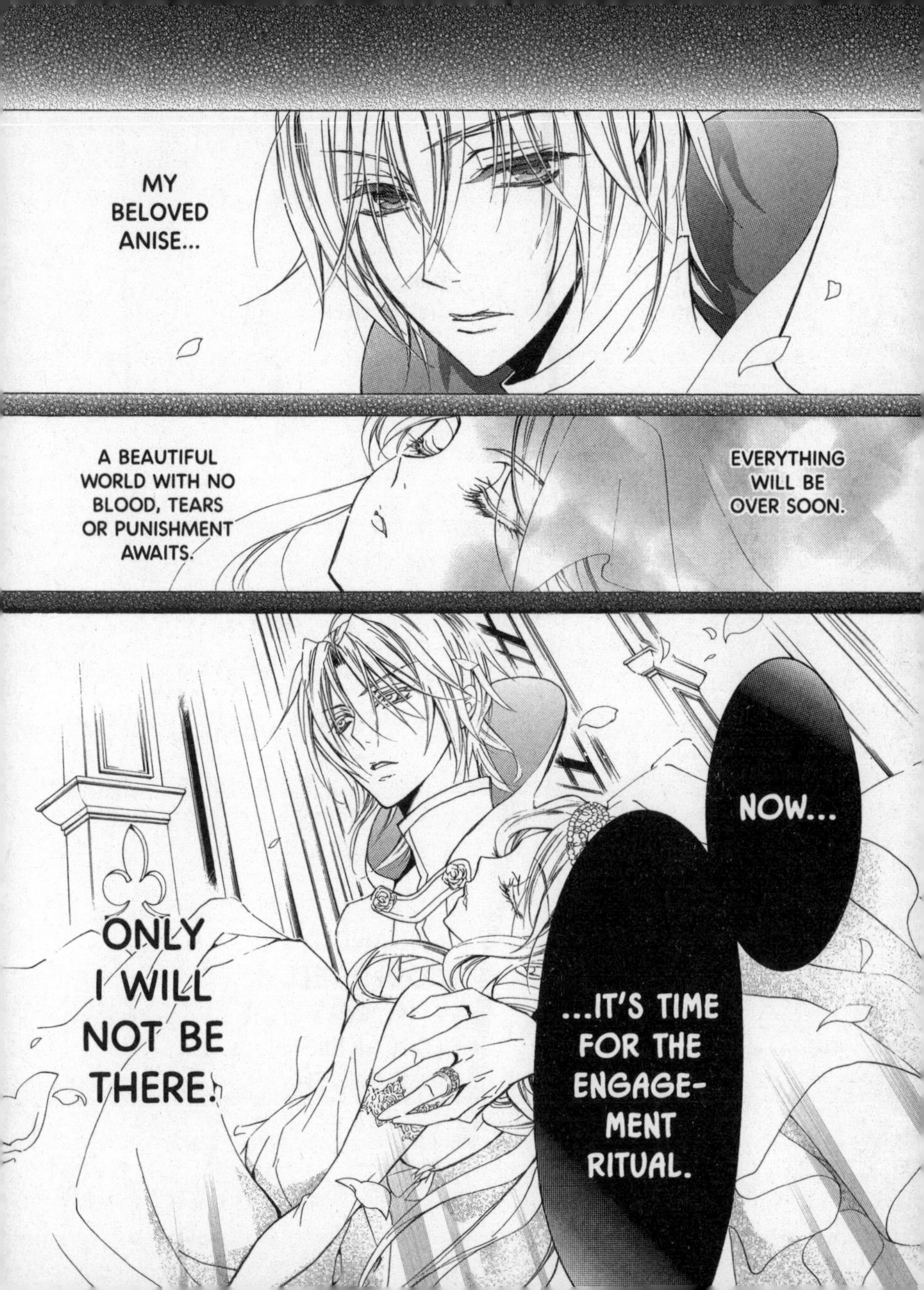
MY BELOVED ANISE...
EVERYTHING WILL BE OVER SOON.
A BEAUTIFUL WORLD WITH NO BLOOD, TEARS OR PUNISHMENT AWAITS.
NOW...
...IT'S TIME FOR THE ENGAGE-MENT RITUAL.
ONLY I WILL NOT BE THERE.

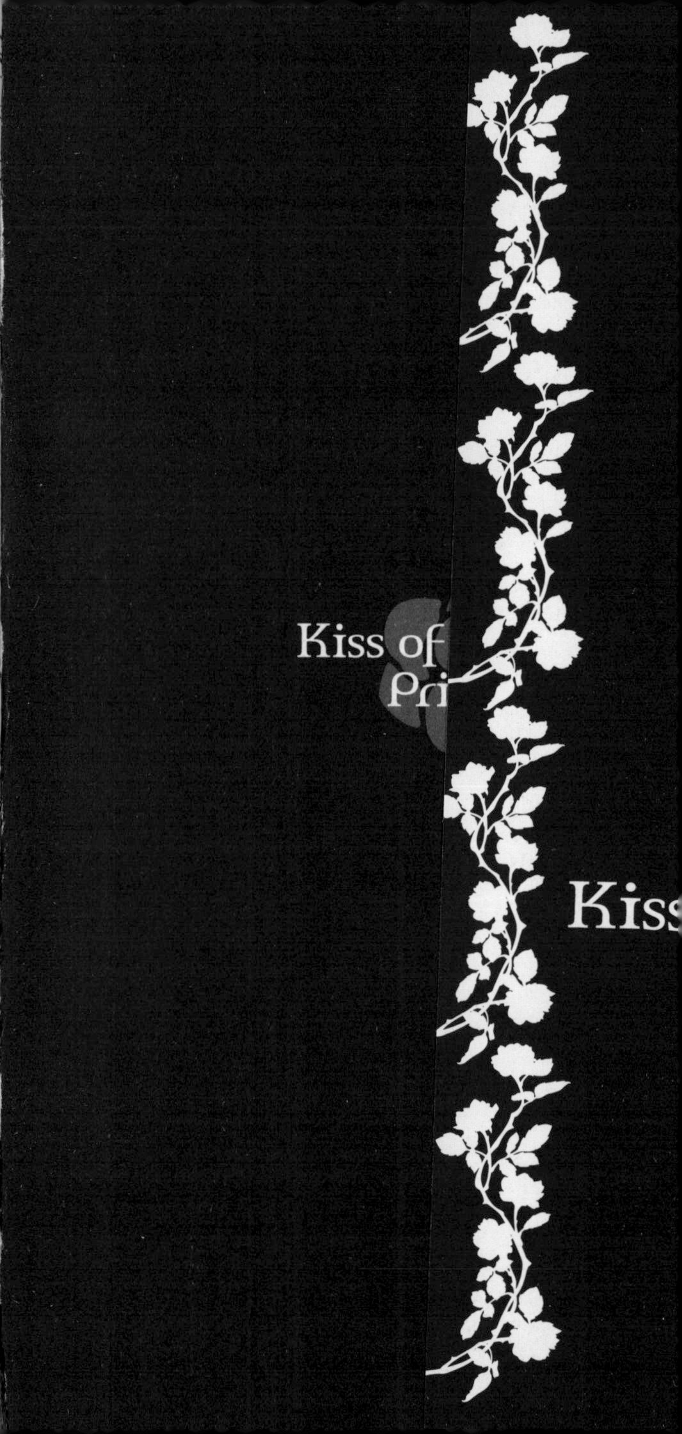
Kiss of
Pri
Kiss

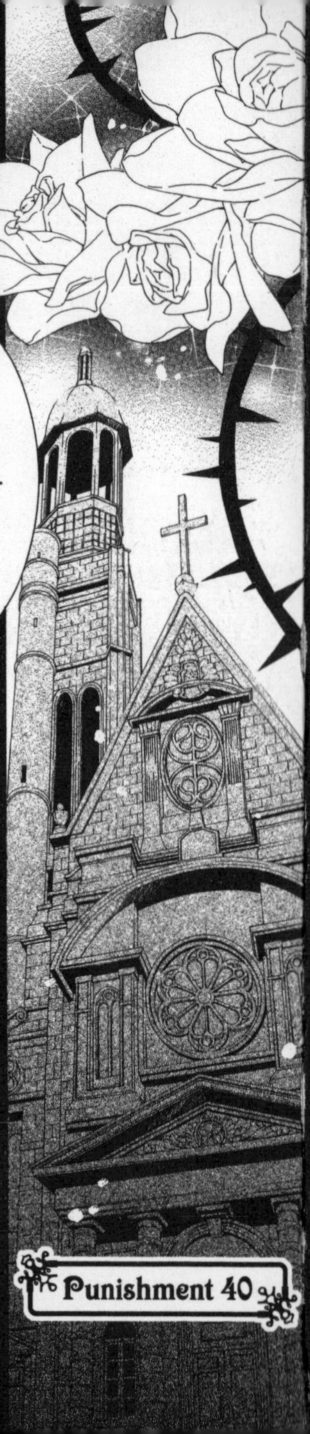
Punishment 40

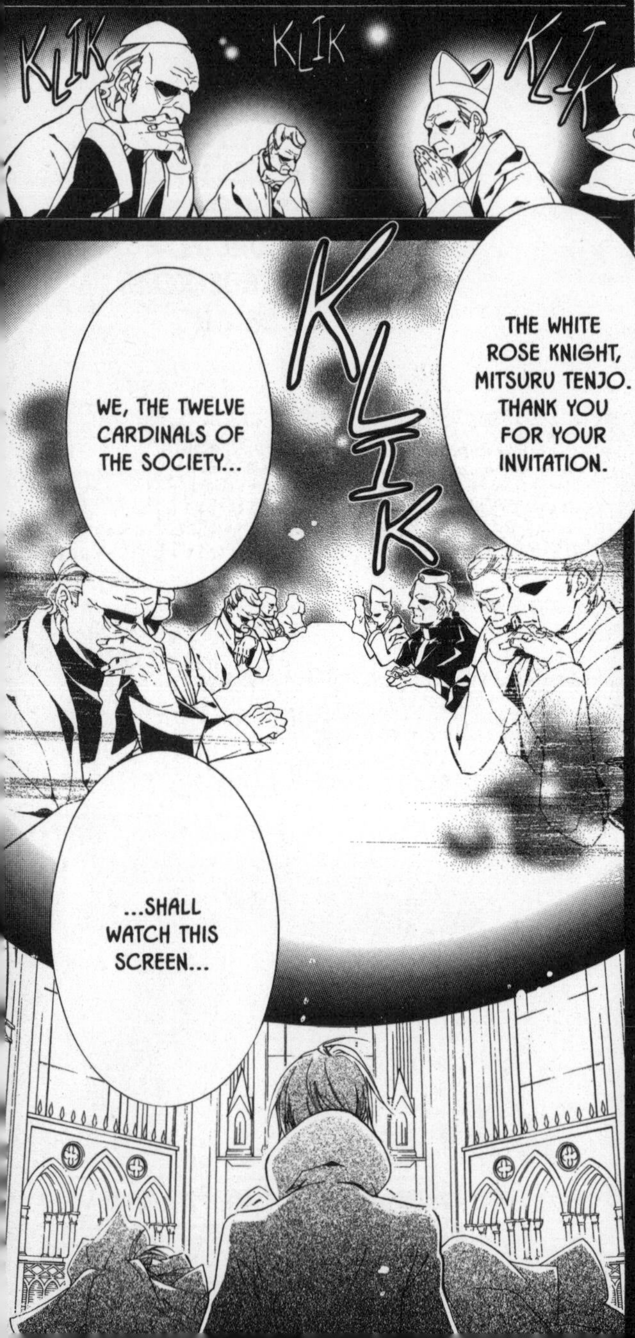
KLIK
KLIK
KLIK
KLIK
THE WHITE ROSE KNIGHT, MITSURU TENJO. THANK YOU FOR YOUR INVITATION.
WE, THE TWELVE CARDINALS OF THE SOCIETY...
...SHALL WATCH THIS SCREEN...

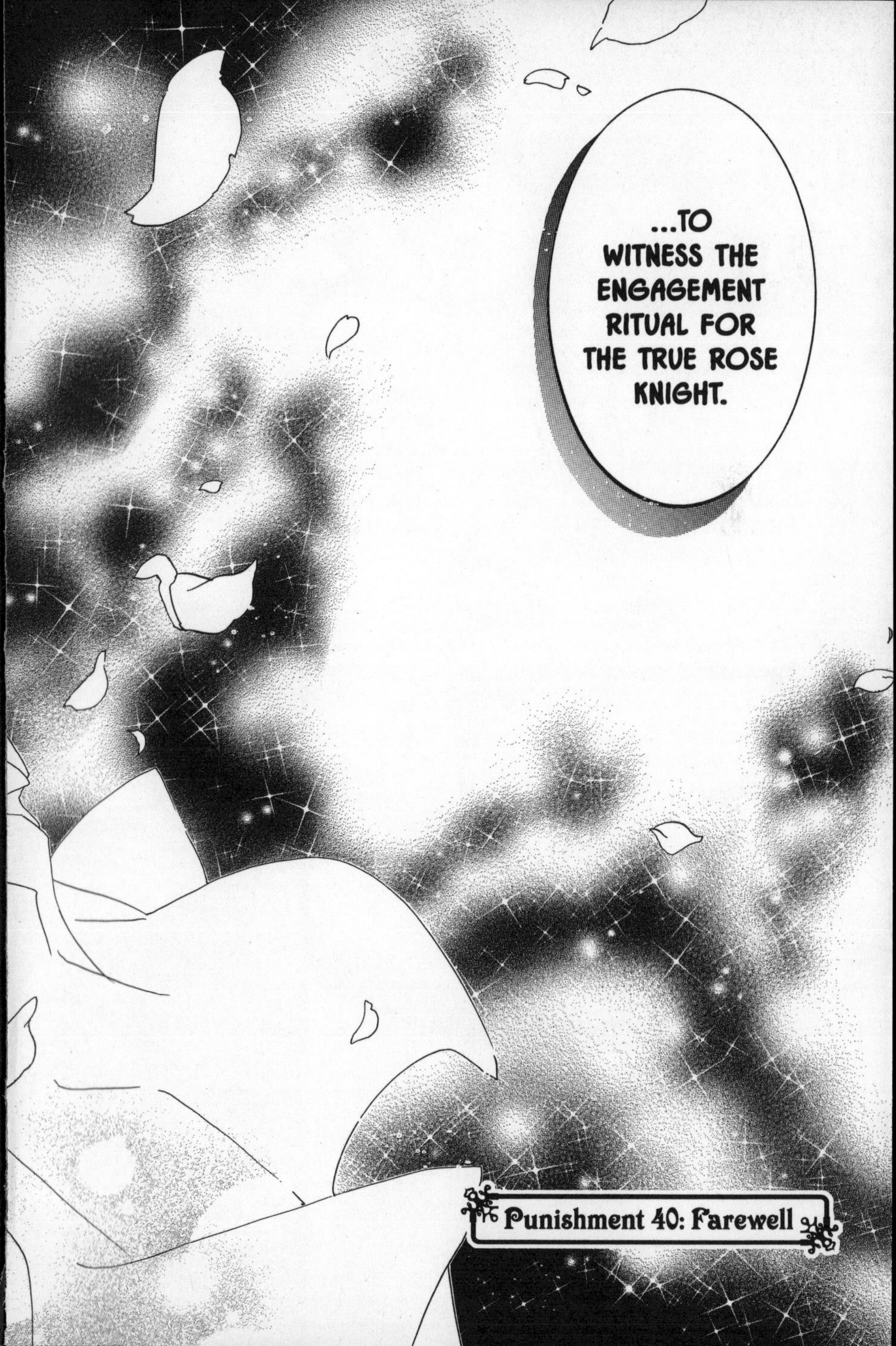
...TO WITNESS THE ENGAGEMENT RITUAL FOR THE TRUE ROSE KNIGHT.
Punishment 40: Farewell

of the Rose Princess

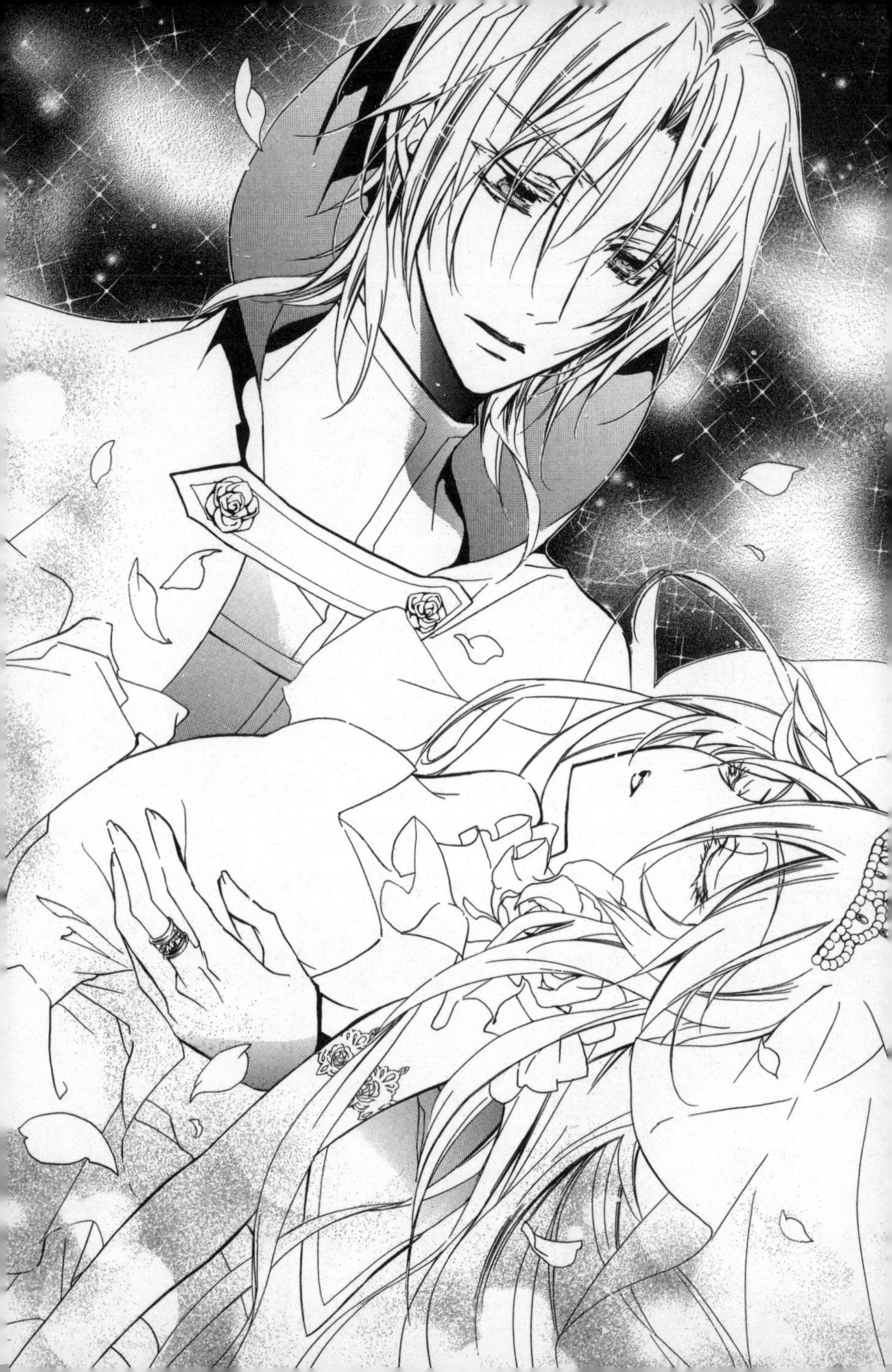

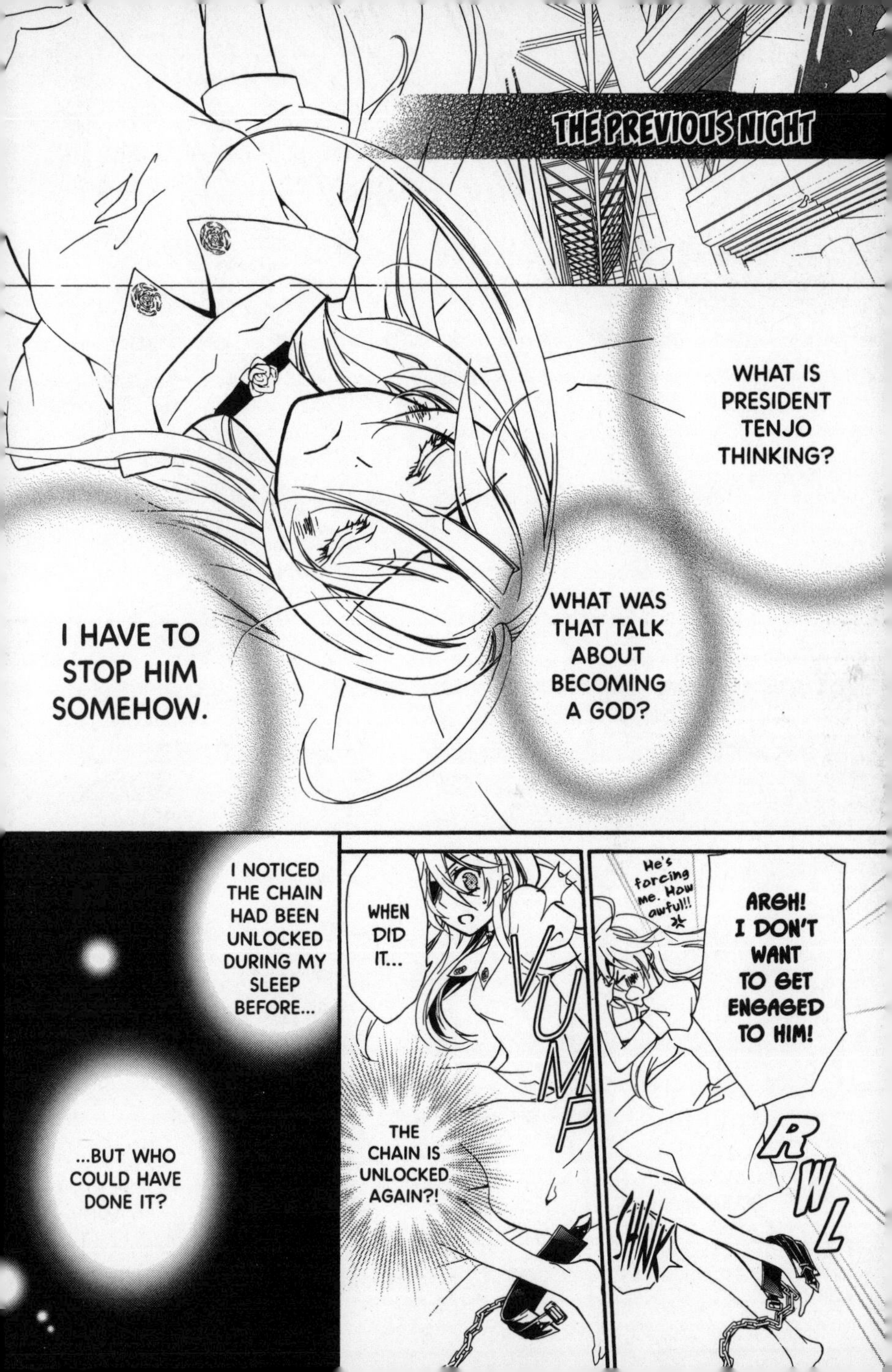
THE PREVIOUS NIGHT
WHAT IS PRESIDENT TENJO THINKING?
WHAT WAS THAT TALK ABOUT BECOMING A GOD?
I HAVE TO STOP HIM SOMEHOW.
ARGH! I DON'T WANT TO GET ENGAGED TO HIM!
He's forcing me. How awful!!
RWL
SHINK
WHEN DID IT...
VUMP
THE CHAIN IS UNLOCKED AGAIN?!
I NOTICED THE CHAIN HAD BEEN UNLOCKED DURING MY SLEEP BEFORE...
...BUT WHO COULD HAVE DONE IT?

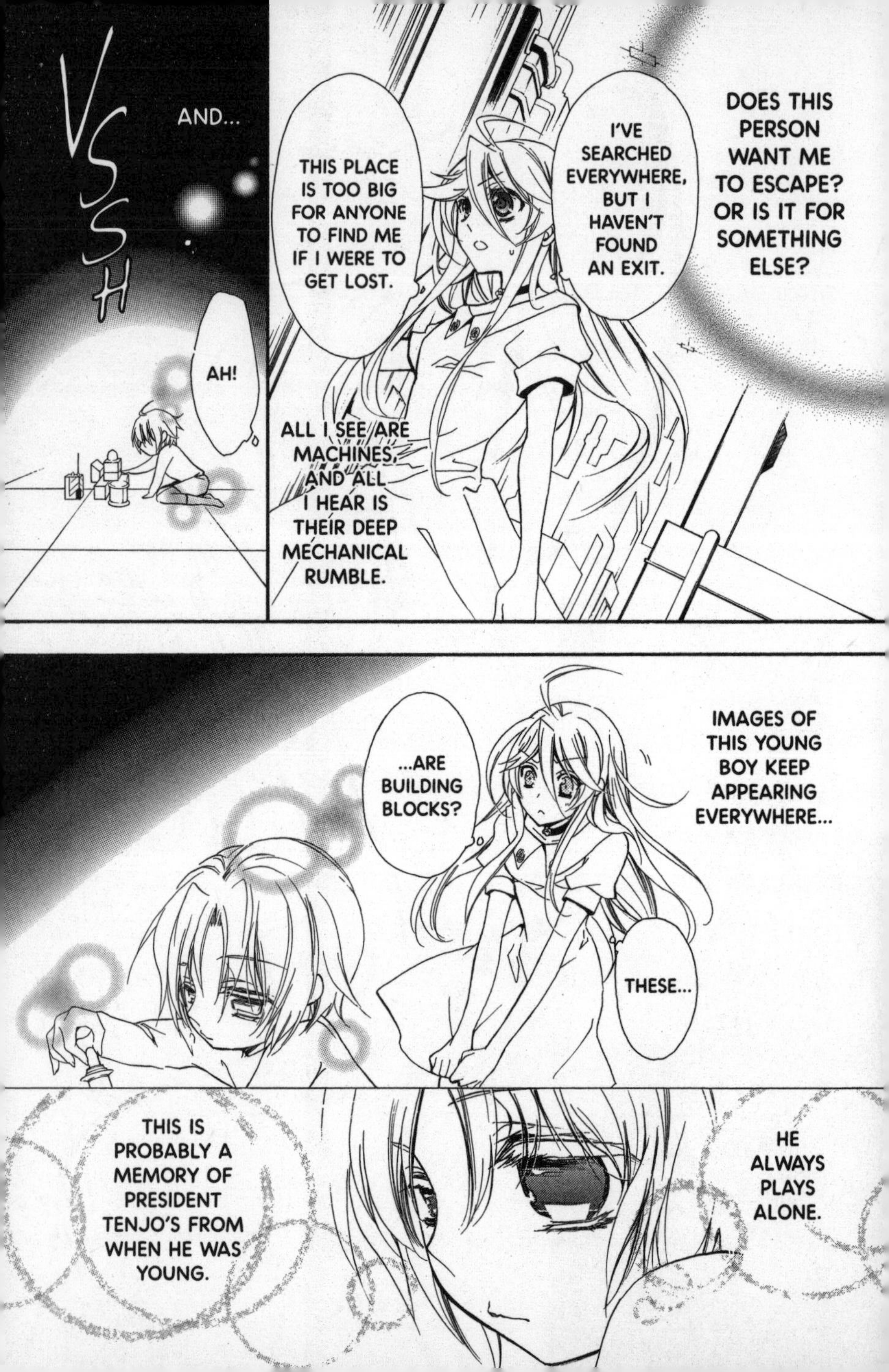
DOES THIS PERSON WANT ME TO ESCAPE? OR IS IT FOR SOMETHING ELSE?
I'VE SEARCHED EVERYWHERE, BUT I HAVEN'T FOUND AN EXIT.
THIS PLACE IS TOO BIG FOR ANYONE TO FIND ME IF I WERE TO GET LOST.
ALL I SEE ARE MACHINES, AND ALL I HEAR IS THEIR DEEP MECHANICAL RUMBLE.
AND...
VSSH
AH!
IMAGES OF THIS YOUNG BOY KEEP APPEARING EVERYWHERE...
THESE...
...ARE BUILDING BLOCKS?
HE ALWAYS PLAYS ALONE.
THIS IS PROBABLY A MEMORY OF PRESIDENT TENJO'S FROM WHEN HE WAS YOUNG.

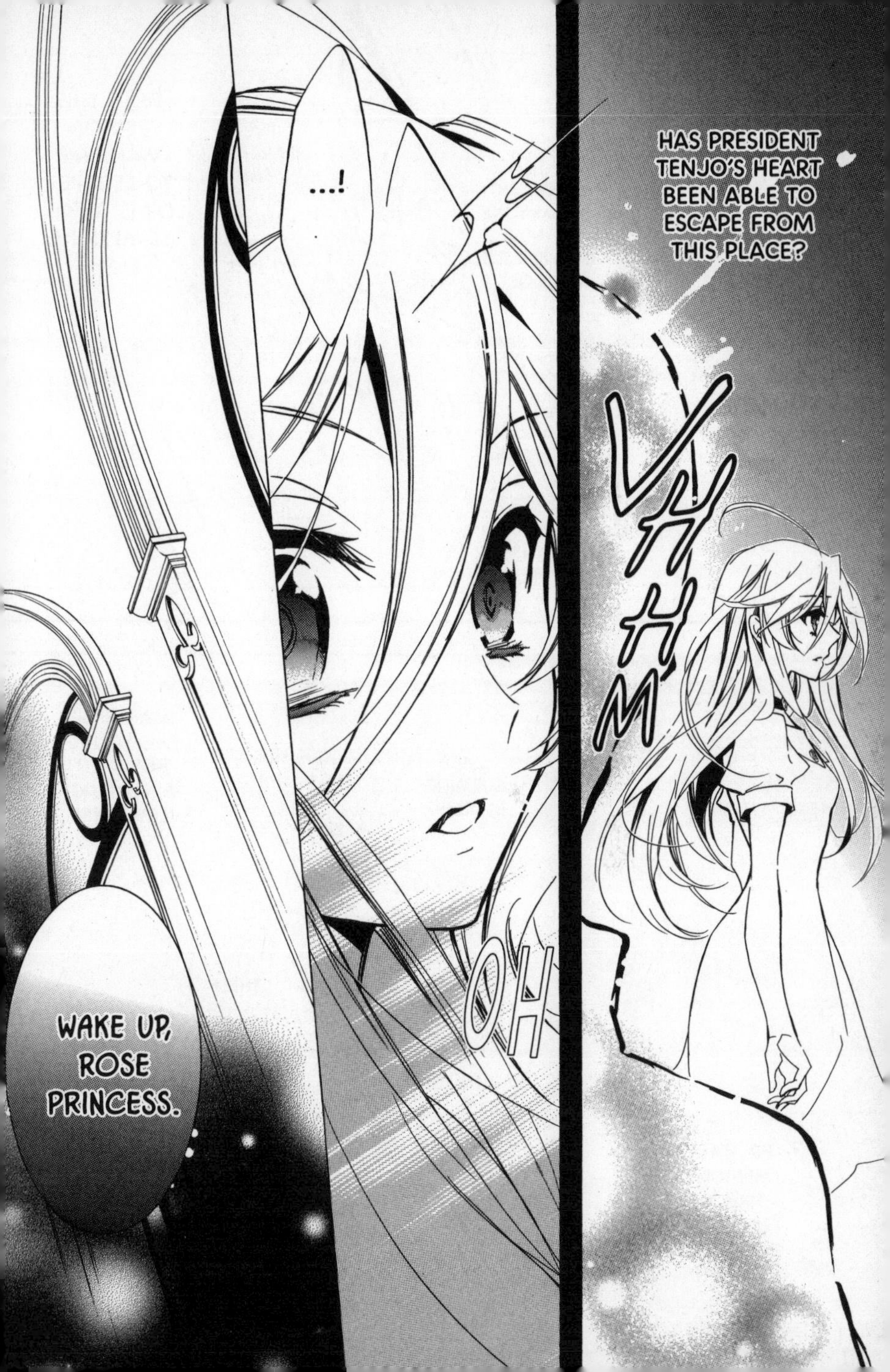
HAS PRESIDENT TENJO'S HEART BEEN ABLE TO ESCAPE FROM THIS PLACE?
VHHM
...!
OH
WAKE UP, ROSE PRINCESS.

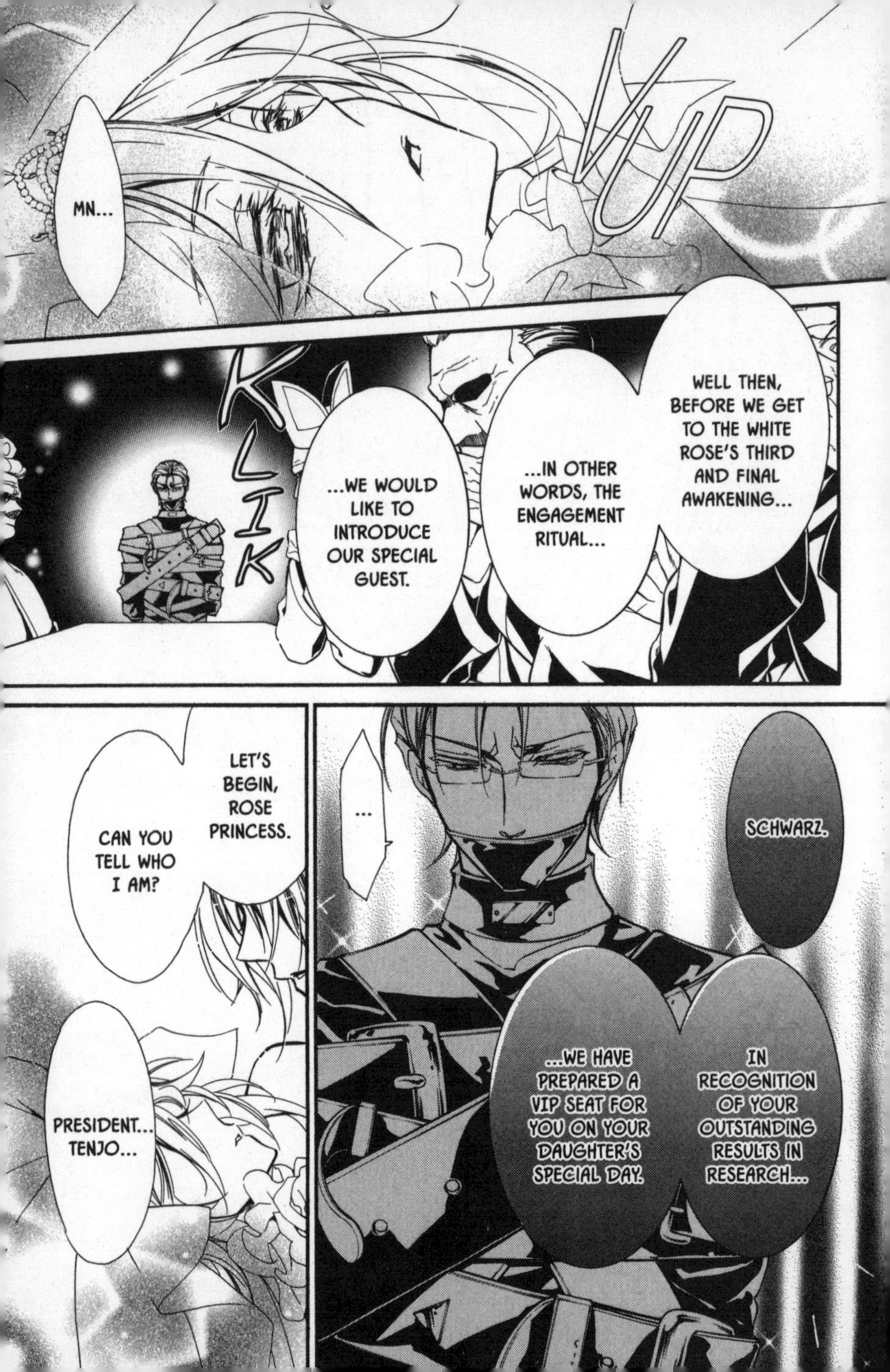
VUP
MN...
WELL THEN, BEFORE WE GET TO THE WHITE ROSE'S THIRD AND FINAL AWAKENING...
...IN OTHER WORDS, THE ENGAGEMENT RITUAL...
...WE WOULD LIKE TO INTRODUCE OUR SPECIAL GUEST.
KLIK
SCHWARZ.
...
IN RECOGNITION OF YOUR OUTSTANDING RESULTS IN RESEARCH...
...WE HAVE PREPARED A VIP SEAT FOR YOU ON YOUR DAUGHTER'S SPECIAL DAY.
LET'S BEGIN, ROSE PRINCESS.
CAN YOU TELL WHO I AM?
PRESIDENT... TENJO...

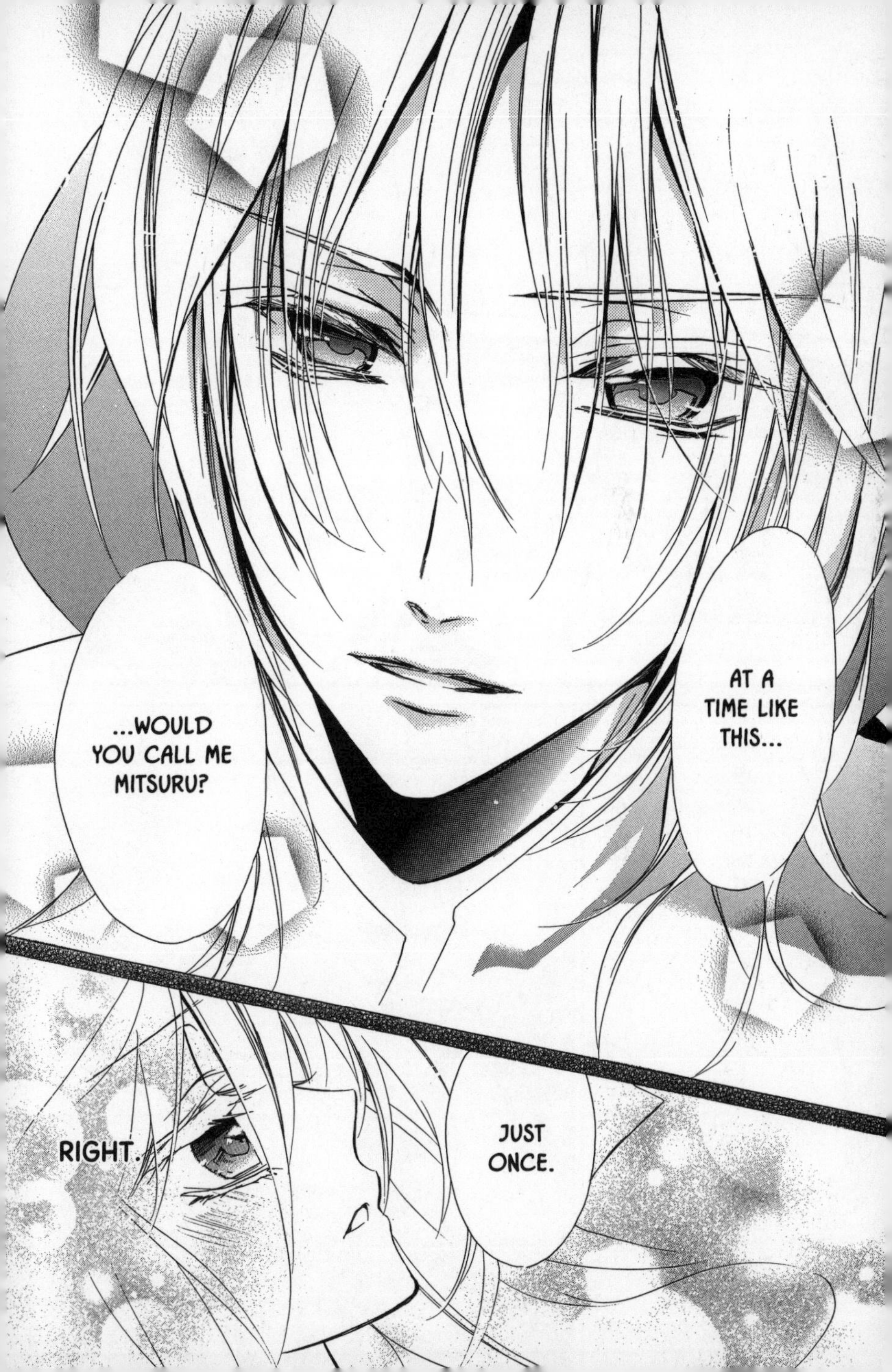
AT A TIME LIKE THIS...
...WOULD YOU CALL ME MITSURU?
JUST ONCE.
RIGHT.

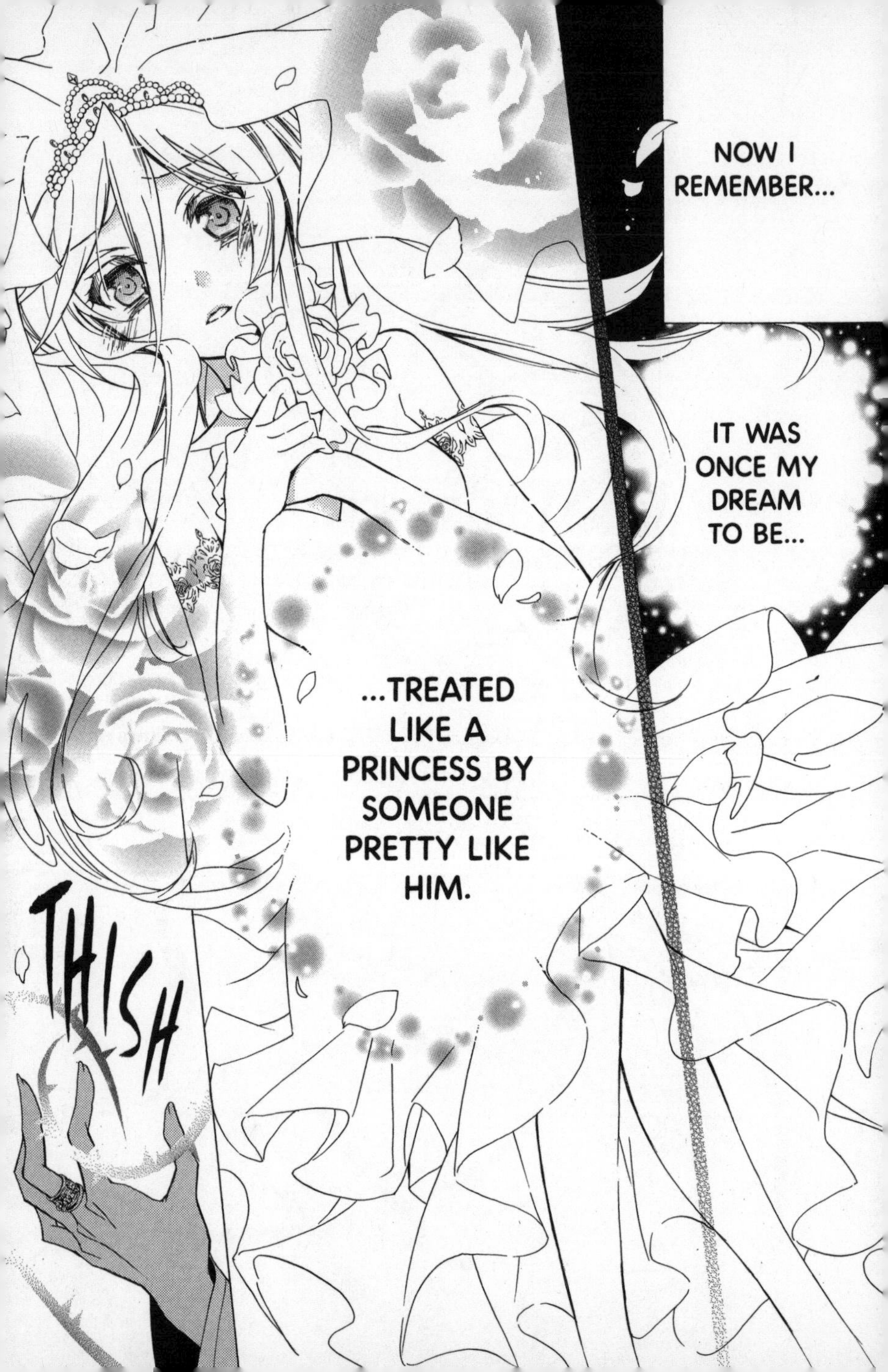
NOW I REMEMBER...
IT WAS ONCE MY DREAM TO BE...
...TREATED LIKE A PRINCESS BY SOMEONE PRETTY LIKE HIM.
THISH

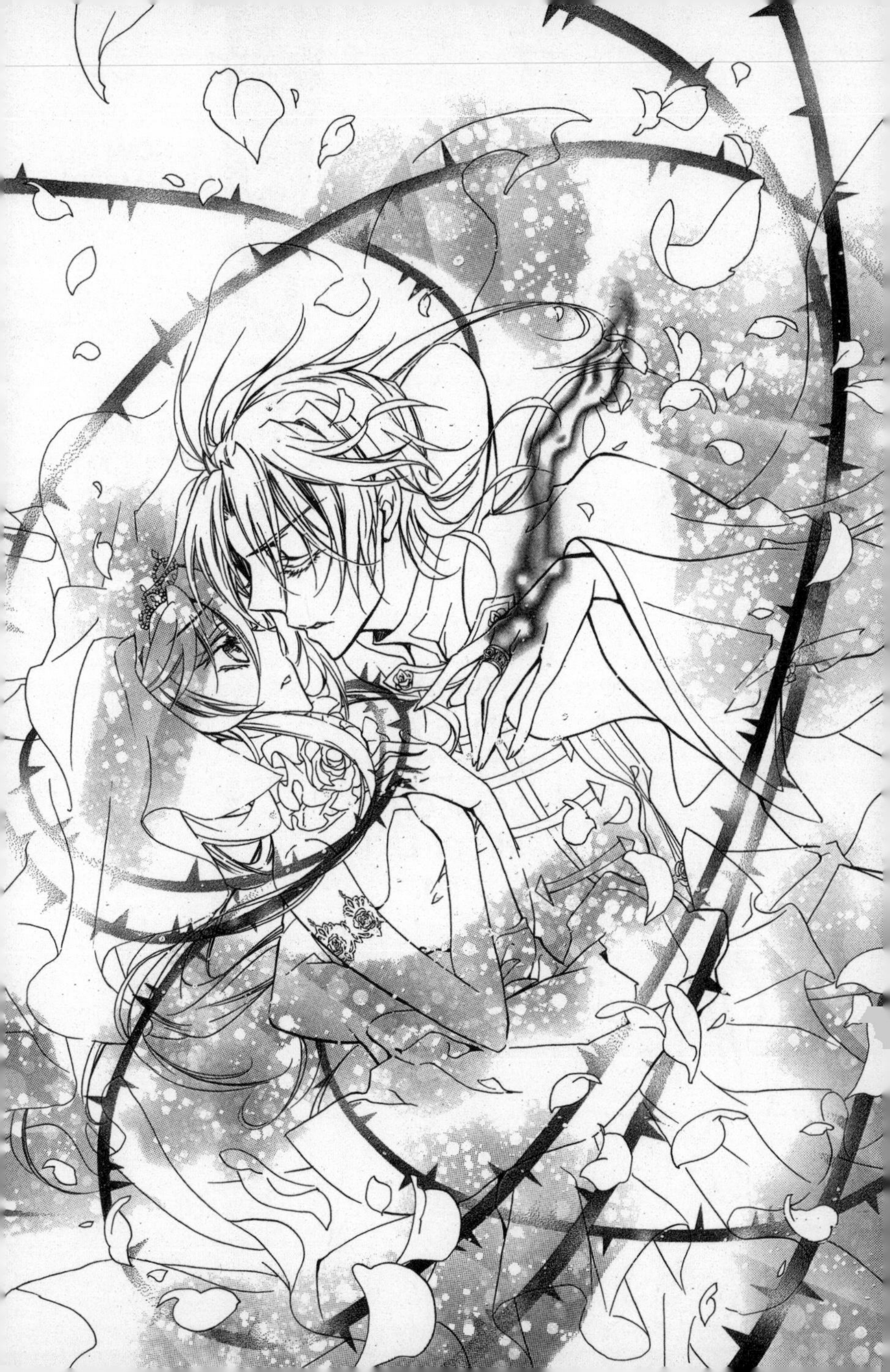

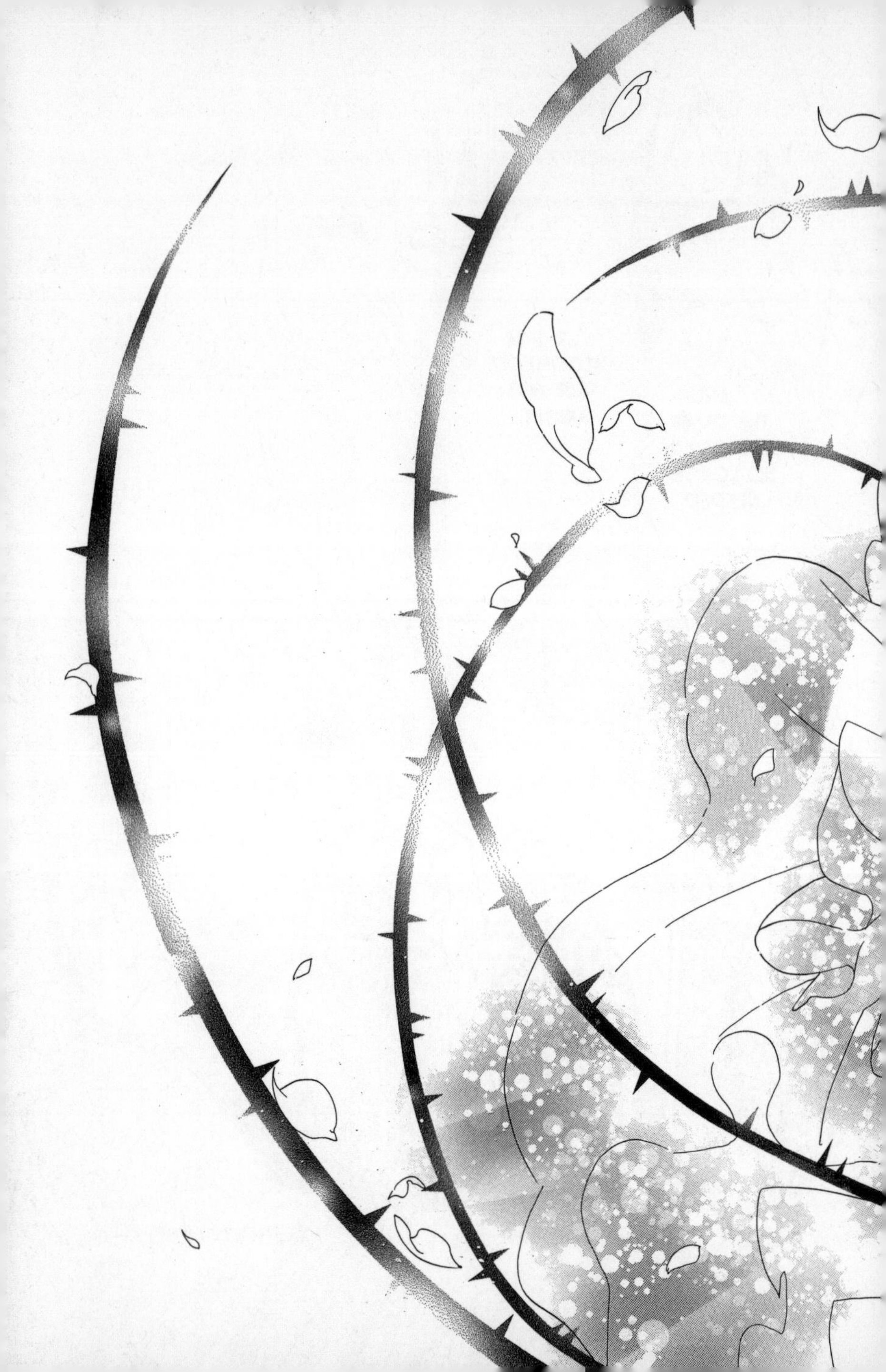

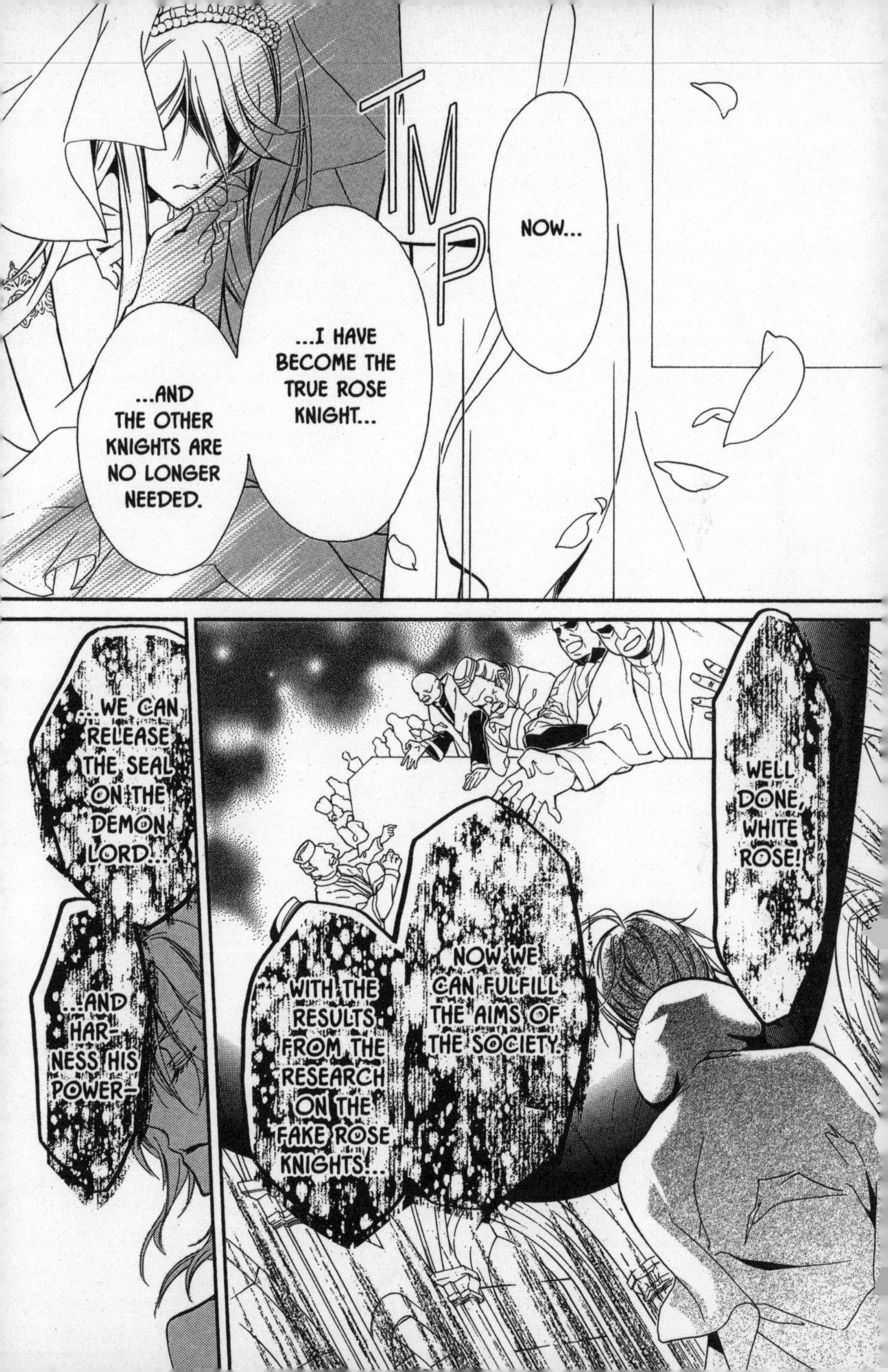
NOW...
TMP
...I HAVE BECOME THE TRUE ROSE KNIGHT...
...AND THE OTHER KNIGHTS ARE NO LONGER NEEDED.
WELL DONE, WHITE ROSE!
NOW WE CAN FULFILL THE AIMS OF THE SOCIETY.
WITH THE RESULTS FROM THE RESEARCH ON THE FAKE ROSE KNIGHTS...
...WE CAN RELEASE THE SEAL ON THE DEMON LORD...
...AND HARNESS HIS POWER—

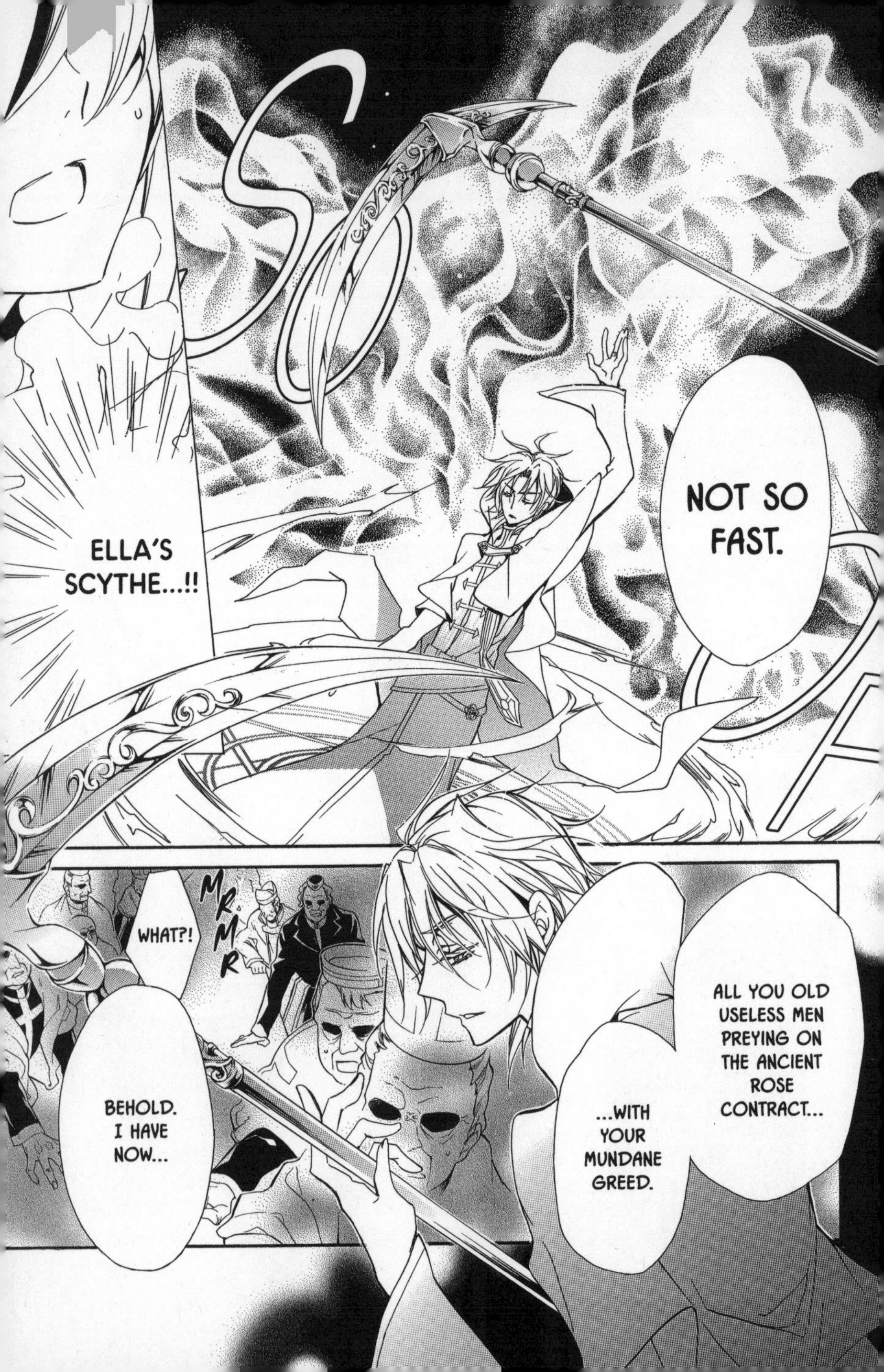
NOT SO FAST.
ELLA'S SCYTHE...!!
ALL YOU OLD USELESS MEN PREYING ON THE ANCIENT ROSE CONTRACT...
...WITH YOUR MUNDANE GREED.
MRMR
WHAT?!
BEHOLD. I HAVE NOW...

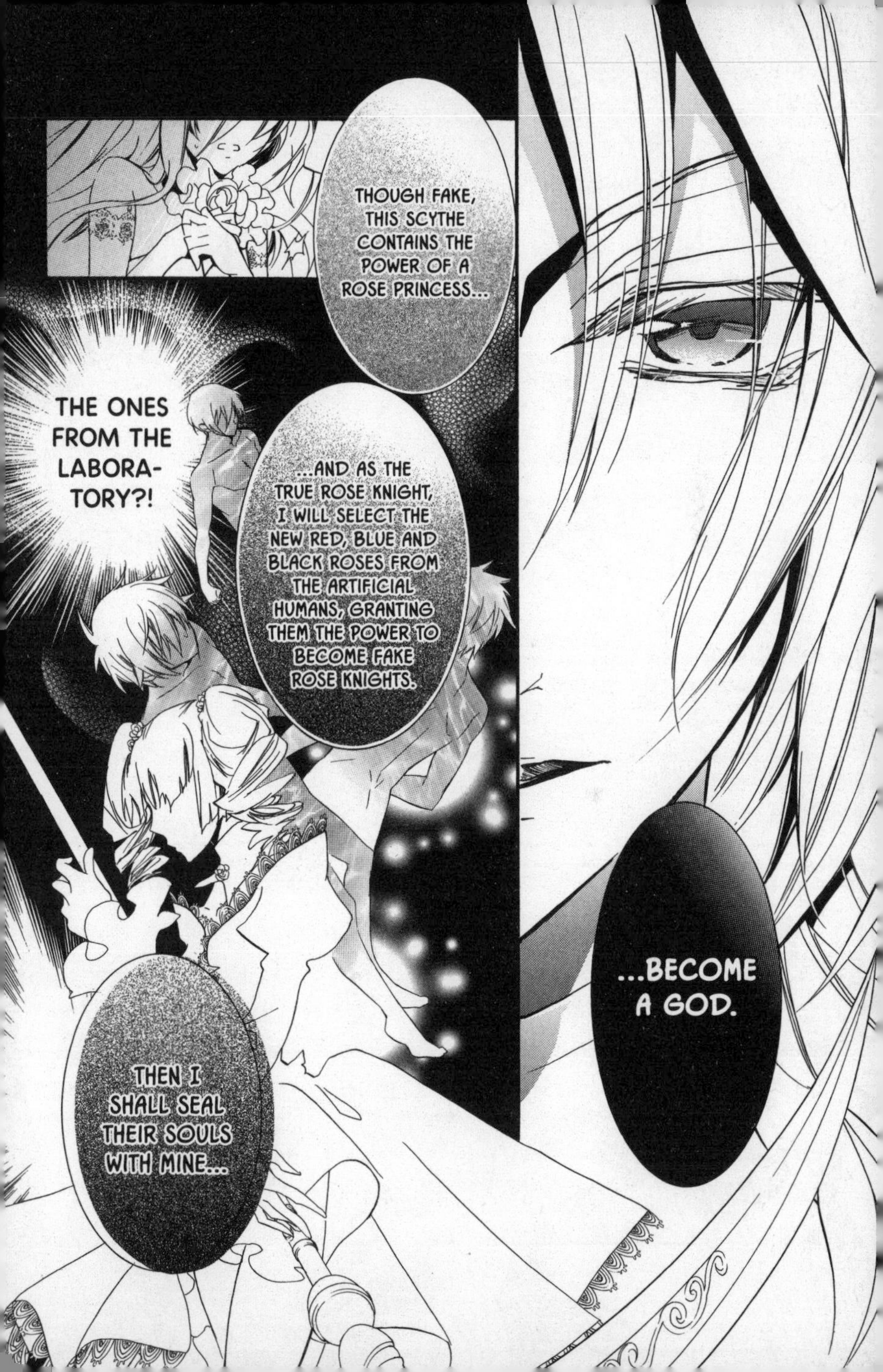
THOUGH FAKE, THIS SCYTHE CONTAINS THE POWER OF A ROSE PRINCESS...
THE ONES FROM THE LABORA-TORY?!
...AND AS THE TRUE ROSE KNIGHT, I WILL SELECT THE NEW RED, BLUE AND BLACK ROSES FROM THE ARTIFICIAL HUMANS, GRANTING THEM THE POWER TO BECOME FAKE ROSE KNIGHTS.
THEN I SHALL SEAL THEIR SOULS WITH MINE...
...BECOME A GOD.

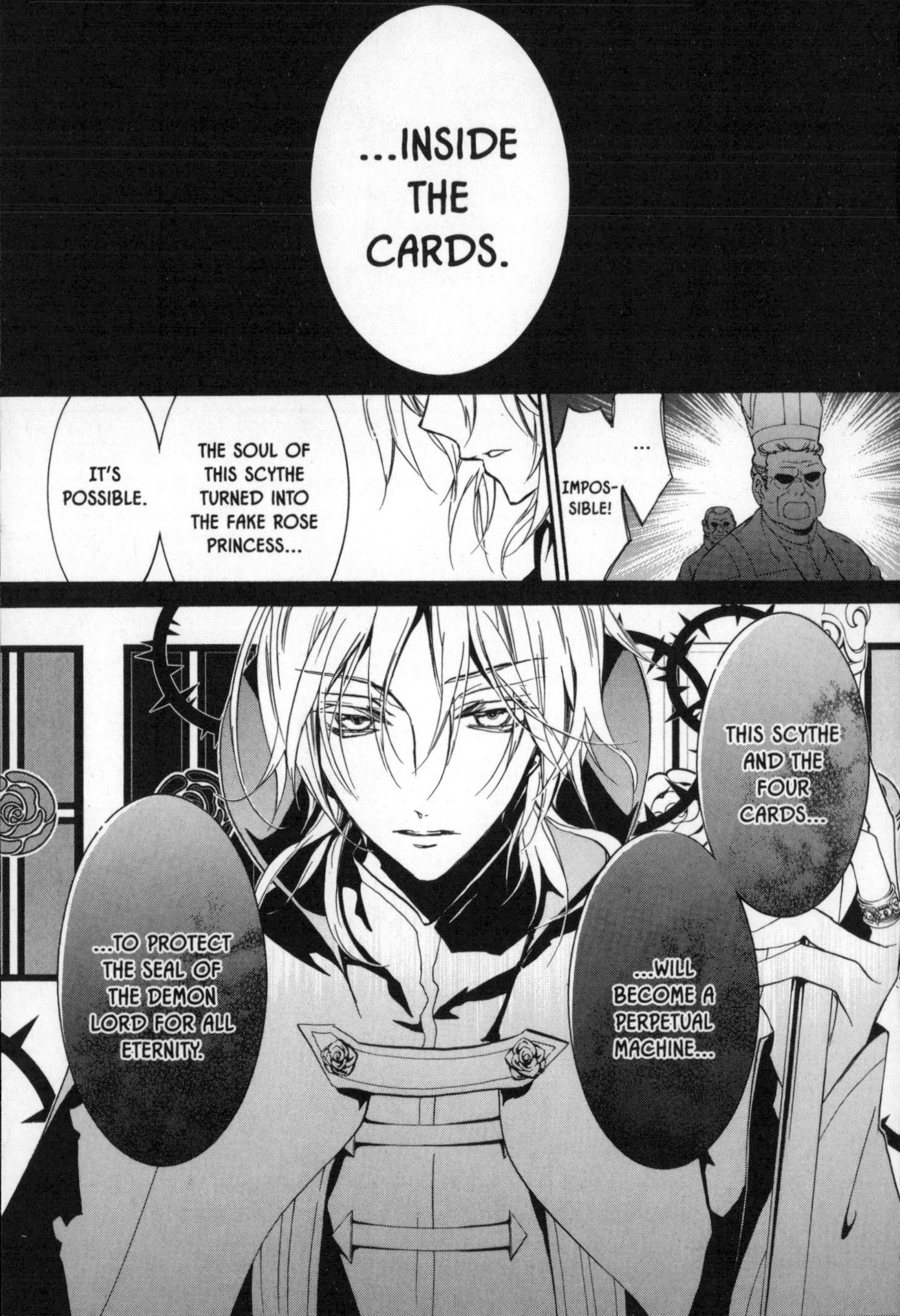
...INSIDE THE CARDS.
...
IMPOS-SIBLE!
THE SOUL OF THIS SCYTHE TURNED INTO THE FAKE ROSE PRINCESS...
IT'S POSSIBLE.
THIS SCYTHE AND THE FOUR CARDS...
...WILL BECOME A PERPETUAL MACHINE...
...TO PROTECT THE SEAL OF THE DEMON LORD FOR ALL ETERNITY.

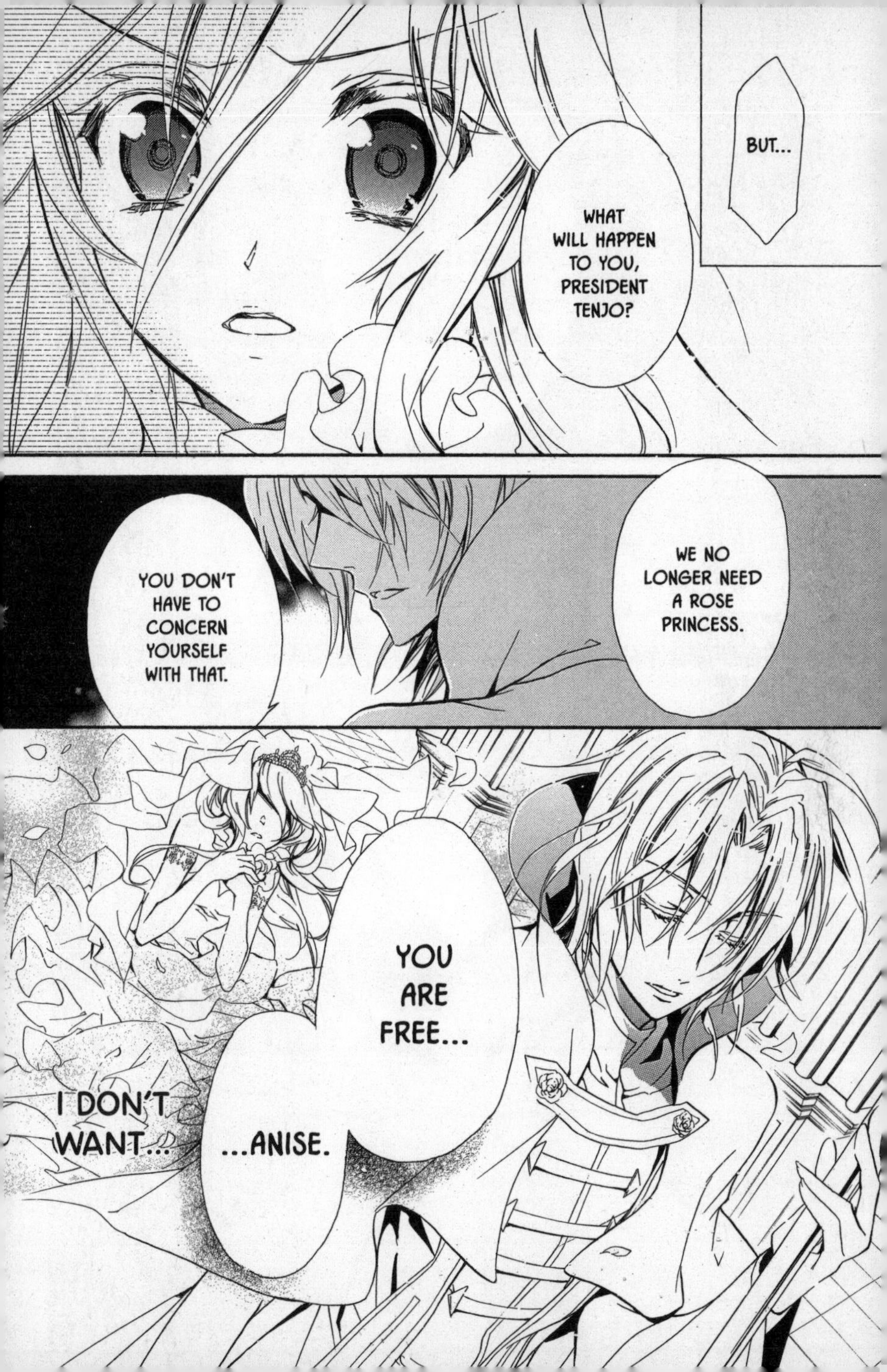
BUT...
WHAT WILL HAPPEN TO YOU, PRESIDENT TENJO?
WE NO LONGER NEED A ROSE PRINCESS.
YOU DON'T HAVE TO CONCERN YOURSELF WITH THAT.
YOU ARE FREE...
...ANISE.
I DON'T WANT...

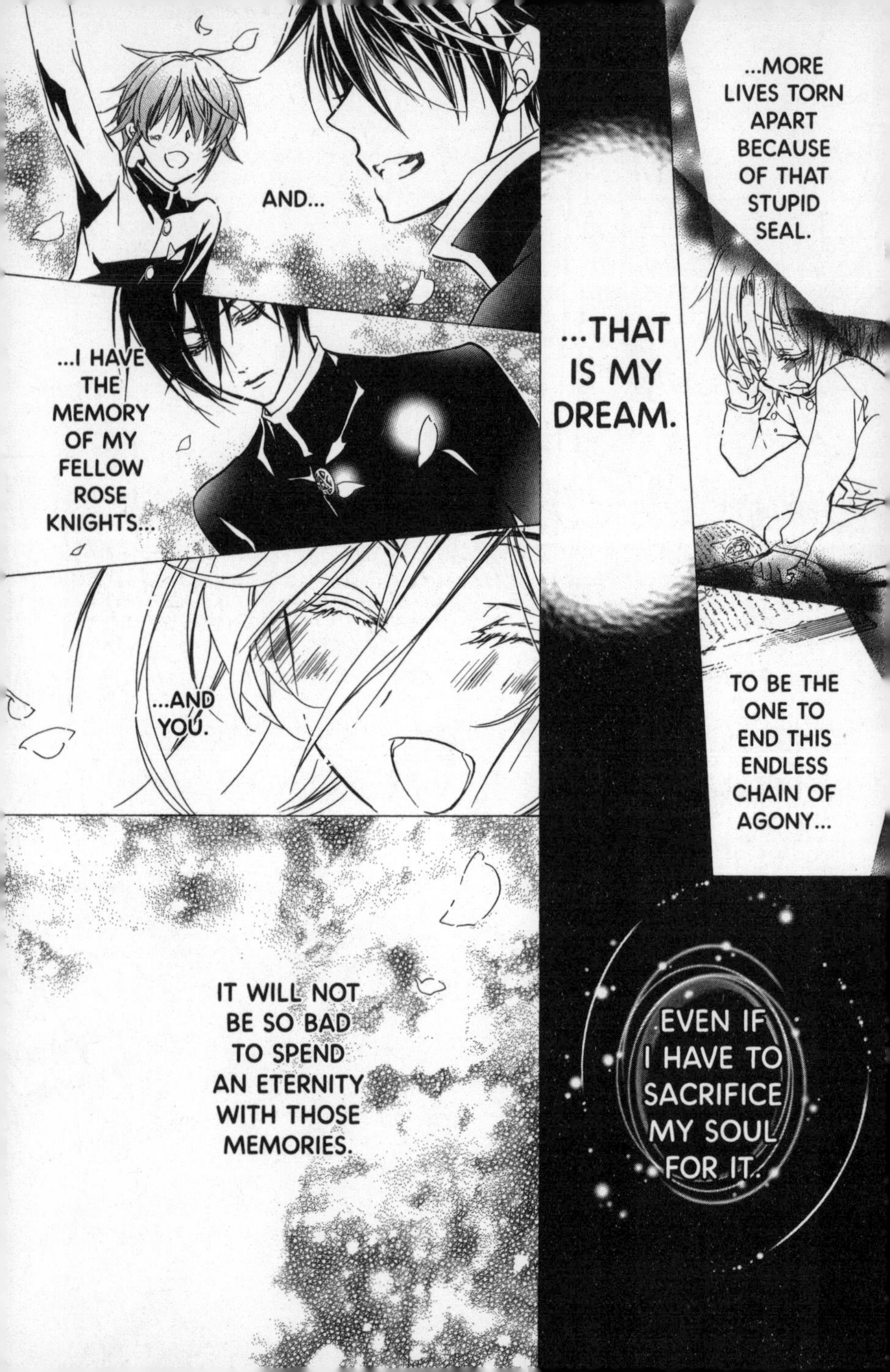
...MORE LIVES TORN APART BECAUSE OF THAT STUPID SEAL.
...THAT IS MY DREAM.
TO BE THE ONE TO END THIS ENDLESS CHAIN OF AGONY...
EVEN IF I HAVE TO SACRIFICE MY SOUL FOR IT.
AND...
...I HAVE THE MEMORY OF MY FELLOW ROSE KNIGHTS...
...AND YOU.
IT WILL NOT BE SO BAD TO SPEND AN ETERNITY WITH THOSE MEMORIES.

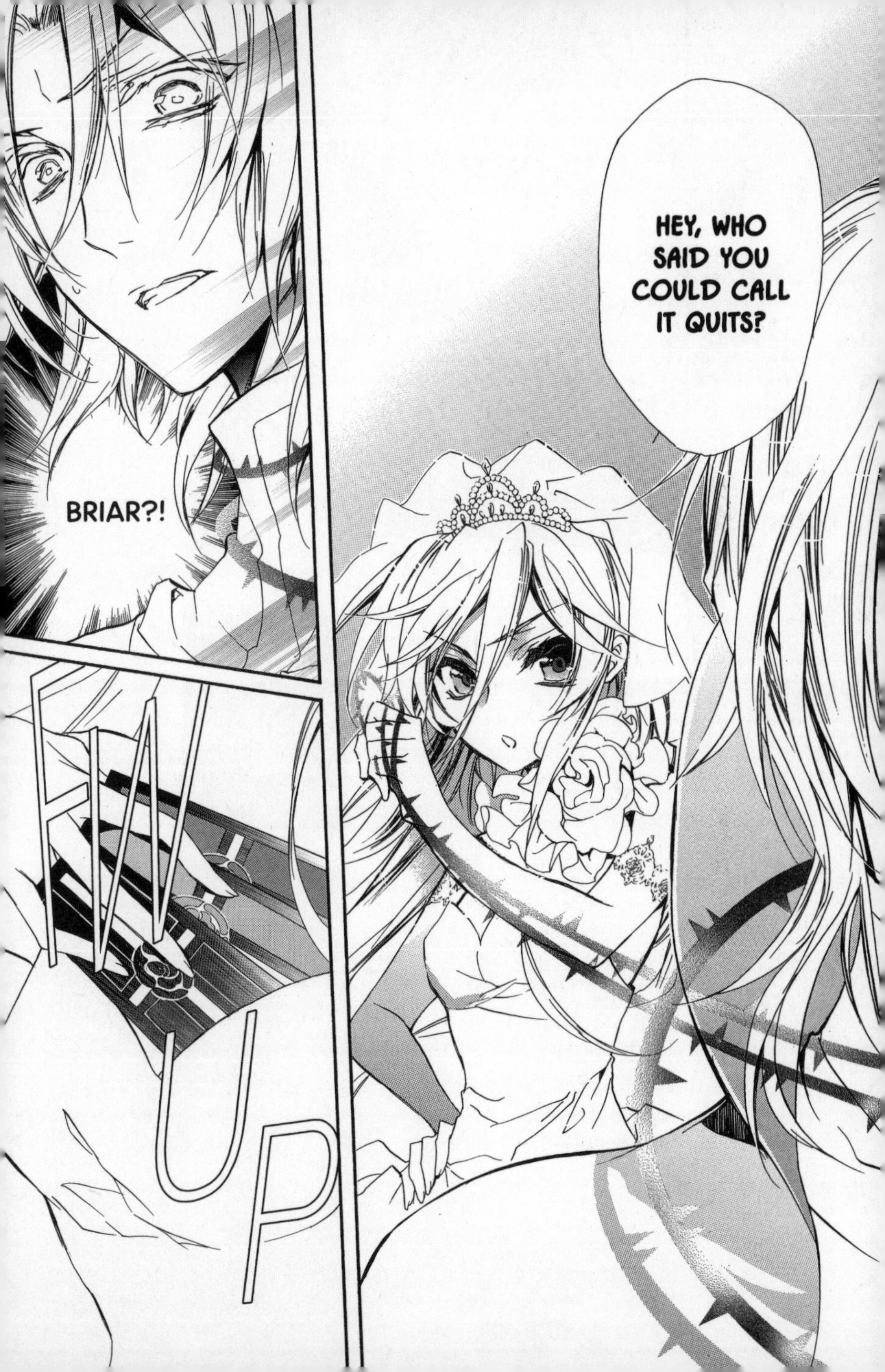
HEY, WHO SAID YOU COULD CALL IT QUITS?
BRIAR?!
FWUP

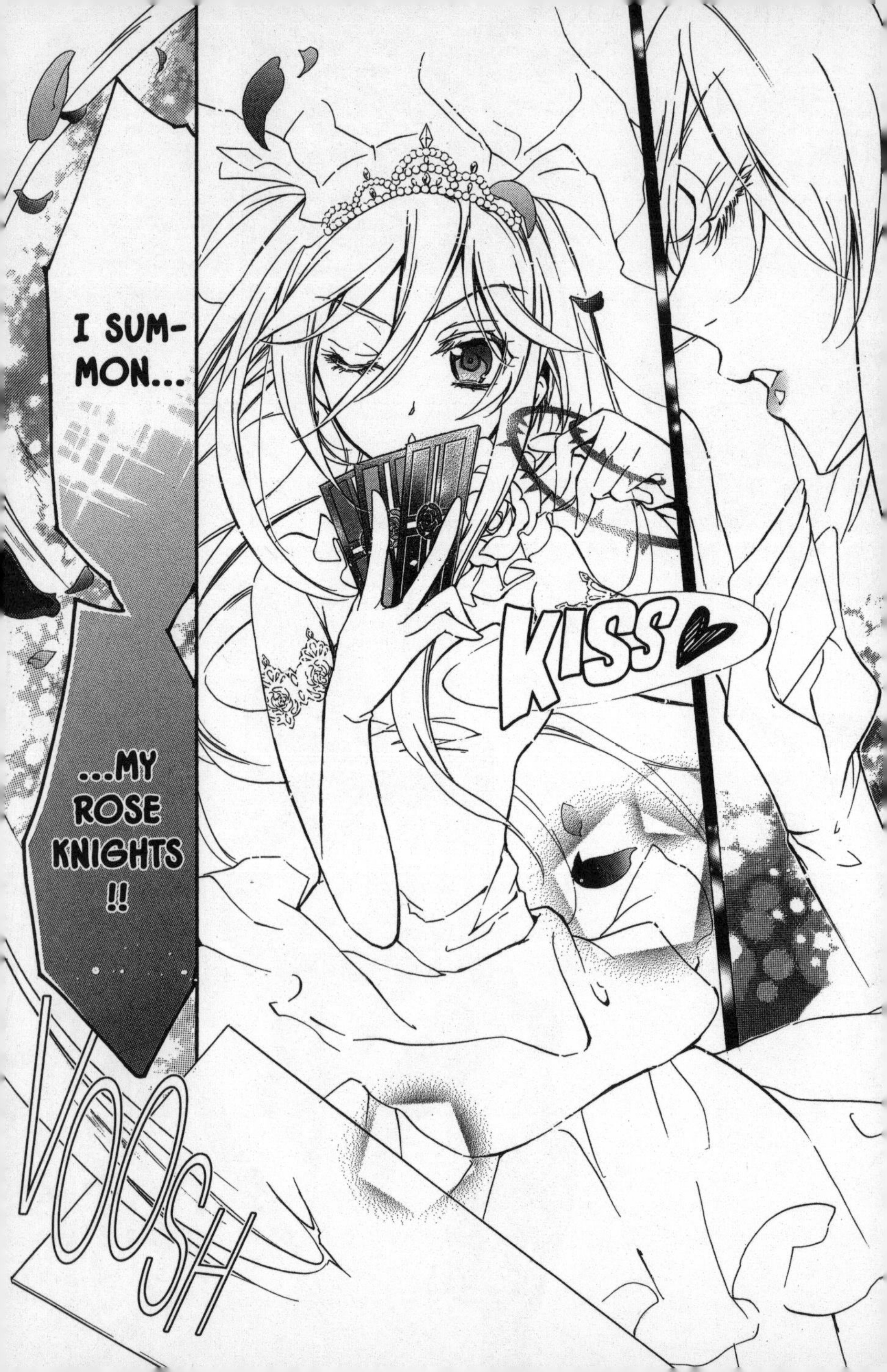
I SUM-MON...
...MY ROSE KNIGHTS!!
KISS
VOOSH

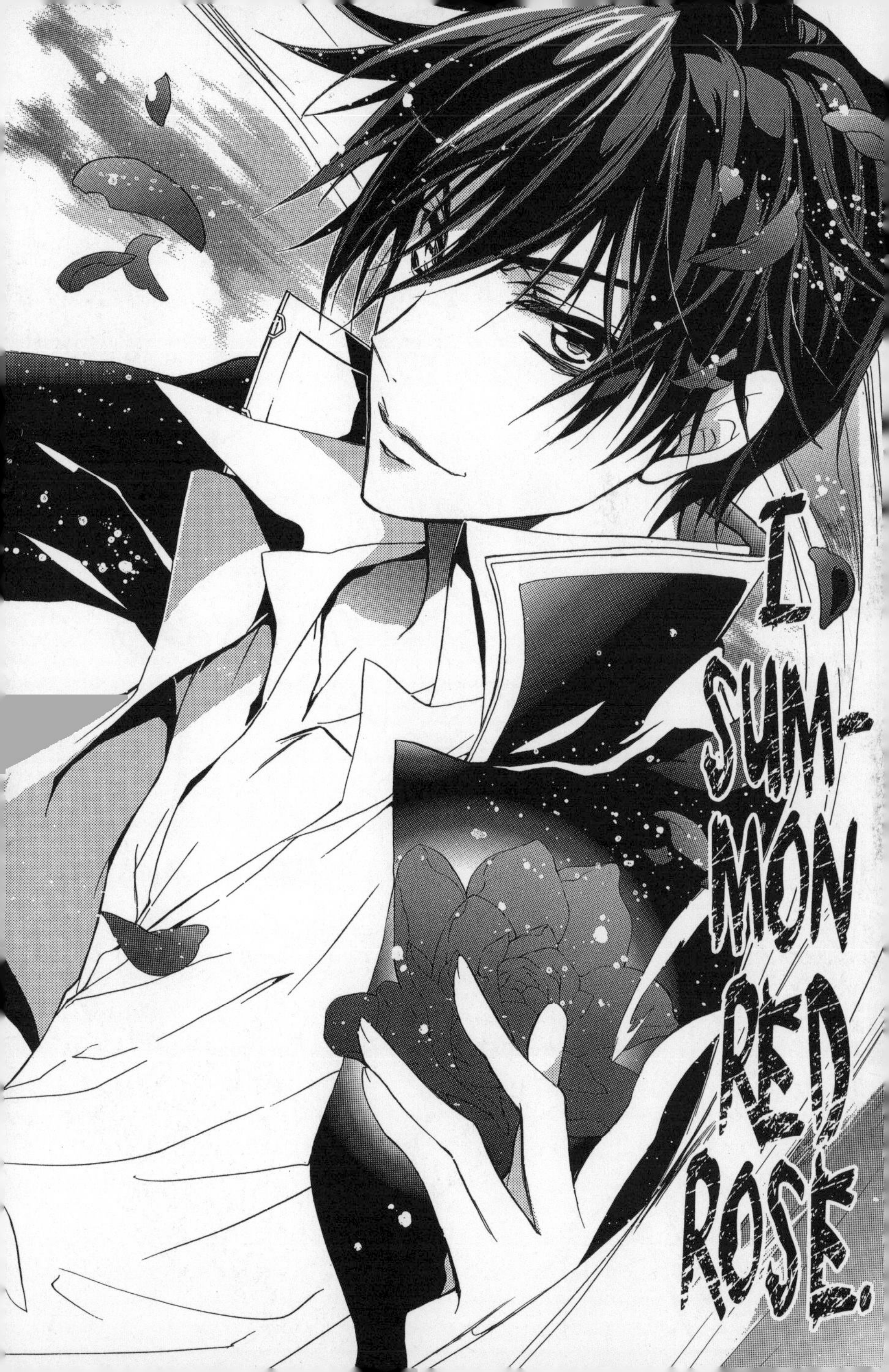
I SUM-MON RED ROSE.

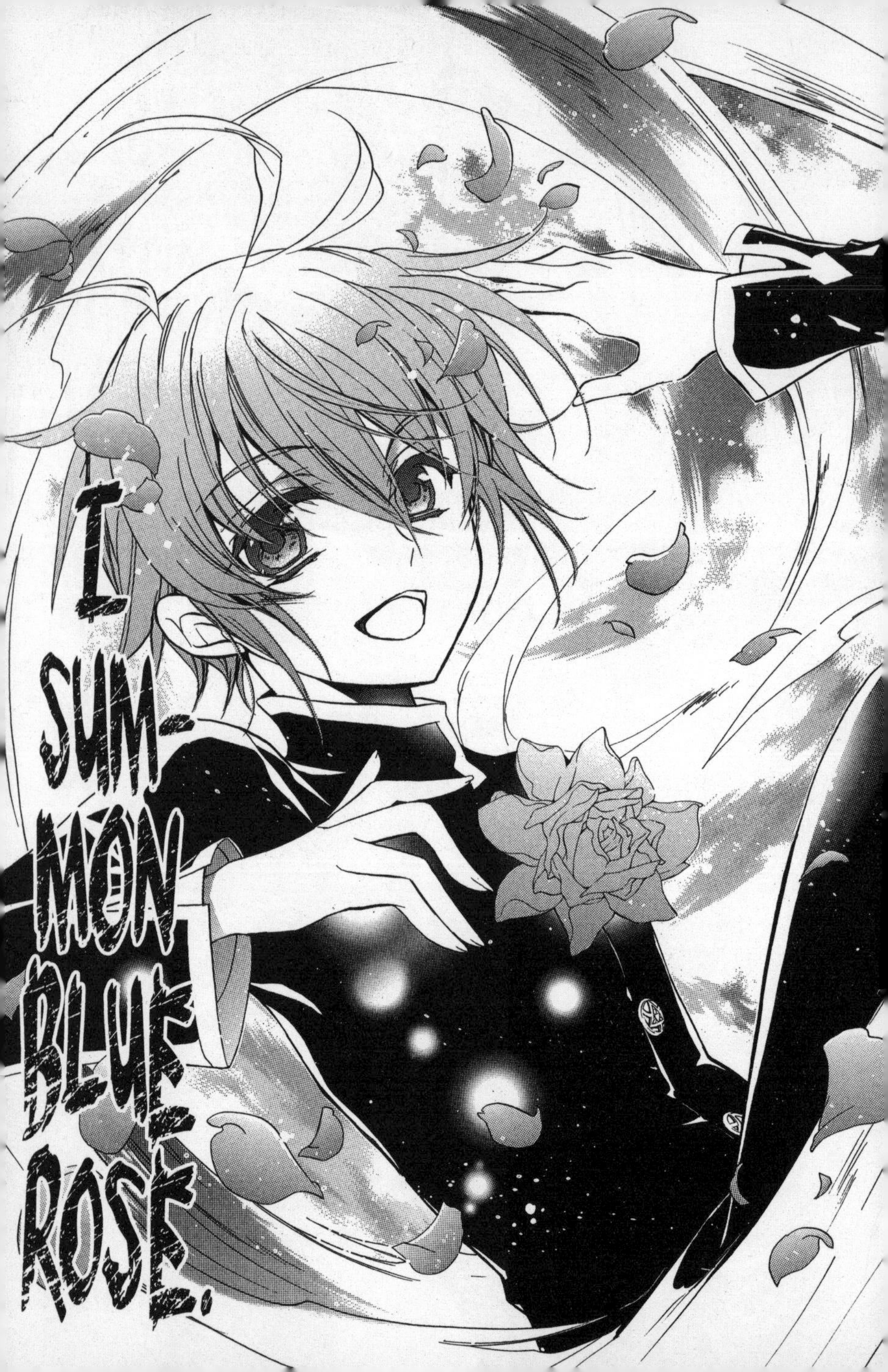
I SUMMON BLUE ROSE.

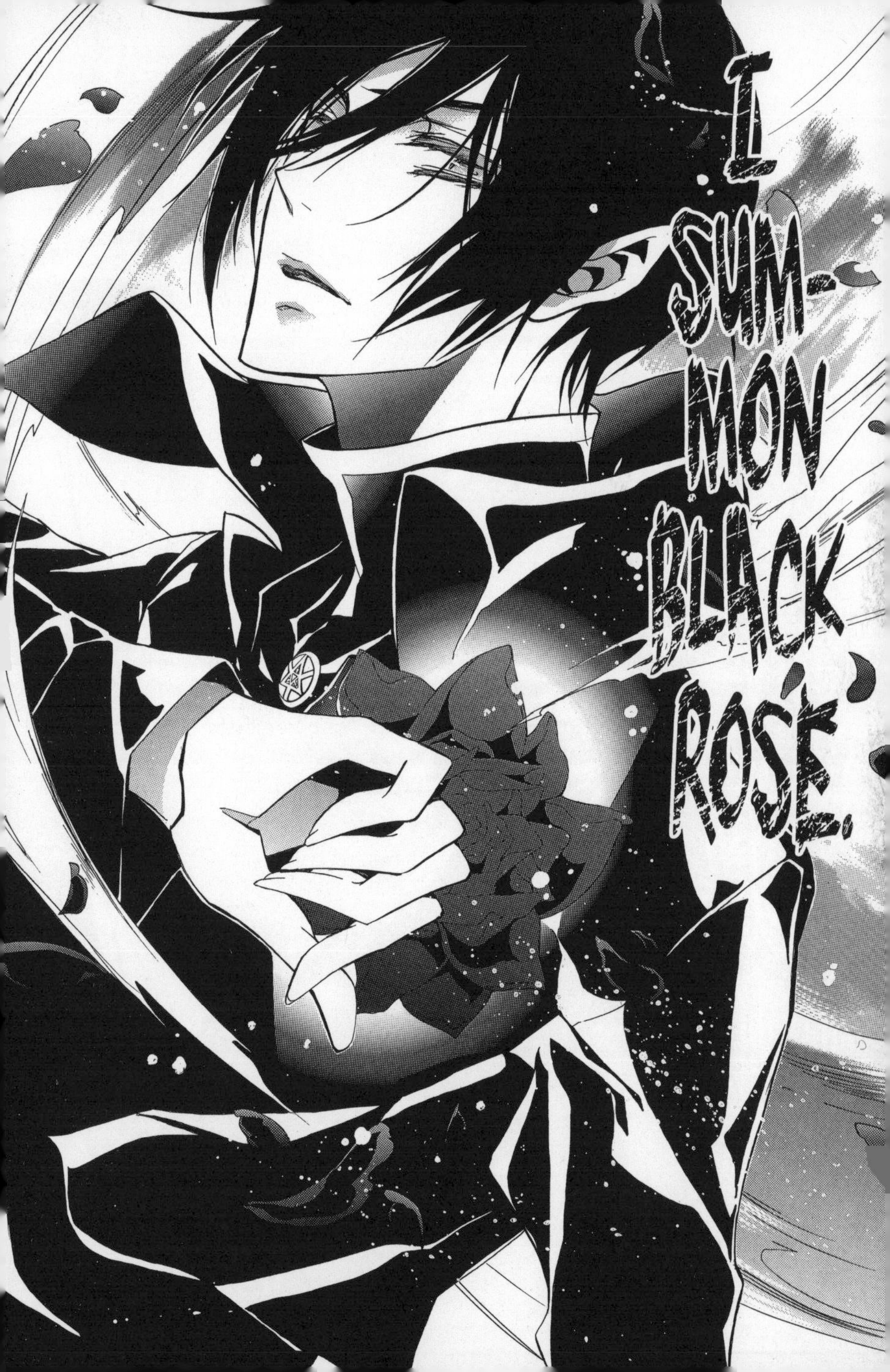
I SUMMON BLACK ROSE.

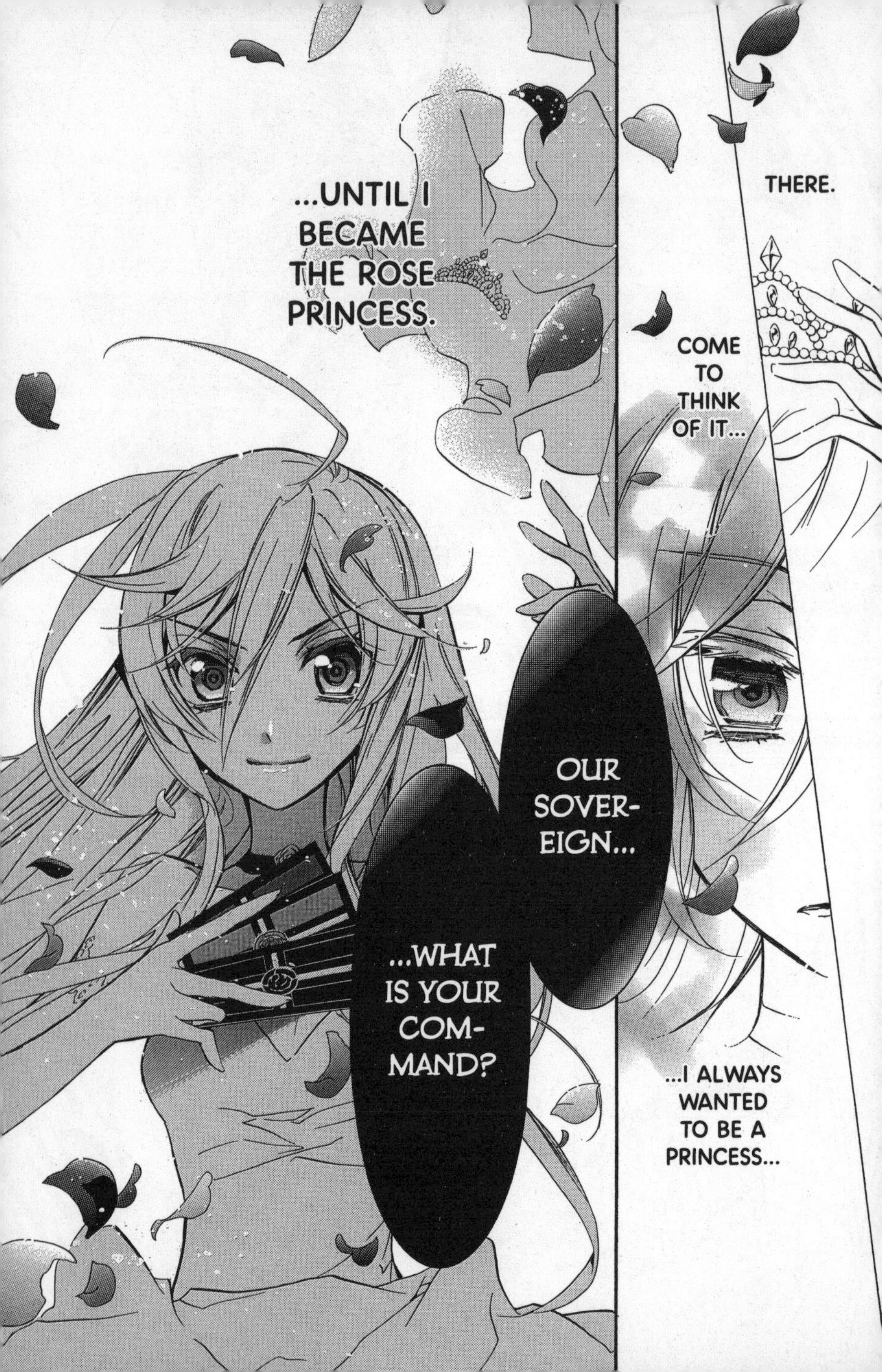
THERE.
COME TO THINK OF IT...
...I ALWAYS WANTED TO BE A PRINCESS...
...UNTIL I BECAME THE ROSE PRINCESS.
OUR SOVEREIGN...
...WHAT IS YOUR COMMAND?

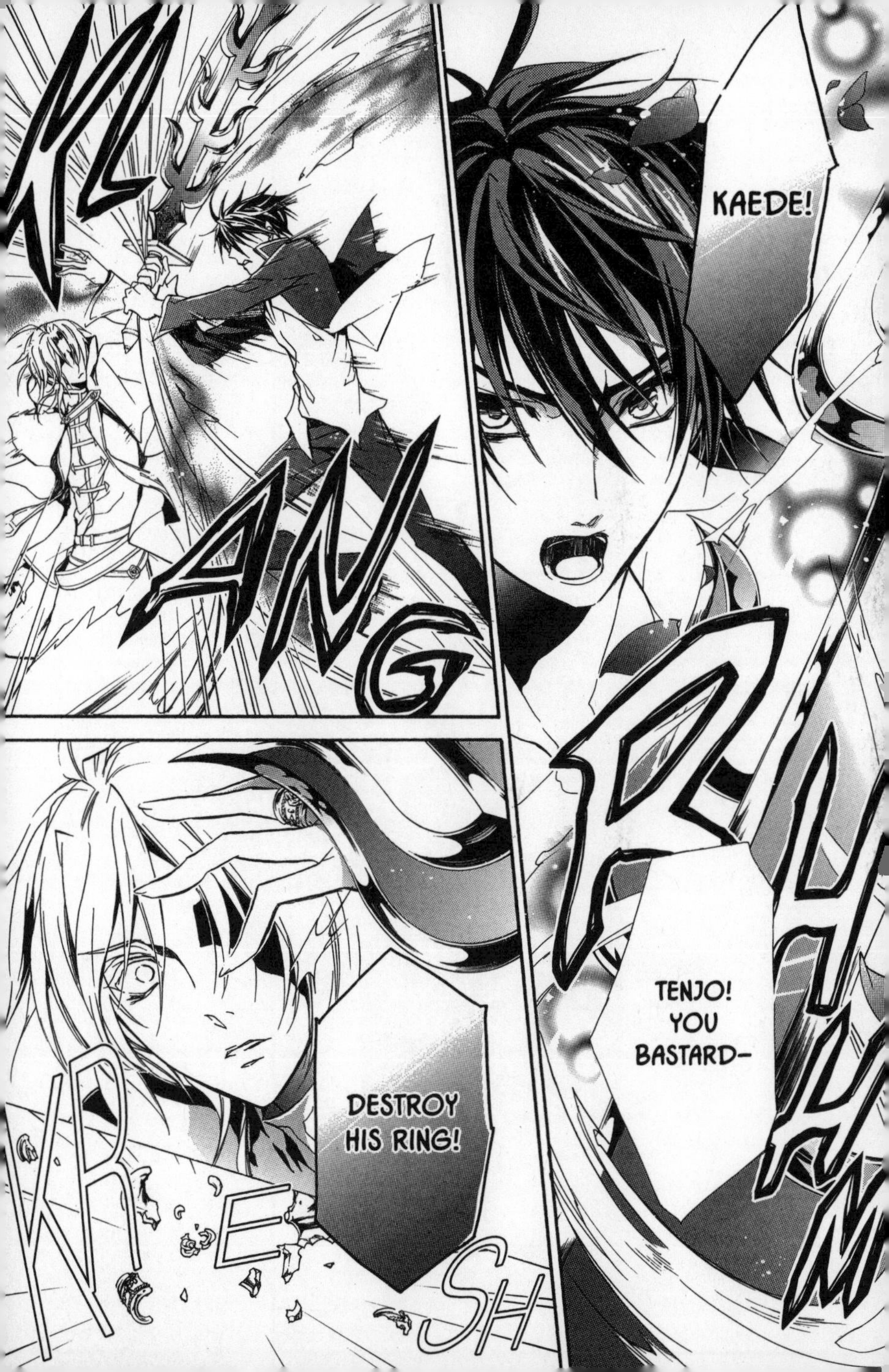
KAEDE!
TENJO! YOU BASTARD–
KLANG
DESTROY HIS RING!
KRESH

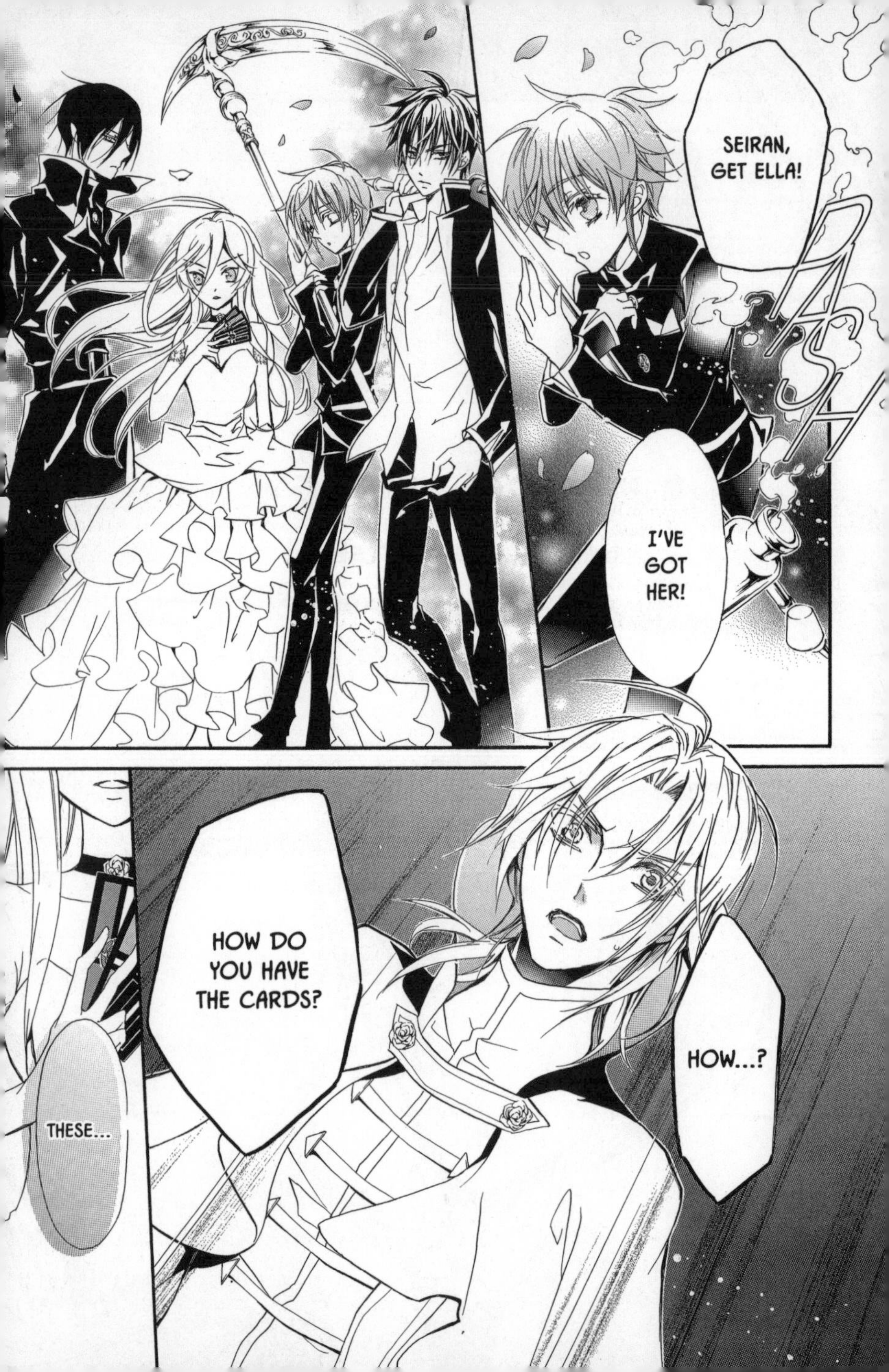
SEIRAN, GET ELLA!
I'VE GOT HER!
HOW...?
HOW DO YOU HAVE THE CARDS?
THESE...

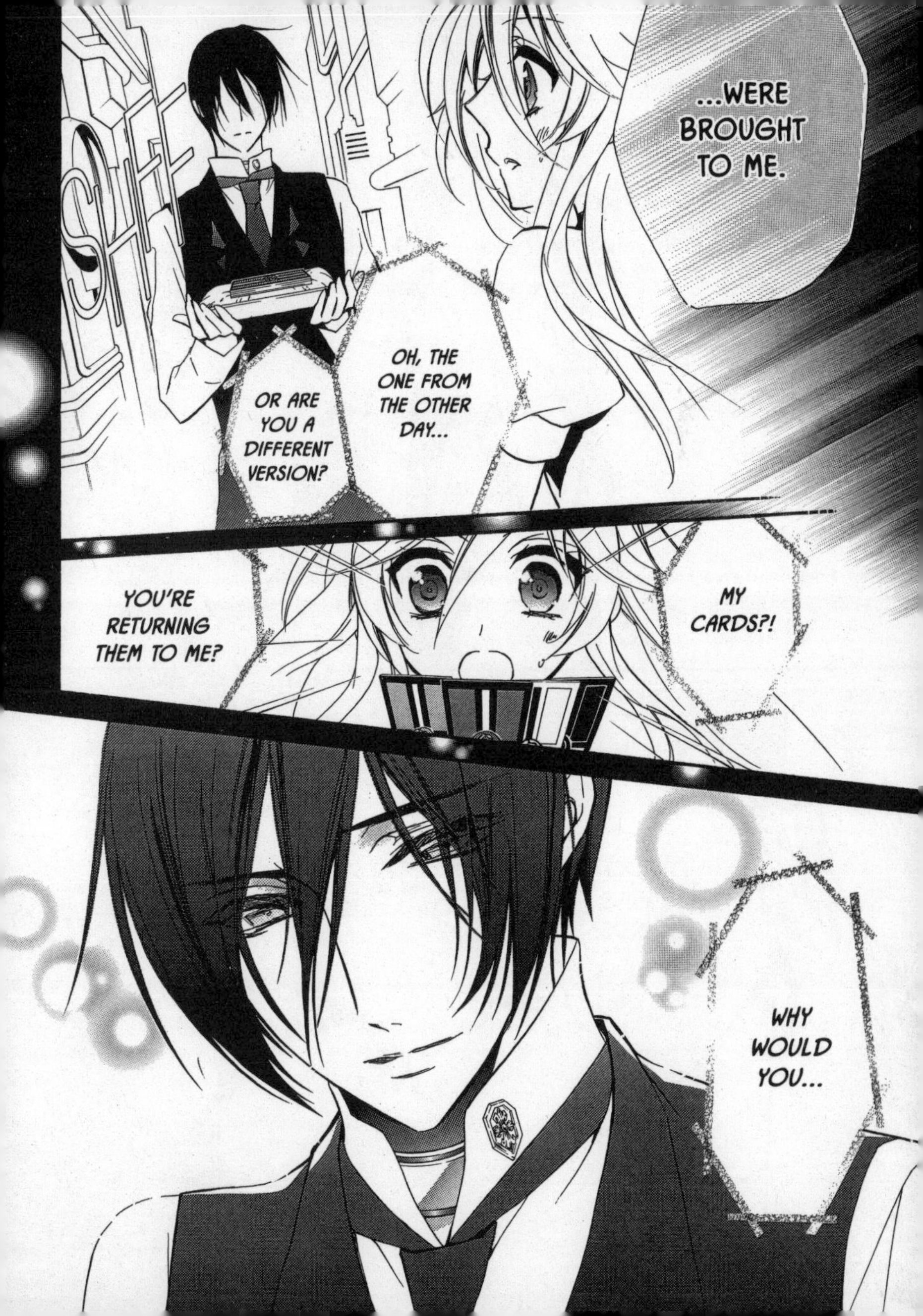
...WERE BROUGHT TO ME.
OH, THE ONE FROM THE OTHER DAY...
OR ARE YOU A DIFFERENT VERSION?
MY CARDS?!
YOU'RE RETURNING THEM TO ME?
WHY WOULD YOU...

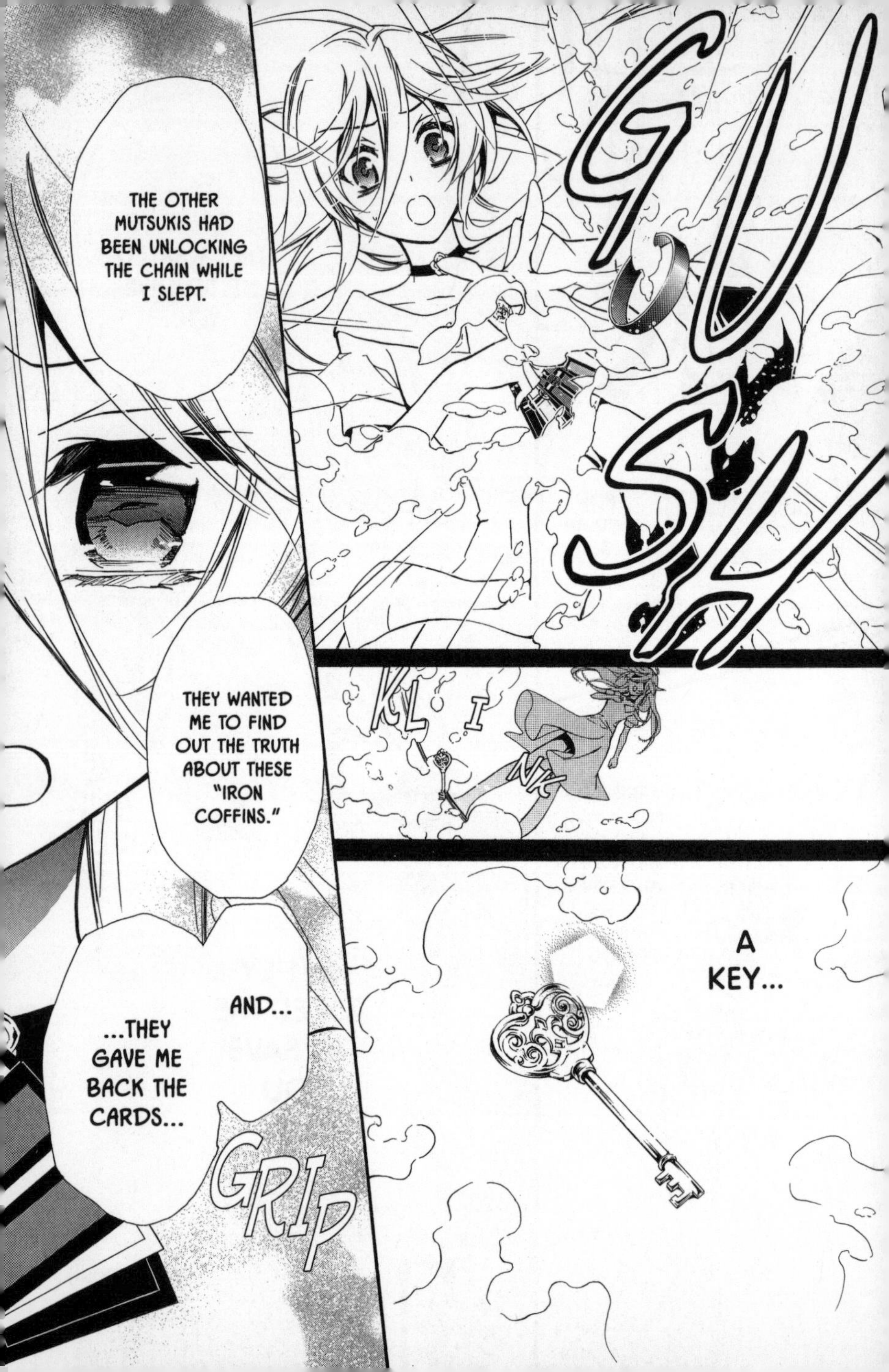
GUSH
KLINK
A KEY...
THE OTHER MUTSUKIS HAD BEEN UNLOCKING THE CHAIN WHILE I SLEPT.
THEY WANTED ME TO FIND OUT THE TRUTH ABOUT THESE "IRON COFFINS."
AND...
...THEY GAVE ME BACK THE CARDS...
GRIP

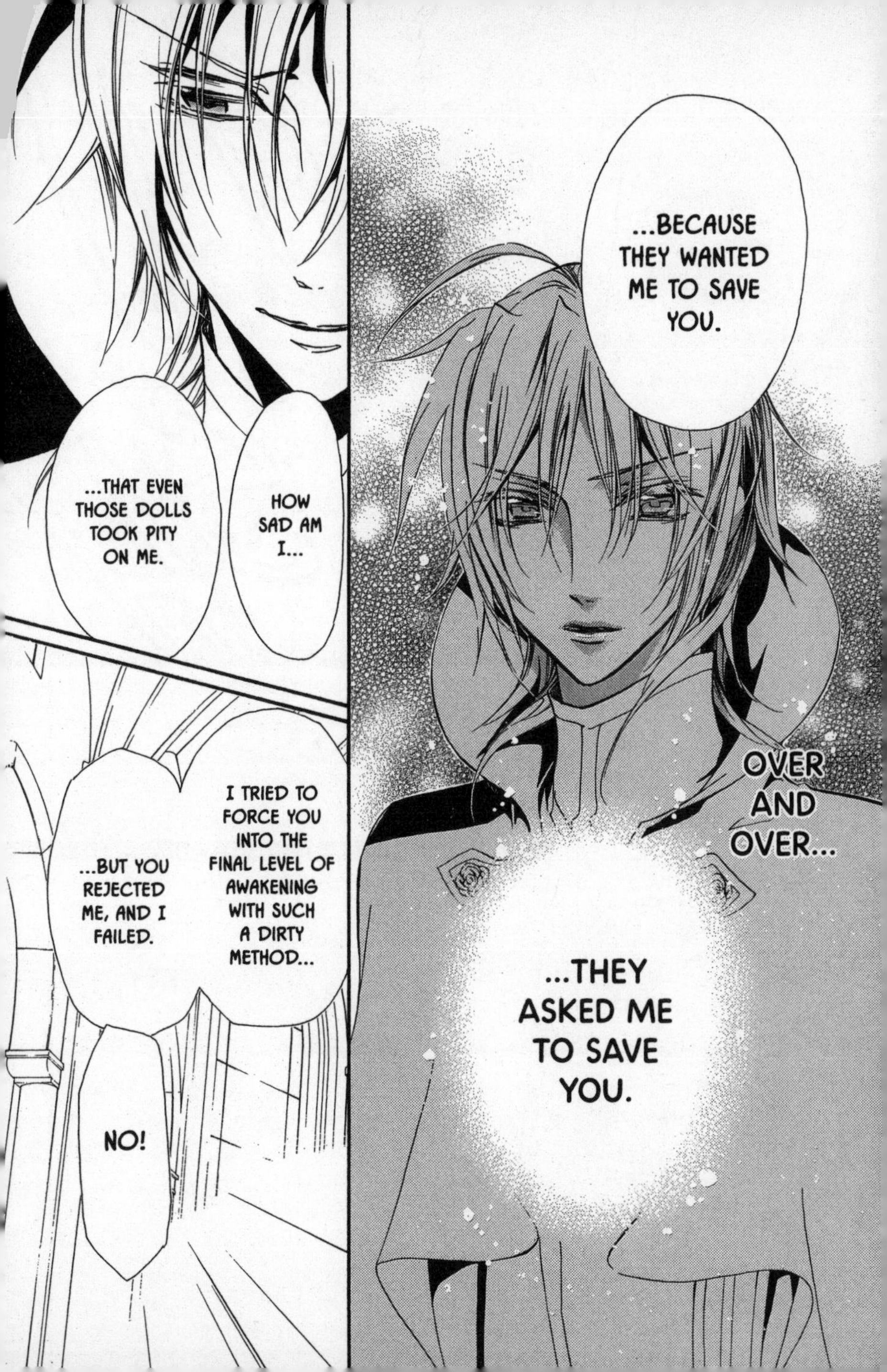
...BECAUSE THEY WANTED ME TO SAVE YOU.
OVER AND OVER...
...THEY ASKED ME TO SAVE YOU.
HOW SAD AM I...
...THAT EVEN THOSE DOLLS TOOK PITY ON ME.
I TRIED TO FORCE YOU INTO THE FINAL LEVEL OF AWAKENING WITH SUCH A DIRTY METHOD...
...BUT YOU REJECTED ME, AND I FAILED.
NO!

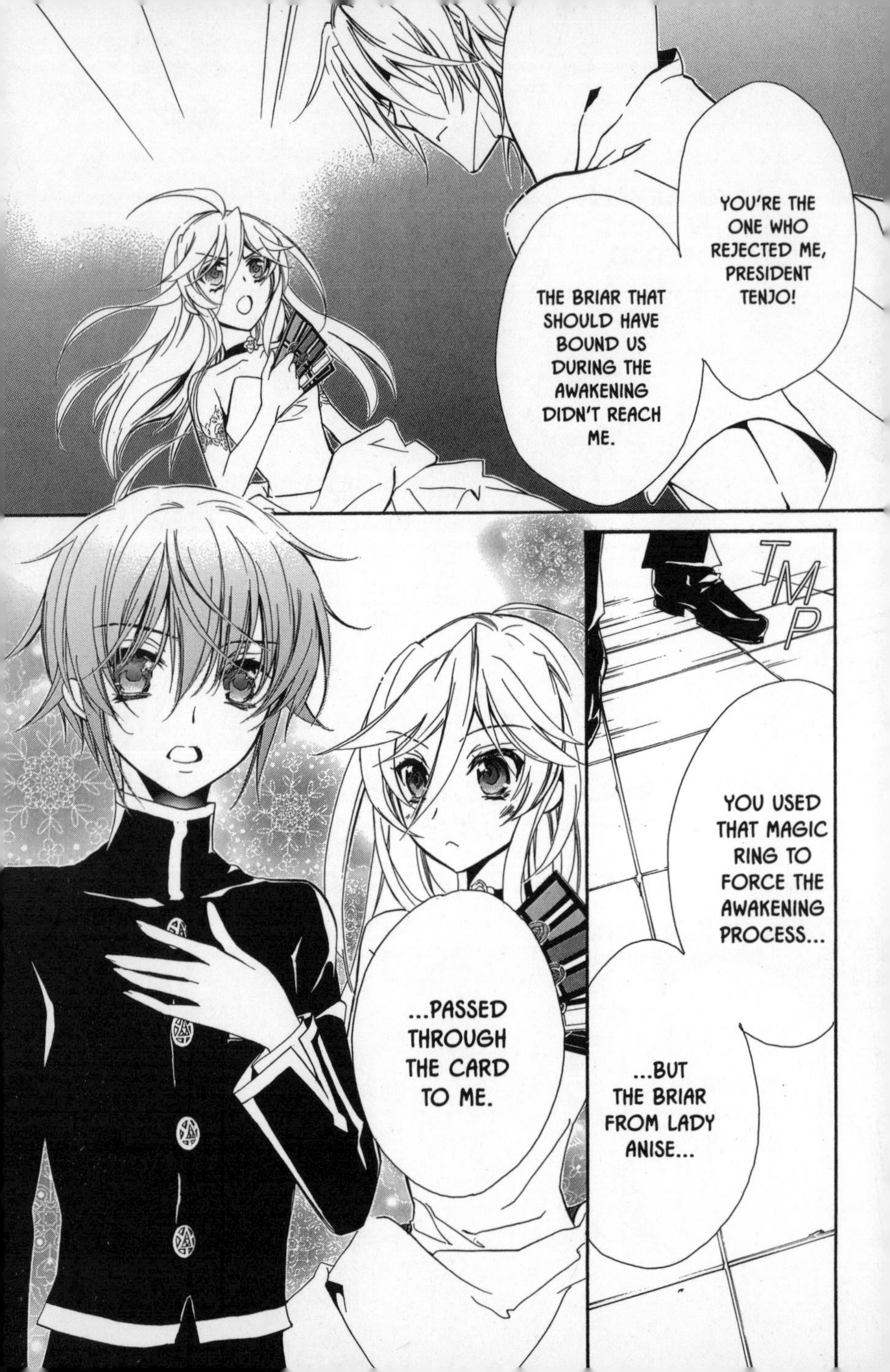
YOU'RE THE ONE WHO REJECTED ME, PRESIDENT TENJO!
THE BRIAR THAT SHOULD HAVE BOUND US DURING THE AWAKENING DIDN'T REACH ME.
TMP
YOU USED THAT MAGIC RING TO FORCE THE AWAKENING PROCESS...
...BUT THE BRIAR FROM LADY ANISE...
...PASSED THROUGH THE CARD TO ME.

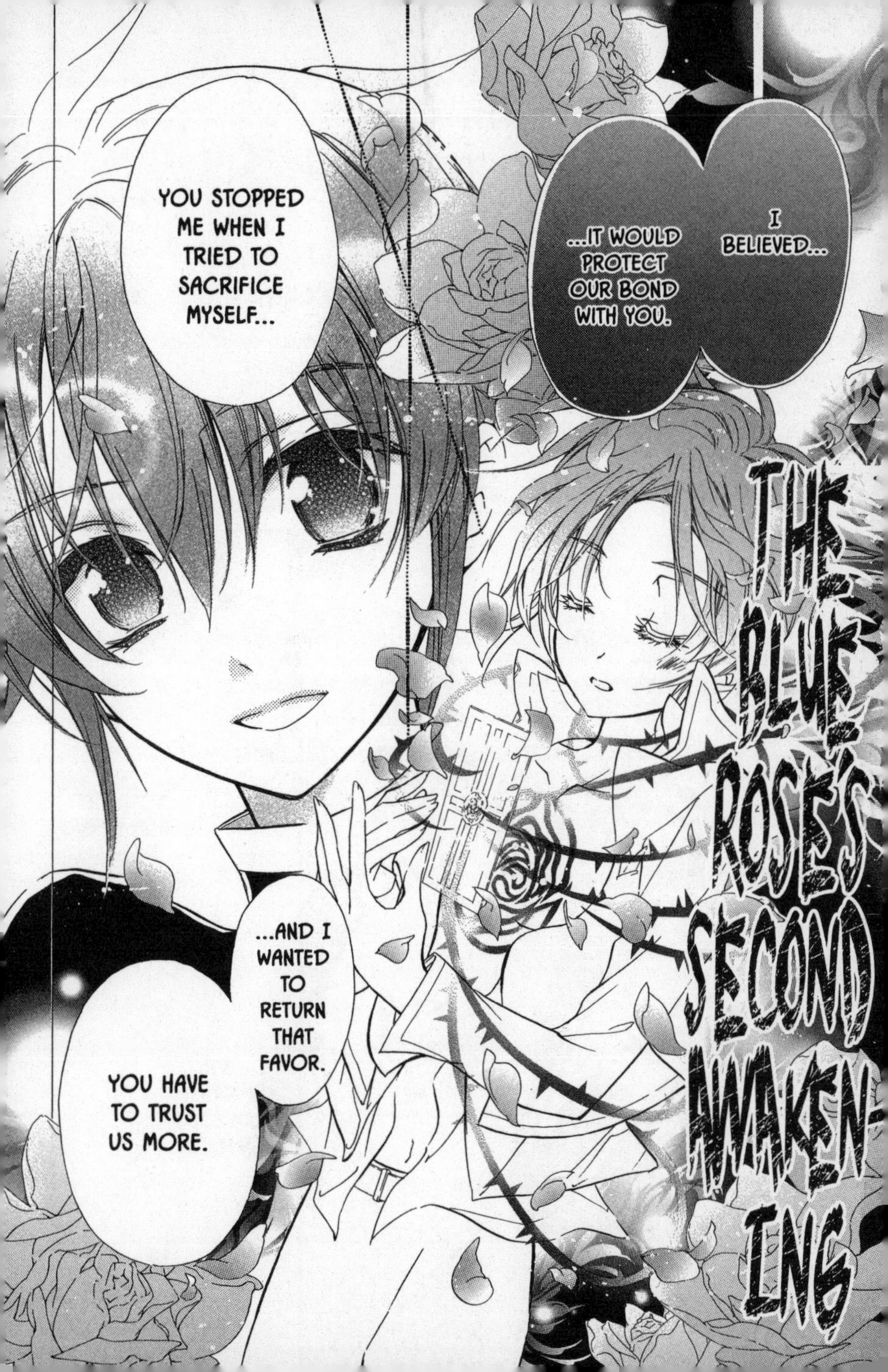
THE BLUE ROSE'S SECOND AWAKENING
I BELIEVED...
...IT WOULD PROTECT OUR BOND WITH YOU.
YOU STOPPED ME WHEN I TRIED TO SACRIFICE MYSELF...
...AND I WANTED TO RETURN THAT FAVOR.
YOU HAVE TO TRUST US MORE.

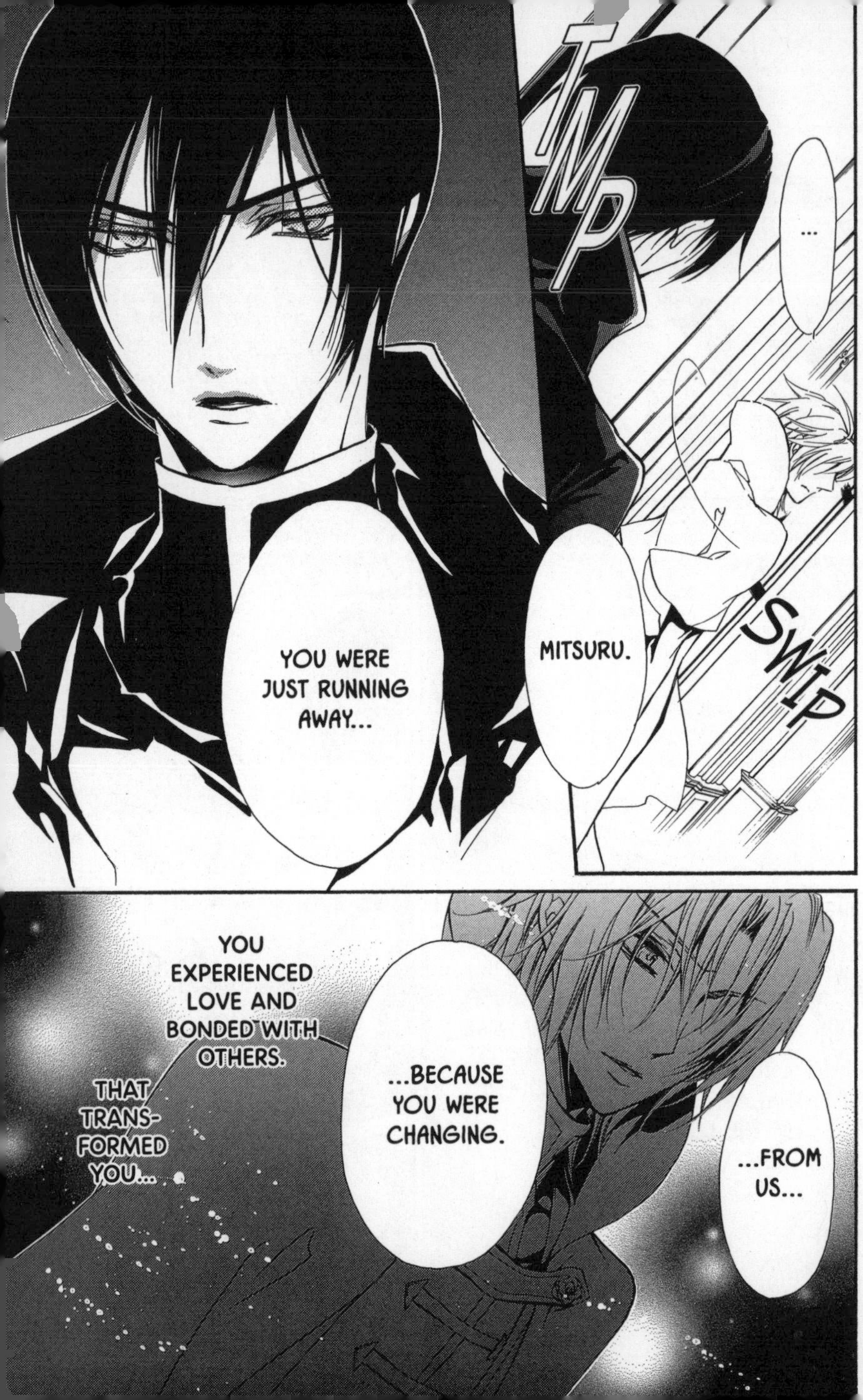
TMP
...
SWIP
MITSURU.
YOU WERE JUST RUNNING AWAY...
...FROM US...
...BECAUSE YOU WERE CHANGING.
YOU EXPERIENCED LOVE AND BONDED WITH OTHERS.
THAT TRANSFORMED YOU...

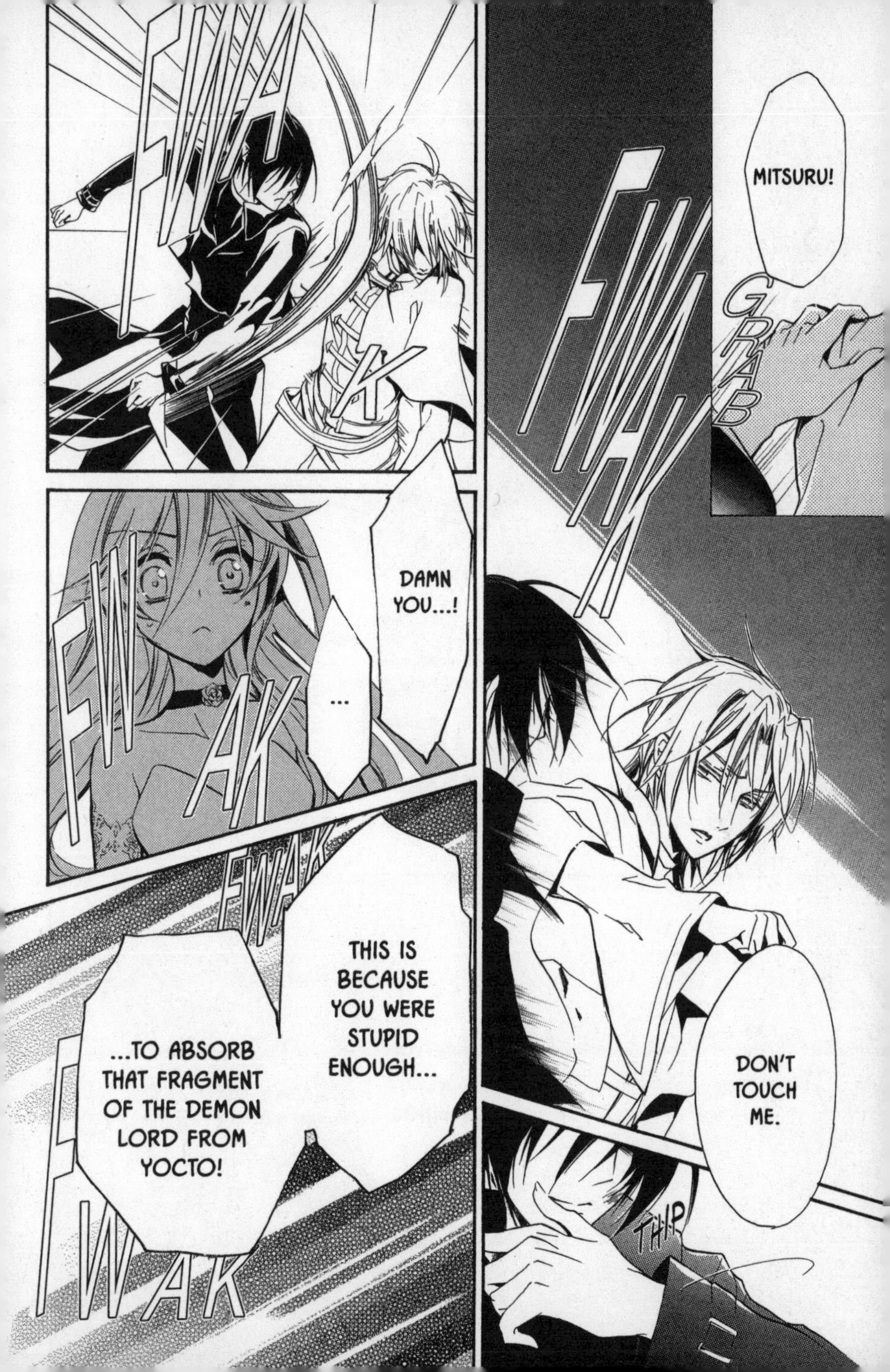

MITSURU!
GRAB
FWAK
FWAK
DAMN YOU...!
...
FWAK
FWAK
THIS IS BECAUSE YOU WERE STUPID ENOUGH...
...TO ABSORB THAT FRAGMENT OF THE DEMON LORD FROM YOCTO!
FWAK
DON'T TOUCH ME.
THIP

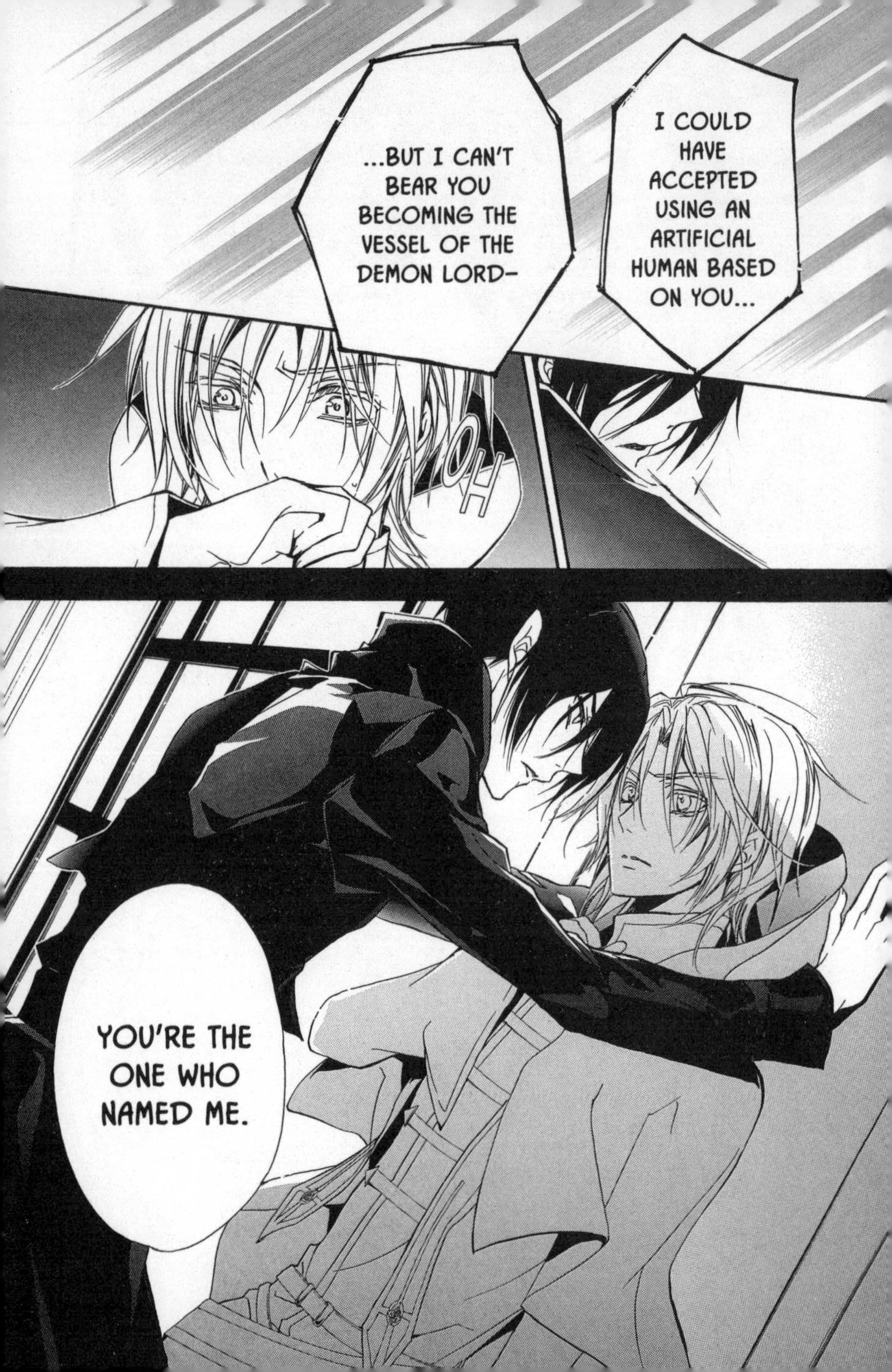
I COULD HAVE ACCEPTED USING AN ARTIFICIAL HUMAN BASED ON YOU...
...BUT I CAN'T BEAR YOU BECOMING THE VESSEL OF THE DEMON LORD–
OH
YOU'RE THE ONE WHO NAMED ME.

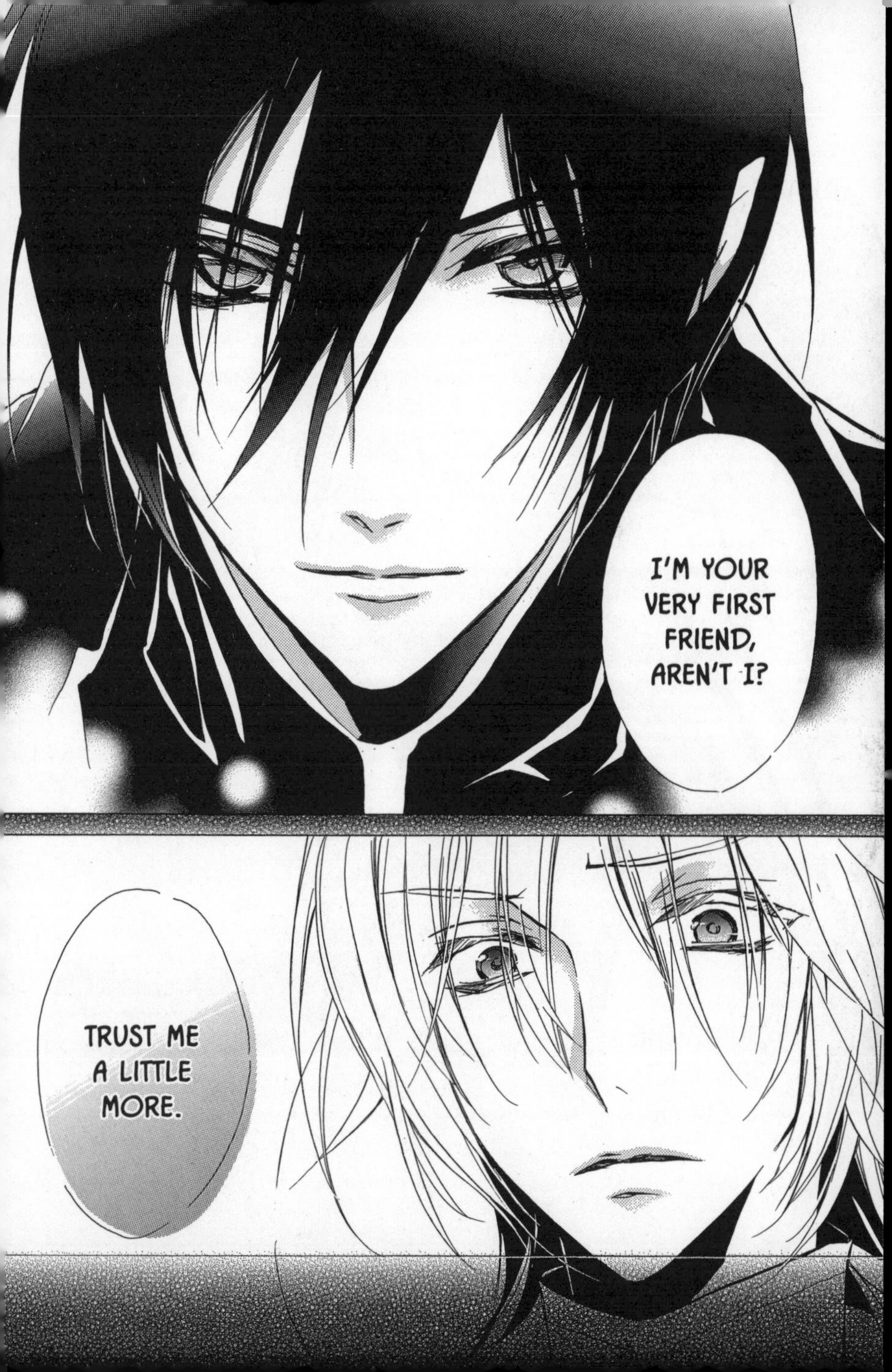
I'M YOUR VERY FIRST FRIEND, AREN'T I?
TRUST ME A LITTLE MORE.

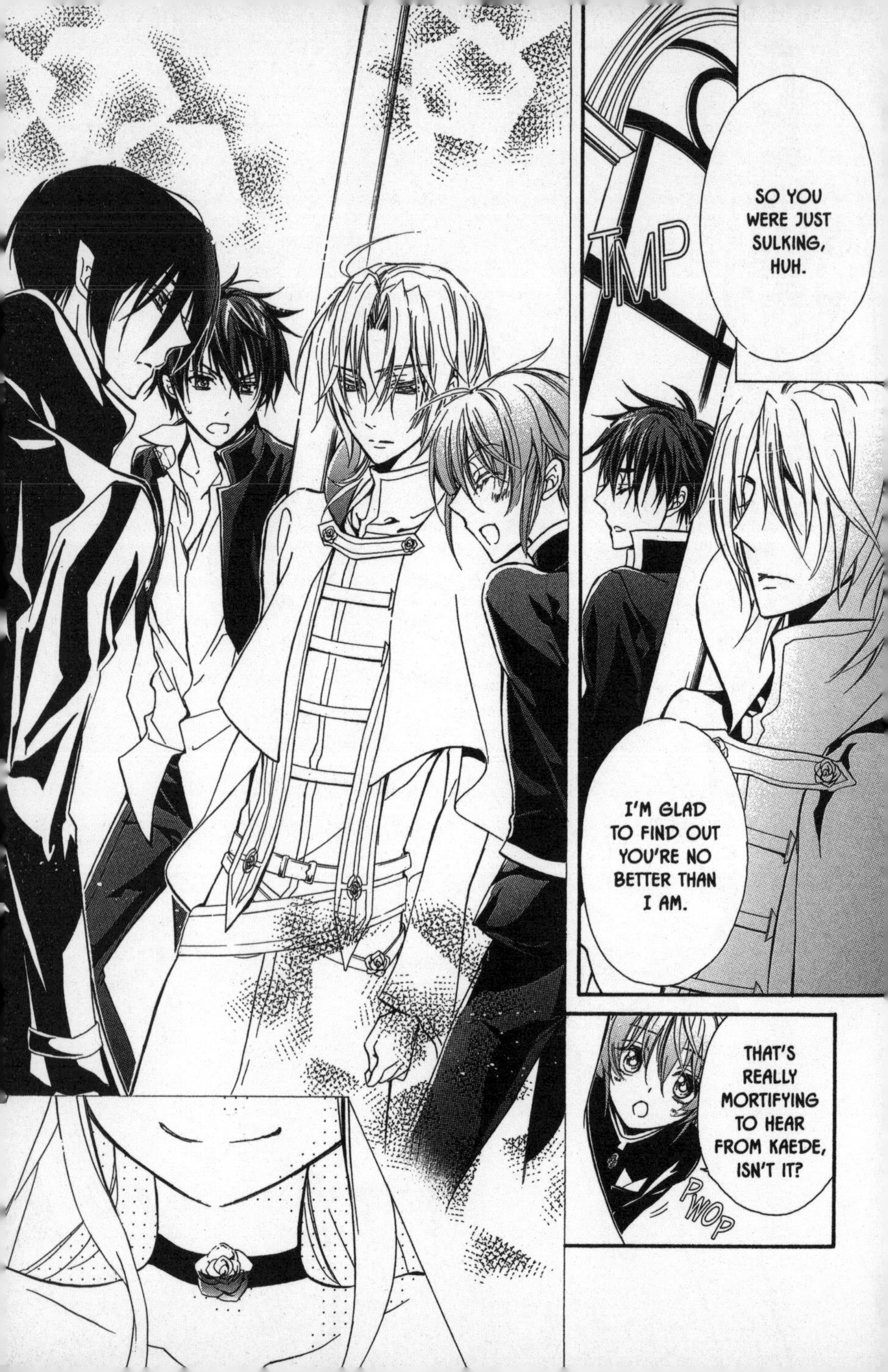
SO YOU WERE JUST SULKING, HUH.
TMP
I'M GLAD TO FIND OUT YOU'RE NO BETTER THAN I AM.
THAT'S REALLY MORTIFYING TO HEAR FROM KAEDE, ISN'T IT?
PWOP

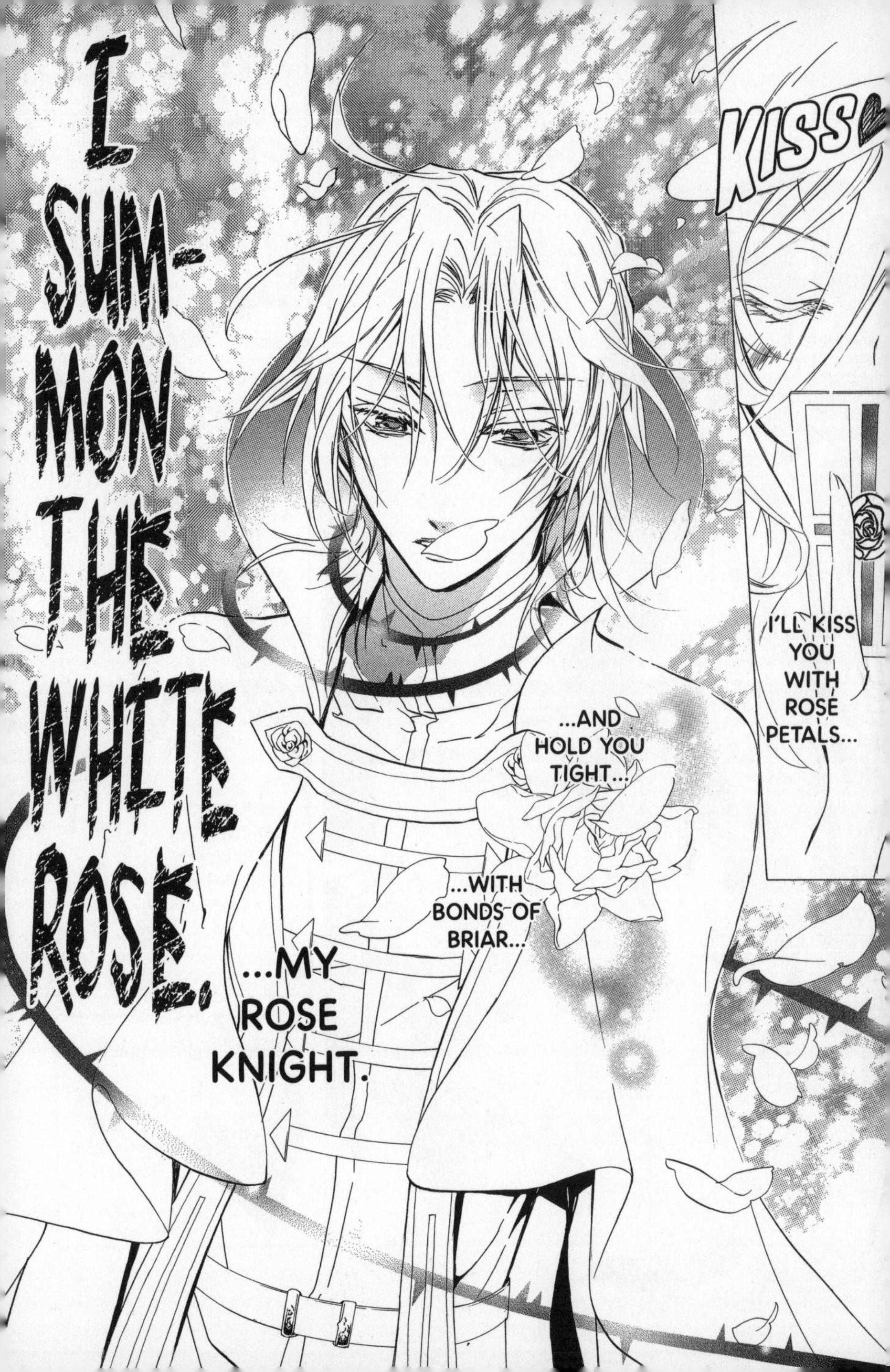
KISS
I'LL KISS YOU WITH ROSE PETALS...
...AND HOLD YOU TIGHT...
...WITH BONDS OF BRIAR...
...MY ROSE KNIGHT.
I SUMMON THE WHITE ROSE.

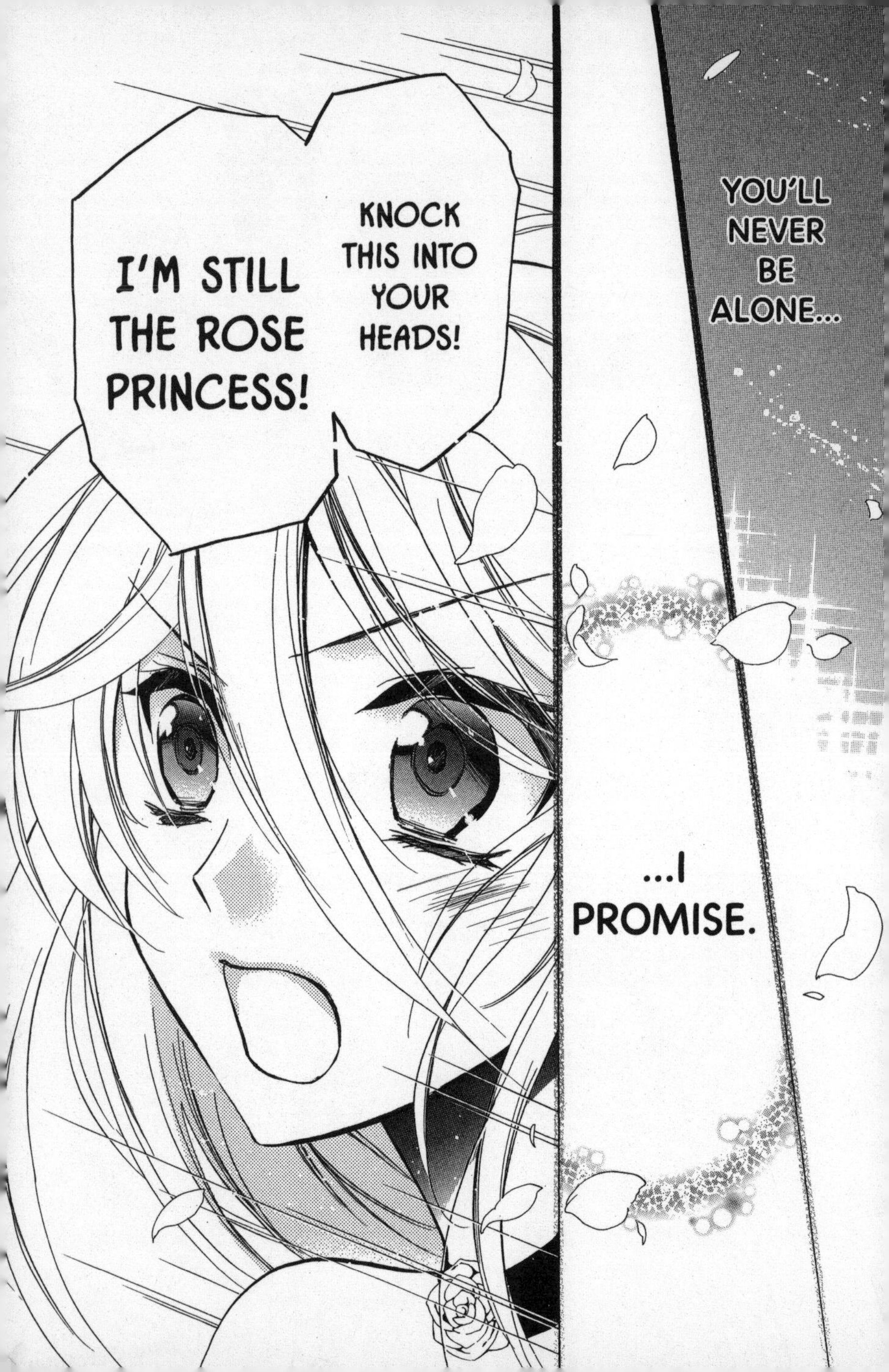
YOU'LL NEVER BE ALONE...
...I PROMISE.
KNOCK THIS INTO YOUR HEADS!
I'M STILL THE ROSE PRINCESS!

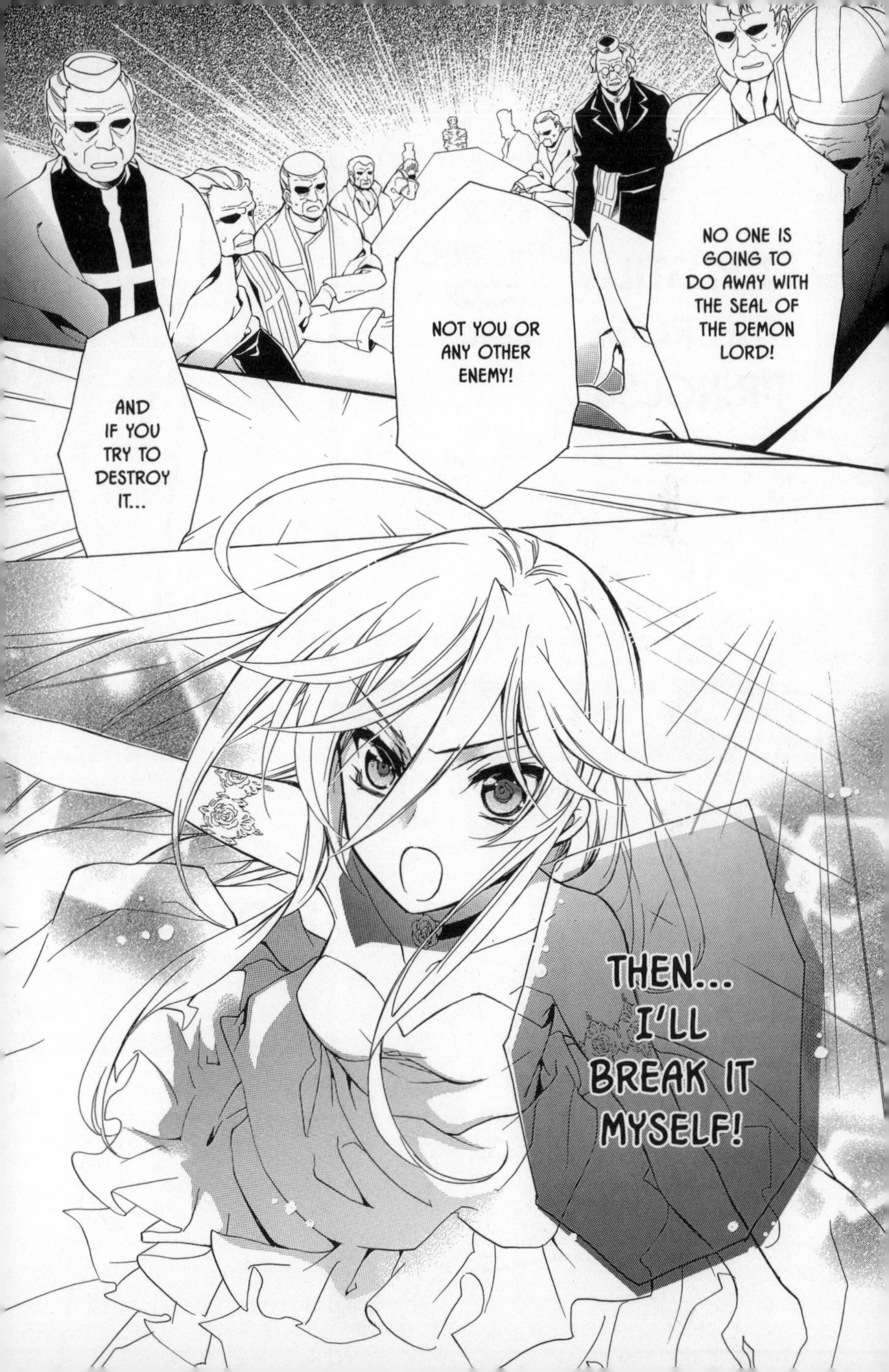
NO ONE IS GOING TO DO AWAY WITH THE SEAL OF THE DEMON LORD!
NOT YOU OR ANY OTHER ENEMY!
AND IF YOU TRY TO DESTROY IT...
THEN... I'LL BREAK IT MYSELF!

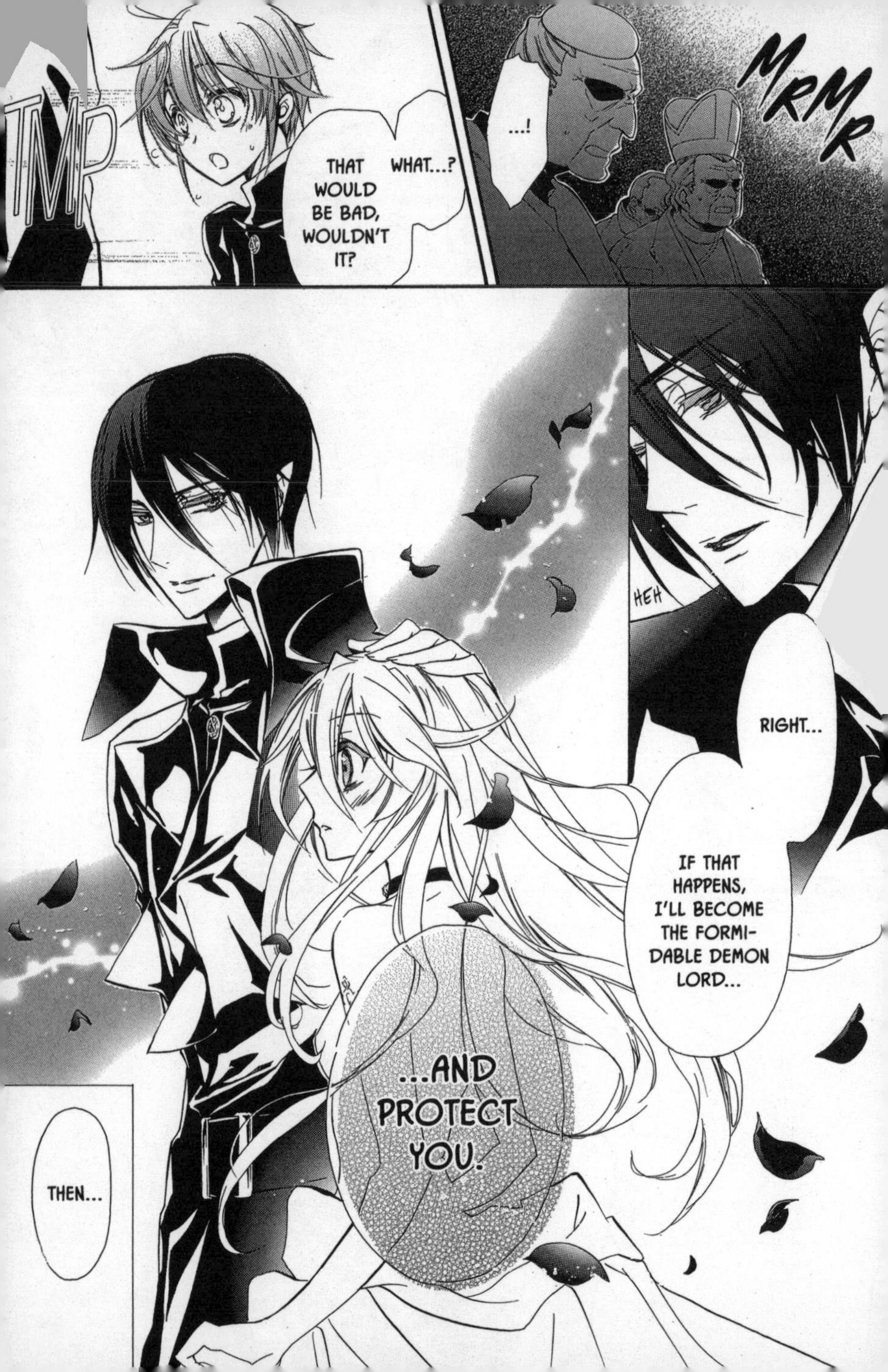
MRMR
...!
WHAT...?
THAT WOULD BE BAD, WOULDN'T IT?
TMP
HEH
RIGHT...
IF THAT HAPPENS, I'LL BECOME THE FORMI-DABLE DEMON LORD...
...AND PROTECT YOU.
THEN...

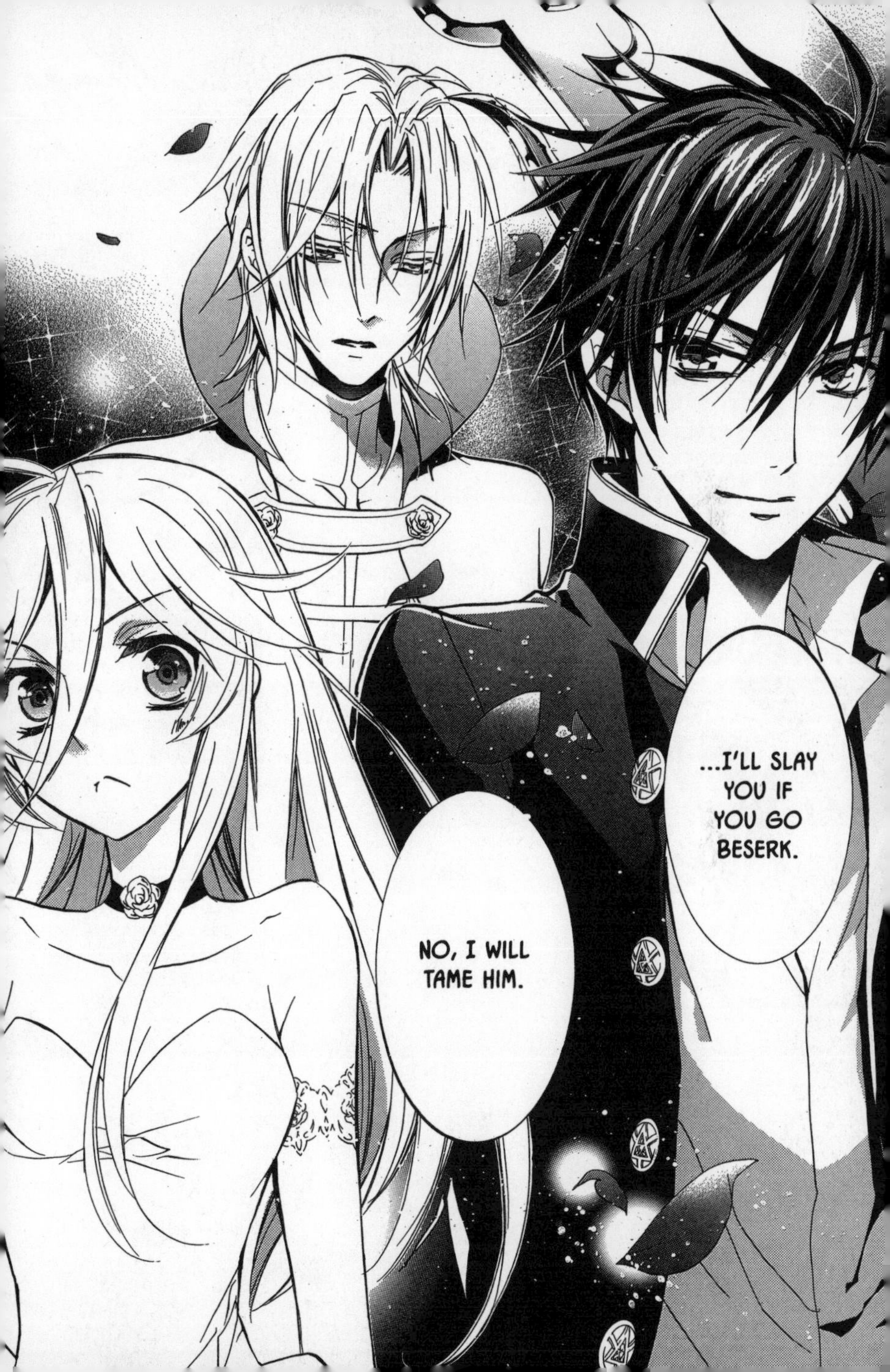
...I'LL SLAY YOU IF YOU GO BESERK.
NO, I WILL TAME HIM.

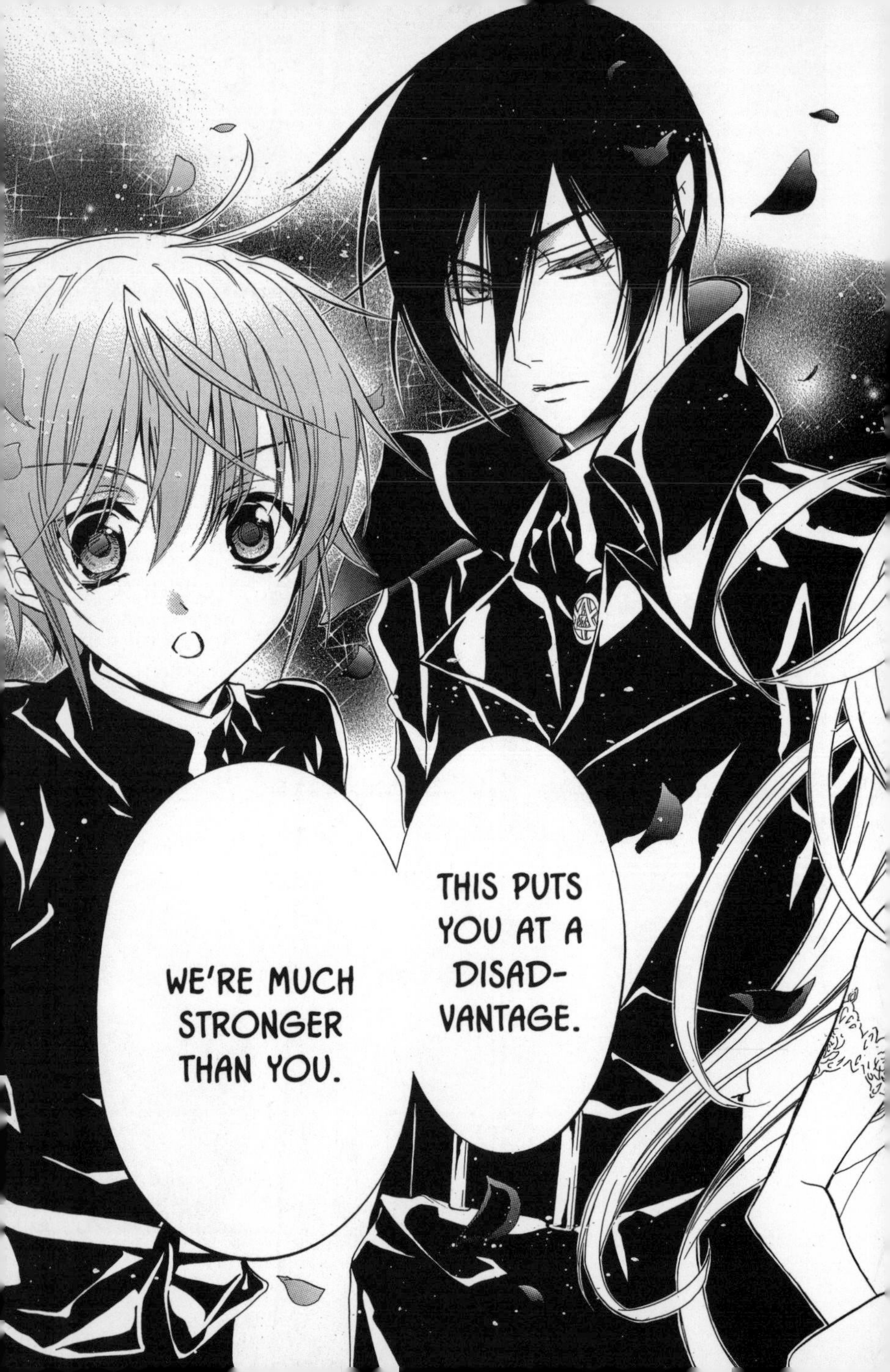
THIS PUTS YOU AT A DISAD-VANTAGE.
WE'RE MUCH STRONGER THAN YOU.

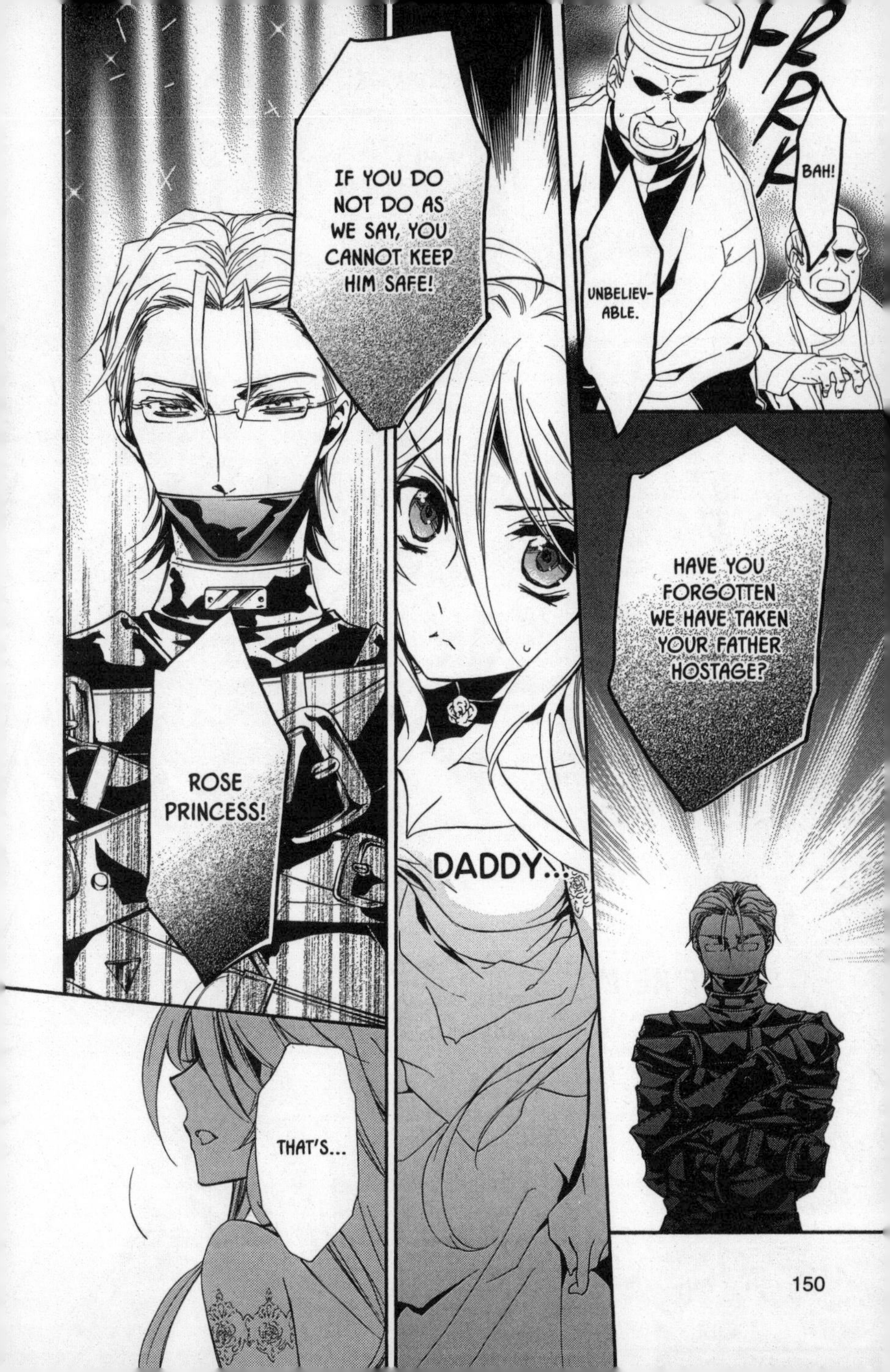
KRRK
BAH!
UNBELIEV-ABLE.
HAVE YOU FORGOTTEN WE HAVE TAKEN YOUR FATHER HOSTAGE?
DADDY...
IF YOU DO NOT DO AS WE SAY, YOU CANNOT KEEP HIM SAFE!
ROSE PRINCESS!
THAT'S...

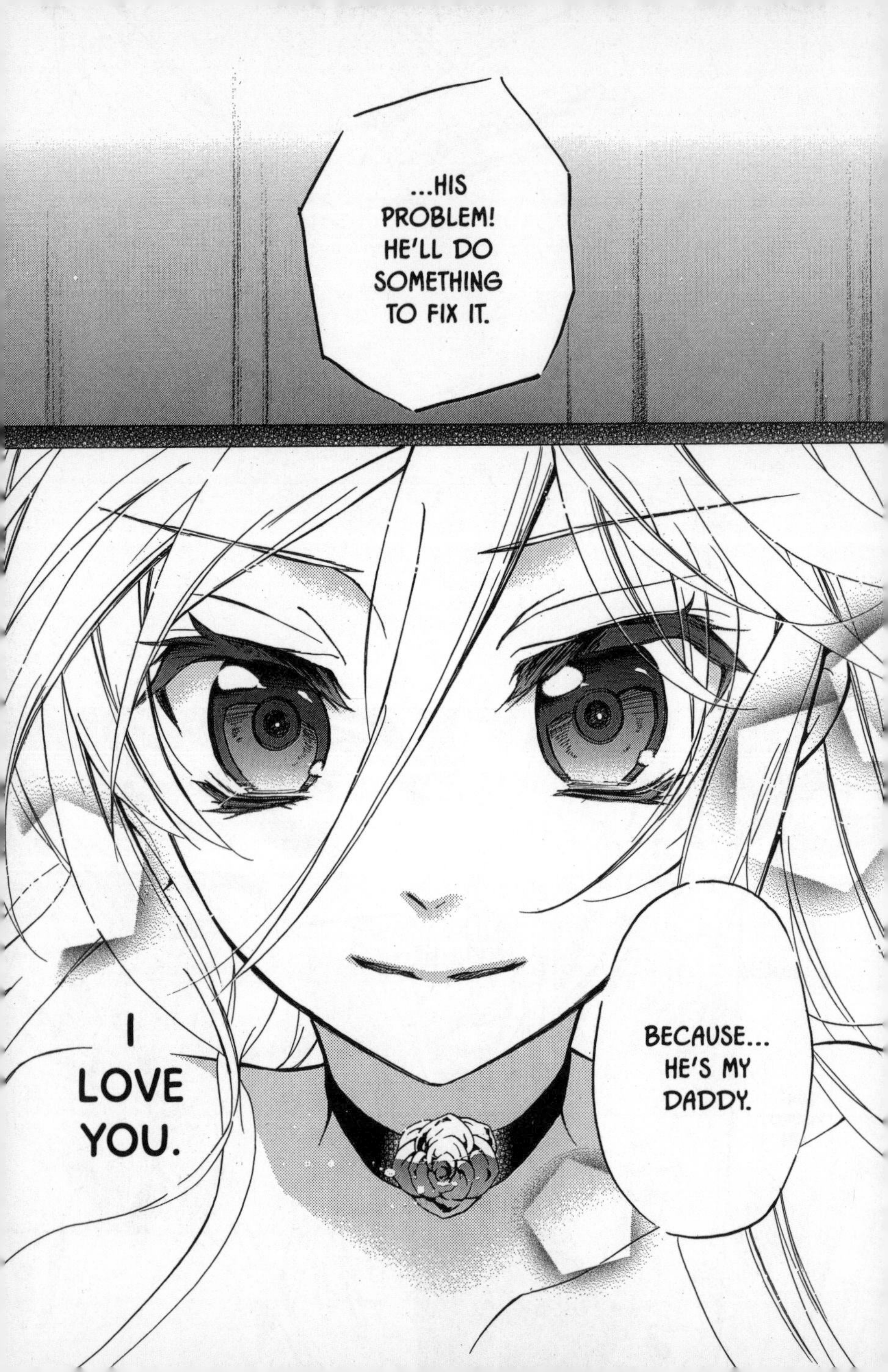
...HIS PROBLEM! HE'LL DO SOMETHING TO FIX IT.
BECAUSE... HE'S MY DADDY.
I LOVE YOU.

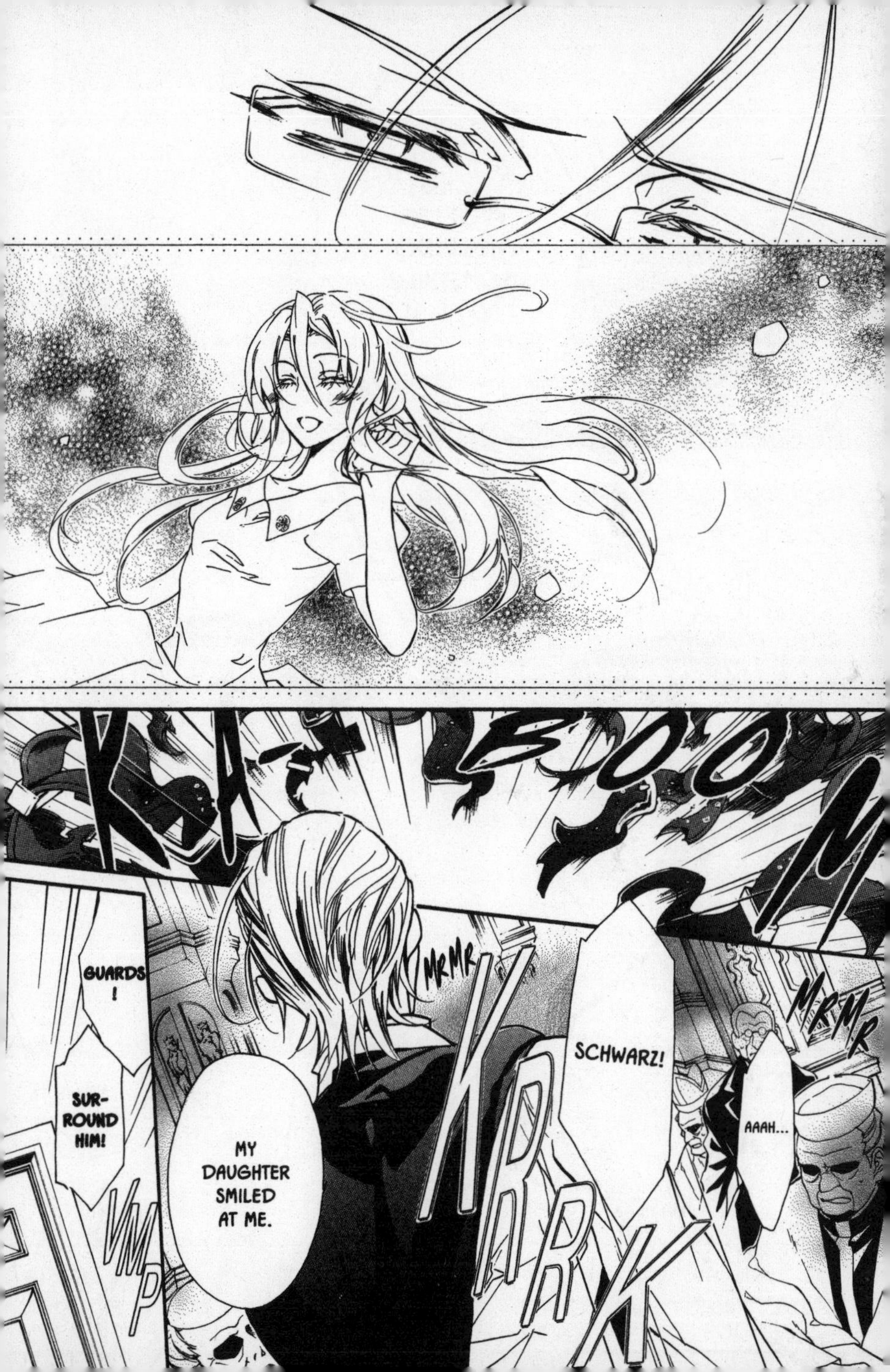
KA-BOOOM
MRMR
AAAH...
SCHWARZ!
MRMR
KRRRK
MY DAUGHTER SMILED AT ME.
GUARDS!
SURROUND HIM!
VMP

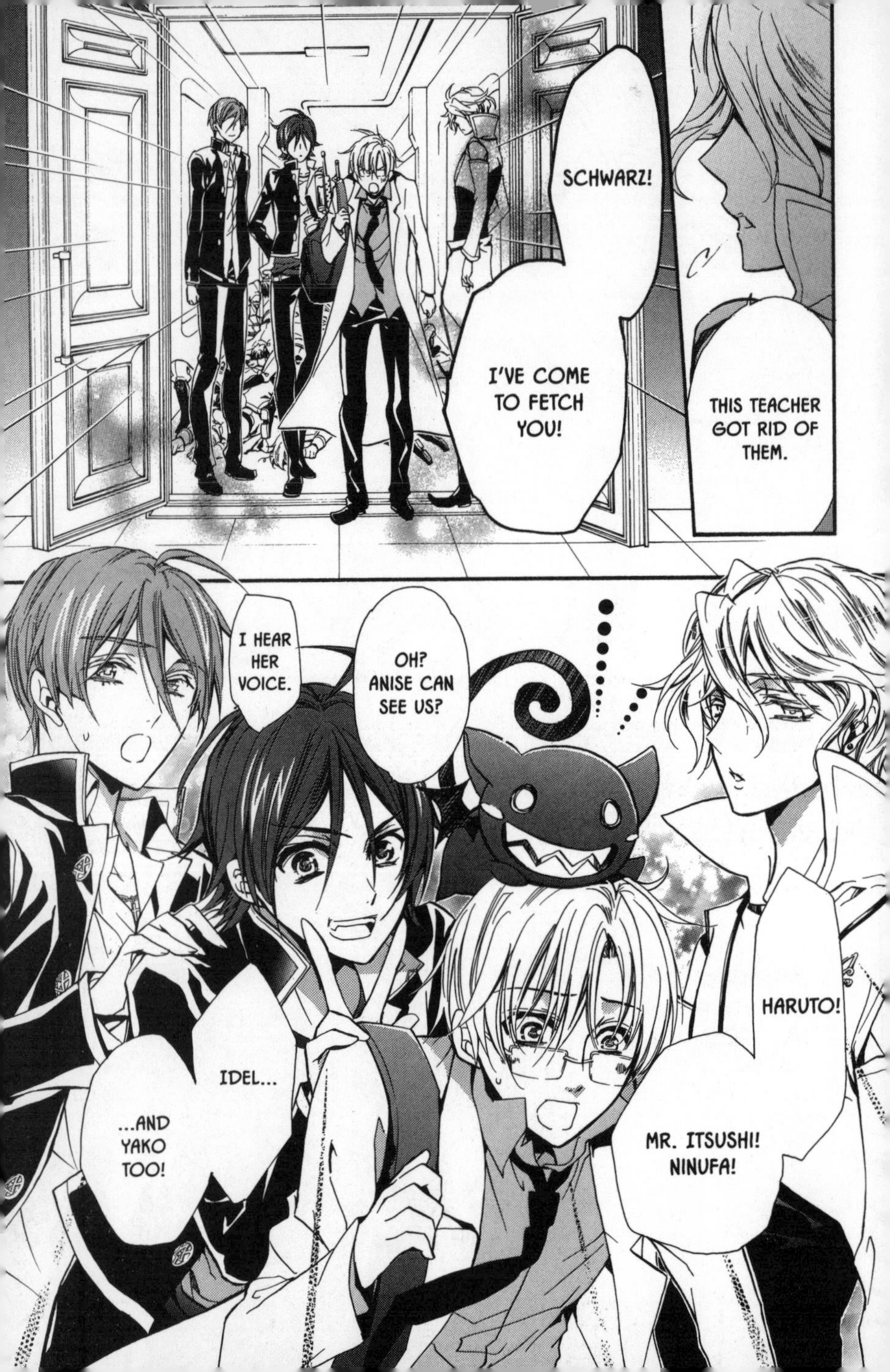
THIS TEACHER GOT RID OF THEM.
SCHWARZ!
I'VE COME TO FETCH YOU!
......
OH? ANISE CAN SEE US?
I HEAR HER VOICE.
HARUTO!
MR. ITSUSHI! NINUFA!
IDEL...
...AND YAKO TOO!

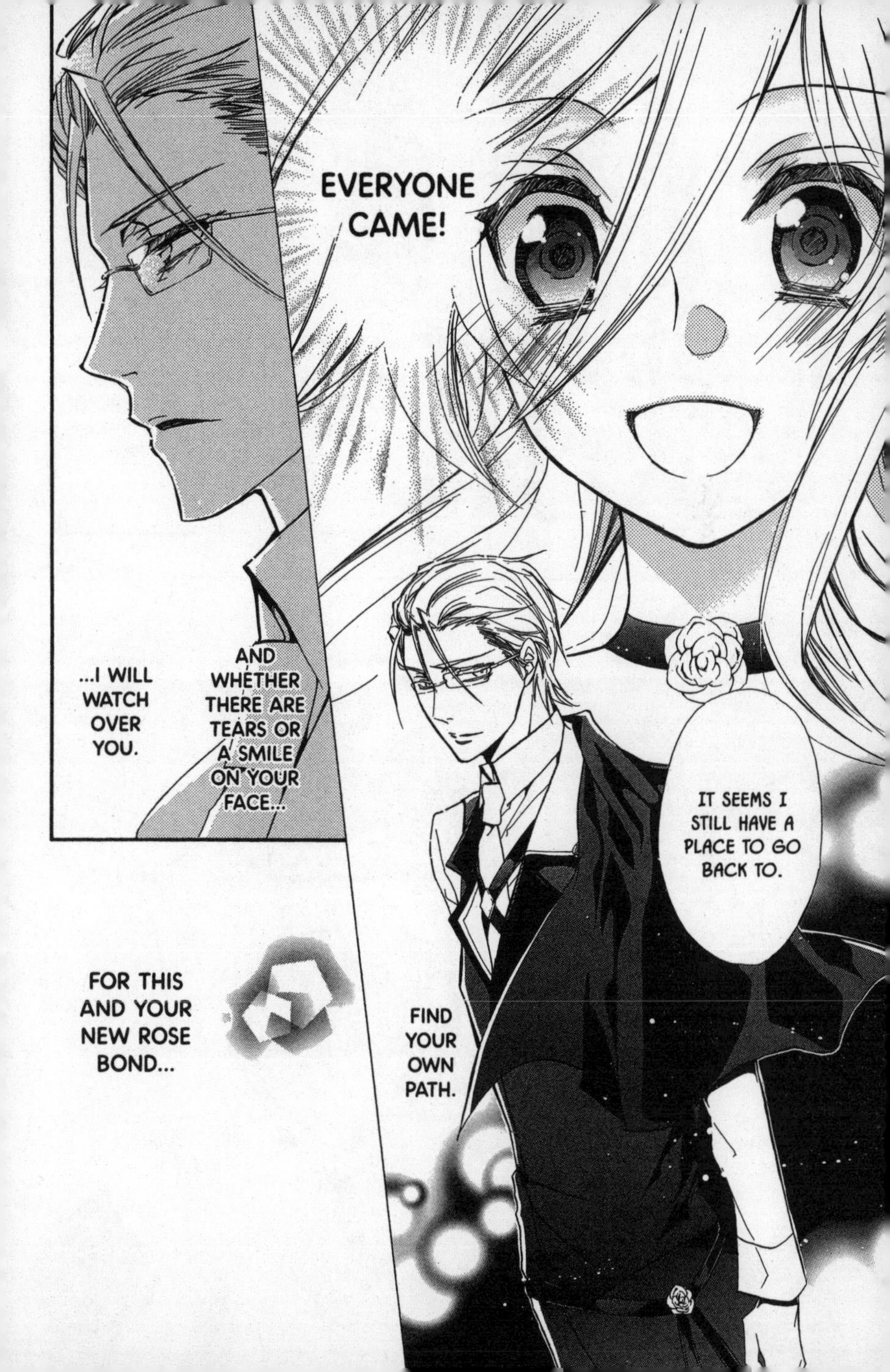
EVERYONE CAME!
IT SEEMS I STILL HAVE A PLACE TO GO BACK TO.
AND WHETHER THERE ARE TEARS OR A SMILE ON YOUR FACE...
...I WILL WATCH OVER YOU.
FIND YOUR OWN PATH.
FOR THIS AND YOUR NEW ROSE BOND...

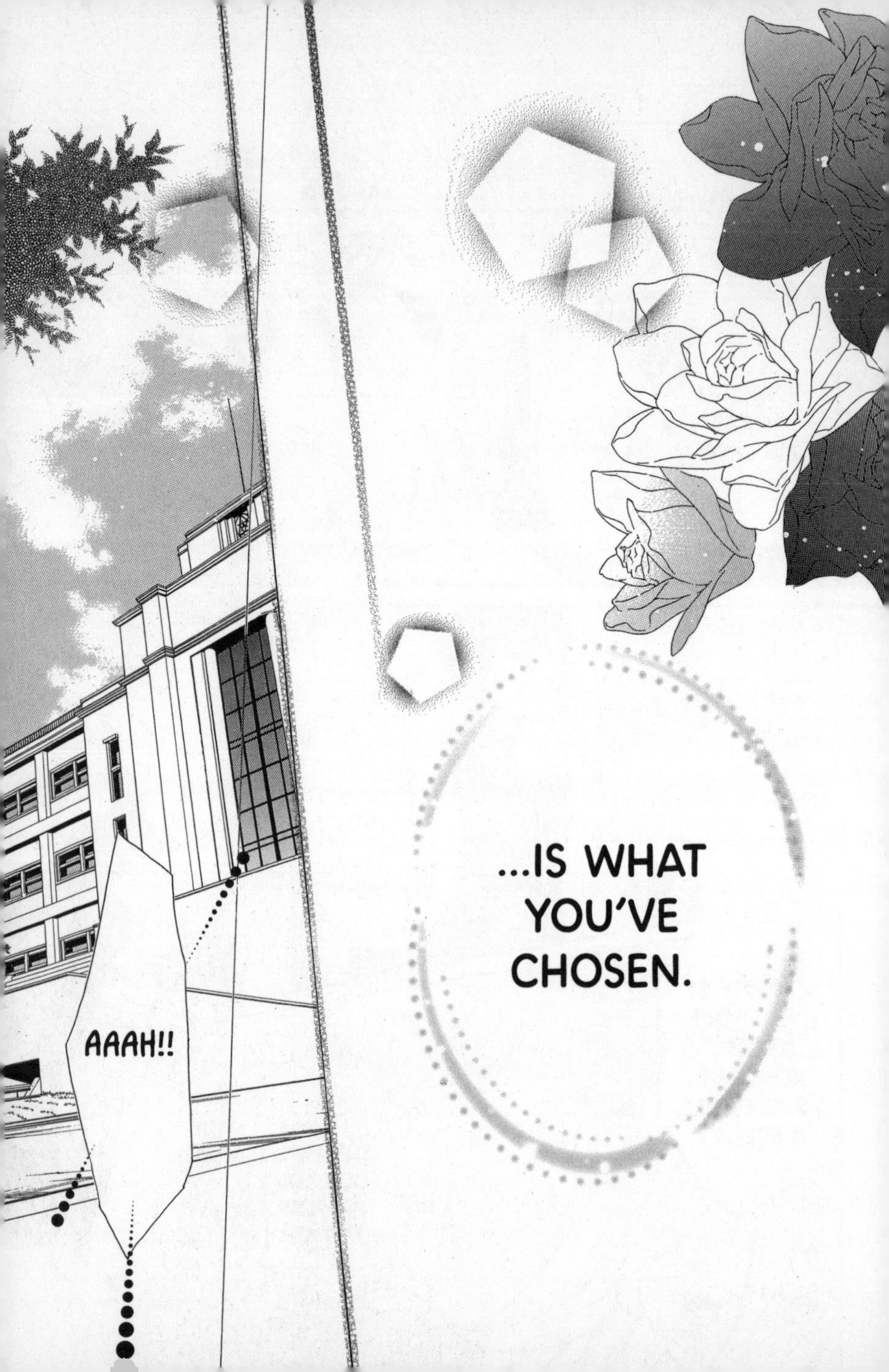
...IS WHAT YOU'VE CHOSEN.
AAAH!!

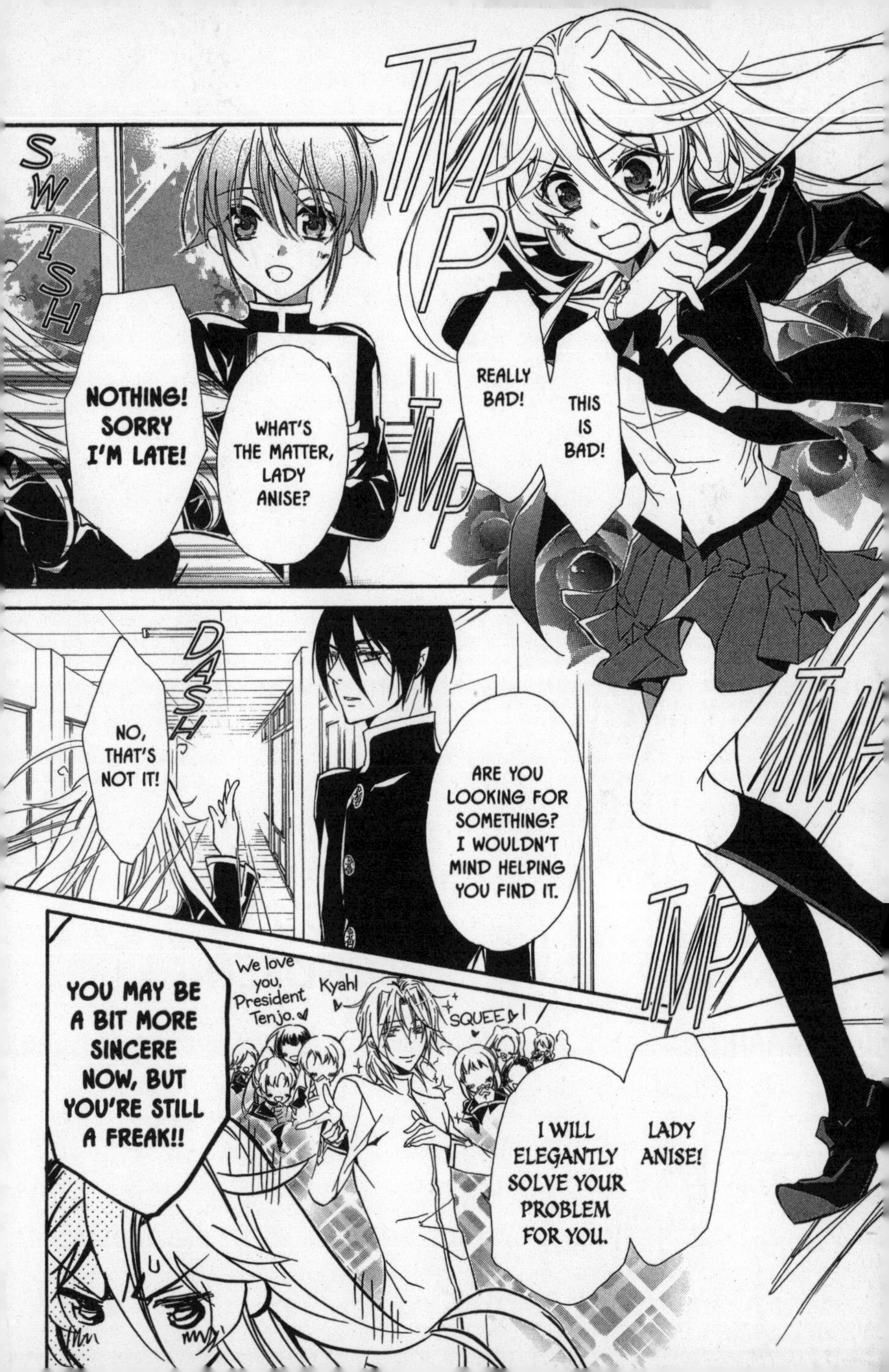
TMP
THIS IS BAD!
REALLY BAD!
TMP
TMP
TMP
TMP
SWISH
WHAT'S THE MATTER, LADY ANISE?
NOTHING! SORRY I'M LATE!
ARE YOU LOOKING FOR SOMETHING? I WOULDN'T MIND HELPING YOU FIND IT.
DASH
NO, THAT'S NOT IT!
LADY ANISE!
I WILL ELEGANTLY SOLVE YOUR PROBLEM FOR YOU.
SQUEE
Kyah!
We love you, President Tenjo.
YOU MAY BE A BIT MORE SINCERE NOW, BUT YOU'RE STILL A FREAK!!

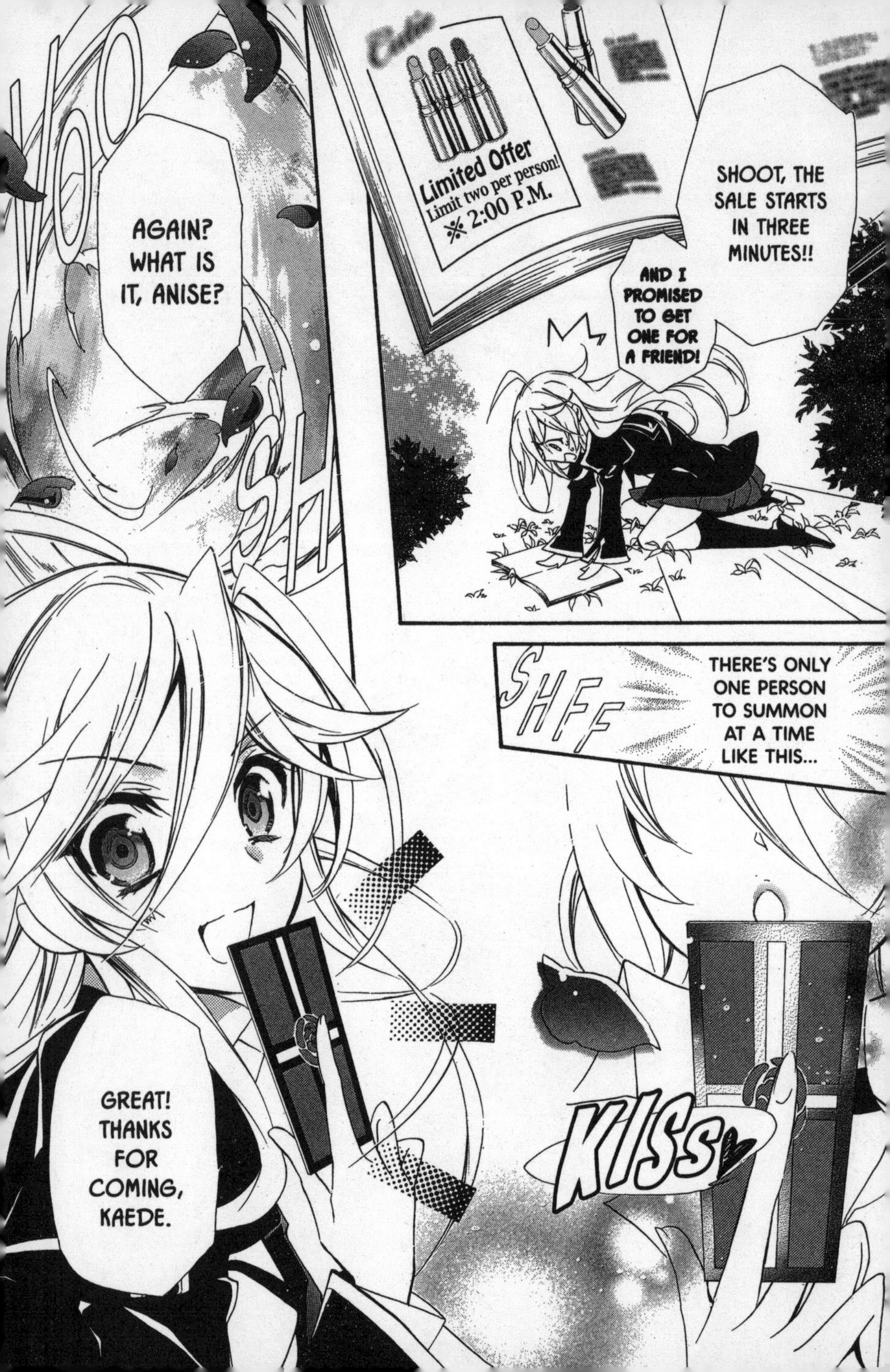
Limited Offer
Limit two per person!
※ 2:00 P.M.
SHOOT, THE SALE STARTS IN THREE MINUTES!!
AND I PROMISED TO GET ONE FOR A FRIEND!
SHFF
THERE'S ONLY ONE PERSON TO SUMMON AT A TIME LIKE THIS...
KISS
WHOO
SH
AGAIN? WHAT IS IT, ANISE?
GREAT! THANKS FOR COMING, KAEDE.

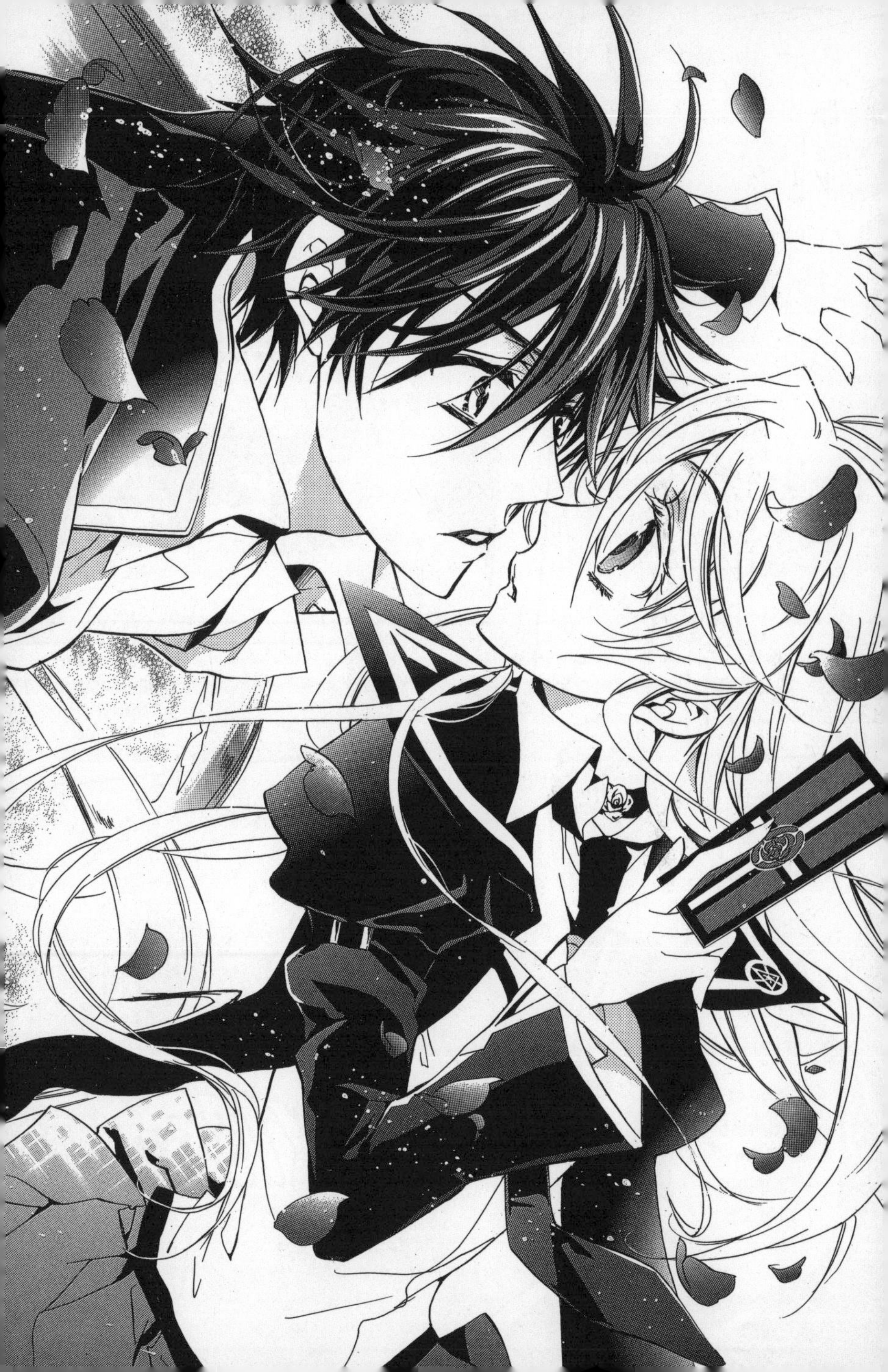

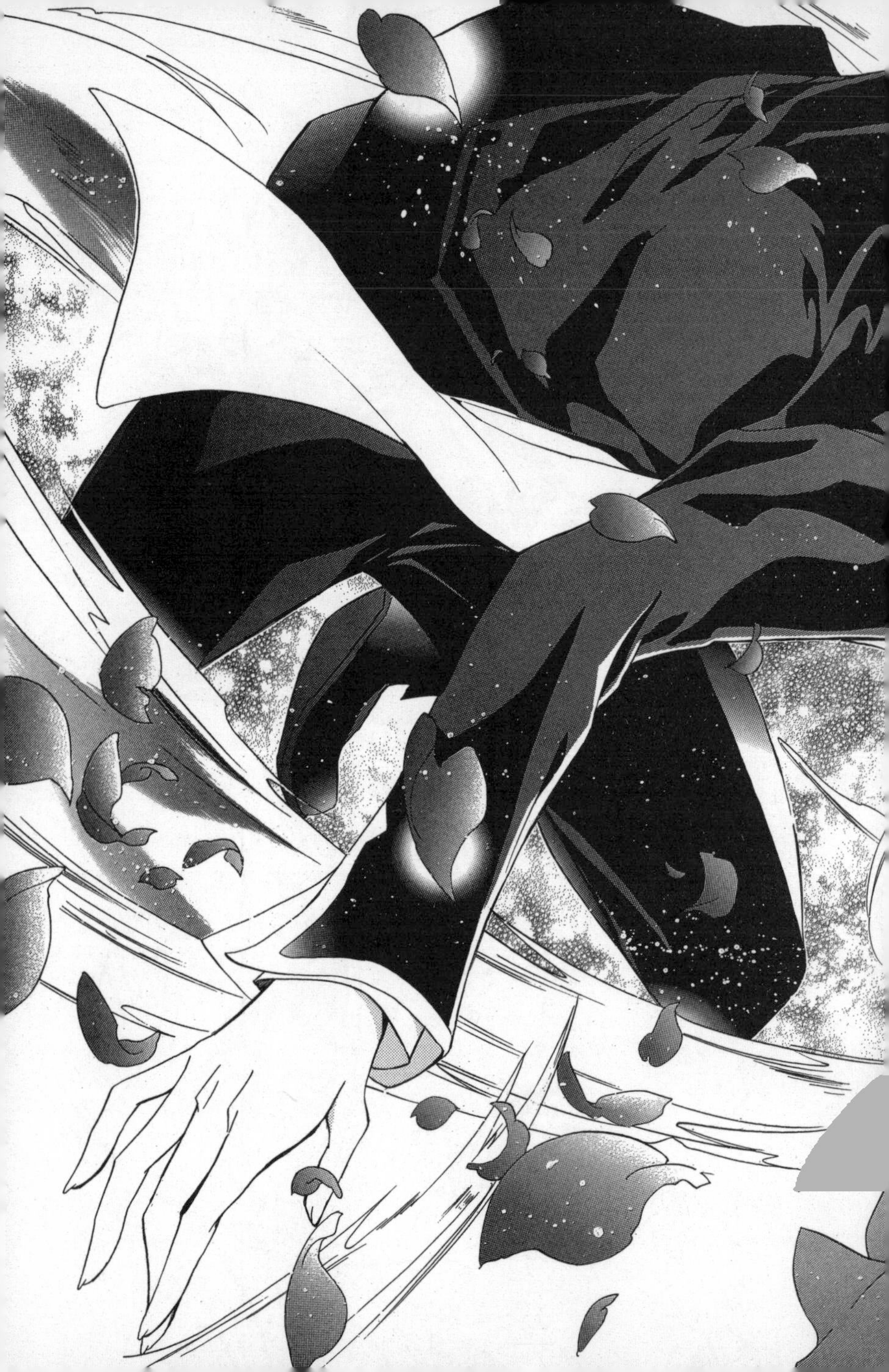

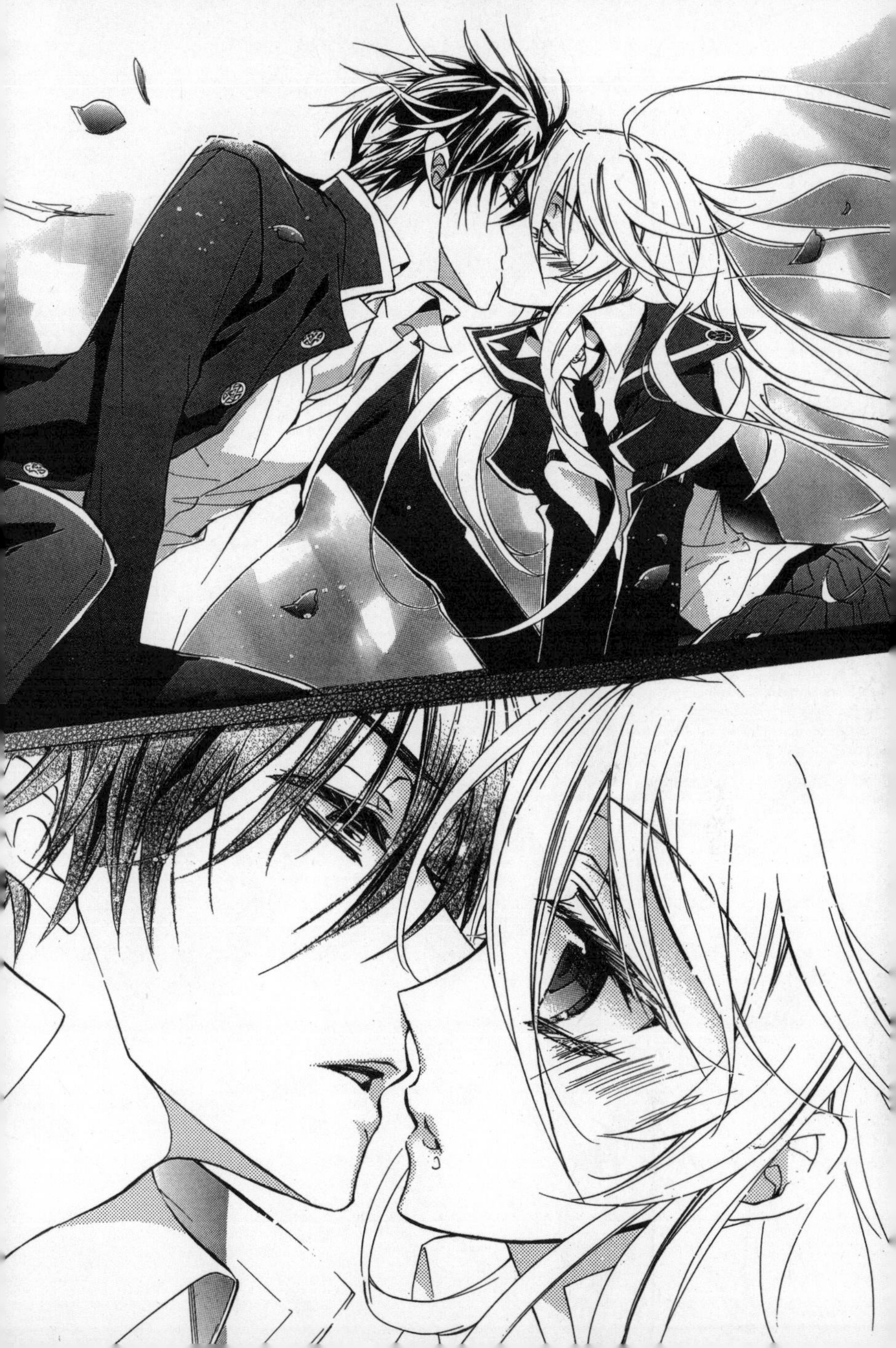

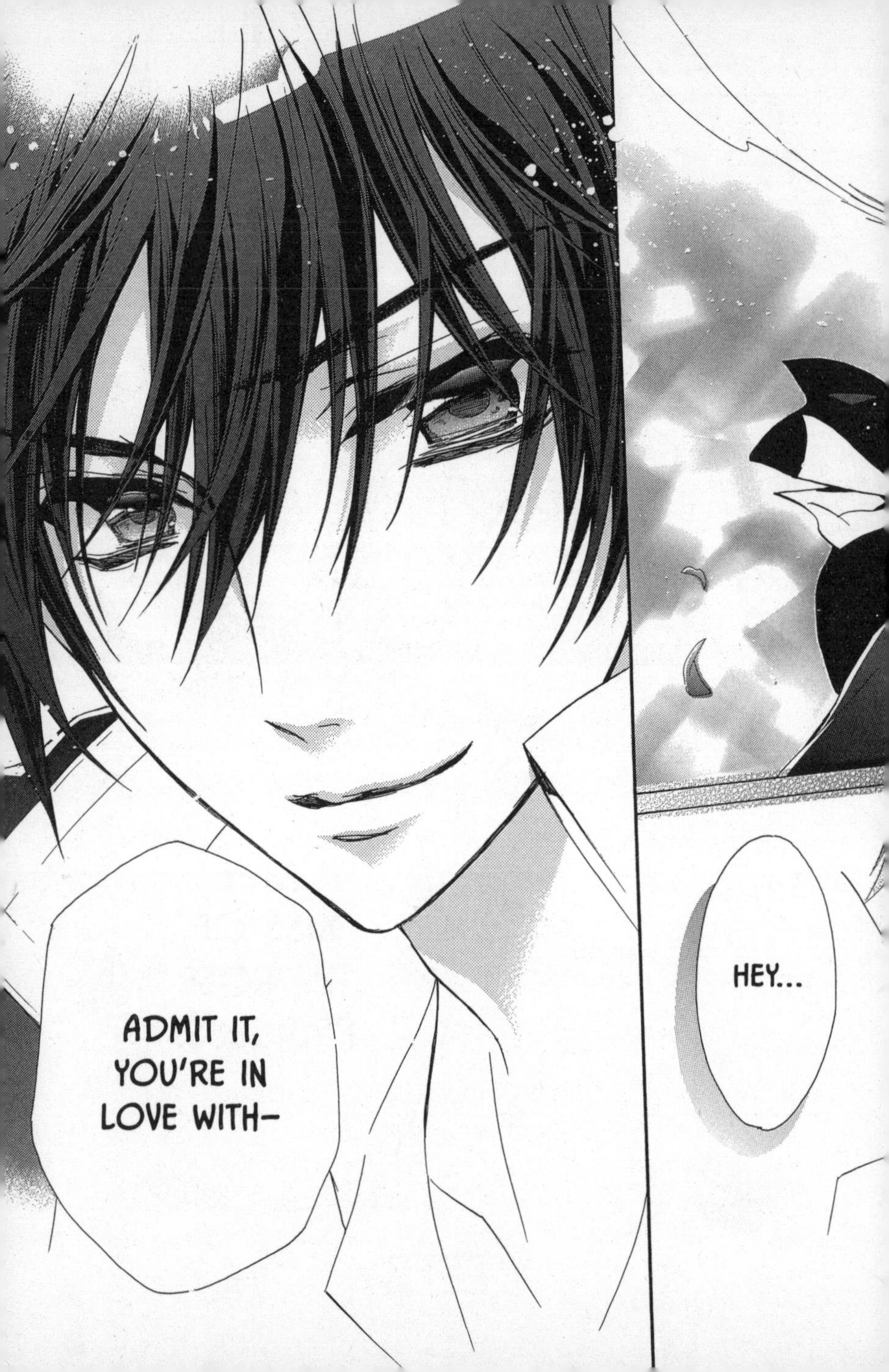
HEY...
ADMIT IT, YOU'RE IN LOVE WITH–

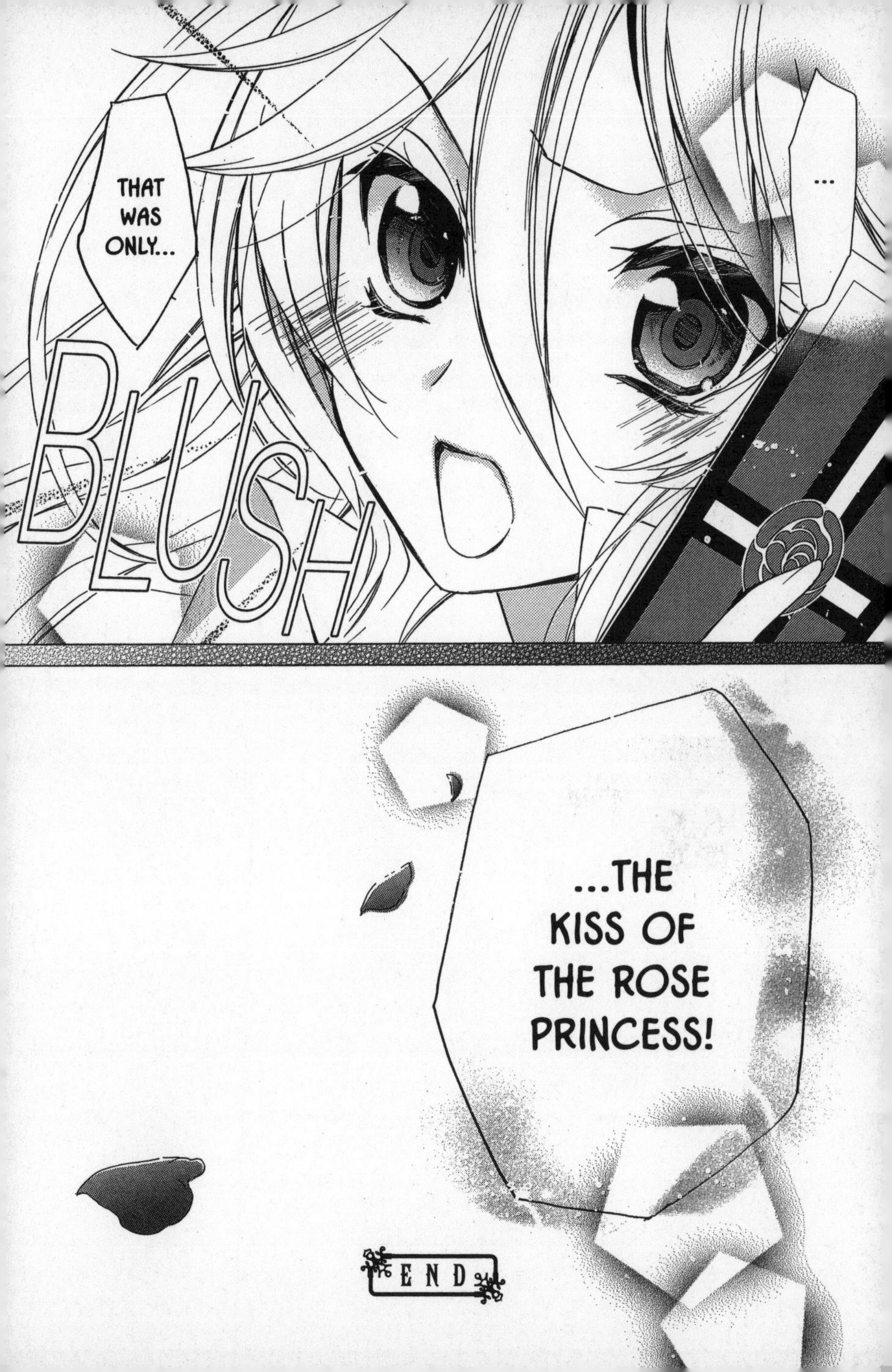
...
THAT WAS ONLY...
BLUSH
...THE KISS OF THE ROSE PRINCESS!
END

Kiss of the Rose Princess

Kiss of the Rose
Princess

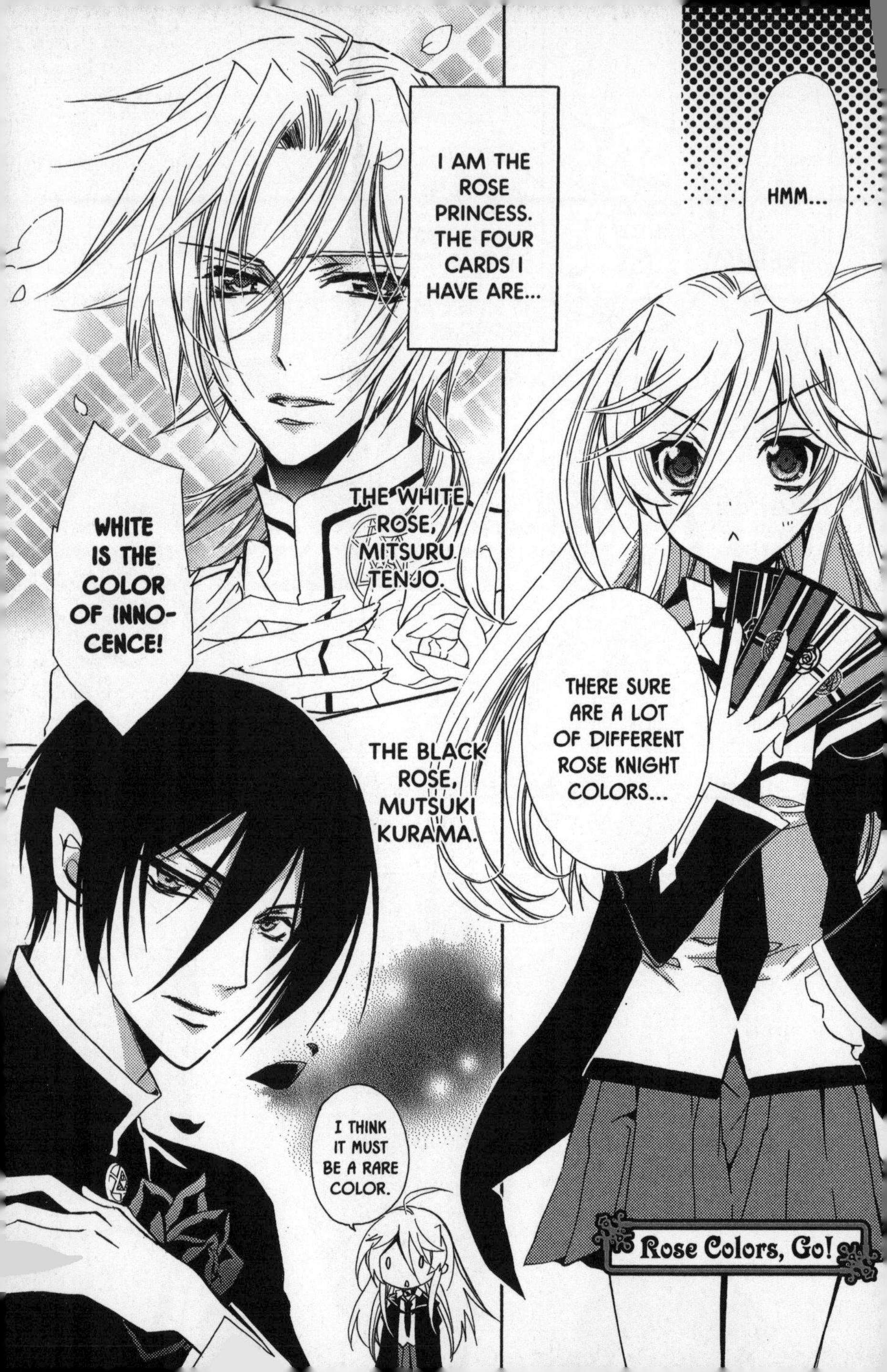
HMM...
THERE SURE ARE A LOT OF DIFFERENT ROSE KNIGHT COLORS...
Rose Colors, Go!
I AM THE ROSE PRINCESS. THE FOUR CARDS I HAVE ARE...
THE WHITE ROSE, MITSURU TENJO.
WHITE IS THE COLOR OF INNO-CENCE!
THE BLACK ROSE, MUTSUKI KURAMA.
I THINK IT MUST BE A RARE COLOR.

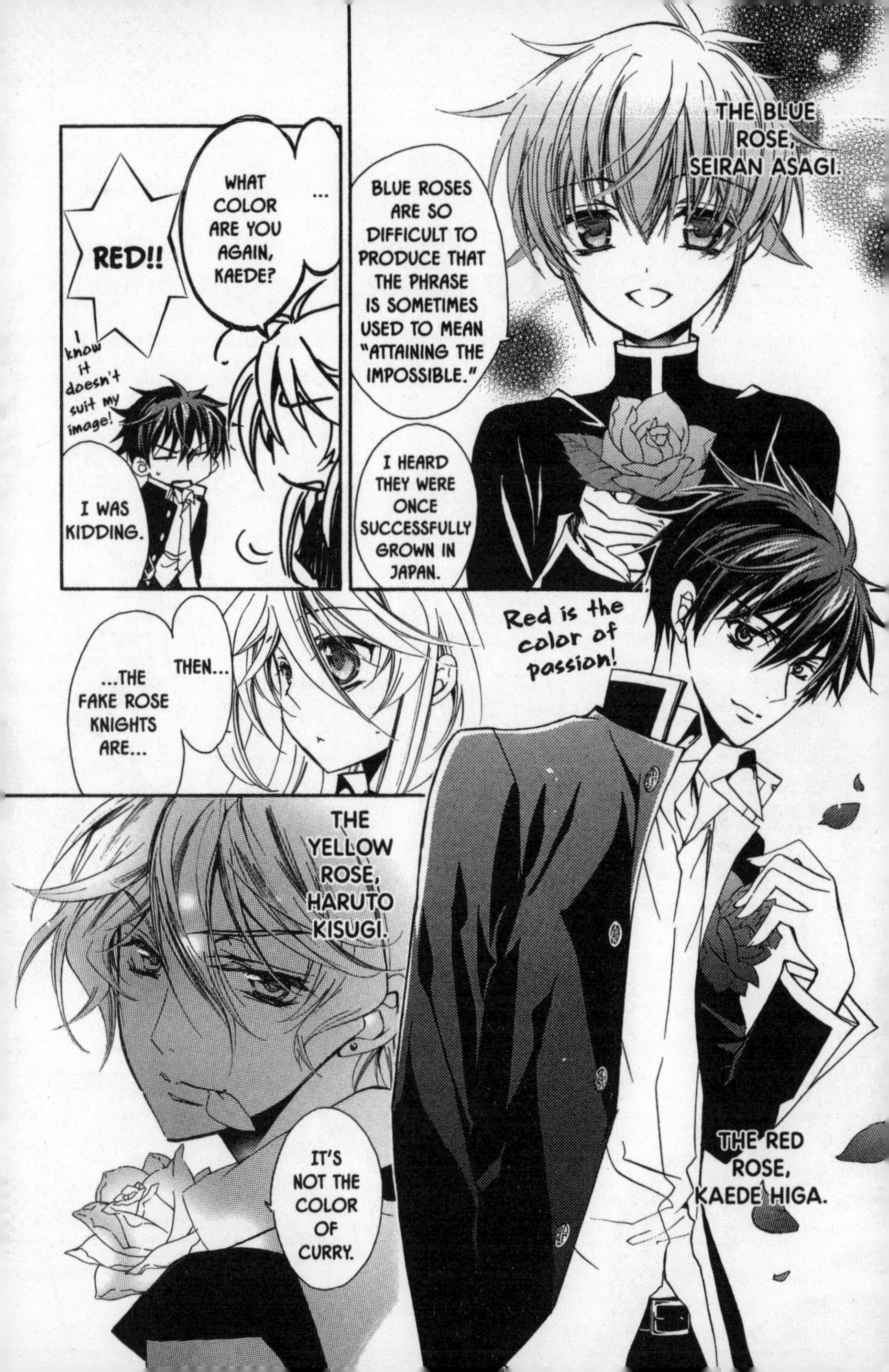
THE BLUE ROSE, SEIRAN ASAGI.
BLUE ROSES ARE SO DIFFICULT TO PRODUCE THAT THE PHRASE IS SOMETIMES USED TO MEAN "ATTAINING THE IMPOSSIBLE."
I HEARD THEY WERE ONCE SUCCESSFULLY GROWN IN JAPAN.
...
WHAT COLOR ARE YOU AGAIN, KAEDE?
RED!!
I know it doesn't suit my image!
I WAS KIDDING.
Red is the color of passion!
THE RED ROSE, KAEDE HIGA.
THEN...
...THE FAKE ROSE KNIGHTS ARE...
THE YELLOW ROSE, HARUTO KISUGI.
IT'S NOT THE COLOR OF CURRY.

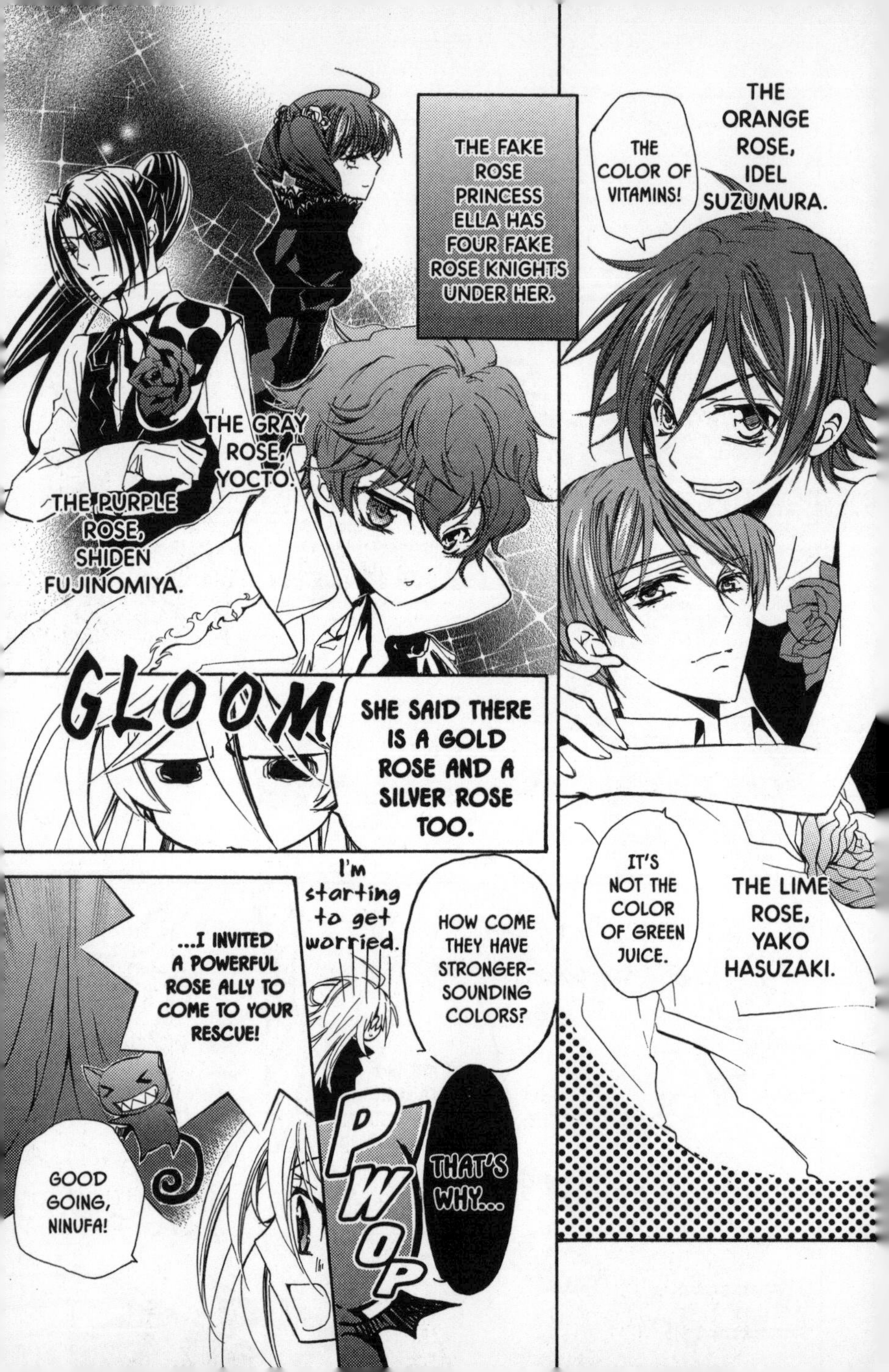
THE ORANGE ROSE, IDEL SUZUMURA.
THE COLOR OF VITAMINS!
THE LIME ROSE, YAKO HASUZAKI.
IT'S NOT THE COLOR OF GREEN JUICE.
THE FAKE ROSE PRINCESS ELLA HAS FOUR FAKE ROSE KNIGHTS UNDER HER.
THE GRAY ROSE, YOCTO.
THE PURPLE ROSE, SHIDEN FUJINOMIYA.
SHE SAID THERE IS A GOLD ROSE AND A SILVER ROSE TOO.
GLOOM
HOW COME THEY HAVE STRONGER-SOUNDING COLORS?
I'm starting to get worried.
THAT'S WHY...
PWOP
...I INVITED A POWERFUL ROSE ALLY TO COME TO YOUR RESCUE!
GOOD GOING, NINUFA!

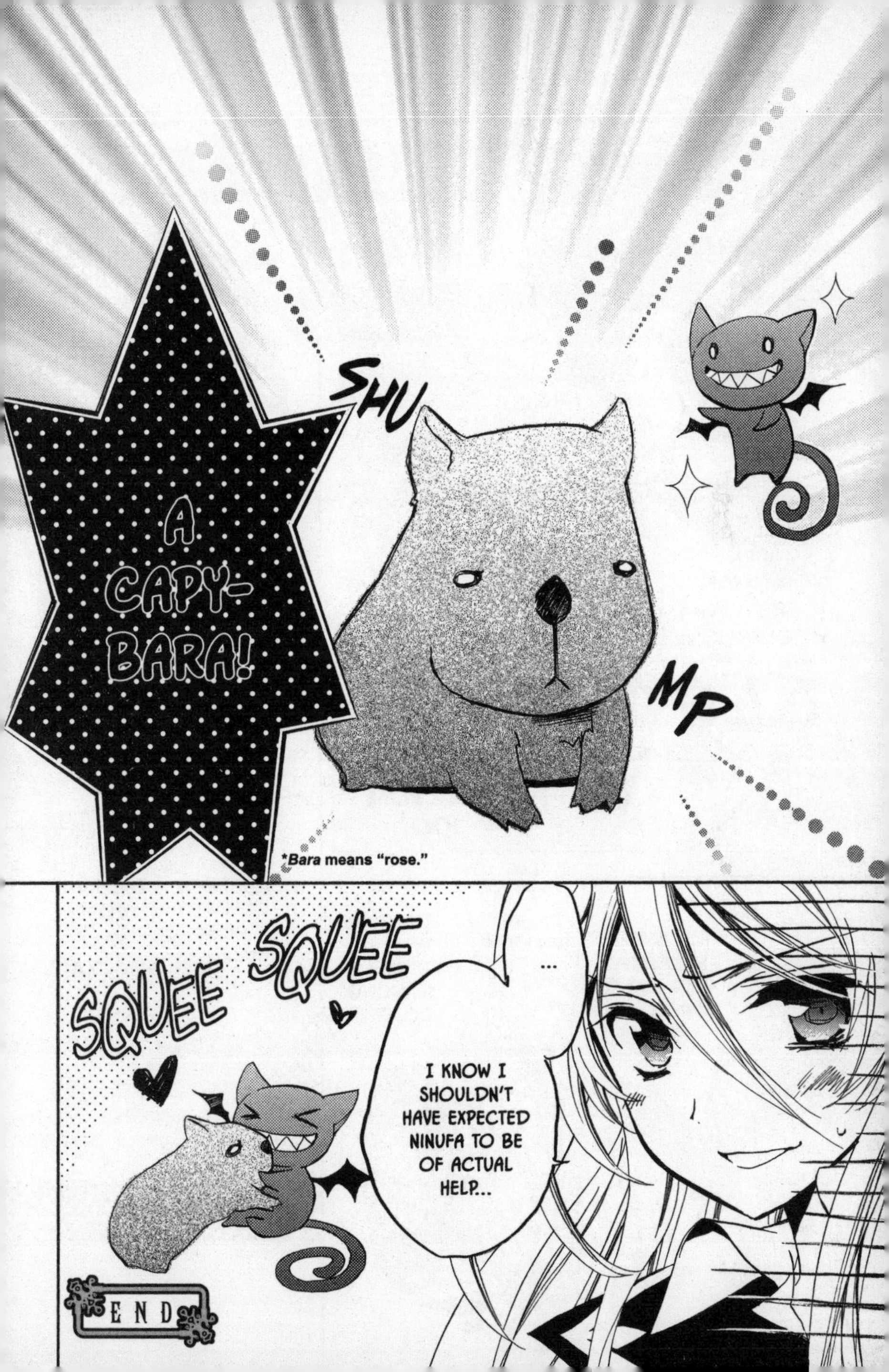
SHU MP
A CAPY-BARA!
*Bara means "rose."
...
I KNOW I SHOULDN'T HAVE EXPECTED NINUFA TO BE OF ACTUAL HELP...
SQUEE SQUEE
END

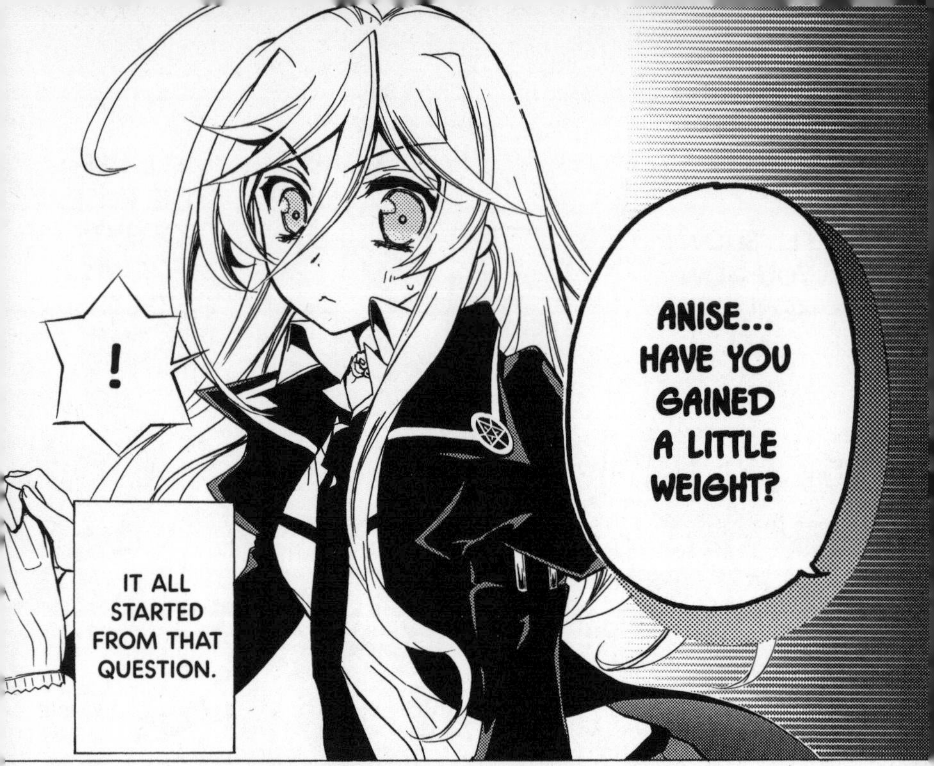
ANISE... HAVE YOU GAINED A LITTLE WEIGHT?
!
IT ALL STARTED FROM THAT QUESTION.

A Certain Girl's Rose Fest

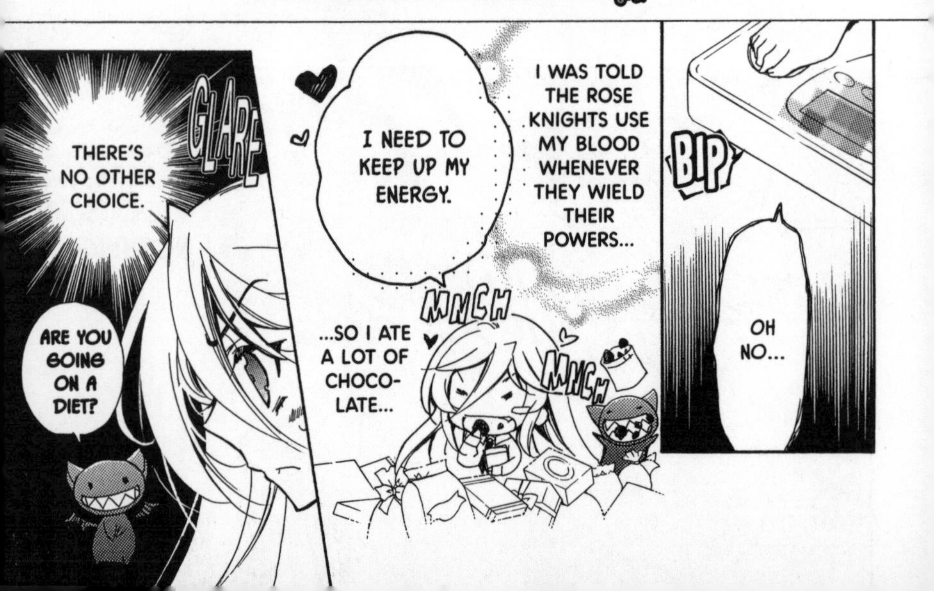
BIP
OH NO...
I WAS TOLD THE ROSE KNIGHTS USE MY BLOOD WHENEVER THEY WIELD THEIR POWERS...
I NEED TO KEEP UP MY ENERGY.
...SO I ATE A LOT OF CHOCO-LATE...
MNCH
MNCH
GLARE
THERE'S NO OTHER CHOICE.
ARE YOU GOING ON A DIET?

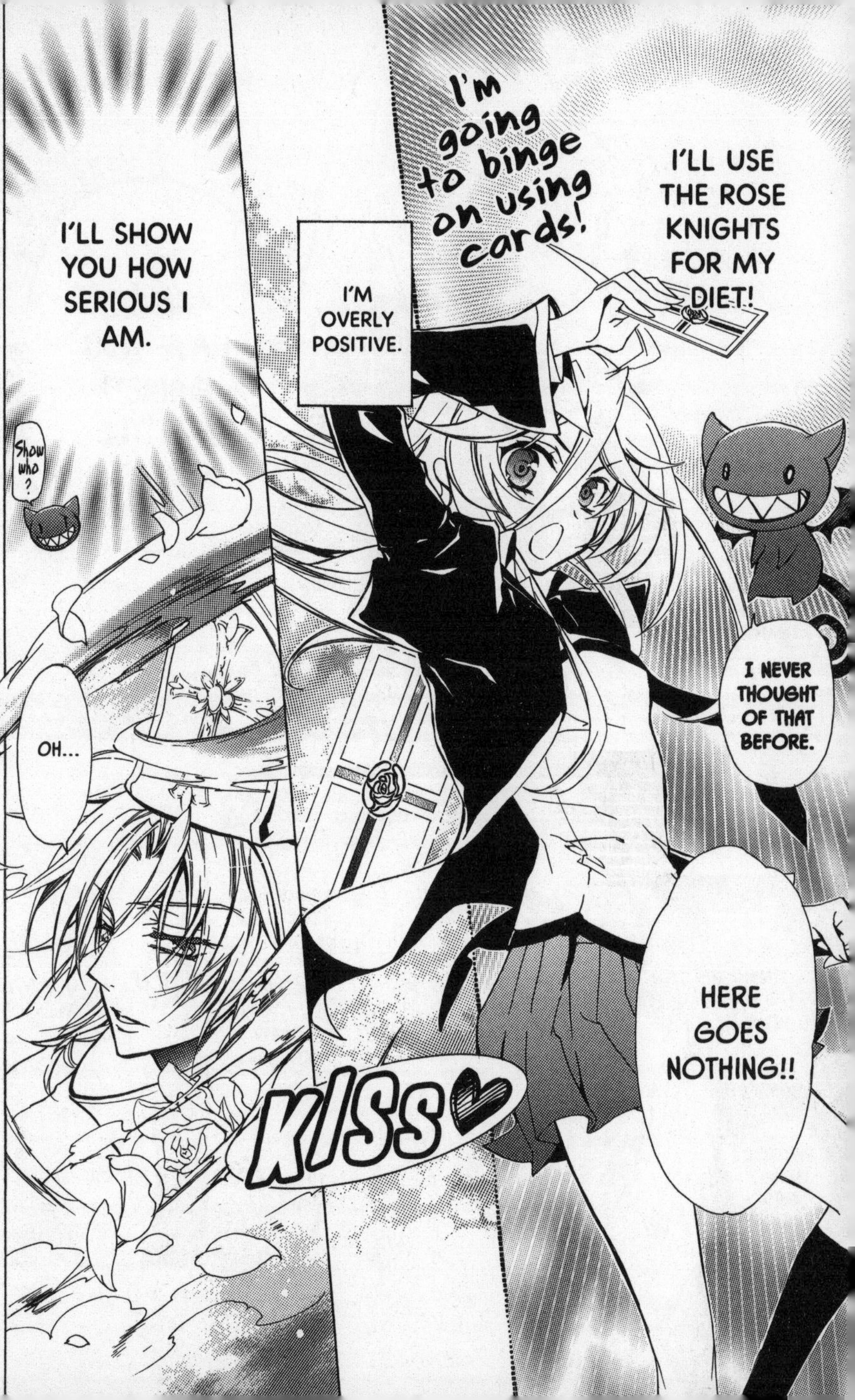
I'LL USE THE ROSE KNIGHTS FOR MY DIET!
I'm going to binge on using cards!
I'M OVERLY POSITIVE.
I NEVER THOUGHT OF THAT BEFORE.
HERE GOES NOTHING!!
KISS♥
I'LL SHOW YOU HOW SERIOUS I AM.
Show who?
OH...

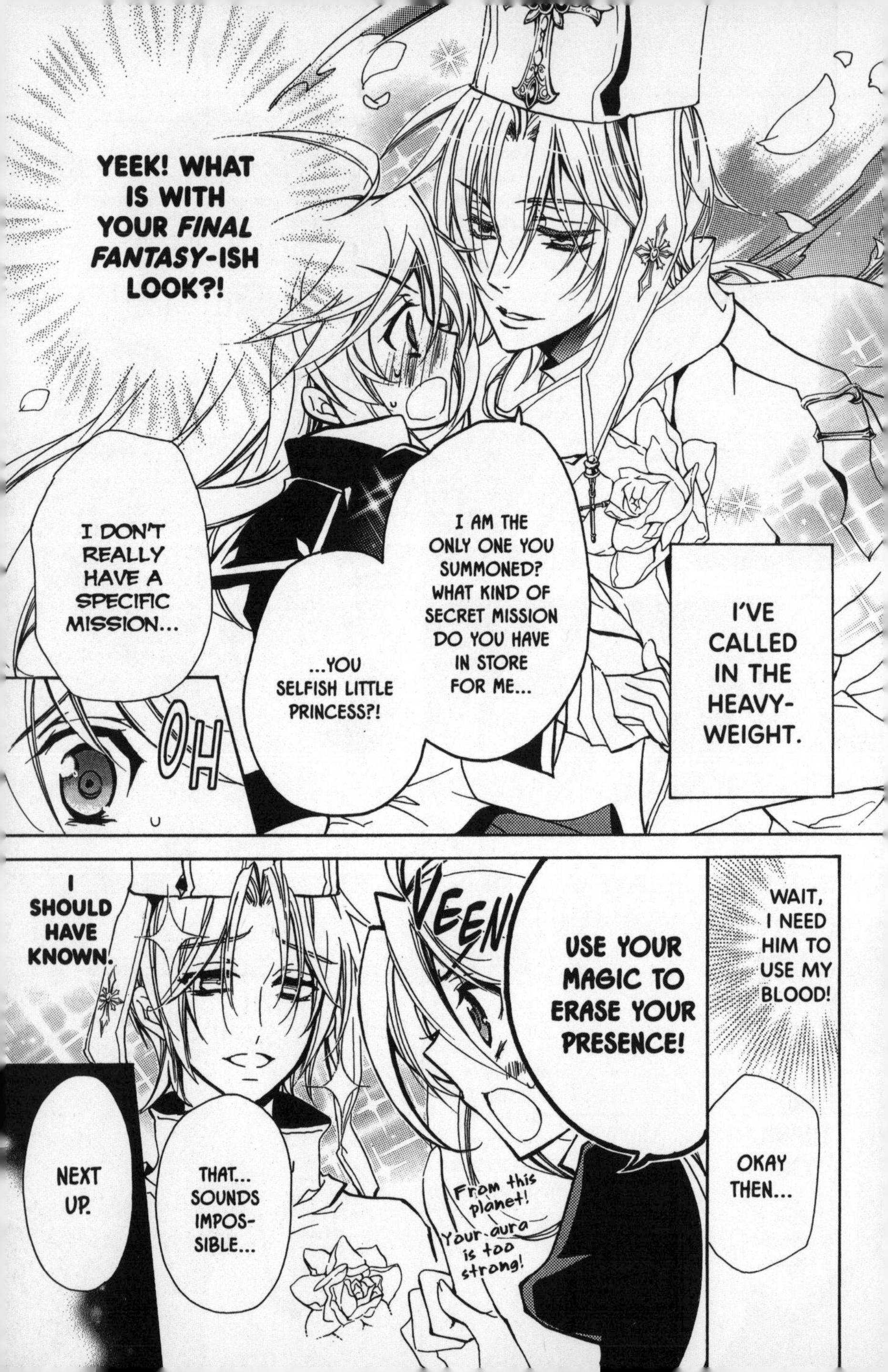
I'VE CALLED IN THE HEAVY-WEIGHT.
YEEK! WHAT IS WITH YOUR *FINAL FANTASY*-ISH LOOK?!
I AM THE ONLY ONE YOU SUMMONED? WHAT KIND OF SECRET MISSION DO YOU HAVE IN STORE FOR ME...
...YOU SELFISH LITTLE PRINCESS?!
OH
I DON'T REALLY HAVE A SPECIFIC MISSION...
WAIT, I NEED HIM TO USE MY BLOOD!
USE YOUR MAGIC TO ERASE YOUR PRESENCE!
VEEN
I SHOULD HAVE KNOWN.
OKAY THEN...
From this planet!
Your aura is too strong!
THAT... SOUNDS IMPOS-SIBLE...
NEXT UP.

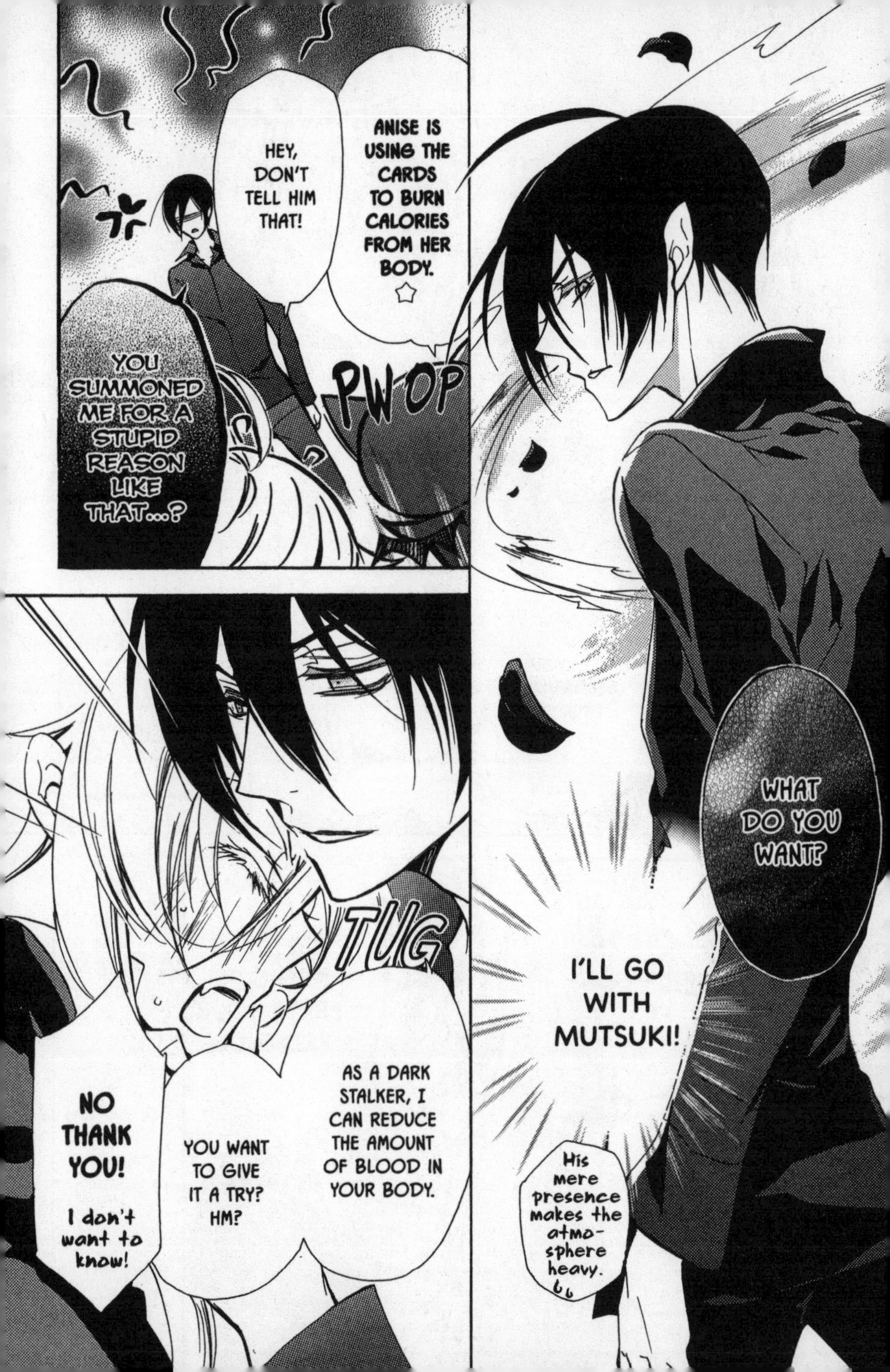
WHAT DO YOU WANT?
I'LL GO WITH MUTSUKI!
His mere presence makes the atmosphere heavy.
ANISE IS USING THE CARDS TO BURN CALORIES FROM HER BODY. ☆
HEY, DON'T TELL HIM THAT!
PWOP
YOU SUMMONED ME FOR A STUPID REASON LIKE THAT...?
TUG
AS A DARK STALKER, I CAN REDUCE THE AMOUNT OF BLOOD IN YOUR BODY.
YOU WANT TO GIVE IT A TRY? HM?
NO THANK YOU!
I don't want to know!

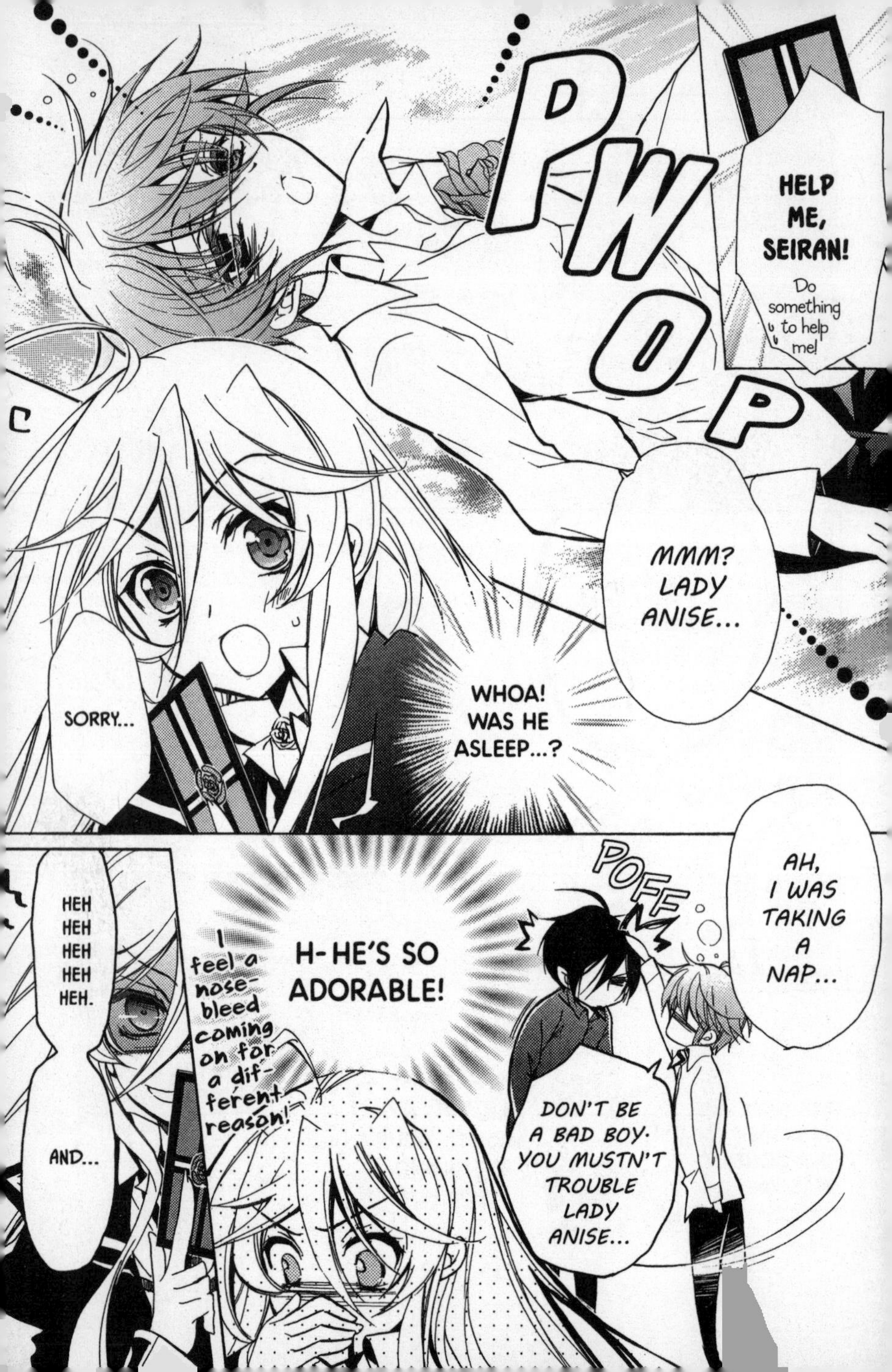
HELP ME, SEIRAN!
Do something to help me!
PWOP
MMM? LADY ANISE...
WHOA! WAS HE ASLEEP...?
SORRY...
AH, I WAS TAKING A NAP...
POFF
DON'T BE A BAD BOY. YOU MUSTN'T TROUBLE LADY ANISE...
H-HE'S SO ADORABLE!
I feel a nose-bleed coming on for a dif-ferent reason!
HEH HEH HEH HEH HEH.
AND...

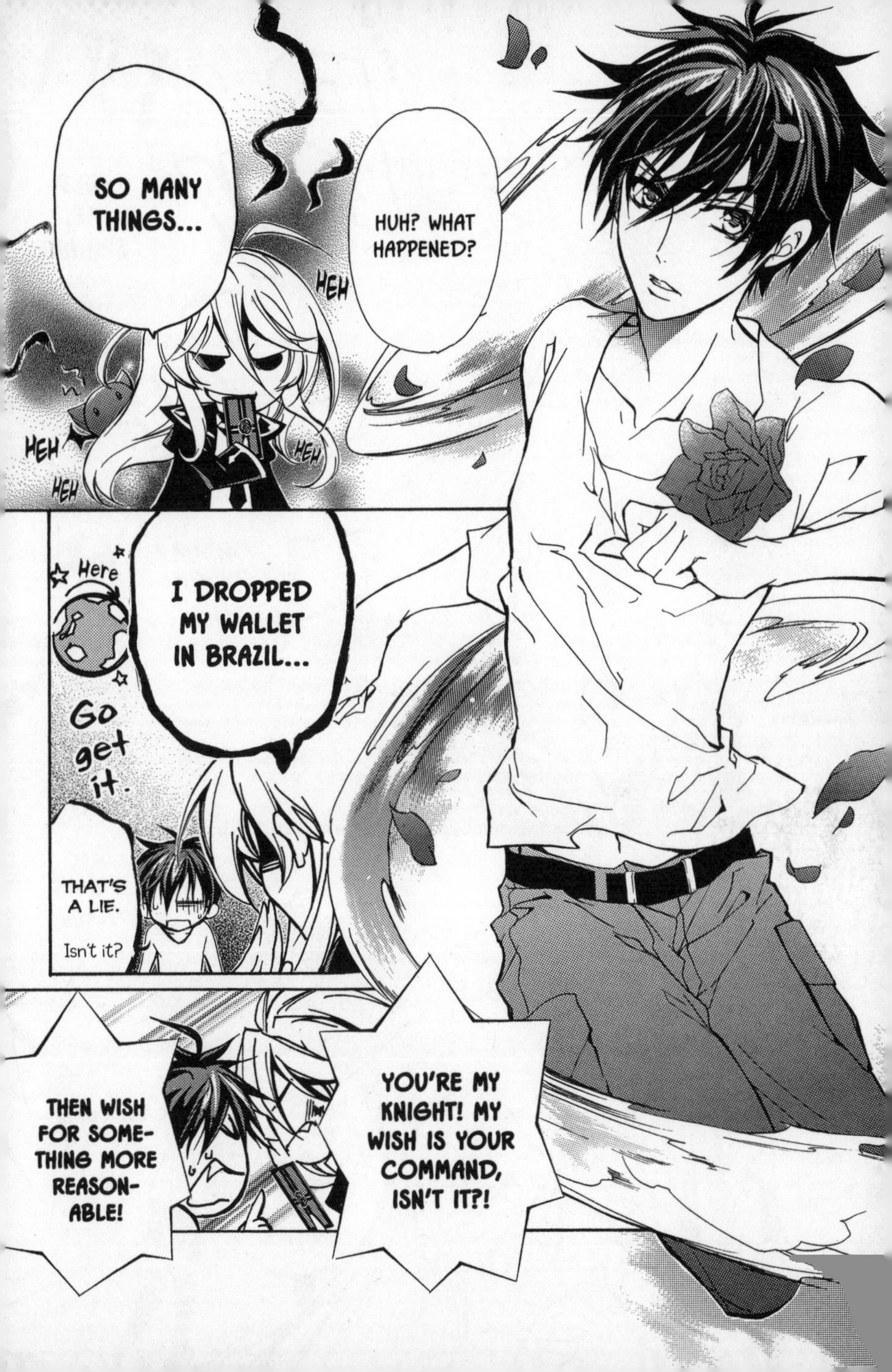
HUH? WHAT HAPPENED?
SO MANY THINGS...
HEH
HEH
HEH
HEH
I DROPPED MY WALLET IN BRAZIL...
Here
Go get it.
THAT'S A LIE.
Isn't it?
YOU'RE MY KNIGHT! MY WISH IS YOUR COMMAND, ISN'T IT?!
THEN WISH FOR SOME-THING MORE REASON-ABLE!

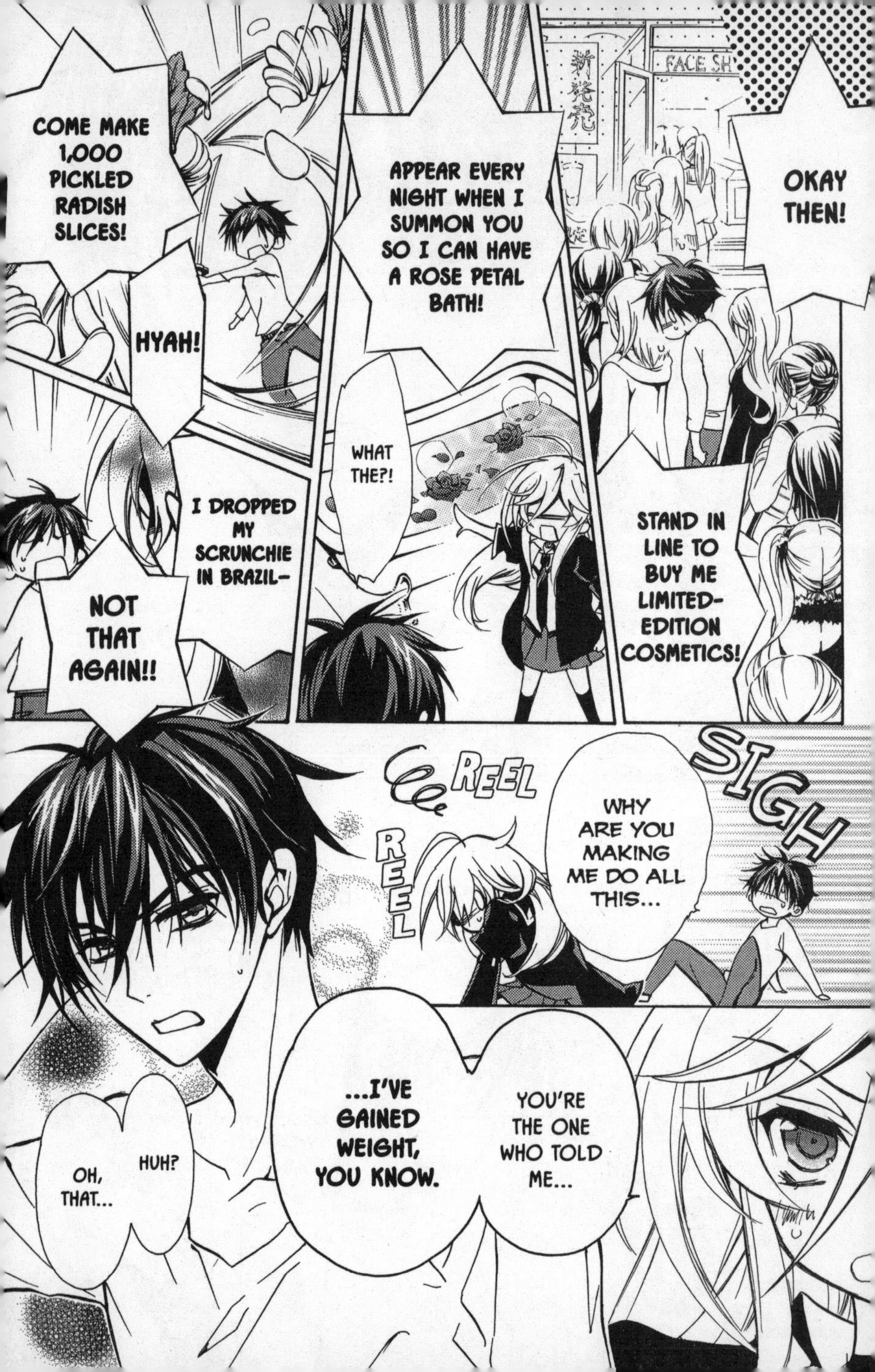
FACE SH
新発売
OKAY THEN!
STAND IN LINE TO BUY ME LIMITED-EDITION COSMETICS!
APPEAR EVERY NIGHT WHEN I SUMMON YOU SO I CAN HAVE A ROSE PETAL BATH!
WHAT THE?!
COME MAKE 1,000 PICKLED RADISH SLICES!
HYAH!
I DROPPED MY SCRUNCHIE IN BRAZIL-
NOT THAT AGAIN!!
SIGH
WHY ARE YOU MAKING ME DO ALL THIS...
REEL
REEL
YOU'RE THE ONE WHO TOLD ME...
...I'VE GAINED WEIGHT, YOU KNOW.
HUH?
OH, THAT...

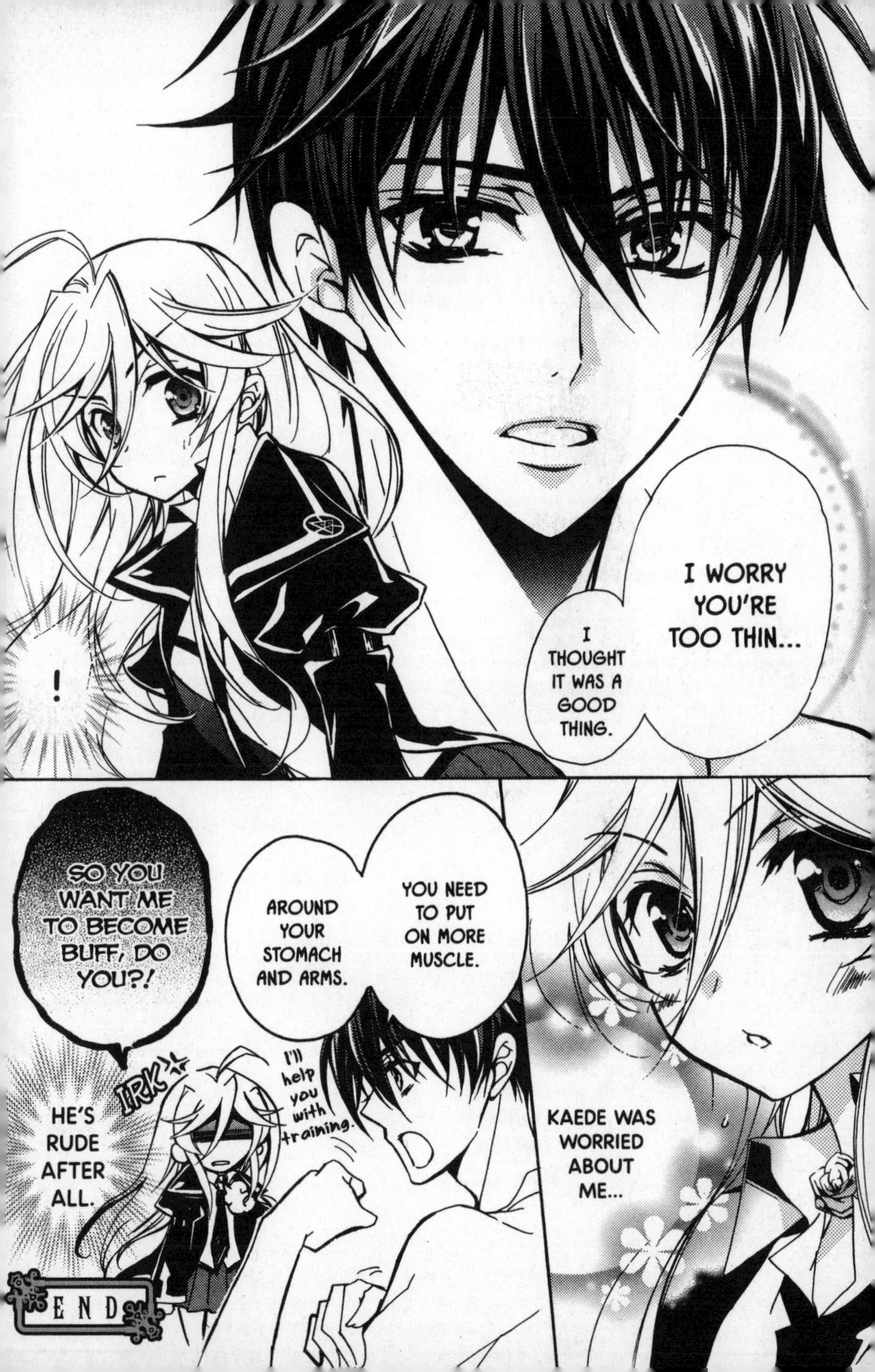
I WORRY YOU'RE TOO THIN...
I THOUGHT IT WAS A GOOD THING.
!
KAEDE WAS WORRIED ABOUT ME...
YOU NEED TO PUT ON MORE MUSCLE.
AROUND YOUR STOMACH AND ARMS.
I'll help you with training.
SO YOU WANT ME TO BECOME BUFF, DO YOU?!
IRK
HE'S RUDE AFTER ALL.
END

Kiss of the Rose Princess

This is the final volume of *Kiss of the Rose Princess*.

Thank you very much for reading this series. Originally it was meant to be only five chapters, but it became a long-running series for over three years thanks to your support. Both the characters and I are very happy. Thank you very much!!

I would also like to thank all the people who sent in fan mail and questionnaires, as well as the people who cheered this series on with their reviews and fan illustrations on their blogs and websites! This series has been published overseas as well, so thank you to all the readers across the sea! And thank you to all the wonderful cosplayers!

To my editor Lady M, the Asuka Editorial Office, my graphic novel editor, the sales representatives and bookstores, Marine Entertainment who created the drama CD, the voice actors who added life to my work with their acting, the people who helped me with the goods: Thank you very much!!

My friends and assistants, my family, thank you!!

Thank you from the bottom of my heart!

I will continue to work hard!

I hope to see you again!!

Aya Shouoto   January 2012

STAFF
NORIE OGAWA
AYA NAKAMURA
MAIKO YOSHISE
AYA MAEDA
RIKA KASAHARA
KANAE SAITOU
YURIKA HONDA
KOU

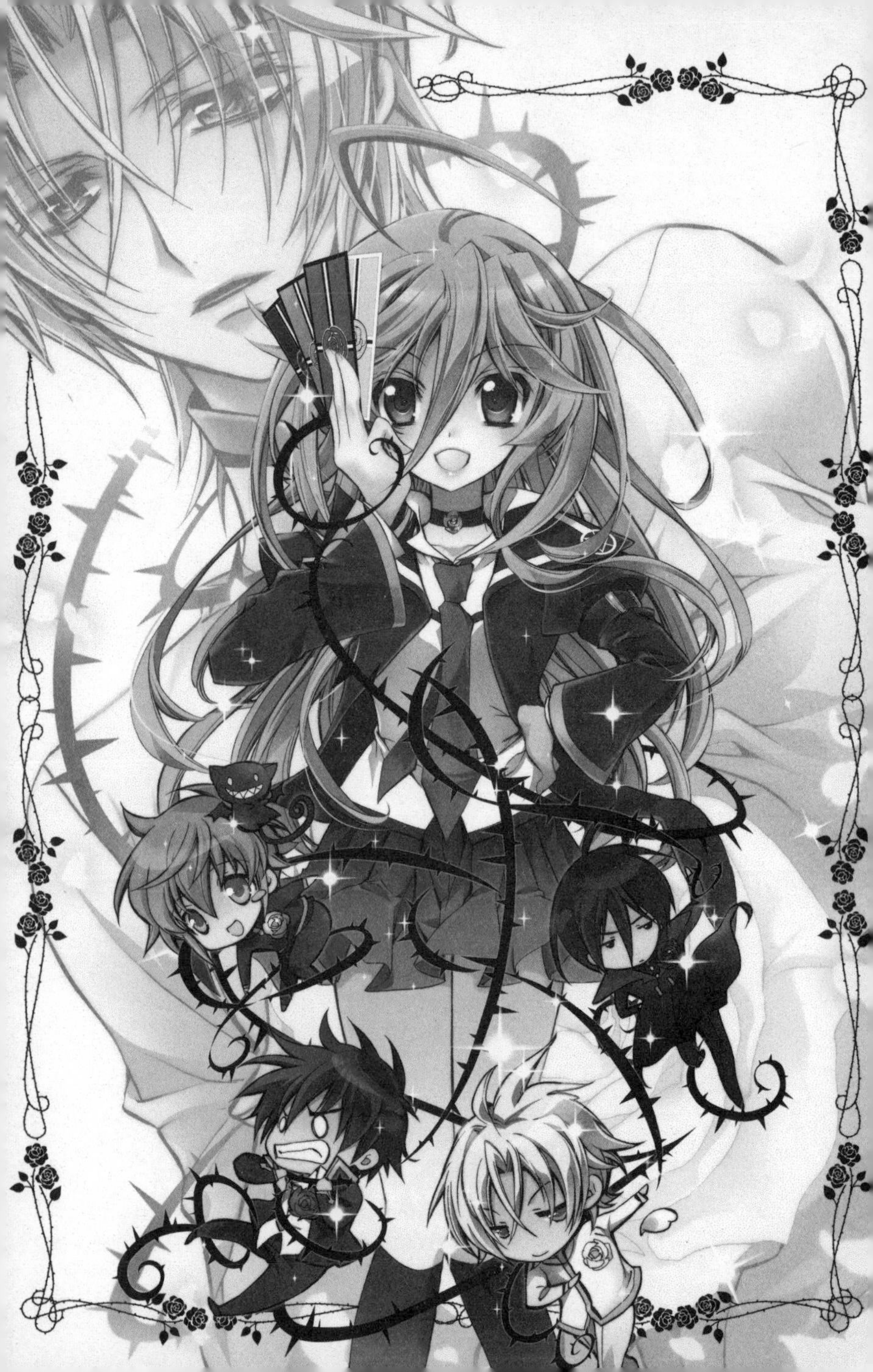

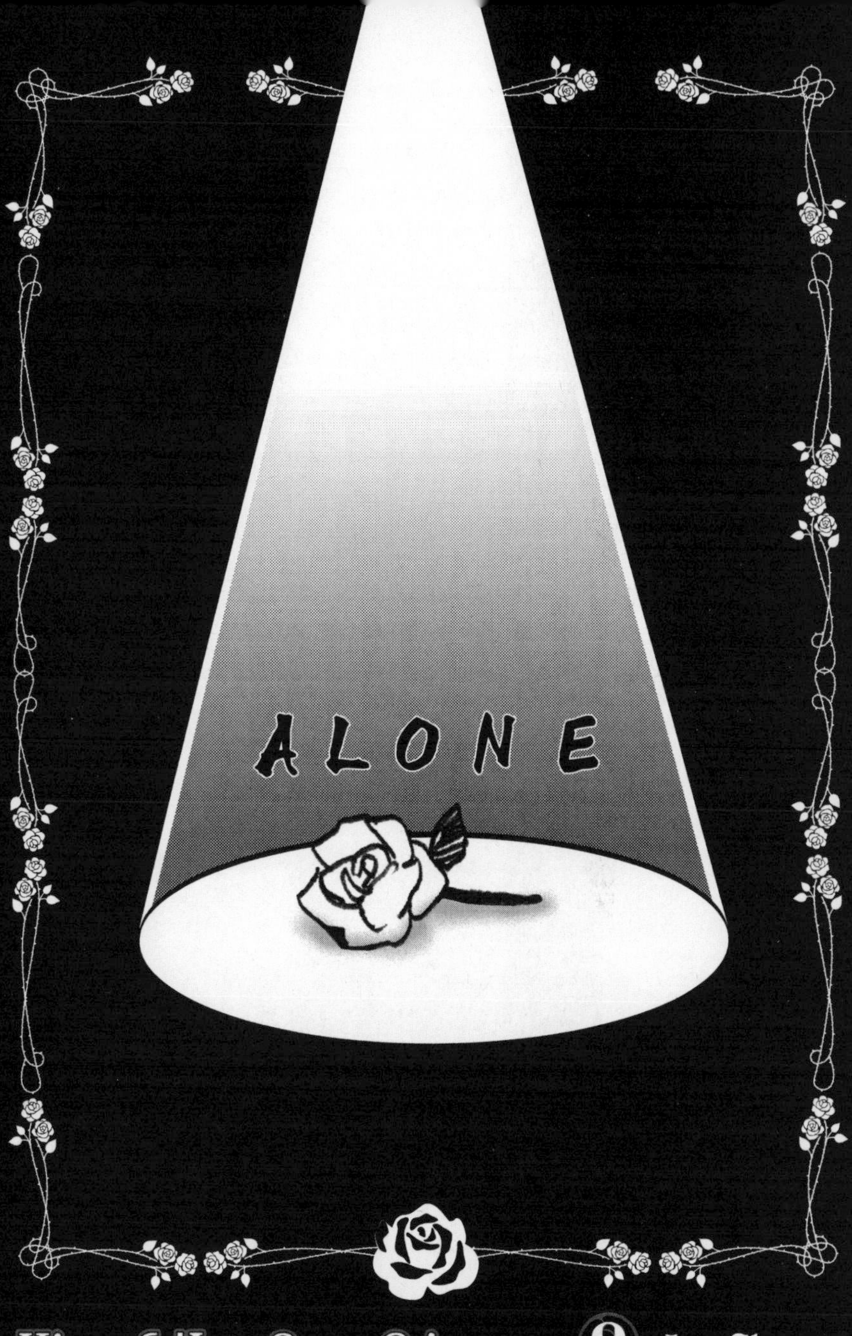
ALONE

Kiss of the Rose Princess 9 Aya Shouoto

Thank you
very much!

LOSS OF
THE ROSE PRINCESS

AYA SHOUOTO

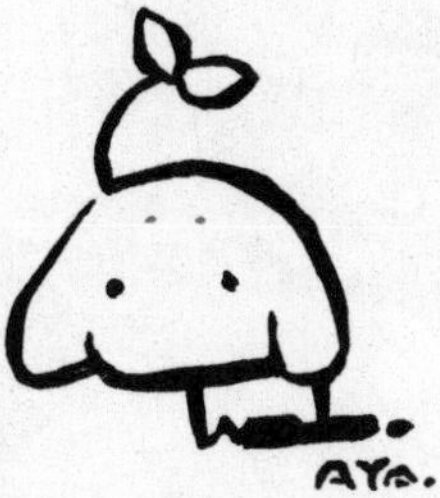
AYA.

I saw the logo of a liquor called Four Roses and thought it looked really cool. I also had the thought, "It'd be fun if boys popped out of cards like in those monster card games." These two ideas were combined to create this series!

-Aya Shouoto

Aya Shouoto was born on December 25. Her hobbies include traveling, staying at hotels, sewing and daydreaming. She currently lives in Tokyo and enjoys listening to J-pop anime theme songs while she works.

This is the last page.

In keeping with the original Japanese comic format, this book reads from right to left, so action, sound effects, and word balloons are completely reversed. This preserves the orientation of the original artwork. Check out the diagram below to get the hang of things, then turn to the other side of the book to get started!

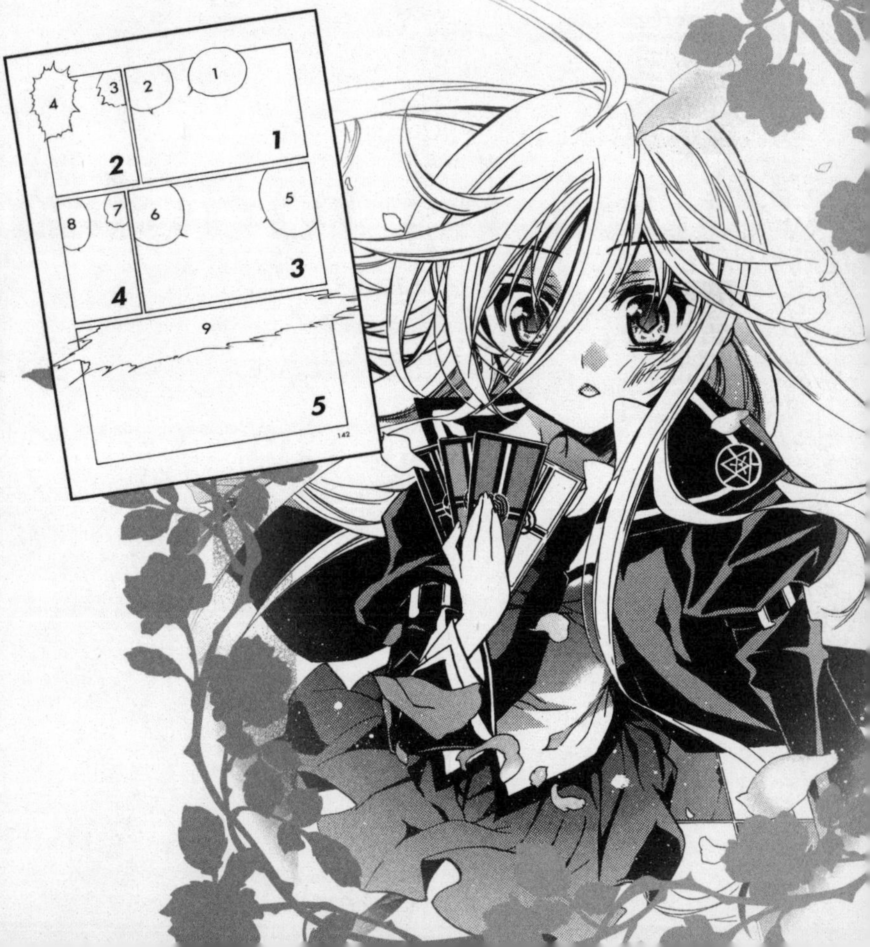
1
2
3
4
1
2
5
6
7
8
3
4
9
5
142

Characters

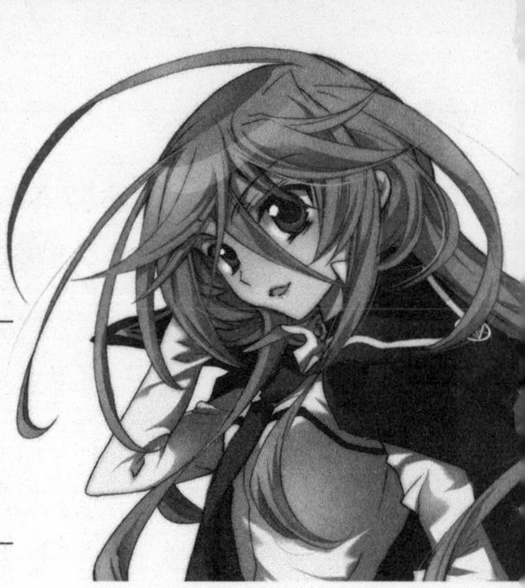

Anise Yamamoto

First-year at Shobi Academy. She's currently striving to free the Rose Knights from the Rose Contract.

Rose Knights

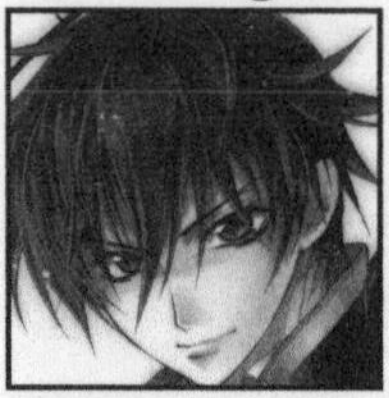

Kaede Higa (Red Rose)

Anise's classmate. He is an excellent athlete who often teases Anise.
Specialty: Offence

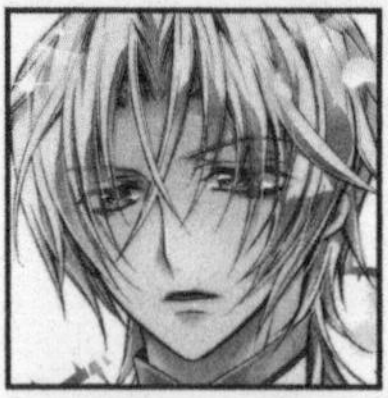

Mitsuru Tenjo (White Rose)

Third-year and Student Council President. He is revered by both male and female students. Super-rich.
Specialty: Healing, Defense

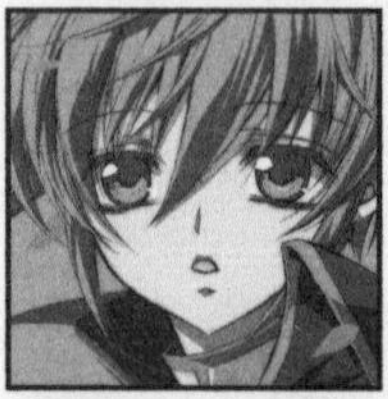

Seiran Asagi (Blue Rose)

First-year. This boy is cuter than any girl at school, and he doesn't know he's the school idol. He's well-versed in a wide range of topics.
Specialty: Alchemy, Science

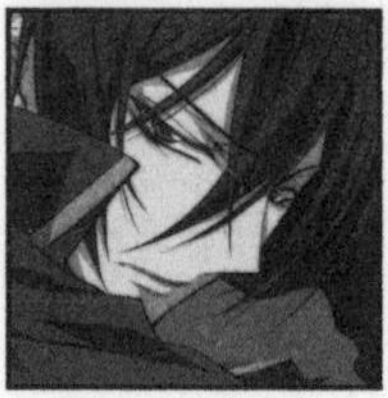

Mutsuki Kurama (Black Rose)

Second-year. There are many frightening rumors about this mysterious student. Apparently he lives in the basement of Tenjo's house.
Specialty: Discovery, Capture

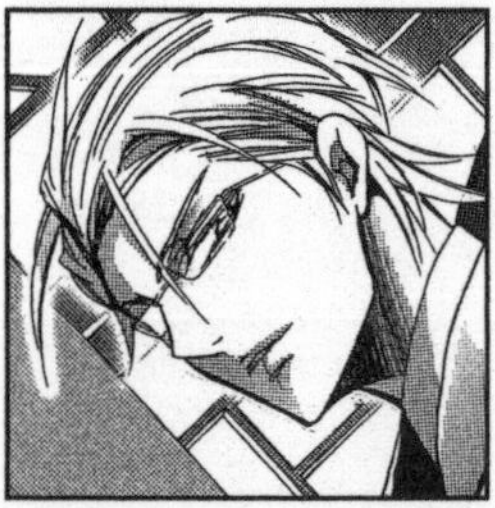

Schwarz Yamamoto (Silver Rose)

Anise's father. It seems he had a motive in putting the rose choker on Anise.

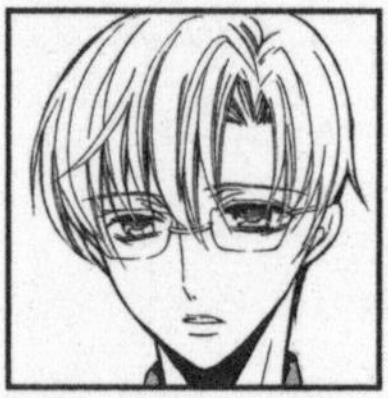

Itsushi Narumi (Classics Teacher)

He is the most knowledgeable about the "Sovereign," her "Rose Knights" and the "Rose Contract" that binds them...

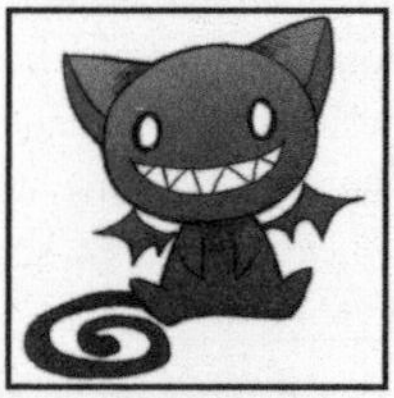

Ninufa (Guardian)

The guardian who has been protecting the cards since ancient times.

Characters

Fake Rose Princess

Ella

She has a strong obsession with Anise. She commands four Fake Rose Knights.

Rhodecia

Idel Suzumura (Orange Rose)

An active and optimistic student at Shobi Academy. He can attack using sound waves.

Yako Hasuzaki (Lime Rose)

A student at Shobi Academy. He uses the power of scent to hypnotize people.

Fake Rose Knights

Shiden Fujinomiya (Purple Rose)

A loyal follower of Ella. He controls water to attack his enemies.

Yocto (Gray Rose)

Mutsuki's older brother. He was taken over by the Demon Lord's curse, but was freed from it by Mutsuki and the others.

Haruto Kisugi (Gold Rose)

Anise's childhood friend. He was dragged into the seal of the Demon Lord, but was saved by Schwarz.

Story Thus Far

In order to save Yako's life, Anise heads for the tower where Schwarz awaits, but the Fake Rose Knights stand before her. Kaede and the others fight a fierce battle against Yocto and his formidable power. Tenjo faces Mutsuki, who had joined Yocto's side in the battle among Rose Knights. Meanwhile, Anise decides she must find a way to destroy the source of Yocto's power, so she heads for the top floor of the tower...

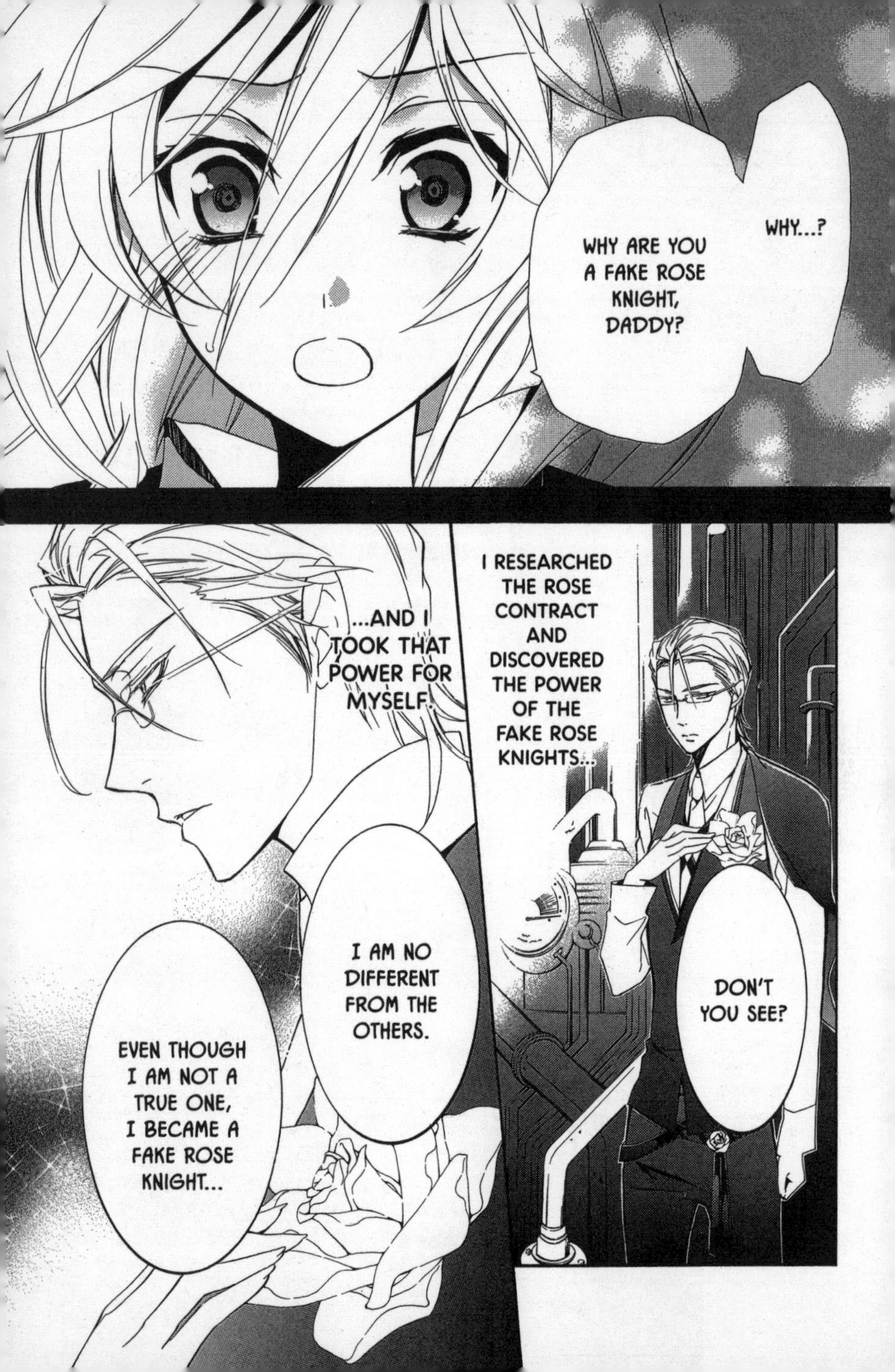
WHY...?
WHY ARE YOU A FAKE ROSE KNIGHT, DADDY?
I RESEARCHED THE ROSE CONTRACT AND DISCOVERED THE POWER OF THE FAKE ROSE KNIGHTS...
DON'T YOU SEE?
...AND I TOOK THAT POWER FOR MYSELF.
I AM NO DIFFERENT FROM THE OTHERS.
EVEN THOUGH I AM NOT A TRUE ONE, I BECAME A FAKE ROSE KNIGHT...

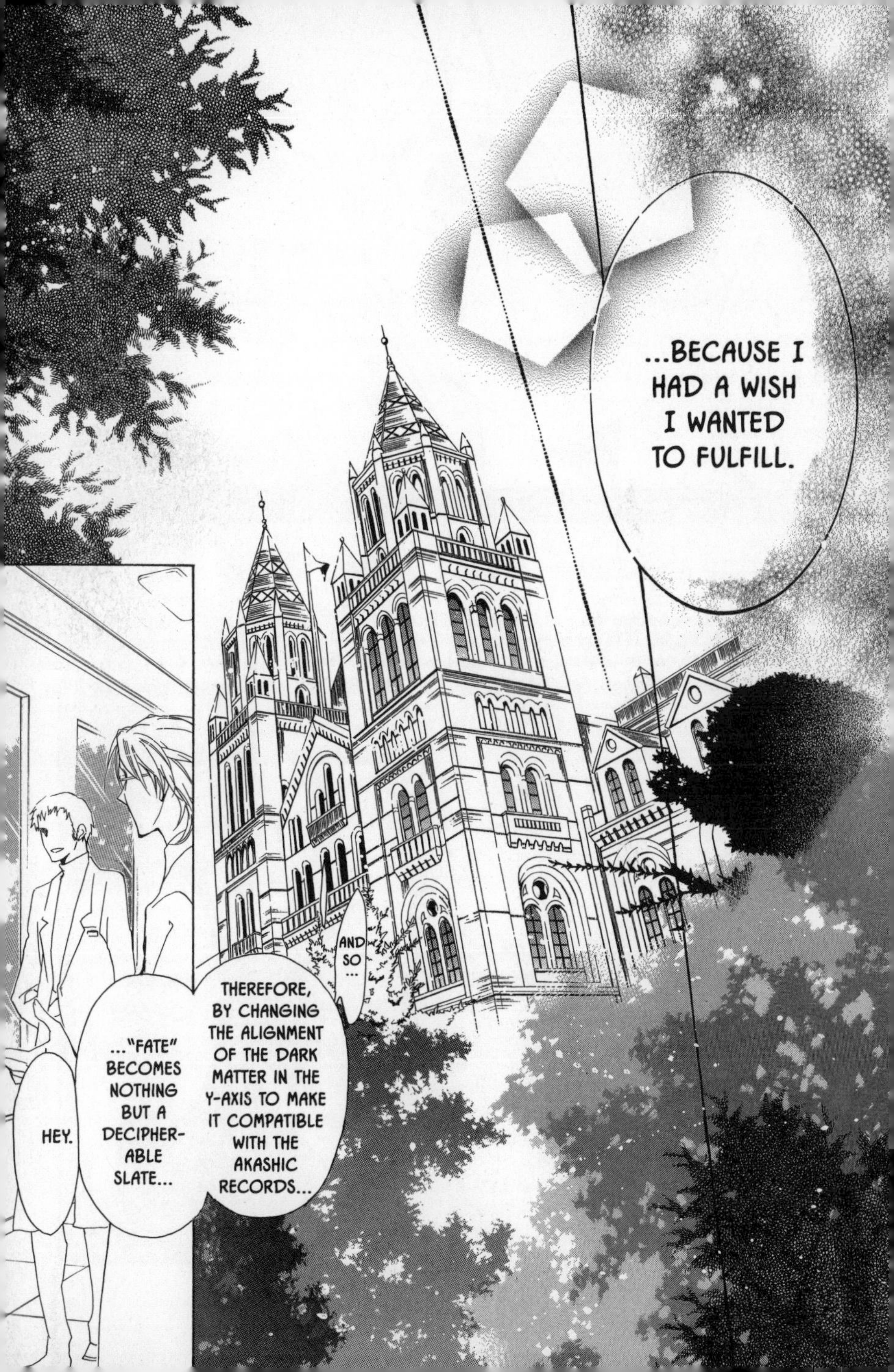
...BECAUSE I HAD A WISH I WANTED TO FULFILL.
AND SO...
THEREFORE, BY CHANGING THE ALIGNMENT OF THE DARK MATTER IN THE Y-AXIS TO MAKE IT COMPATIBLE WITH THE AKASHIC RECORDS...
..."FATE" BECOMES NOTHING BUT A DECIPHER-ABLE SLATE...
HEY.

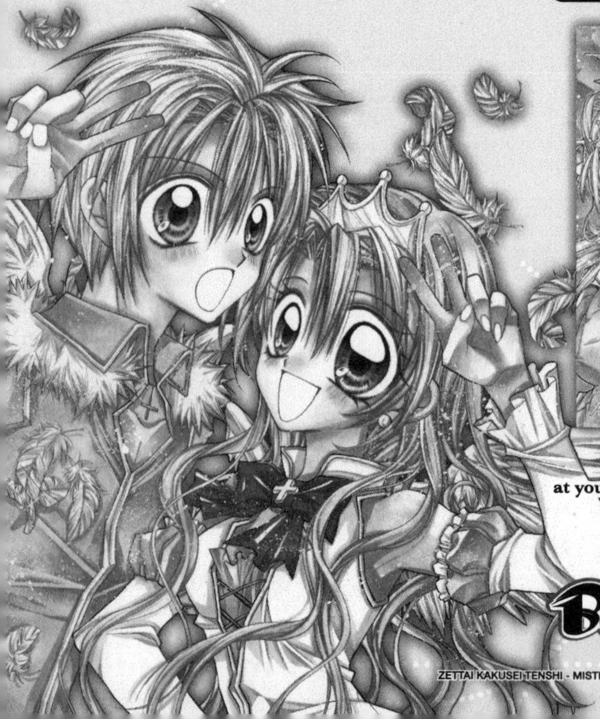

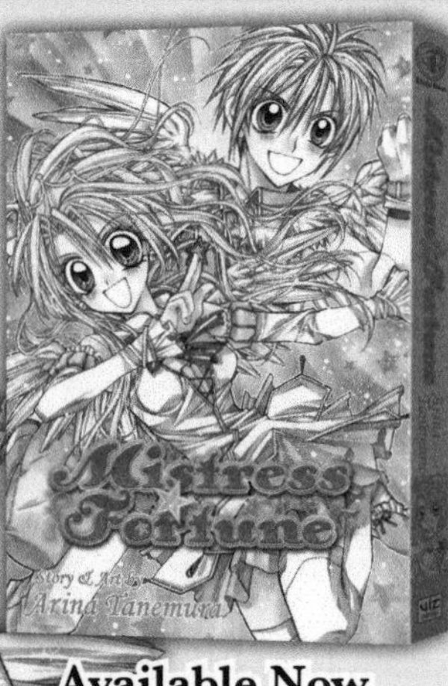
Mistress Fortune
Story & Art by
Arina Tanemura

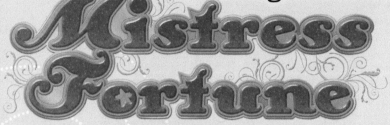

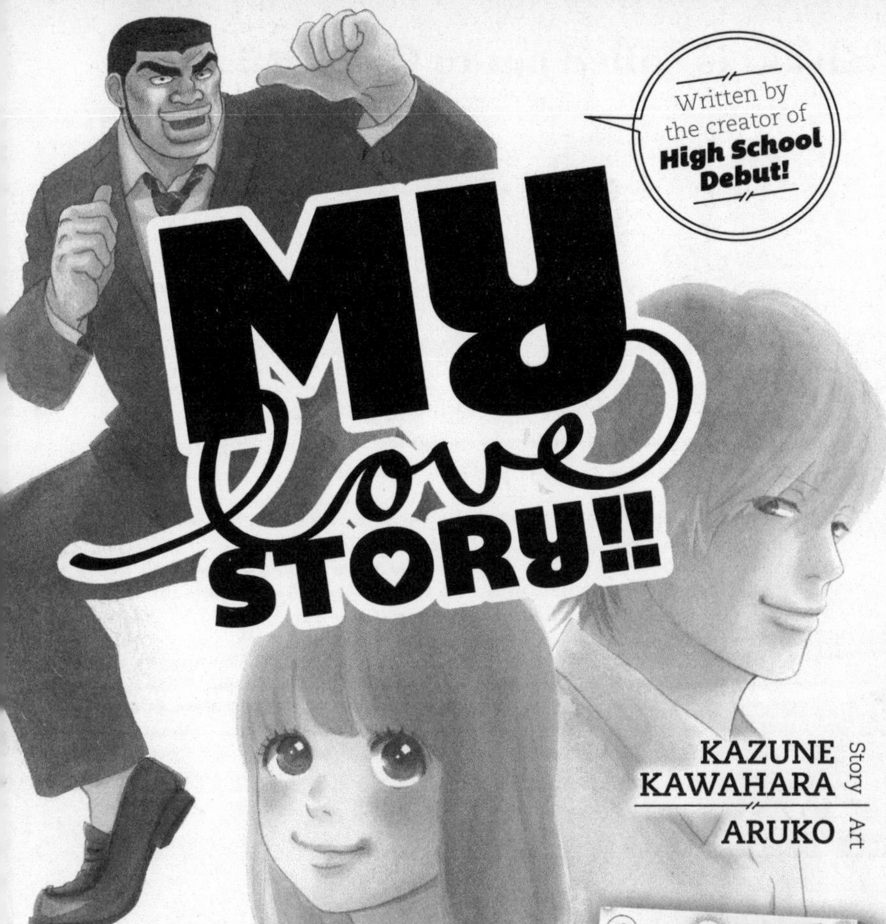
Written by the creator of
High School Debut!
MY Love STORY!!
KAZUNE KAWAHARA Story
ARUKO Art